MODERN STUDIES IN PROPERTY LAW: VOLUME 12

This edited collection of papers comes from the well-established Modern Studies in Property Law biennial conference. It examines a diverse range of topics in property law, using a variety of methodological approaches to reflect on current and emerging problems and on important issues that have often been overlooked. Its new analysis and insights will be valuable for property lawyers, academics and students. It considers new developments in property law, including those connected with digital assets, proprietary estoppel, and co-housing. The contributors are leading academics and practitioners from several common law jurisdictions, which expands the book's focus and enhances its value to the reader.

Previous volumes in this series:

Modern Studies in Property Law: Volume 1
Edited by Elizabeth Cooke

Modern Studies in Property Law: Volume 2
Edited by Elizabeth Cooke

Modern Studies in Property Law: Volume 3
Edited by Elizabeth Cooke

Modern Studies in Property Law: Volume 4
Edited by Elizabeth Cooke

Modern Studies in Property Law: Volume 5
Edited by Martin Dixon

Modern Studies in Property Law: Volume 5
Edited by Susan Bright

Modern Studies in Property Law: Volume 6
Edited by Susan Bright

Modern Studies in Property Law: Volume 7
Edited by Nicholas Hopkins

Modern Studies in Property Law: Volume 8
Edited by Warren Barr

Modern Studies in Property Law: Volume 9
Edited by Heather Conway and Robin Hickey

Modern Studies in Property Law: Volume 10
Edited by Ben McFarlane and Sinéad Agnew

Modern Studies in Property Law: Volume 11
Edited by Sue Farran, Russell Hewitson and Adam Ramshaw

Modern Studies in Property Law

Volume 12

Edited by
Natalie Mrockova
Aruna Nair
and
Luke Rostill

• HART •
OXFORD • LONDON • NEW YORK • NEW DELHI • SYDNEY

HART PUBLISHING

Bloomsbury Publishing Plc

Kemp House, Chawley Park, Cumnor Hill, Oxford, OX2 9PH, UK

1385 Broadway, New York, NY 10018, USA

29 Earlsfort Terrace, Dublin 2, Ireland

HART PUBLISHING, the Hart/Stag logo, BLOOMSBURY and the Diana logo are trademarks of Bloomsbury Publishing Plc

First published in Great Britain 2023

A catalogue record for this book is available from the British Library.

A catalogue record for this book is available from the Library of Congress.

Library of Congress Control Number: 2001272703

ISBN: HB: 978-1-50996-366-9
ePDF: 978-1-50996-368-3
ePub: 978-1-50996-367-6

Typeset by Compuscript Ltd, Shannon

Preface

THIS TWELFTH VOLUME in the Modern Studies in Property Law series is a product of a well-established biennial conference that brings together property law scholars and practitioners from around the world. After the many lockdowns and restrictions imposed to contain the spread of COVID-19 – which led to, inter alia, the cancellation of the previous conference – we were very lucky to be able to host a well-attended hybrid conference at the University of Oxford in March 2022. It provided a wonderful opportunity to discuss new ideas, exchange views, listen to and learn from others, and to offer and collect valuable feedback on a wide range of topics presented in 16 sessions, with a total of 33 papers being presented. It also provided a chance to meet old friends and make new ones.

This book contains 13 chapters: 10 are peer-reviewed and edited papers from the conference presenters and three are kindly contributed by our wonderful keynote speakers. The book is divided thematically into four parts. Part I of the book considers the fundamental question how the subject-matter of property is to be defined and illustrates the practical importance of that question in the varied contexts in which it arises. The first two chapters examine the quintessentially modern problem of defining the role, if any, that property should play in regulating access to and control of 'digital assets.' Professor Sarah Green's keynote address, drawing on her experience as the Law Commissioner for England and Wales responsible for the Commission's ongoing project on this question, critiques conventional objections to treating at least some digital assets ('DIDOs', or Discrete Instantiation Digital Objects) as objects of property that are analogous in important ways to tangible things. She argues for the law's recognition of a 'tertium quid' between the traditional categories of things in action and things in possession to accommodate the distinctive features of this class of digital asset. Meanwhile, Andrew Ray, Dr Damian Clifford and Dr Heather Roberts examine the question whether the task of addressing the novel problems posed by digital assets is properly one for the courts or the legislature, concluding that the 'property question' is a question that the judges are ill-equipped to answer. Finally, Professor William Swadling's chapter, 'Treehold', reminds us that the problem of defining the subject-matter of property is not confined to the realm of the intangible; he examines the extent to which the common law can treat standing trees as themselves the object of property, apart from the land to which they are attached, and concludes that no right to possess trees as such can be recognised.

Part II of the book then turns to the moral justification of private property or of particular private property rules or institutions. Professor Jeremy Waldron's keynote address examines the core question whether property is merely a convention, and challenges the view that 'natural law' or 'natural rights' theories of property have nothing to tell us about the reasons why the law recognises private property in the first place. Dr Susan Pascoe then considers whether the law should recognise novel types of negative easement (such as the right to privacy by not being overlooked, solar and wind easements, and rights to receive broadband and mobile signals). She draws on an important new account of the moral foundations of private property – Hanoch Dagan's *A Liberal Theory of Property* – to argue that the law's commitment to enhancing private autonomy suggests that such an expansion ought to take place. Finally, Professor Heather Conway looks at a different aspect of the law's regulation of private autonomy in relation to property, the freedom to disinherit adult children, and considers how the legal limits on that freedom reflect prevailing social norms. She identifies a basic tension between the law's commitment to testamentary freedom and widespread public support for a duty to provide for adult children, and the absence of a clear 'normative template' for the courts in adjudicating this tension.

Part III of the book deals with issues pertaining to leases and co-housing. Dr Natalie Mrockova and Dr Luke Rostill consider co-ownership of leases. They examine the interaction of the rules on co-ownership and the rules on leases, and examine in particular the nature of, and the relationship between, unity of possession (a requirement of co-ownership) and exclusive possession (a requirement of leases) in cases involving a co-owned lease. They go on to analyse whether two or more parties can be equitable tenants in common in respect of a lease following the changes introduced by the Law of Property Act 1925, and the legal effect of such a co-ownership arrangement both internally and externally. Dr Fabiana Bettini considers several legal questions concerning co-housing, ie, resident-led housing projects which feature common areas and shared facilities. She provides a very useful account of co-housing as well as a comparative analysis of property arrangements used in England and France to set-up co-housing sites. Within this framework, she then examines whether the property arrangements recognise and support the co-housing values of its members. She concludes by offering some thoughts on the implications of these property arrangements for property theory. Finally, Professor Helen Carr, Professor Caroline Hunter, Carl Makin and Dr Gwilym Owen critically evaluate responses to the crisis of leasehold. They suggest that recent reform proposals clearly show a shift to a consumerist response to the crisis. They use newly collected data to illustrate what leaseholders want, and conclude that the proposed reforms may address some, but not all, of leaseholders' concerns.

Part IV of the book focuses on property and equity. Lord Sales, a Justice of the UK Supreme Court, shares his thoughts about the role of equity, proprietary estoppel, and the recent decision of his Court in *Guest v Guest*. Like the Court in *Guest v Guest*, Lord Sales asks whether the doctrine of proprietary estoppel rests on protecting promisee's expectations or their 'reliance interest'.

Aside from its theoretical importance, this issue is also vital for determining appropriate remedies. To answer that, Lord Sales first considers the competing concepts of predictability and flexibility in equity, and positions his discussion of the right approach to proprietary estoppel as an illustration of how these competing concepts, these tensions, have been dealt with and balanced in this particular area. He concludes by calling for a clearer justification for remedies granted under the auspices of a proprietary estoppel, and suggests that a clearer correlation between the grounds of the relief and the remedy is needed. Dr Joyman Lee considers the nature of express trusts. He argues that, in spite of the different legal pathways used to create the trusts, the English express trust and the trust as found in the mixed legal systems of Japan and Quebec are functionally similar. This shows, he suggests, that express trusts operate as a nexus or a system of rules. He argues that the core features of the English express trust are not contingent on the distinctive attributes of English equity, and that they have been reproduced through a limited modification of civilian property law. Joshua Teng critically examines the alternative conceptions of the *Pallant v Morgan* equity as offered in subsequent case law. He first discusses the conventional explanation and situation in which the *Pallant v Morgan* equity arises. He then rejects the proposed explanations for the equity founded on the common intention constructive trust and under the law of agency. Instead, he argues that the basis of the *Pallant v Morgan* equity may be found in the pre-existing fiduciary obligations owed by one party to the other, or between the parties, and the breach of these fiduciary obligations. Finally, Dr Rory Gregson investigates the nature and relationship of subrogation and marshalling. He discusses various justifications for subrogation and marshalling, and suggests that while the former may justifiably create property rights, the latter cannot. He concludes by discussing the implications of his analysis for commercial practice.

Sir Robert Megarry, in a lecture to the Holdsworth Club at the University of Birmingham, maintained that '[l]aw is not just something stored away in books, an ossified abstraction. It is a living force that only yesterday changed the lives of some of our neighbours, and tomorrow may change our own.' The technical nature of the subject sometimes obscures what should never be forgotten: that Sir Robert's observation applies to the law of property. It is a body of law that has profound implications for all to whom it applies. For this reason, among others, the law of property needs its academic community. We believe – and we hope the reader will agree – that this volume indicates that this community is in very good shape and shows the significance, strength, and breadth of modern property law research.

We wish to record that neither the conference nor this volume would have been possible without the hard work and dedication of many people. We would like to thank Hart Publishing – and especially our wonderful editor, Kate Whetter – for their enthusiasm and continued support for this series. We also wish to thank our contributors for writing such interesting and impressive pieces, responding efficiently and sensitively to feedback, and adhering to deadlines.

We are also grateful to the many peer reviewers and conference attendees who gave their time, provided thoughtful and constructive criticism, and shared their views. Our thanks also go to the Events Team at St John's College in Oxford, and especially Susie Power, who went above and beyond the call of duty and worked tirelessly with us to make this large-scale hybrid conference a success. We are also thankful to the MSPL board, in particular Warren Barr and Sue Bright, and to Ben McFarlane, for their guidance, support, and encouragement. We would also like to thank Jason Chau for his excellent assistance with proofreading and formatting the chapters. Finally, we would also like to thank our families for their understanding and unwavering support throughout this process.

Dr Natalie Mrockova, Dr Aruna Nair and Dr Luke Rostill
Oxford

Contents

List of Contributors

Fabiana Bettini is a Lecturer in Property Law at University College London, England.

Helen Carr is Professor of Property Law and Social Justice at the University of Southampton., England.

Damian Clifford is a Senior Lecturer at the ANU College of Law, Australia.

Heather Conway is a Professor of Law at Queen's University Belfast, Northern Ireland.

Sarah Green is Law Commissioner for Commercial and Common Law at the Law Commission of England and Wales.

Rory Gregson is a Junior Research Fellow at Trinity College, Cambridge, England.

Caroline Hunter is a Professor of Law at the University of York, England.

Joyman Lee is a Lecturer in Common Law at the University of Glasgow, Scotland.

Carl Makin is an ESRC Doctoral Candidate in the Law School at the University of York, England.

Natalie Mrockova is a Career Development Researcher and Lecturer in Law at Merton College, Oxford, England.

Aruna Nair is an Associate Professor of Law in the Oxford Law Faculty and a Tutorial Fellow in Law at Hertford College, Oxford, England.

Gwilym Owen is a Senior Lecturer in Law at the University of Bangor, Wales.

Susan Pascoe is an Associate Professor of Law in the School of Law at Middlesex University, London, England.

Andrew Ray is a Visiting Fellow at the ANU College of Law, Australia.

Heather Roberts is an Associate Professor at the ANU College of Law, Australia and an ARC DECRA Fellow.

Luke Rostill is an Associate Professor of Property Law in the Oxford Law Faculty and a Tutorial Fellow in Law at Trinity College, Oxford, England.

Lord Sales JSC is a Justice of the Supreme Court of the United Kingdom.

William Swadling is a Professor of Law in the Oxford Law Faculty and the Senior Law Fellow at Brasenose College, Oxford, England.

Joshua Teng is an Associate at Skrine and an Advocate and Solicitor of the High Court of Malaya.

Jeremy Waldron is a Professor of Law at New York University School of Law, United States.

Table of Cases

United Kingdom

Australia

Canada

Canada (Province of Quebec)

France

Japan

New Zealand

Singapore

United States

Table of Legislation

Primary Legislation

United Kingdom

Table of Secondary Legislation

Part I

Boundaries of Property

1

A 'bit' Too Much? The Common Law's Digital Dilemma

SARAH GREEN

IT IS PERHAPS not immediately obvious why the digitisation of personal property presents such a challenge to the common law, a creature that has, after all, been defined by its capacity for evolution, incremental development, and flexibility – in a comparative sense at least. But that challenge certainly exists. And it is a thorny one.

In terms of personal property alone, the common law has shown itself equal to accommodating the emergence of bank money, intermediated securities, and the mercantile use of documents that embody the rights to which they refer. All of these commercial and social developments required significant conceptual creativity and latitude on the part of common lawyers, and yet none was regarded as a step too far. The emergence and increased use of digital assets, however, does seem to have generated something of a blocker to incremental common law development, with appeals being made, at least in some quarters, to Parliament and to the Law Commission, to provide some form of guidance. What is it then, about bits and about bots, that presents such a challenge to the law of property?

I refer of course to the way in which the law has apparently struggled to categorise digital assets of various kinds. Such assets have so far been excluded from the category of things in possession and have fallen therefore, rather by default, into the category of things in action. This they definitely are not.

In any event, 'digital assets' is not a particularly homogenous class, and there are many, many different ways in which such assets can be constructed, used, transferred and stored. Their functions, and perhaps their legal classification, will often therefore be context-specific in a way that other 'categories' of personal property will not. This in itself gives rise to another question: why are digital assets so often grouped together – ie, what is their common denominator? It seems only to be that they exist in the digital realm; that they are 'soft' or 'electronic'; that their atoms take the form of bumps and troughs on computer hardware rather than the form of, say, stitches in cloth, DNA within cells or minerals within precious stones. The language used is often not helpful in facilitating an authentic understanding of digital things. 'Cloud storage' is just one example, leading many to believe that digital things are somehow ethereal and lacking in physical substance. 'The cloud' is of course nothing more or less than hardware located remotely from users – it is in fact just as physical as any other computer system.

In any event, there is a tendency to regard everything that has an electronic form as being homogenous: in form, in function and in type. The first step towards ensuring the appropriate legal treatment of digital assets is therefore to challenge this idea, and to differentiate clearly between digital assets on the basis of their particular characteristics; characteristics that are no less variable between types simply by virtue of being in electronic form.

It is a specific type of digital asset that gives rise to the most difficult classification problem in terms of personal property: a type whose novel characteristics are as revolutionary as they are disruptive. For present purposes, I will refer to these as Discrete Instantiation Digital Objects (DIDOs) – not the snappiest of monikers, but it highlights the features most relevant for classification purposes. What is distinctive about DIDOs is that they:

- exist independent of persons and legal systems;
- are unique and discrete units of value;
- are fully transferable (in the sense that they are divestible);
- are amenable to exclusive control.

They also meet the four criteria set out in Lord Wilberforce's classic definition of property in *National Provincial Bank v Ainsworth*[1] as being definable, identifiable by third parties, capable in their nature of assumption by third parties, and having some degree of permanence.

Nobody has ever really cared about the existence or nature of the personal property rights that they have in their Word documents because those documents are highly reproducible, scalable, interchangeable and therefore not (for practical purposes) scarce. They could be used and 'spent' many thousands of times and it would not matter. They sit on a reasonably inexpensive operating system and are generated by a reasonably inexpensive program. They are not practically exclusive or excludable and are valuable as means rather than as ends in themselves. That is not to say anything conclusive at this stage about whether they could in any context ever be the object of possessory rights, but merely to point out why the question has never really been asked.

Because they were mostly means and not ends, the questions that did arise in relation to those digital forms were rather different to the ones the law currently faces in relation to the latest generation of digital assets. What was important to users of word and data processing programs was the ability to use, rather than

[1] *National Provincial Bank v Ainsworth* [1965] 1 AC 1175.

to exchange, their wares. The standard acquisition of such programs was done so that those programs could be kept and employed as functional tools, rather than transferred or kept for their intrinsic value. A licence to use has always been, therefore, a perfectly adequate interest for such users to have in relation to those assets.

Even here, though, the seeds of conceptual confusion were somehow sown. The fact that such use value was, empirically, almost always both appropriate and sufficient seemed to distract from the point that such functionality did not constitute the *logical* limit of digitised value. Somewhere in cyberspace, personal and intellectual property interests were conflated. In cyberspace, it seems, everyone can share your screen. Whether I buy a paperback novel or its digital, downloadable version, I only (in the standard case) aim to acquire the *use value* of my copy. In neither instance would I intend, hope or expect that I also thereby acquire the intellectual property rights in that book, and accrue to myself therefore its exchange value. The distinction is so clear in the case of a paperback novel purchase, for example, that nobody ever considers it – there is no question that I acquire personal property rights in my copy of the book, and that nobody, not even the author, has the right to take that from me or otherwise to interfere with my possessory rights in it. As soon as electronic copies enter the picture, however, the line between intellectual and personal property rights for some reason becomes blurred and arguments start being made that a discrete copy in electronic form can never be sold because the intellectual property rights in it remain with the transferor (again, this refers to the standard case: it is of course perfectly possible for both intellectual property and personal property rights, or just intellectual property rights to be transferred if that is what the parties agree). Why this happens in the digital realm and not the analogue realm has never been clear to me, but it is problematic; threatening, as it does, a coherent development of the law in relation to digitised things. The other common error made in relation to the conceptualisation of digital things is their conflation with pure information. Perhaps this is because of the label, applied since the late 1980s to anything computer-related, of 'information technology', whatever that means. DIDOs are definitely not information and understanding this is crucial to a proper legal treatment of them. There are several points of distinction between pure information and DIDOs (all of which are to some extent interdependent):

- Pure information is not separable or independent from persons but DIDOs are.
- Divestibility. This is why the distinction of DIDOs from pure information is crucial. Pure information, such as the knowledge of the question on the exam paper in *Oxford v Moss*[2] (in which the student took a copy of an

[2] *Chief of Merseyside Police v Moss* (1979) 68 Cr App Rep 183, [1979] Crim LR 119.

engineering exam paper, acquired the questions and then replaced the paper: an action deemed not to be theft because all that was permanently appropriated was pure information, in which there can be no property rights) is not divestible because, having passed such information on to another party, the transferor nonetheless still retains it, and therefore has the ability to use it and to control it. That control, as we know, has not been moved or transferred, but merely spread further and wider. DIDOs on the other hand are fully divestible: when I transfer my NFT or digital coin to another party, I do not retain the ability to use or control it – this has *transferred* in the true sense of the term to, rather than having been shared with, the transferee. Control has been moved and not spread. In order fully to appreciate this, it is necessary also to understand the distinction which follows.

- Functionality. The value of pure information lies in knowing it. As the student in *Oxford v Moss* anticipated, the pure fact of his having such knowledge was likely to give him an advantage over those who did not know the same information (to the extent that this ever helps any student). Such advantage as he was seeking results simply and directly from the fact of having that knowledge. The point is that the knowledge itself is all that is needed to access, use or exploit its value.

This is not true of the functionality of DIDOs. Whilst digital coins, for example, are often described as strings of data, this data is not information in the same way as is a civil engineering exam question, or an investment tip, or the location of buried treasure. Knowledge of the contents of the digital coin data string alone is *not* intrinsically valuable: its value lies only in its specific instantiation within the protocol by which it has been generated. In other words, were I to memorise the string of characters that might, on a given protocol, represent a particular digital coin, this is no good to me as bare knowledge. Whilst that string of characters is *eo ipso* pure information, it does not amount to the digital coin. It is rather just one element of that coin and, although it is a necessary element, it is most definitely not a sufficient one. It has no value outside of its unique instantiation within that protocol. Nobody would want it in that form because it is good to nobody. To suggest that it is the same as suggesting that my knowing the serial number of a ten-pound note gives me the power to spend that particular note, without having possession of the note itself. The serial number on the ten-pound note identifies a unique instantiation of discrete value but is not valuable in its own right. The same is true of the characters that make up a digital coin. The coin itself (which is made up of the character string – the pure information part – plus its unique instantiation within the program) is discrete, unique and has an independent existence in its own right, outside of human minds, in a way that pure information does not. I could, for instance, acquire knowledge of the code underlying a crypto-whale's entire fortune. If I did, I would have all of the same pure information as she does. But I still would not be a penny richer, because only the unique instantiation of that data in the relevant software (broadly, the digital analogue of holding a serial number in the form of its being printed on a banknote of legal tender) has any dynamic function and therefore any value. I do not, simply by knowing the data element, have the ability to use, transfer or dispose of that fortune. In fact, I cannot do anything with it: it is not the same as an idea at all.

These two elements of a DIDO (pure information plus its unique instantiation within the protocol or program) are an indivisible unit in terms of their value. Pure information in the buried treasure location sense can of course be written down and recorded, either on paper or in electronic form, but it is valuable even when it is not. So pure information and its medium do not form an indivisible unit: pure information does not require a particular medium to function in the way that DIDOs do. Except, of course, for the medium of human cognition, but that is precisely why pure information and DIDOs need to be distinguished: human cognition facilitates sharing but not transfer; it can neither truly give nor truly take, and so personal property rules (as opposed to intellectual property rules) are therefore not a proper fit for the things to which it gives value. In requiring more than human cognition, DIDOs are able to assume the qualities that make them fully independent of persons, fully transferable between those persons and therefore capable of exclusive control following transfer.

So why, given that these things are so, have DIDOs found it so difficult to be admitted to the choses in possession club, alongside all the other familiar and conventional things that exhibit those qualities? First, there is the presumption of homogeneity, alluded to above: the tendency to conclude that, because *some* things in digitised form do not have, say, the quality of true divestibility, the same must be true for *all* digital forms. The very fact that we have for centuries maintained a distinction between choses in action and choses in possession tells us that we do not do this with non-digital things. We do not, for instance, prevent the transfer of oxygen cylinders from being a sale simply because oxygen in the atmosphere is not something to which that analysis could ever be appropriate. And yet, as I have said, we do this in the digital realm all the time. Or at least we have historically.

Second, there are the nefarious beginnings of DIDOs to consider. Cryptocurrencies, so the argument goes, are used by thieves, rogues and money launderers. But so is cash, and the internet, and bank money. To be diverted by arguments such as these from the need to ensure that a particular technology's legitimate use is safe, resilient and effective is to deny that most of our commercial and technological developments started, or were at least accelerated, by those with an incentive to find new ways to get rich. But what begins on the edge soon becomes both mainstream and inevitably a force for good. Yes, Bitcoin itself is at the moment colossally environmentally damaging, but it is far from the only cryptocurrency and not all such currencies use proof of work (the process that requires enormous processing power) in this way. In fact, the Ethereum blockchain, easily one of the most globally significant networks, has recently 'merged' with a proof of stake chain, meaning that its energy consumption has been reduced by more than 99.95 per cent. (As the name suggests, proof of stake does not require extensive data processing in the way that proof of work does, relying instead on capital 'skin in the game'.) Others are bound to follow suit. What is more, cryptocurrencies can provide access to finance and funding to huge numbers of the planet's population, who have hitherto been excluded from conventional banking services. Distributed Ledger Technology, which has made the creation of DIDOs possible, is not intrinsically bad: it is only as bad as its uses and users. And those uses are getting better and better. Recently, for example, US$13 million dollars has been raised in Bitcoin through crowdfunding for those affected and displaced by the war in Ukraine. Even were this not to be the case, it does not follow that 'bad' things should be denied proper legal recognition and understanding. Knowing one's enemy is always to be recommended.

Third, there is the bare fact that some of these digital assets are simply not like anything we have seen before. Analogies, for so long the lubricant of common law development, are of limited use in this context, and are actually liable to confuse rather than to clarify. When bank money became the payment medium of choice, for instance, it looked and behaved in some ways very differently from cash, but not at all differently from the debt and its long legal pedigree. When documents started to be used by merchants to embody the rights to which they referred, those documents were treated as a fusion of the right (in terms of value) and the thing (in terms of transferability). These things could all be made to fit existing categories because they were analogous to current things and current forms of things.

Some digital assets, however, are not analogous with anything we know and with which the law currently deals. Take cryptocurrencies (and for the minute, let us not consider their existence or otherwise as true currencies – that is a lecture for another day. Neither is it unrealistic: they are currently more commonly used by parties as commodities and investment vehicles than they are as a means of exchange). In some ways, cryptocurrencies are like banknotes in that they are (strictly) individually identifiable and therefore technically non-fungible, but practically fungible.

In other ways, however, they are not. They are not transferred by the passing of one completely unchanging thing from one hand to another. Whilst the protocols on which different cryptocurrencies sit do not all operate in exactly the same way, the usual means of 'transfer' is achieved through a sort of extinction of the transferor's thing and the creation of a new thing that accrues to the account of the transferee. I say 'sort of' extinction because the data string that the transferor held still exists on the ledger, but it is stripped of its transactional potential. It is, therefore, sort of like an empty wallet, but again, only sort of, because physical wallets themselves can often have their own intrinsic value as objects. 'Spent' data strings are unlikely to be an object of desire for anyone because they have no physical, functional, or aesthetic value. Any interest in them would be niche, to say the least.

This process, which is akin to extinction and novation, is, I expect you are thinking, just what happens with bank money. This is true, but it does not mean that, simply because DIDOs share a form of transfer process with choses in action that they themselves are choses in action. Choses in action are of course those things that only exist by virtue of enforcement by parties and recognition by a legal system. A debt is nothing if nobody claims it and/or if no legal system recognises it. A digital asset, on the other hand, does have an existence independent of both persons and the legal system. It exists, like a database or digital photograph repository, regardless of whether anyone lays a claim to it, or whether any legal system recognises it. It exists regardless of 'action'.

So, DIDOs are not things in action, but they do not always behave or look like things in possession either, not least because they do not subsist as one single form that is passed from hand to hand. The analogies on which we have relied for so long are of limited assistance to us here. DIDOs are independent things that can be subject to exclusive control, fully transferred and divested, and yet we cannot touch them, see them or perceive them with the unaided senses. Should we give greater emphasis to their factual characteristics and physical appearance, or to their functionality; to the way that parties use them and the expectations they have of them? The real problem, I think, for the common law of personal property is that the dichotomy on which it has always been based no longer provides an exhaustive account of the things that we want to own.

It is time therefore for a tertium quid.

This might sound like a bold move, but the current digital economy operates in a whole new paradigm. So the law that supports it needs to do the same. I get that the Romans did not do it, but, as paragons of progressive thinking, I have no doubt that they would have embraced a digital revolution with vigour and enthusiasm. And with legal development. There really are more things in Heaven and Earth than have yet been dreamt of in legal philosophy.

2

Digital Assets as Property and the Challenges of Forced Judicial Activism

ANDREW RAY, DAMIAN CLIFFORD
AND HEATHER ROBERTS*

I. INTRODUCTION

DO PROPERTY RIGHTS attach to digital assets? Should different tests apply depending on the form and content of the digital asset,[1] for example, where the asset contains personal data? Who decides which digital assets are things to which property rights attach and what test (or tests) should they apply in doing so?

As we enter a world of web 3.0, courts and governments are increasingly grappling with these questions as consumers embrace digital assets such as cryptocurrencies.[2] These assets are, at their core, different forms of stored data or information. Significant questions arise as to the legal status of these digital

* The chapter outlines our personal views only. We would like to thank the anonymous reviewers and attendees at the Modern Studies in Property Law Conference for their comments which strengthened the chapter. We would also like to separately thank Katie Mccay for her helpful comments on an earlier draft. All errors remain our own.

[1] Here we take a wide definition of digital assets to consider not just blockchain based assets, but also wider forms of data used by businesses and consumers.

[2] See, eg, M Polasik et al, 'Price Fluctuations and the Use of Bitcoin: An Empirical Inquiry' (2015) 20(1) *International Journal of Electronic Commerce* 9; E Prasad, *The Future of Money: How the Digital Revolution is Transforming Currencies and Finance* (Cambridge, MA, Harvard University Press, 2021); International Monetary Fund, 'The Crypto Ecosystem and Financial Stability Challenges' (October 2021) www.imf.org/-/media/Files/Publications/GFSR/2021/October/English/ch2.ashx (last accessed 3 December 2022); A Ferreira, 'The Curious Case of Stablecoins – Balancing Risks and Rewards?' (2021) 24(4) *Journal of International Economic Law* 755.

assets as, traditionally, and for good reason, information is not a thing to which property rights attach.[3]

Several matters complicate the resolution of these questions. First, traditional legal rules and principles are not easily applicable in online realms.[4] Second, the speed of the uptake of digital assets has created regulatory uncertainties, leaving gaps in the law which may be exploited.[5] Third, digital assets are, by definition, not constrained by geographic or legal boundaries and consumers increasingly operate across jurisdictions. Fourth, rapid technological development, especially growth in computing power, is leading to significant increases in the breadth of the categories of digital assets, hampering efforts to categorise or value digital assets.

This chapter explores the question of when data are things to which property rights attach through the lens of the crypto-asset cases. In doing so, it discusses whether the current approaches used by courts are sufficient to distinguish between different categories of data (and by extension different categories of digital assets). The chapter focuses on the broader question of *who* should be making these decisions, noting that the position to date in many jurisdictions has been to leave these decisions to judges to resolve. In particular, this chapter questions whether these decisions are ultimately 'judicial' in nature or whether they are more akin to policy determinations which fall in the purview of the executive or legislative branches of government.

In exploring how property law applies to information we note that our discussion focuses on the concept of property in law only and not broader philosophical questions as to whether a digital asset *should* be property.[6]

The chapter proceeds in four parts. First, we briefly review how property law tests have been applied by courts to information. Second, we analyse the recent crypto-asset cases and assess the tests that courts have applied in resolving those disputes.[7] Third, we consider whether these are issues that fall within the judicial role or whether another body would be better suited to resolve these issues. Ultimately, we suggest that the determinations should be left to legislative or quasi-legislative bodies which are better equipped to navigate the policy issues inherent in property classifications surrounding data and information.

[3] Sir J Mummery, 'Property in the Information Age' in W Barr (ed), *Modern Studies in Property Law: Volume 8* (Oxford, Hart Publishing, 2018) 3.

[4] C Engel, 'The Role of Law in the Governance of the Internet' (2006) 1(2) *International Review of Law, Computers and Technology* 201.

[5] A Ferreira and P Sander, 'EU Search for Regulatory Answers to Crypto Assets and their Place in the Financial Markets' Infrastructure' (2021) 43 *Computer Law and Security Review* 105632.

[6] A Rahmatian, 'Intellectual Property and the Concept of Dematerialised Property' in S Bright (ed), *Modern Studies in Property Law: Volume 6* (Oxford, Hart Publishing, 2011) 362–63.

[7] By extension, we argue that it is likely that courts would apply similar tests in determining whether other digital assets are things to which property rights attach.

II. PROPERTY LAW AND INFORMATION

A. The Benefits of Proprietary Remedies

Before turning to discuss how property law principles have been applied to digital assets, it is necessary to outline why this question is important. In particular, if there were suitable alternative approaches to protecting digital assets, the question whether a digital asset is a thing to which property rights attach may be purely academic.

In the context of digital assets, the question is important for at least three reasons. First, the easily transportable nature of digital assets makes other legal avenues for protection ill-suited compared to proprietary remedies. Proprietary remedies offer consumers and businesses certainty around the status of transactions and a clear framework to resolve disputes. Bennett Moses aptly describes the situation:

> where certain things fall partly or entirely outside the realm of property law, only specially tailored (or sui generis) rules can perform a similar function. In the absence of a sufficient sui generis framework, a failure to apply property rules leads to wrongs without remedies and pervasive uncertainty.[8]

In the case of digital assets such as cryptocurrencies, the risk of a 'wrong without a remedy' is heightened where consumers are forced to rely on contractual or other legal rights. For example, the cases discussed in section III demonstrate the risks that consumers face given the high-risk nature of digital transactions in part due to the rapid ease of portability of digital assets which permits digital assets to be rapidly on-sold, copied or moved outside of a jurisdiction.[9] In such cases, consumers must be able to access freezing orders and tracing remedies to be able to recover their stolen asset. Elevating the need for remedies is the significant volatility in the value of digital assets.[10] Where a stolen asset increased rapidly in value, absent a proprietary remedy, a consumer will be unable to recover the 'true' value of the stolen asset. Similarly, as we will discuss later, contractual remedies may not protect the holders of the digital tokens in a liquidation scenario caused by the collapse of a trading exchange.[11]

[8] L Bennett Moses, 'The Applicability of Property Law in New Contexts: From Cells to Cyberspace' (2008) 30 *Sydney Law Review* 639, 641.

[9] *Chen v Blockchain Global Ltd; Abel v Blockchain Global Ltd* [2022] VSC 92.

[10] C Strohm, O Kharif and T Schoenberg, 'US says $5b seizure of stolen bitcoin is largest in history', *Australian Financial Review* (online, 9 February 2022) www.afr.com/world/north-america/us-says-5b-seizure-of-stolen-bitcoin-is-largest-in-history-20220209-p59uvp (last accessed 3 December 2022).

[11] We note that similar concerns do not generally arise in relation to currency in banks in advanced economies, which are often government-backed or in stocks or other similar assets which attract the protection of proprietary remedies.

In turn, absent the protections afforded by property law, consumers and businesses may be more cautious in investing in the novel technologies underpinning digital assets. Viewed in this light, there are arguably strong policy reasons that favour the extension of property law doctrines to digital assets.[12]

The second reason that the question is important is the fact that the rapidly evolving market for digital assets means that existing statutory protections such as consumer or privacy frameworks may not readily or universally apply to digital assets.[13] It may therefore be easier for a legislature to extend property law frameworks to those assets, avoiding the need for wholesale revision of other forms of protection.

The third reason the question is of significance concerns the implications for government regulation if digital assets are *not* classed as things to which property rights attach. Relevantly, in the Australian context, the acquisition of *property* can activate a constitutional guarantee that can require the federal government to provide compensation to the owner.[14] This is a broader limitation than is present in the UK, where similar limitations only apply to the 'taking' of real property.[15]

Overall, it is apparent that the questions posed in this chapter are not merely of academic interest. Rather, whether digital assets are things to which property rights attach will have consequences for consumers, businesses, and governments. While standalone regulation may be able to afford *some* of the protections afforded by proprietary remedies, there are significant hurdles to adopting a course where no digital assets attract proprietary remedies. That is not to say, however, that legislation will not have an important role to play in the regulation of digital assets.

[12] We note there is mixed evidence as to whether regulation increases or impedes innovation: L Hashimy and P Sandner, 'The Impact of Financial Regulation on the Development of Distributed Ledger Technology (DLT) Firms' (2020) 3 *Frontiers in Blockchain* 21; A Moore, 'Measuring Economic Uncertainty and Its Effects' (Research Paper, Reserve Bank of Australia 2016) 93 Econ Rec 550, available at www.rba.gov.au/publications/rdp/2016/pdf/rdp2016-01.pdf (last accessed 3 December 2022).

[13] For example, mining or trading crypto-assets continues to be banned in China, although there is evidence that these bans can be (and are) circumvented: MA Nadeem et al, 'Investigating the Adoption Factors of Cryptocurrencies – A Case of Bitcoin: Empirical Evidence from China' (2021) 11(1) SAGE Open, available online at journals.sagepub.com/doi/10.1177/2158244021998704 (last accessed 3 December 2022).

[14] Australian Constitution, s 51(xxxi) which requires 'just terms' to be provided for the acquisition of property; See *Houston v State of New South Wales (No 2)* [2021] FCA 637; *JT International SA v Commonwealth* (2012) 250 CLR 1.

[15] Compulsory Purchase Act 1965 (UK) and Land Compensation Act 1961 (UK). For a detailed theoretical engagement with the 'takings' jurisprudence and theoretical conceptions of property, see K Gray, 'Recreational Property' in S Bright (ed), *Modern Studies in Property Law: Volume 6* (Oxford, Hart Publishing, 2011) 3.

B. Property Law and Information

Property has traditionally fallen into two categories: real and personal. For the purposes of this chapter, we are concerned solely with personal property.[16] Personal property itself falls into two categories: '[a]ll personal things are either in possession or action. The law knows no tertium quid between the two'.[17] *Halsbury's Laws of England* outlines the distinction:

> The expression 'chose in action' or 'thing in action' in the literal sense means a thing recoverable by action, as contrasted with a chose in possession, which is a thing of which a person may have physical possession.[18]

It is apparent that information cannot be a chose in possession (as, by its nature, information is not tangible). The question is then whether the information itself can form a chose in action or some other form of intangible property right. In addressing this question courts have historically been reticent to find that information is something to which property rights attach.[19] For example, in *Your Response Ltd v Datateam Business Media Ltd*, the English Court of Appeal rejected arguments that information in a database is a thing to which property rights attach *at common law*.[20] This situation can be readily distinguished from a circumstance where the relevant information is in the form of a copyrighted work or a patent, which are creatures of property created by statute.[21] These statutorily-recognised rights differ from those recognised by the common law. In particular, patents are recognised as personal property but are not recognised as choses in action or choses in possession.[22]

If the character of information is not enough, the question that then arises is whether there are circumstances in which property characteristics will nevertheless attach to information. Courts have, for example, accepted that where information is a trade secret (or to a lesser extent confidential) certain proprietary characteristics may attach to it. For example, the Australian High Court in *Farah Constructions*, in discussing whether property acquired through misuse of information should be treated as trust property, stated:

> Even if the information were confidential, that would not make it property for the purposes of the first limb of *Barnes v Addy. The protection given by equitable doctrines and remedies causes confidential information sometimes to be described as having a proprietary character, 'not because property is the basis upon which that*

[16] As information would not amount to real property.
[17] *Colonial Bank v Whinney* [1885] 30 ChD 261 (Fry LJ).
[18] (5th edn, 2021) vol 13, para 1.
[19] *Farah Constructions Pty Ltd v Say-Dee Pty Ltd* (2007) 230 CLR 89, [118].
[20] *Your Response Ltd v Datateam Business Media Ltd* [2015] QB 41.
[21] See, eg, *University of Western Australia v Gray (No 20)* [2008] FCA 498, [89].
[22] Patents Act 1977 (UK), s 30(1).

protection is given, but because of the effect of that protection'. Certain types of confidential information share characteristics with standard instances of property. Thus trade secrets may be transferred, held in trust and charged. However, the information involved in this case is not a trade secret.[23]

C. Common Law Tests

In determining whether a thing is something to which property rights attach, courts have generally relied upon the *Ainsworth* indicia, found in Lord Wilberforce's opinion in *National Provincial Bank v Ainsworth*,[24] where his Lordship stated:

> [I]t must be definable, identifiable by third parties, capable in its nature of assumption by third parties, and have some degree of permanence or stability.[25]

While this approach is not the only one used by courts to assess whether a thing is something to which property rights attach,[26] as will be outlined further below, it has been the 'test' applied by courts in the recent crypto-asset cases. By extension, it is highly likely that that approach will be influential in future digital asset cases.

As a general comment, many cases concerning information/data would struggle to satisfy the *Ainsworth* indicia of property.[27] This is because information is replicable, is often comprised of information that is public knowledge (or, at a minimum, is hard for a party to show is not public knowledge), and can be easily destroyed or deleted and hence fails to satisfy the requirement of permanence or stability.[28] Information can also easily be added to or lost from a particular asset, or the digital access key to that information may be lost or corrupted – in effect eroding the value of the asset.[29]

Further, the question of assumption also poses challenges. After all, if an individual possesses a copy of some information and hands it to another person,

[23] *Farah Constructions* (n 19) [118] (emphasis added, citations omitted).

[24] *Provincial Bank v Ainsworth* [1965] 1 AC 1175.

[25] ibid 1248.

[26] See generally Bennett Moses (n 8). See further *Yanner v Eaton* (1999) 201 CLR 351, 339; *Smith, Kline & French Laboratories (Australia) Ltd v Secretary, Department of Community Services and Health* (1990) 95 ALR 87, 135. These principles were recently discussed in *Hocking v Director-General of the National Archives of Australia* (2020) 271 CLR 1, in which Professor Hocking sought access to archival records containing letters relating to the dismissal of Prime Minister Gough Whitlam by Sir John Kerr between the Queen and the Governor General. This case is worth emphasising as Professor Hocking was likely after the *information* in those letters, rather than the physical copies themselves. Kiefel CJ, Bell, Gageler and Keane JJ discussed the concept of property at [89]–[91]: stating in part '[p]roperty is not "a monolithic notion of standard content and invariable intensity"'. See further Edelman J's judgment at [201]–[206].

[27] *Fairstar Heavy Transport NV v Adkins & Anor* [2013] EWCA Civ 886, [47].

[28] *Boardman v Phipps* [1967] 2 AC 46, 127: '[i]n general, information is not property at all. It is normally open to all who have eyes to read and ears to hear'.

[29] *Chen* (n 9) [10].

has the information changed hands (possession), or has a new copy of that information simply been created?

For example, in *Fairstar Heavy Transport NV v Adkins & Anor* Lord Justice Mummery (with whom Patten LJ and Black LJ agreed) said:

> … The claim to property in intangible information presents obvious definitional difficulties, having regard to the criteria of certainty, exclusivity, control and assignability that *normally* characterise property rights and distinguish them from personal rights.[30]

However, reducing the weight that can be attributed to this statement, his Lordship later went on to state:

> … It would be unwise, for example, for this court to endorse the proposition that there can never be property in information without knowing more about the nature of the information … and the circumstances in which a property right was being asserted. Some kinds of information, such as non-patentable know-how, are more akin to property in their specificity and exclusivity than, say, personal information about private life.[31]

As the cases we have discussed so far demonstrate, there are at least *some* circumstances in which information is something to which property rights attach. To further explore this boundary, we turn now to consider the recent crypto-asset cases. As we will argue, these cases demonstrate that courts appear to be increasingly willing to accept that information (at least in some cases) can be a form of intangible personal property.

III. CRYPTO-ASSET CASES

This Part focuses on analysing the approaches taken by courts in Singapore, the UK and New Zealand in assessing whether crypto-assets are things to which property rights attach. These jurisdictions were chosen as they reflect common law countries where more significant analysis of the question has been undertaken by courts. While there have been some cases in Australia and Canada that have briefly discussed the issue, those decisions occurred at preliminary stages of the respective litigation.[32] Given the limited legal argument advanced at preliminary hearings for injunctive relief, the cases did not require the courts to explain their reasoning.

This Part focuses *solely* on the approach taken by the courts, rather than on analysing any factual differences between the types of crypto-asset that each

[30] *Fairstar* (n 27) [47] (Mummery LJ, Patten and Black LJ agreeing).

[31] ibid [48].

[32] *Re Blockchain Global Limited (Admins Apptd)* [2021] VSC 762; *Shair.Com Global Digital Services Ltd v Arnold* [2018] BCSC 1512.

court was considering.[33] In our view, it is likely that courts will take a similar approach in determining whether other forms of digital assets are property. As such, consideration of the tests applied in these cases will inform our later analysis.

A. Singapore

i. First Instance Decision

In a 2019 decision, the Singapore International Commercial Court became one of the first courts to assess whether Bitcoin ('BTC') and Ethereum ('ETH') are things to which property rights attach in *B2C2 Ltd v Quoine Pty Ltd*.[34] The facts of the case are (for our purposes) largely straightforward. Quoine operated a digital asset exchange platform through which individuals could buy and sell crypto-assets. B2C2 was a UK-based company that bought and sold large volumes of BTC and ETH through the platform as a 'market maker'.[35] Through a mistake in one of the digital contracts underpinning the Quoine platform,[36] on 19 April 2017, there was an error in the market exchange rate at which BTC and ETH could be exchanged (reflecting approximately 250 times their value).[37] As a result of the operation of various automatic contracts, B2C2 entered trades with other users of the Quoine platform, receiving 3,100 BTC at a cost of around 310 ETH. When made aware of the trades, Quoine unilaterally cancelled the trades and reversed the transactions.[38] Subsequently, B2C2 commenced action against Quoine alleging breach of contract (for the unilateral cancellation of the trades) and breach of trust.

While the first of these claims is itself interesting and raised novel questions concerning the doctrine of mistake and its application to automated systems,[39] it is not relevant for our discussion. Instead, it is the second claim which is relevant – as it relied on a determination that the crypto-assets were things to which property rights attach. If they were not, then the action would fail.

Before the Singapore International Commercial Court, Quoine 'was prepared to assume that cryptocurrencies may be treated as property that can

[33] Such a question is beyond the scope of this chapter.

[34] *B2C2 Ltd v Quoine Pty Ltd* [2019] SGHC(I) 03 ('*B2C2 First Instance*').

[35] Quoine's role was to provide liquidity across several exchanges by buying and selling large volumes of crypto-assets: see ibid [10] for discussion. It made these transactions through automated trading software that could rapidly make large numbers of transactions over the multiple currency exchanges it operated on.

[36] The parties did not dispute the fact that this was a genuine and systemic error in the pricing algorithm underpinning the Quoine system.

[37] ibid [4].

[38] ibid [5].

[39] V Ooi and KP Soh, 'Rethinking Mistake in the Age of Algorithms: Quoine Pte Ltd v B2C2 Ltd' (2020) 31(3) *King's Law Journal* 367.

be held on trust'.[40] Nevertheless, Simon Thorley IJ made comments in obiter supporting that position, relevantly stating at [142] that:

> ... Cryptocurrencies are not legal tender in the sense of being a regulated currency issued by a government but do have the fundamental characteristic of intangible property as being an identifiable thing of value. Quoine drew my attention to the classic definition of a property right in the House of Lords decision of *National Provincial Bank v Ainsworth* [1965] 1 AC 1175 at 1248:
>
>> 'it must be definable, identifiable by third parties, capable in its nature of assumption by third parties, and have some degree of permanence or stability'.
>
> Cryptocurrencies meet all these requirements. Whilst there may be some academic debate as to the precise nature of the property right, in the light of the fact that Quoine does not seek to dispute that they may be treated as property in a generic sense, I need not consider the question further.[41]

It is worth noting here that Thorley IJ made no comment as to the *type* of property or what rights may (or may not) attach to BTC/ETH, merely that they met the requirements. His Honour then went on to consider whether on the facts a trust was made out, and whether any of Quoine's defences applied. His Honour ultimately held that B2C2 succeeded on both of its claims. Quoine subsequently appealed the decision.

ii. Court of Appeal Decision

The Court of Appeal engaged an amicus, Professor Goh Yihan, to provide an expert opinion outlining whether the contracts were void for unilateral mistake and whether the relevant crypto-assets were a species of property to which a trust applied.[42] The majority of the Court of Appeal upheld the primary judge's findings that the underlying contracts did not permit the unilateral cancellation of the transactions, and that there was no mistake that Quoine could rely upon to cancel the contracts. The majority of the Court did, however, uphold the appeal in relation to the breach of trust, and, in doing so, commented on the discussion by the primary judge on the property issue.

Having outlined how Quoine 'belatedly' raised the issue of whether BTC was a thing to which property rights attach on appeal, the majority reviewed the existing case law on the issue from other Commonwealth jurisdictions noting that '[t]here have been some other cases in the Commonwealth that have implicitly accepted that cryptocurrency may be regarded as property, although we are not aware of any court that has attempted to identify the precise nature

[40] *B2C2 First Instance* (n 34) [142].
[41] ibid.
[42] *Quoine Pte Ltd v B2C2 Ltd* [2020] SGCA(I) 02, [6] ('*B2C2 Appeal*'). Professor Goh Yihan is now a Judicial Commissioner of the Supreme Court of Singapore.

of the property right if any'.[43] The appellate Court, however, went on to say that:

> There may be much to commend the view that cryptocurrencies should be capable of assimilation into the general concepts of property. There are, however, difficult questions as to the type of property that is involved. It is not necessary for us to come to a final position on this question in the present case …[44]

B. United Kingdom

The approach taken in the UK is similar to that taken by the primary judge in *B2C2*. In the UK, this approach was, prior to judicial consideration, advanced in the *Legal Statement on Cryptoassets and Smart Contracts* authored by a specially appointed UK Jurisdiction Taskforce in 2019.[45] In its statement, the Taskforce adopted an approach that focused on the *Ainsworth* indicia, reasoning that the correct approach would be to assess whether a thing met the *Ainsworth* indicia and, if so, that 'the law [would then] treat them as property unless there is some special legal reason to disqualify them'.[46] The Taskforce ultimately concluded that the things that distinguished crypto-assets from other more 'traditional' forms of property were insufficient to deny them status as some form of property.[47]

The approach taken by the Taskforce, was subsequently endorsed implicitly in two cases (one concerning the grant of a worldwide freezing order[48] and one an asset preservation order[49]), however neither of those decisions assessed the issue in depth.

In the 2019 decision of *AA v Persons Unknown*,[50] however, the High Court had the opportunity to consider whether a proprietary injunction could be sought over a specified Bitcoin 'wallet' that contained 96 BTC. The BTC had been traced (in the layperson sense) from payments originally made by an insurance company to hackers to regain access to their company systems following an anonymous 'ransomware' demand. The insurance company's insurer brought

[43] ibid [139].

[44] ibid [144] (Menon CJ, Leong and Prakash JJ and French IJ). The dissenting judge did not make findings on this issue.

[45] UK Jurisdiction Taskforce, *Legal Statement on Cryptoassets and Smart Contracts* (Report, November 2019), available online at technationio.wpenginepowered.com/wp-content/uploads/2021/04/Lawtech-Amplifi-Roundtables-Report-FINAL2.pdf (last accessed 3 December 2022). The members of the panel included the Chancellor of the High Court, a Justice of the High Court and senior lawyers and civil servants.

[46] ibid [39].

[47] ibid [77], [84].

[48] *Vorotyntseva v Money-4 Limited* [2018] EWHC 2596 (CH).

[49] *Liam David Robertson v Persons Unknown*, CL-2019-000444, unreported, 15th July 2019 (Moulder J).

[50] *AA v Persons Unknown* [2019] EWHC 3556 (Comm).

an action against four separate respondents[51] seeking to recover the BTC in partial payment for the amounts they had paid out under their insurance policy.

The action itself is noteworthy for at least two reasons. First, it clearly demonstrated the ability to trace/track BTC payments (including through several transfers), and (at least in part) refutes calls concerning the alleged un-traceability of BTC transactions.[52] Second, the action was brought by an insurer who wished to remain anonymous (a request which was granted by the Court), with the action heard in private.[53]

More relevant for this chapter is how Bryan J determined the property law question. His Honour stated at [55]–[56] that:

> Prima facie there is a difficulty in treating Bitcoins and other crypto currencies as a form of property: they are neither chose in possession nor are they chose in action. They are not choses in possession because they are virtual, they are not tangible, they cannot be possessed. They are not choses in action because they do not embody any right capable of being enforced by action. That produces a difficulty because English law traditionally views property as being of only two kinds, choses in possession and choses in action.
>
> …
>
> On that analysis Bitcoins and other crypto currencies could not be classified as a form of property, which would prevent them being the subject of a proprietary injunction or a freezing injunction …[54]

His Honour went on to consider the Taskforce Report, noting that the authors of the Report were not endorsing its contents in their capacity as judicial officers, nor was the report 'a statement of the law'.[55] Nevertheless his Honour said that:

> [I]n my judgment, it is relevant to consider the analysis in that Legal Statement as to the proprietary status of crypto currencies because it is a detailed and careful consideration and, as I shall come on to, I consider that that analysis as to the proprietary status of crypto currencies is compelling …[56]

His Honour then applied the *Ainsworth* indicia (the same approach taken in the Taskforce Report), stating at [59] that:

> The conclusion that was expressed was that a crypto asset might not be a thing in action on a narrow definition of that term, but that does not mean that it cannot

[51] First, the persons unknown who demanded the bitcoin, second, the persons unknown who control the wallet currently holding the tracked BTC, and third and fourth, the trading exchanges on which those wallets were stored. There was no suggestion that the exchanges were involved in the original hack.

[52] See, eg, S Foley, JR Karlsen and TJ Putniņš, 'Sex, Drugs, and Bitcoin: How Much Illegal Activity Is Financed Through Cryptocurrencies?' (2019) 32(5) *The Review of Financial Studies* 1798.

[53] *AA v Persons Unknown* (n 50) [27]–[28], [30]–[37].

[54] ibid [55]–[56].

[55] ibid [56]–[57].

[56] ibid [57].

> be treated as property. Essentially, and for the reasons identified in that legal statement, I consider that a crypto asset such as Bitcoin are property. They meet the four criteria set out in Lord Wilberforce's classic definition of property in *National Provincial Bank v Ainsworth* [1965] 1 AC 1175 as being definable, identifiable by third parties, capable in their nature of assumption by third parties, and having some degree of permanence. That too, was the conclusion of the Singapore International Commercial Court in *B2C2 Limited v Quoine PTC Limited* [2019] SGHC (I) 03 [142].[57]

There are three key points to highlight from the above. First, the Court rejected an approach limited to the two 'traditional' conceptions of property, finding that while crypto-assets do not fall into these categories they can nonetheless be *some* form of property. This approach accords with much of the academic literature on these points, with most commentators noting that the real contention is what rights attach to this property and what form those rights take rather than whether crypto-assets are *capable* of being property.[58]

Second, and relevant to our analysis below, the Court has given judicial weight to the statement from the UK Jurisdiction Taskforce.[59] It is interesting to hypothesise about what path the Court would have taken in the absence of that statement – while his Honour did point to the *B2C2 First Instance* decision, that approach was reversed on appeal. In contrast to the Singapore Court of Appeal,[60] the UK Court had a clear quasi-legislative statement that it could draw on in support of its ultimate determination that, notwithstanding that BTC fell outside the traditional realms of property, it could be considered *some* form of property. As we will discuss below, such decisions lend themselves more easily to the realm of policy determinations than judicial.

Third, the UK decision applied the same test that was suggested in the *B2C2* first instance decision – namely the *Ainsworth* criteria. While such an approach may have worked with crypto-assets that, in some respect, function in ways similar to other speculative asset classes, the application of that test will likely become more strained as further technological breakthroughs occur and different (more complex) forms of digital assets are created.

[57] ibid [59].

[58] This was the conclusion of the Singapore Appeal Court in *B2C2 Appeal* (n 42) [141] citing J Bacon et al, 'Blockchain Demystified: A Technical and Legal Introduction to Distributed and Centralised Ledgers' (2018) 25(1) *Richmond Journal of Law and Technology* 1; KFK Low and EGS Teo, 'Bitcoins & Other Cryptocurrencies as Property?' (2017) (21) Singapore Management University School of Law Research Paper Series.

[59] '[s]hould be adopted by the Court' being the approach that Bryan J took.

[60] Which notably decided not to issue a concluded view on the topic given the narrow available grounds to base its decision.

C. New Zealand

A similar approach to that adopted in *AA v Persons Unknown* was followed in the NZ case of *Ruscoe v Cryptopia*.[61] In that case the Court was considering a factual situation similar to that in *AA v Persons Unknown* where an individual(s) had hacked a crypto-asset exchange and stolen around NZ$30 million[62] of crypto-assets.[63] The company behind the exchange went into liquidation and the Court was asked to consider whether the remaining crypto-assets held by the exchange were held on trust for the benefit of the individuals who had purchased the assets. If they were, then the property would need to be returned to the individual controllers. If not, they would form part of the general pool of assets available to creditors.

The Court was called on to answer two different questions (only the second of which will be analysed below):

1. whether the crypto-assets were property pursuant to section 2 of the Companies Act 1993 (NZ);[64] and
2. whether the crypto-assets were property under general principles.

In considering general principles of property law, the NZ Court applied the *Ainsworth* indicia,[65] and accepted that all of the requirements could be met in the case of BTC, and, as such, that BTC fell within the concept of property.[66] The Court then went on to consider (and reject) specific arguments against BTC being property[67] as well as wider policy arguments against that proposition (notwithstanding that such arguments had not been advanced by the respondent in the case).[68]

IV. IS THE CURRENT APPROACH SUFFICIENT?

It is worth pausing here to summarise some key points about the approaches taken in the cases analysed above. First, only in the UK case was the Court provided with clear guidance as to whether crypto-assets were property. In the other cases the courts turned to first principles. Second, in most of the cases no

[61] *Ruscoe v Cryptopia Limited (in liquidation)* [2020] NZHC 728 ('*Ruscoe*').
[62] The value at the time of the theft.
[63] *Ruscoe* (n 61) [1].
[64] The section states: property means property of every kind whether tangible or intangible, real or personal, corporeal or incorporeal, and includes rights, interests, and claims of every kind in relation to property however they arise.
[65] *Ruscoe* (n 61) [75].
[66] ibid [102], [120].
[67] ibid [122]–[128].
[68] ibid [129]–[132].

significant argument was advanced against the proposition that the *Ainsworth* test should be applied. Third, despite the increased use of crypto-assets especially in the mid-2010s,[69] these decisions were not heard until late 2019 or early 2020. Fourth, in all cases the private parties themselves bore the cost of litigation and there was no government intervention. Fifth, apart from the New Zealand decision, none of the cases considered in-depth any policy implications flowing from their conclusions. Sixth, the courts struggled with placing digital assets into existing property classification systems. In doing so, it is worth noting that were a statutory regime created that recognised digital assets as things to which property rights attach, there would be no need for courts to create a novel property category in order to address the (otherwise) narrow legal dispute before them.

Flowing from these points, a number of practical and normative issues arise. The first, and most important, matter is whether these types of determinations are truly ones that fall within the judicial function.

A. Are these Decisions Judicial?

One argument against leaving these decisions to courts alone is that as technology continues to advance, the applicability of the existing property law tests will continue to stretch. As can be seen from the above cases, the courts have universally applied traditional property law principles and, in particular, the *Ainsworth* indicia (or test) to resolve the legal issue before them. As can be seen in the divergent approach taken by the Singapore Court of Appeal compared to the UK and NZ courts, how the *Ainsworth* indicia apply to crypto-assets has already been stretched.

Such a statement is not to critique any of the courts involved (which must resolve the questions brought before them), but rather to highlight that there are limits to the current tests that are being applied. A sensible question to ask is what occurs when these limits are reached. Fundamentally, courts must do justice between the parties before them. In doing so, the role of a court is to 'finally dispose of the rights of the parties',[70] or to '[impartially and dispassionately] decide cases brought before the court by parties, and to do so, by applying law to fact'.[71]

It is worth remembering that in exercising their function, courts are not called on, or at liberty to dispose of, the wider social policy issues at stake.

[69] Polasik et al (n 2).

[70] *Hall v Nominal Defendant* (1966) 117 CLR 423, [439] (Taylor J).

[71] K Mack et al, 'The Judiciary and the Public: Judicial Perceptions' (2018) 39(1) *Adelaide Law Review* 1, 4.

Instead, courts are only required to answer the legal questions *necessary* to dispose of the particular controversy before them.[72]

The question of judicial involvement in policy decisions was recently considered by the Full Federal Court of Australia in upholding an appeal against a judgment which had established that the government owed a novel duty of care to protect young people from the impacts of climate change. Chief Justice Allsop, in outlining why a court should not intervene in broad policy debates, stated:

> so-called core policy, or at least the making of it, is not, or is unlikely to be, the province of the Judiciary in its role of quelling private controversies or controversies between individuals and government.[73]

The difference between these broader policy matters and the proper judicial role (of addressing the legal issue before it to resolve the rights between the parties) was similarly discussed by the Full Court in the case of *Commissioner of Patents v Thaler*, which concerned the issue of AI inventorship. The Court stated at [119]–[120]:

> First, in filing the application, Dr Thaler no doubt intended to provoke debate as to the role that artificial intelligence may take within the scheme of the Patents Act and Regulations. *Such debate is important and worthwhile. However, in the present case it clouded consideration of the prosaic question before the primary judge, which concerned the proper construction of s 15 and reg 3.2C(2)(aa).* In our view, there are many propositions that arise for consideration in the context of artificial intelligence and inventions. …
>
> Those questions and many more require consideration. Having regard to the agreed facts in the present case, it would appear that this should be attended to with some urgency. However, the Court must be cautious about approaching the task of statutory construction by reference to what it might regard as desirable policy, imputing that policy to the legislation, and then characterising that as the purpose of the legislation.[74]

There are two related points to note from the above cases. First, the Court accepted that it is not the role of judges to decide core policy questions. Instead,

[72] This is drawn from the requirement that there be a 'justiciable controversy … comprised of the substratum of facts and claims representing or amounting to the dispute or controversy between or amongst them [the parties to the dispute]': Justice James Allsop, 'An Introduction to the Jurisdiction of the Federal Court of Australia' (Speech, 1 October 2007) www.fedcourt.gov.au/digital-law-library/judges-speeches/chief-justice-allsop/allsop-cj-200710 (last accessed 3 December 2022), citing *Re Wakim* (1999) 198 CLR, 585–86, [139]–[142]. See also *Clubb v Edwards & Anor; Preston v Avery & Anor* [2019] HCA 11, [35] quoting *Attorney-General for NSW v Brewery Employees Union of NSW* (1908) 6 CLR 469, 590.

[73] *Minister for the Environment v Sharma* (2022) 400 ALR 203, 251.

[74] *Commissioner of Patents v Thaler* [2022] FCAFC 62 (Allsop CJ, Nicholas, Yates, Moshinsky and Burley JJ) at [119]–[120] (emphasis added, citations omitted).

such matters fall into the role of the executive and legislative branches of government. Second, judges, in deciding legal disputes, cannot and should not have regard to broader significant policy considerations in resolving the dispute.

The rationale for these propositions has been succinctly put by US judges, who have noted that restraint in the judicial function is what gives courts their legitimacy; in essence, the role of a court is not to make a policy decision.[75] A second point worth considering is that courts lack the expertise to satisfactorily resolve these broader disputes. This matter was pointed out by Allsop CJ in *Sharma* where his Honour quoted with approval the New Zealand Court of Appeal decision in *Smith v Fonterra Co-operative Group Limited*[76] at [255]:

> … 'Courts are … ill-equipped to address the issues that the claim raises', which call for 'a level of institutional expertise, democratic participation and democratic accountability that cannot be achieved through a court process'.[77]

In considering the crypto-asset cases discussed above, judges are arguably determining broad questions of public policy as to how property law interacts with emerging technology. In particular, the UK court decisions (although based on quasi-legislative statements) have recognised an entirely new category of personal property. How this new category of property and the increasing application of the *Ainsworth* test will interact with pre-existing rules (namely, that information is not a thing to which property rights can attach) is not yet known. Indeed, these implications will not be known until we see how digital assets, and the technology underpinning them, continue to evolve.

This broader question is critical, given the significant reliance that societies place on the free flow of data and information.[78] Similar issues arise when considering how personal information or industrial data would overlap or interact with new categories of property rights.[79]

It is also worth noting that courts in the crypto-asset cases have generally not had the benefit of drawing on significant public sector or academic expertise and debate in their decisions. The exception to this was the Singapore Court of Appeal which had appointed an amicus to aide in its decision-making process. The Court in its decision *did not decide the property law issue*. Rather, as noted

[75] *Obergerfell v Hodges* 576 US ___ 3 (2015) Roberts CJ dissenting: '"courts are not concerned with the wisdom or policy of legislation." … The majority today neglects that restrained conception of the judicial role. It seizes for itself a question the Constitution leaves to the people … And it answers that question based not on neutral principles of constitutional law, but on its own "understanding of what freedom is and must become."'

[76] *Smith v Fonterra Co-operative Group Limited* [2021] NZCA 552 at [116].

[77] *Sharma* (n 73) 255.

[78] Indeed, the free transference of information underpins significant economic activity.

[79] See generally PM Schwartz, 'Property, Privacy, and Personal Data' (2005) 117(7) *Harvard Law Review* 2055. See also A Quodling, 'Shadow profiles – Facebook knows about you, even if you're not on Facebook', *The Conversation* (online, 13 April 2018) theconversation.com/shadow-profiles-facebook-knows-about-you-even-if-youre-not-on-facebook-94804 (last accessed 3 December 2022).

above, the case was decided on narrower grounds. In doing so, it appears that the Court resolved the 'prosaic question' before it *without* considering (or intervening in) matters of broader public policy.

Ultimately, as we will explore further below, where judges continue to be called on to determine these novel property law questions there are increasing risks of courts stepping beyond their judicial function, whether intentionally or accidentally. The rapid expansion of technology in this area in particular is one that calls for a cautious and expert-driven parliamentary-led approach.[80]

B. Practical Concerns

i. Speed of Decision-making

One challenge that courts face in making these determinations is that they are limited to the cases and arguments brought before them. Satoshi Nakamoto first authored their White Paper explaining the technical underpinnings of Bitcoin in 2008.[81] Despite the early explanation of principles, it took over a decade for the first of the crypto-asset cases to come before the courts for determination. In the context of rapidly advancing technology, delay in providing certainty and clarity around a transaction's status may unduly impede innovation.

The fact that courts are restricted to the arguments of the parties may also limit the development of legal principles if these types of legal disputes continue to be resolved solely by judges. For example, let us assume a start-up company is developing a new data product. As part of an employee-incentive scheme it pays part of its wages by way of that data product. It fails to make the payments one year, and some of its employees sue arguing that that data product is property held on trust for them. Neither party would have an interest in arguing against the proprietary character of the product and would be unlikely to advance such an argument before a court. In contrast, if instead the company had become insolvent and was in liquidation, the liquidator may well now argue that the data product is not property held on trust and that the employees who opted into the scheme ought not be in any different position to the other employees with regards to any entitlements they may have. In both scenarios, the issues facing the court would be the same; however, in the first, the court would be required to make a determination without any argument advanced, or expert evidence against, the contention that the digital asset was property.

Such a position is not a hypothetical one. In many of the freezing order cases, no argument was advanced *against* the proposition that BTC could be property.

[80] For an example of such an approach see Law Commission of England and Wales, 'Digital Assets: Consultation Paper' (Law Com No 256, 28 July 2022).

[81] S Nakamoto, 'Bitcoin: A Peer-to-Peer Electronic Cash System' (White Paper, 2008) bitcoin.org/bitcoin.pdf (last accessed 3 December 2022).

This was likely in part because the respondent parties were themselves crypto-asset exchanges, and so could face a competitive disadvantage were the assets determined *not* to be property. Faced with such a scenario, a party may choose to sacrifice immediate advantage in the instant case in return for expected benefits in the medium to longer term.

ii. Costs and Commencing Actions Generally

One apparent challenge to relying on litigation to establish whether a particular digital asset has proprietary characteristics is the issue of costs. In most disputes in the jurisdictions we consider, the costs must be borne by one of (or some combination of) the parties to it.[82] In the case of a speculative property right and resultant legal uncertainty, parties may be unwilling to bear the resulting risk of commencing that proceeding.

This can also act as a significant disincentive to commence a legal action, especially in jurisdictions such as Australia and the UK where litigants may face adverse costs orders if they do not win their dispute.[83] Many commentators have critiqued both the need for, and complexity of, the litigation necessary to establish novel property rights. For example, Low and Lin critiqued the need for litigation to determine whether carbon credits had status as property (and therefore whether certain rights did or did not attach to them), arguing that clearer definition in the initial creation of carbon credits could have prevented protracted and complex litigation.[84]

A further issue that arises in the context of these types of disputes is *when* in the litigation costs need to be incurred. In some cases, it may be necessary for a party to litigate to establish the existence of a property right even at a very preliminary stage of proceedings in order to seek particular asset-protection or freezing orders. Absent the ability to fund these up-front costs, parties may be unable to pursue a substantive claim or may face risks in doing so where an opposing party is able to dissipate assets.

In addition to the costs faced by the parties, are the costs borne by the state (and taxpayers) through the resources necessary to hear and determine cases.[85]

[82] Leaving to the side matters of significant public importance, or where specific statutory rules allow for costs to be paid by governments: see, eg, *Lopez v Gold Titan Pty Ltd (No 2)* [2022] FCAFC 146.

[83] *Summers v Repatriation Commission (No 2)* [2015] FCAFC 64, [14]. See also *Ruddock v Vadarlis (No 2)* (2001) 115 FCR 229, [11] (Black CJ and French J).

[84] See, eg, KFK Low and J Lin, 'Carbon Credits as EU Like It: Property, Immunity, TragiCO_2medy?' (2015) 27(3) *Journal of Environmental Law* 377.

[85] Australian court funding for 2020 was estimated at nearly AUS$2 billion. See Productivity Commission, 'Report on Government Services 2020' (Government Report, 29 January 2020) Part C Section 7, www.pc.gov.au/research/ongoing/report-on-government-services/2020/justice/courts (last accessed 3 December 2022). Beyond cost, it is worth noting that the *time* spent hearing and deciding property cases is time not spent resolving, for example, migration or criminal matters where individual liberty is at stake.

In litigation involving novel (and resultingly complex) cases concerning property rights, these costs may be greater than more 'standard' cases as courts may opt to hear appeals with larger benches to bring greater judicial scrutiny to the issue.[86] Such an approach may be seen as desirable to give greater weight to a decision and to reduce the impact that individual judges can have on an entire area of future law reform. While the cost of judicial officers is rarely considered in assessments of barriers to litigation, given the increasing adoption of a wider array of data products and digital assets these costs should not be discounted.

This is especially the case where minor technical variances in products may mean they fall inside or outside of the *Ainsworth* indicia. For example, despite the UK Jurisdictional Taskforce statement and *AA v Persons Unknown* settling the issue of whether BTC is property in the UK, it is not readily apparent that the same approach would readily apply to other crypto-assets, NFTs or other forms of digital asset classes. Given the significant array of slightly different products, the generalisation of universally applicable rules from such cases may not be possible. If true, this would mean that every new asset will need to reach a court determination to resolve its property status, and, if a court decides a case on narrower grounds,[87] further litigation may be necessary.

iii. Consistency in Decision-making

The final practical challenge addressed in this chapter is that of consistency. As in many areas of law that are addressing rapidly emerging technologies, one challenge that different jurisdictions are facing is that of consistency. In the context of digital assets this challenge arises both intra and inter-jurisdictionally. As noted above, the crypto-asset cases provide little practical guidance that could be extrapolated to different digital assets. This means that within a single jurisdiction, challenges could arise between potentially inconsistent authorities on differing asset types.

This is especially the case for property law determinations if different judges rely on different tests. While the cases we analysed above relied on the *Ainsworth* indicia, as commentators have noted, there are an array of tests that Commonwealth courts can apply. These tests can, in turn, result in potentially divergent outcomes.[88] For example, in her paper, Bennett Moses used the example of digital 'tokens' or 'assets' in video games and suggested that courts would reach differing views depending on *which* test they applied to determine whether those assets were property.[89]

[86] For example, the Singapore Court of Appeal empanelled five judges to hear the appeal in *Quoine Pte Ltd v B2C2 Ltd* [2020] SCGA(I) 02.

[87] See, eg, *B2C2 Appeal* (n 42).

[88] Bennett Moses (n 8).

[89] ibid.

One obvious challenge here is that there is no clear hierarchy of tests. While we have seen courts use the *Ainsworth* criteria recently, there is nothing to stop a differently constituted court using a different test to reach a different outcome. As we will discuss further below, such a position would not arise were the legislature to impose clearer more practical guidance for courts to follow.

Inter-jurisdictionally, even greater issues arise. In particular, given the decentralised nature of digital assets, their holders appear to intend for these asset types to move fluidly across country and state borders.[90] Issues may then arise where an asset is property in one state but not another, and a case is brought on that basis. Such a dispute may raise complex choice of laws questions, especially where a party to a contract had included a forum clause which may impact not just the contractual law that would apply, but also the treatment of the assets involved. Recent litigation in Australia highlights this point, with significant litigation recently before the Federal Court concerning a dispute between Epic Games and Apple and Epic Games and Google as to whether the disputes should be heard in Australia or the US.[91] Where the property status of different assets differed by jurisdictions, the stakes involved in a choice of law dispute would be significantly higher, with parties able to access significantly different remedies depending on which forum the dispute was heard in.

iv. Who Decides?

In our view, the question whether a particular digital asset is a thing to which property rights attached is a question best resolved by a legislative body. This is so for four key reasons. First, and most importantly, the broader policy questions that arise are matters that fall outside the judicial function and expertise. In particular, there are significant flow-on implications from a decision that a specific form of data is property including:

- taxation consequences on the disposal of the data;
- different treatment of transactions under contract law;[92]
- different treatment of digital assets for the purpose of securities law;[93]
- different statuses for the purpose of trusts law; and
- different constitutional status regarding the seizure of property by government.

[90] Y Chen and C Bellavitis, 'Blockchain Disruption and Decentralized Finance: The Rise of Decentralized Business Models' (2020) 13 *Journal of Business Venturing Insights* 151.

[91] B Smith, '"Strong Reasons": The Epic Litigation and the Primacy of Public Policy over Exclusive Jurisdiction Clauses' (2022) 49(5) *Australian Business Law Review*.

[92] Particularly in relation to security aspects of transactions.

[93] See, eg, I H-Y Chiu and JG Allen, 'Exploring the Assetisation and Financialisation of Non-fungible Tokens (NFTs): Opportunities and Regulatory Implications' [2022] *Banking and Finance Law Review* (forthcoming).

The legislative or executive branches are better equipped to address these questions cohesively and have the expertise necessary (or can readily access that expertise) to consider the implications of different approaches. It is also worth noting that, unlike courts, policymakers are not limited by the particular factual matrix or arguments advanced before them.

Second, the digital asset cases demonstrate that differently constituted courts (applying the same traditional English legal principles) can reach divergent conclusions. Leaving such questions to differently constituted benches of judges risks cascading inconsistency, fatal to assets which operate freely across legal borders and boundaries. Third, in the context of rapidly evolving fields of technology, it is unclear whether there will be sufficient cases brought before the courts to enable that tension to be resolved naturally, consistently, and efficiently. Fourth, and finally, the courts in making these decisions are in effect being forced to address policy issues to resolve the legal questions before them.

V. FUTURE STEPS

Pausing here, it is worth noting that the policy analysis will vary depending on the *type* of digital asset being considered. For example, while the treatment and use of crypto-assets likely means that commercial interests should trump other considerations, this will not be so for *all* asset types. In particular, the focus on whether a thing is property considers only the *economic* outcomes and implications to a transaction, rather than considering the holistic circumstances.

While such a focus is created by our economic system and its reliance on property, this does not mean that such a focus should always be applied to the digital realm. In particular, there may be better methods of protecting individuals, without resorting to property rights. Indeed, focusing on property interests alone may lead to a failure to consider the core interests or emotions that underpin the use of a particular digital asset. This only further strengthens our above analysis as to why a legislative regime ought to be considered, as courts *cannot* (in exercising their function) and are not *equipped* to assess these wider concerns.

Broader consideration of the interests of stakeholders should also be considered by regulatory bodies, with the crypto-asset community itself divided over whether greater government regulation is required or desirable – or if such an approach simply moves away from the anarchist roots that underpin the technology.[94]

[94] GM Volpicelli, 'New Regulation Could Cause a Split in the Crypto Community', *Wired* (online, 17 August 2021) www.wired.com/story/regulation-split-crypto-community/ (last accessed 3 December 2022).

That is not to say however that governments should *never* act. Instead, they will need to take an approach that attempts to balance the competing policy considerations to assess whether a particular type of asset *is* property. In making such an assessment, governments (and courts) will, as discussed above, need to move away from traditional legal tests as digital assets continue to evolve. In doing so, they will be able to consider the wider policy points we highlighted above to assess to what degree something is property and what other regulation (if any) is needed.

While, ultimately, the matters a legislative body should consider in determining what (if any) measures should be implemented is a matter beyond the scope of this chapter, as a starting point, we consider that legislatures will need to consider the following questions in determining whether a particular asset should (or should not) be considered property:

1. what protections does that asset already have under existing law (eg, consumer law or data protection law);
2. what protections do individuals using that asset need to conduct their business that are not already included in (1);
3. are there any policy considerations that tend against the creation of a property right; and
4. if a right is to be created, should it be limited in any way.

In making such an assessment, it is worth noting that legislatures have additional control over the *type* of property rights they award to a particular digital asset. That is, digital assets could be placed onto a spectrum of weaker (thinner) or stronger (thicker) property rights. As the property right becomes stronger (or more recognised), additional remedies become available. For example, a weaker property right might permit a tracing exercise to occur, or for a trust to be established but would not extend to (or would be extinguished in) a bankruptcy or insolvency situation. Similarly, limits could be placed on how property rights in information *could* be traded – limiting the ability of individuals to alienate unless certain conditions are met (for example, requiring all buyers and sellers to be over 18 or to indicate that they have obtained financial advice). In designing a broader system, policymakers could rely on different levers to balance competing interests, options not open to a judge required to answer a definitive yes or no question.

VI. CONCLUSION

Ultimately, this chapter has explored how courts are increasingly being forced to grapple with the question of how and when property rights attach to information in a digital age. This has led to significant tensions as courts grapple, on the one hand, with the historic position that information is not something to which property rights attach and emerging asset classes where businesses and consumers place significant value and trust in novel asset types.

As we have demonstrated through the lens of the crypto-asset cases, such questions are best left to legislative bodies who are equipped to balance the competing interests of personal and commercial rights. Such an approach may mirror that taken to patent or copyright law and would circumvent the issues associated with a broadening of the categories of information to which property rights attach. As noted by Lord Mummery:

> The courts should stick to their constitutional role: developing the case law principles as clearly and simply as possible and adapting them in a common sense and cautious way to concrete situations, one case at a time. That is far preferable to attempting to achieve too much by ambitious judicial activism and probably failing in the process.[95]

Although, in the eyes of some, legislative bodies may themselves struggle to adopt suitable regulation, they at least have the constitutional legitimacy to define the future policy direction. We believe it is time for policy makers to step in and find a balance.

[95] Mummery (n 3).

3

Treehold

WILLIAM SWADLING*

I. INTRODUCTION

WHAT PROPERTY RIGHTS, if any, can exist with respect to standing trees? Is it possible to have a personal property right in a standing tree or even a freehold estate to the tree distinct from any title to the soil to which it is attached, what might be called a 'Treehold'?[1]

Why does this matter? Trees are environmentally friendly organisms, soaking up carbon from the atmosphere. Many companies run schemes encouraging the planting of trees, attractive to, for example, airlines needing to offset the negative effects of their carbon-producing activities. Some companies allow customers to pay for the planting of trees on the company's own land. An alternative is for customers to 'buy trees', enabling them to leave 'the trees' by will or purchase them for others, such as grandchildren.[2] At first glance, this second model seems impossible: once planted, the doctrine of accession dictates that the trees become part of the land to which they are attached and lose their separate identities; any pre-existing property right in the tree is therefore extinguished; only later, when physically severed, can a property right in the tree arise.

However, it was said by Duff J in the Canadian Supreme Court case of *Beatty v Mathewson* that not only can standing trees be the subject-matter of personal property rights, there can be 'an estate in fee simple in growing trees'.[3] The purpose of this chapter is to question this statement. The conclusion reached is that, though there can be a property right to trees in the form of a *profit à prendre*, a right to take trees from the land, and that such right may exist for the same length of time as a freehold title to land, it is impossible to have either a personal property right or a freehold title to a tree whilst it is attached to land. Duff J can therefore only have been speaking of a freehold profit.

* I am indebted to Paul Brand, Mike Mcnair, Llewellyn Morgan, and Ian Williams for their comments.

[1] I thank Simon Douglas for the suggested name.

[2] For example, see ecotree, ecotree.green/en/ (last accessed 3 December 2022).

[3] *Beatty v Mathewson* (1908) 40 SCR 557, 567.

The discussion proceeds as follows. First, the doctrine of accession is examined. Second, an ambiguity with respect to the word 'chattel' is noticed; it is sometimes used to describe a type of right and at other times to describe the physical object that is the subject of the right; the same is true of 'realty'. Third, given that land is capable of horizontal and vertical division, the question is asked whether such a device might allow freehold interests in trees. Fourth, attention turns to the *profit à prendre*, and its specific application to trees. Fifth, the so-called 'general' and 'particular' property rights to trees in the case of leases and the grants of lesser estates are discussed. Finally, arguments for both personal and real property interests in standing trees are assessed and rejected.

II. THE DOCTRINE OF ACCESSION

The objection to any separate property right, real or personal, in standing trees is the doctrine of accession. A physical thing attached to land, a 'fixture', becomes part of the land, thereby losing its separate physical identity: 'whatever is annexed to the soil is given to the soil' (*quicquid plantatur solo, solo cedit.*) Thus, in *Lancaster v Eve*, Williams J said that fixtures become 'incorporated with the soil',[4] while in *Moody v Steggles*, Fry J said that a wall was to be taken as 'part of the soil'.[5] As a consequence, any property rights in respect of the previously unattached physical thing are destroyed on accession. As Lord Chelmsford said in *Bain v Brand*, 'the person who was the owner of it when it was a chattel loses his property in it'.[6]

Moreover, parties cannot contract out of accession. Though it might be expressly agreed that title shall not be lost when the thing is affixed, this will be of no effect. In *Melluish v BMI (No 3) Ltd*,[7] a finance company entered into a number of contracts purporting to lease to a local authority central heating equipment for installation in council houses, swimming pool equipment, replacement cremators for crematoria, alarm systems for installation in sheltered housing, lifts for installation in car parks, and boiler equipment. The agreements provided that the leased equipment would remain personal or moveable property, continuing in the ownership of the lessor, notwithstanding that it might become affixed to any land or building of the lessee. A unanimous House of Lords endorsed the statement of Dillon LJ in the Court of Appeal that 'the concept of a fixture which remains personal or removeable property is

[4] *Lancaster v Eve* (1859) 5 CB (NS) 717, 729.
[5] *Moody v Steggles* (1879) 12 Ch D 261, 267.
[6] *Bain v Brand* (1876) 1 App Cas 762, 772.
[7] *Melluish v BMI (No 3) Ltd* [1996] 1 AC 454.

a contradiction in terms and an impossibility in law'.[8] Lord Browne-Wilkinson, with whom Lords Goff, Slynn, Nicholls, and Steyn agreed, said:

> The terms of such agreement will regulate the contractual rights to sever the chattel from the land as between the parties to that contract. ... But such agreement cannot prevent the chattel, once fixed, becoming in law part of the land and as such owned by the owner of the land so long as it remains fixed.[9]

Trees are no different to central heating equipment. Thus, in *Bewick v Whitfield*,[10] Talbot LC said that 'timber, while standing, is part of the inheritance', ie, the land. Likewise, in *re Ainslie*, Lord Halsbury LC said that if trees 'are attached to and form part of the soil, they are realty' and he was 'unable to frame words which will express this proposition more clearly than the familiar maxim, "*quicquid plantatur solo, solo cedit*"'.[11]

Once physically severed, whether deliberately or not,[12] trees have an identity separate from the land, and any newly-arising right to their possession will be a personal property or 'chattel' right.[13] As to who holds this right, the assumption is that it vests by operation of law in the freeholder, no matter whether it was they or a third party who did the physical severing.[14] The question as to the vesting of title in a severed tree where there are competing interests in the land, as, for example, in the case of landlord and tenant, is less straightforward and is discussed below. Moreover, the default rule can, as seen, be changed by contract.[15]

III. RIGHTS AND PHYSICAL THINGS

We need to be careful with the word 'chattel'. When Lord Chelmsford in *Bain v Brand* used the word, he was describing the unattached physical thing as the 'property' which was lost. We see the same usage in the leading case of *Holland v Hodgson*, where Blackburn J spoke of things affixed to land being 'considered as part of the land, unless the circumstances are such as to show that it was intended all long to continue a chattel ...'.[16] By contrast, 'chattel' is also used to describe a type of right. So, for example, a right to the exclusion possession of a cow or horse would be a chattel interest. Chattel interests are opposed to

[8] [1995] Ch 90, 115.
[9] *Melluish* (n 7) 473.
[10] *Bewick v Whitfield* (1734) 3 P Wms 267.
[11] *re Ainslie* (1885) 30 Ch D 485, 487; see also ibid 488 (Cotton LJ).
[12] The trees might, for example, be blown down in a storm.
[13] *Re Ainslie* [1894] 1 QB 714.
[14] Even where there is a legal right to sever: *Mills v Brooker* [1919] KB 555 (lawful abatement of nuisance by neighbour of overhanging branches).
[15] *Melluish* (n 7) 473, cited above, text to n 9.
[16] *Holland v Hodgson* (1872) LR 7 CP 328, 335.

other types of right known as 'realty'. Examples of rights classified as realty are freehold estates, fees tail, and life estates in land. Though most rights classified as 'realty' pertain to land, the difference is not one of subject-matter but of the remedy for dispossession of the subject matter of the right. In the case of chattel interests, the common law will not order the defendant to put the plaintiff back in possession, but instead give a money judgment. In the case of realty, an order to restore possession of the thing (*res*) will be made. This difference in procedure, in the nature of the court order, explains the difference between 'real' and 'chattel' property.

There was a substantive difference as well. Until 1540, realty on death descended automatically to the deceased's heir, whereas chattel interests, also known as 'personal property' or simply 'personalty', descended to their executors where they had made a will or to their administrators in the event of intestacy. After the passing of the Statute of Wills in 1540, realty also descended to the executors in the case of a will, only going to the heir on intestacy.[17] Leases of land, which were not classified as realty but personalty, and confusingly described by the hybrid 'chattels real' because the common law did, at least from the sixteenth century, award specific recovery of the land,[18] had always gone to the administrator, not the heir, on intestacy.

The ambiguity just noticed, between chattels as physical things and chattels as rights, is also encountered with its taxonomical opposite, realty. It is common to find judges talking of a person having a title to the 'realty', the physical thing, but at the same time speaking of a person having 'realty' in the form of a fee simple or life estate. We will encounter this dual usage with respect to trees below. Sometimes, the talk is of the trees as physical things; in others, it is in terms of rights with respect to those trees, whatever those rights might be.

IV. HORIZONTAL AND VERTICAL DIVISION OF LAND

It is sometimes said that we can have a freehold estate in trees because of the possibility of the horizontal and vertical division of land. Thus, Professor Gray writes:

> [R]ealty is capable of horizontal division and it is, in this sense, feasible to own and to convey a freehold or leasehold estate in a tree which is separate from estate ownership of the subjacent soil, provided that the tree has not yet been severed from the realty.[19]

[17] By the Administration of Estates Act 1925, a uniform method for the administration of the rights of a deceased person was introduced and the concept of the heir abolished. Realty thereafter went, as with chattel interests, to the administrator.

[18] AWB Simpson, *A History of the Land Law*, 2nd edn (Oxford, Oxford University Press, 1986) 74–77.

[19] K Gray and SF Gray, *Elements of Land Law*, 5th edn (Oxford, Oxford University Press, 2008) 49.

The same thinking is expressed by Dr Mynors in the only specialist work in the area.[20]

There is no doubt that a freehold or leasehold title to land can be divided both vertically and horizontally: 'A man may have an inheritance in an upper chamber though the lower buildings and soil be in another.'[21] It is thus possible, though uncommon, to have a freehold title to a flat.[22] However, the crucial thing to note is that we would now be talking about a freehold, not of the tree itself, but of the space occupied by it. The question then is how such a freehold of tree-space would work. Does the space grow with the tree, diminishing the space over which other titles to the land extend?[23] What happens when roots penetrate neighbouring soil, or branches overhang boundaries? Are the neighbour's rights thereby reduced? What happens when the tree is transplanted to a different area? Does the freehold title to the space previously occupied by the tree move with it or stay put? Likewise, what happens to the freehold title to the space when the tree is felled and turned into goods?

In this regard, it is helpful to note the rejection of a similar claim in relation to the central heating and other equipment in *Melluish v BMI (No 3) Ltd*,[24] discussed above.[25] There, a convoluted argument that the goods somehow 'belonged' to the hirer in equity on the basis of a vendor-purchaser constructive trust was also rejected. It was described as 'wholly unrealistic and unsustainable' because, inter alia, there was no subject matter of the alleged sale. Lord Browne-Wilkinson asked:

> Is it the equipment alone? If so, who owns the airspace occupied by the equipment while it remains fixed? If it is the equipment and the airspace occupied by it, who owns the airspace formerly occupied by it when, pursuant to the rights under the master lease, the equipment is removed?[26]

The same problems arise here. The assumption made by those advocating freehold titles to trees is that the interest comes to an end when the tree is felled. Yet even when the tree is felled, the space formerly occupied remains, so the estate must subsist.

[20] D Mynors, *The Law of Trees, Forests and Hedges*, 2nd edn (London, Sweet and Maxwell, 2011) [2.5.4].

[21] Co Litt 48b. This has, however, been described as heretical: See C Sweet, *Challis's Law of Real Property*, 3rd edn (1911) 54.

[22] The reason is because of problems concerning the running of positive covenants.

[23] In this respect, it might be argued that since the doctrines of accretion and dilution allow the boundary of lands abutting the sea, inland lakes, or rivers to change with the natural forces of erosion, so too with relation to trees. These doctrines, however, give 'recognition to the fact that where land is bounded by water, the forces of nature are likely to cause changes in the boundary between the land and the water'; and is based on 'grounds of convenience and fairness': *Southern Centre of Theosophy Inc v South Australia* [1982] AC 706, 716 (Lord Wilberforce). There is no need for such a rule here.

[24] *Melluish* (n 7).

[25] Text to nn 8–9.

[26] *Melluish* (n 7) 474.

V. PROFITS A PRENDRE

Though the consequence of the doctrine of accession is that there can be no separate right to possession of standing trees, there is no doubt that there can be a real property right, an *incorporeal hereditament*, to take trees from the land, a *profit à prendre*.[27]

There are many different types of profits, some of which have specific names, including the right to take fish (piscary or 'a fishery'),[28] to dig turf or peat in another person's ground for fuel (turbary), to take fowl (auceptary), to release pigs onto the land to feed on acorns (pannage),[29] to graze sheep (sheepwalk), to take ice from a canal, to graze cattle (variously pasture, herbage, or vesture), to hunt game (venery), and to take sand, stone, gravel, brick-earth, coal, and minerals.

Profits can be either 'appurtenant' or 'in gross'. A profit appurtenant pertains to land of the profit-holder, the dominant tenement. In such cases, the amount to be taken from the servient tenement is usually limited to the needs of the dominant tenement. Thus, a profit of pasture appurtenant might be limited to the number of animals which the dominant tenement can maintain throughout the winter, the cattle *levant et couchant* (getting up or lying down) on the land. Profits appurtenant might alternatively have a 'stint' or fixed number. A profit in gross, by contrast, is not attached to any land of the profit-holder and can be with or without stint.[30]

Though profits in gross are freely assignable,[31] the common perception until recently was that profits appurtenant ran automatically with the profit-holder's title to the dominant tenement; they could not be severed therefrom and turned into profits in gross.[32] However, in *Bettison v Langton*,[33] a case concerned with a profit of pasture, Robert Walker LJ, after an extensive review of the authorities, held that the restriction only applied to profits defined by reference to the needs of the dominant tenement. Where there was a stint, severance

[27] A *profit à prendre* has been defined as 'a right to take from the servient tenement some part of the soil of that tenement or minerals under it or some part of its natural produce, or the animals ferae naturae existing on it': *Alfred F Beckett Ltd v Lyons* [1967] Ch 449, 482 (Winn LJ).

[28] For a recent example, see *Pearson v Foster* [2017] EWHC 107 (Ch).

[29] Delightfully described by Sir George Jessel MR in *Chilton v Corporation of London* (1878) 7 Ch D 562, 565, as 'a right granted to an owner of pigs … to go into the wood of the grantor of the right and to allow the pigs to eat the acorns or beech-mast which fall upon the ground. … The pigs have no right to take a single acorn or any beech-mast off the tree, either by themselves or by the hands of those who drive them. There is not even a right to shake the tree. It is only a right to eat what has fallen to the ground.'

[30] However, if without stint, the profit must not be so extensive as to 'tend to the entire destruction of the property': *Lord Chesterfield v Harris* [1908] 2 Ch 397, 421 (Cozens-Hardy MR).

[31] *Welcome v Upton* (1840) 6 M & W 536.

[32] *Sir Henry Nevil's Case* (1570) Plowd 377.

[33] *Bettison v Langton* [2000] Ch 54. The decision was affirmed by the House of Lords on a different ground: [2002] 1 AC 27.

from the estate of the profit-holder was possible because it did not prejudice the servient owner. It is important to note that, when speaking of 'severance', Robert Walker LJ was talking only of the conversion of the profit from one appurtenant to the dominant tenement to one existing in gross. He was not speaking of any legal severance of the grass the cows might in future chew; he was not saying the growing grass could be turned into the subject-matter of a chattel interest.

Profits can be created for the same periods as estates in land. Thus, it is possible to have a perpetual profit (a profit in fee or freehold profit) or a profit for the life of the grantee. There can also be leases of profits, either of an existing profit or the grant of a fresh profit for a term of years.[34] As with leases of land, 'chattels real', profits for terms of years are personalty. As with any chattel interest, they would until 1926 pass to their holder's administrators on intestacy, rather than the heir.

As to creation, profits are either granted or 'excepted and reserved'. However, an 'exception and reservation' is in truth a grant, for the simple reason that the profit did not exist beforehand.[35] Thus, in *Douglas* v *Lock*,[36] Lord Denman held that a 'reservation' by a landlord in a lease of 'the privilege of hawking, hunting, fishing, and fowling' was a grant by the lessee. It was neither 'a reservation or an exception in point of law; it is only a privilege or right granted to the lessor, though words of reservation and exception are used'.[37] This has the consequence that third parties to the grant can take the benefit of such rights. Thus, in *Wickham v Hawker*,[38] a decision to which we shall return, A and B by deed conveyed to D and his heirs a fee simple title to certain lands, 'excepting and reserving' to A, B, and C, their heirs and assigns, the 'liberty to come into and upon the lands, and there to hawk, hunt, fish, and fowl'. As this was not a reservation by A and B, but a grant by D, it enured to the benefit of C, despite C not being party to the conveyance.

[34] There are many examples of leases of incorporeal real rights, eg, advowsons (*Cottington v Fletcher* (1740) 2 Atk 155) and markets (*Keech v Sandford* (1726) Sel Cas Ch 61). As to profits, Chambre J said of a profit of pasturage in *Bunn v Channen* (1813) 5 Taunt 244 that 'the habit of letting these rights, and for the time converting them into common in gross' was prevalent. Leases of other profits are also common, eg, *Bayley v Conyngham* (1863) 15 ICLR 406 (fishery); *Fitzgerald v Firbank* [1897] 2 Ch 96 (fishery); *Peech v Best* [1931] 1 KB 1 (shooting rights).

[35] E Cooke, S Bridge and M Dixon, *Megarry and Wade: The Law of Real Property*, 9th edn (London, Sweet & Maxwell, 2019) [27-009]. A true exception concerns an area of the land itself ('if a man makes a lease for life of a manor, excepting one acre, and afterwards grants the reversion of the manor to another in fee, the acre in possession shall not pass, but is severed from the manor for ever': Coke CJ, *Liford's Case* (1614) 11 Co Rep 46b, 47b), while a reservation was of some new right which was to issue out of the land granted, such as a rentcharge.

[36] *Douglas* v *Lock* (1835) 2 Ad & Ell 705.

[37] ibid 743. The same thinking applies to easements. Thus, in *Durham & Sunderland Rly v Walker* (1842) 2 QB 940, 967–68, Tindal CJ said: 'A right of way reserved (using that word in a somewhat popular sense) to a lessor, as in the present case, is, in strictness of law, an easement newly created by way of grant from the grantee or lessee.'

[38] *Wickham v Hawker* (1840) 7 M & W 63.

Holders of profits can protect their rights by bringing tort claims against those physically interfering with their exercise. Thus, in *Holford v Bailey*,[39] the holder of a profit of piscary was able to bring trespass against a third party who took five salmon from a stretch of the river over which the plaintiff had rights.[40] In appropriate circumstances, the profit-holder can also bring nuisance. In *Fitzgerald v Firbank*,[41] the plaintiffs were granted 'the exclusive right of fishing' in a defined part of a river. The defendant discharged water loaded with sediment into a stream feeding into the river, which had the effect of driving away the fish and injuring their breeding. To the plaintiffs' claims in trespass and nuisance, the defendant argued that they had merely a licence to fish, with no right to take any fish away, which licence did not bind third parties. The Court of Appeal held that the plaintiffs had a *profit à prendre* and that both claims were available.

Does the availability of these tort claims mean that the holder of a profit has a right to possession of the things to be taken before any taking, for example, to the fish in the river to which a profit of piscary is attached? There is certainly *dicta* to that effect. Thus, Holt CJ in *Smith v Kemp* described the holder of a profit of piscary as having 'a property in the fish, and may bring a possessory action for them'.[42] However, this 'property' cannot be a right to possession. The grantors themselves have no property until the fish are caught,[43] and so cannot give such right to the grantee. In *Fitzgerald v Firbank*, Lopes LJ, after citing Holt CJ's dictum, described the profit as 'the right to fish in the water; *and when the fish are caught* it is a right to the property in the fish'.[44] That must be right; Holt CJ can only be using the word 'property' to describe an interest sufficient to sue for interference with the right to fish. Though the profit is a property right, there can be no property in the fish themselves until reduced into possession.

Since profits 'savour of the realty', they would, when in gross, and before 1926, pass on intestacy to the heir rather than the deceased's administrators,[45] unless, of course, they were for a term of years, and so a chattel interest. Where appurtenant, they would pass automatically with the relevant estate. A contract for the grant of a profit is a contract for the sale of an interest in land, which nowadays means such contract will be void for want of writing signed by both parties.[46] Previously, the restrictions on enforceability contained in section 4 of the Statute of Frauds 1677, re-enacted as section 40 of the Law of Property Act 1925, applied. Thus, in *Webber v Lee*,[47] a contract allowing the plaintiff

[39] *Holford v Bailey* (1850) 13 QB 426.
[40] This led the Court of Appeal in *Monsanto plc v Tilly* [2000] Env LR 313 to wrongly conclude that the holder of a right of herbage had a right to possession of the land itself.
[41] *Fitzgerald v Firbank* [1897] 2 Ch 96.
[42] *Smith v Kemp* (1692) 2 Salk 637.
[43] *Young v Hichens* (1844) 6 Ad & El 606.
[44] *Fitzgerald* (n 41) 102 (emphasis added).
[45] *Buckeridge v Ingram* (1795) 2 Ves Jr 652.
[46] See Law of Property (Miscellaneous Provisions) Act 1989, s 2.
[47] *Webber v Lee* (1882) 9 QBD 315.

entry to land to take game was held to be for the grant of a profit in gross and therefore unenforceable for want of the requisite writing.

Profits come to an end in four main ways: by effluxion of time in the case of profits for life or years; by statute; by release; and by unity of ownership and possession.[48] As to the last, where a freeholder, for example, grants a profit of piscary to another in fee and that other acquires the grantor's freehold, the profit will be extinguished,[49] for one cannot have a right against oneself. However, if the profit-holder were to instead take a lease of the burdened land, the profit would be merely suspended during the currency of the lease,[50] reviving at its end. We see the same rule with respect to easements. Thus, in *Simper v Foley*,[51] Page-Wood VC held that the taking of a lease of the servient tenement by the holder of a freehold title to the dominant tenement did not extinguish a right to light but only 'suspend it so long as the union of ownership continues; and that upon a severance of the ownership the easement revives'.[52]

VI. PROFITS OF 'TREES'

There can undoubtedly be profits of trees. According to *Challis*, 'a grant of growing trees apart from the soil, to a man and his heirs, confers the right to cut them, which is an incorporeal hereditament'.[53] It is important to note that this gives no right to possession of the trees whilst standing, only to enter the land to cut and take the trees. Typical is *Barrington's Case*,[54] where a fee simple holder granted to A and his heirs 'all woods, underwoods, etc. then growing, and of all timber trees, woods, etc. which thereafter should grow in a certain part of the forest of Hatfield, (except the land and soil of the same wood)'. It was held that the grantee had 'an inheritance as profit apprender in alieno solo,' but that 'the soil remains to the [grantor]'.[55] It was thus a profit, not the grant of a fee simple title to the land on which the trees stood.[56] It is important

[48] See generally, *Megarry and Wade* (n 35) 28-007–28-016.

[49] *Tyrringham's Case* (1584) 4 Co Rep 36b, 38a. See JDA Brooke-Taylor, 'Perdurable Estates' (1977) 41 *Conv* 107.

[50] *Canham v Fisk* (1831) 2 Cr & J 126; *Thomas v Thomas* (1835) 2 Cr M & R 34.

[51] *Simper v Foley* (1862) 2 J & H 555.

[52] ibid 564.

[53] C Sweet, *Challis's Law of Real Property*, 3rd edn (1911) 58, citing 11 Co 49b.

[54] *Barrington's Case* (1610) 8 Co Rep 136b.

[55] ibid 137b. Unfortunately, this phrase is often abbreviated to simply 'an estate of inheritance'. As we will see, this can give the impression that something more than a profit is involved.

[56] Whether what is involved is the grant of a right to possession of the land on which the trees stand or merely a right to enter and cut and take the trees can be a difficult question of construction, since the area of land may be described as, for example, 'the Brasenose Wood'. This was the issue in *Ive's Case* (1596) 5 Co Rep 11a, a lease for 30 years of a manor 'except all woods and underwoods growing or being on the manor'. It was held that 'By the exception of the woods and underwoods growing or being on the manor, the soil itself is excepted.' The difference seems to be between 'woods' and 'trees'.

to note that though 'the soil' remains in the grantor, 'sufficient nutriment out of the land is reserved to sustain the vegetative life of the trees, for without that, the trees, which are excepted, cannot subsist ....'.[57] Though having no right to possession of the land itself, and *a fortiori* no right to possession of the trees, profit-holders therefore have an 'interest' in the soil in the sense of being able to restrict the grantor and their successors in title in what they can do with it. They can also sue third parties who interfere with it, for example, by poisoning it, just as the holder of a profit of piscary can sue those polluting the river.[58]

Like other profits, profits of trees can be appurtenant or in gross. Where appurtenant, they have various names, all determined by the amount of wood to be taken, called 'estovers' or 'botes'.[59] Where the profit is in gross, it is simply one 'of trees'. Like other profits, profits of trees in gross may be with or without stint.[60] In the case of the grant of a profit of trees in gross, the 'trees' are said to be 'severed' from the land, though this only means that a profit has been created, not that a right to possession of the trees now exists separate from the right to possession of the land on which they stand.

The final issue is the location of property rights in a tree once physically severed from the land. We saw with a fishery that the best title to fish, once caught, vests in the holder of the profit, not the person doing the catching.[61] Though these cases involved third parties, there is no reason to think the result would be any different were it the holder of a title to the servient land doing the catching. So too with trees.[62]

VII. 'GENERAL' AND 'SPECIAL' PROPERTY IN TREES

What happens as a matter of property law when a fee simple title-holder grants to another a lease for life or lives, an estate of freehold,[63] or a term of years of land, a chattel real, on which trees are standing? Here, the parties' relationship is mediated through the doctrine of waste, the object of which is to prevent those with temporary rights to possession despoiling the land to the prejudice of those with future entitlements.[64] In the case of freehold

[57] *Liford's Case* (1614) 11 Co Rep 46b, 49b, Coke CJ. The case is discussed in detail below, text to n 79.

[58] *Liford's Case* (n 57) text to n 79.

[59] 'Estover' derives from 'estoffer', a Norman-French word meaning 'to supply with necessaries', while 'bote' is an Anglo-Saxon word meaning 'satisfaction or recompense'.

[60] *Mellor v Spateman* (1669) 1 Saund 343; *Lord Chesterfield v Harris* [1908] 2 Ch 397, 423 (Buckley LJ).

[61] Text to n 43.

[62] *Douglas* (n 36).

[63] M Wonnacott, *The History of the Law of Landlord and Tenant in England and Wales* (Lawbrook Exchange, 2011) 127–136.

[64] *Megarry and Wade* (n 35), [3-066]–[3-071], [18-051]–[18-056].

land,[65] there are three possible scenarios: where the tenant is unimpeachable for waste; where the tenant is impeachable for waste; and where there is an 'exception of trees' by the lessor.

A. Unimpeachable for Waste

Where the tenant is by the terms of the lease made unimpeachable for waste, they do no wrong if they chop down trees on the demised land. When cut, title to what are now goods vests in the tenant.

B. Impeachable for Waste

In the absence of any specific provision in the lease, the rule is that neither tenant for life nor years can cut down and appropriate to their own use trees which are 'timber'.[66] If they do, they commit the wrong of 'voluntary waste',[67] and the lessor will have an action for damages.[68] 'Timber', according to Blackstone, is 'part of the inheritance'. The tenant is, however, entitled to underwood and 'sufficient estovers [from timber] of common right for house-bote and cart-bote'.[69] Additionally, both tenant for life and years have rights to the mast[70] and fruit of trees and to use them as shade for their cattle. These limited rights with respect to the trees were described by Coke CJ in *Liford's Case* as a 'special property' or 'particular interest' in the trees.[71] Its presence means that the lessor cannot deal with the trees at will. According to Coke CJ, though 'the property of great trees, *scil* the timber, is reserved by the law to the lessor, but he cannot grant it without the termor's licence, for the termor has an interest in it'.[72] The landlord in such cases is said to have the 'general property' in the trees. Where trees are felled, they become goods. If the felling was by the tenant for fuel and repairs, they will have the best title. Otherwise, the best title vests in the landlord.[73]

[65] The position in copyhold land was that the tenant had no right to cut the trees, but the lord could not get to them either: *Eardley v Granville* (1876) 3 Ch D 826, 832–33 (Jessel MR). The copyhold tenant thus had no incentive to cultivate the trees, leading to the comment that 'the oak scorns to grow except on free land': T Cyprian Williams, *Principles of the Law of Real Property*, 23rd edn (1920) 506.

[66] *Honywood v Honywood* (1874) LR 18 Eq 306. The general rule was that 'oak, ash, and elm are timber; provided they are of the age of twenty years and upwards, provided also they are not so old as not to have a reasonable quantity of useable wood in them, sufficient … to make a good post': at 309 (Jessel MR).

[67] ibid.

[68] *Woodhouse v Walker* (1880) 5 QBD 404.

[69] Bl *Comm* II, 281-2.

[70] *Douglas* (n 36). The 'mast' are acorns of oak trees and beech nuts, used for feeding animals.

[71] *Liford's Case* (1614) 11 Co Rep 46b, 48.

[72] ibid 48a-b.

[73] *Douglas* (n 36) 750 (Denman CJ).

C. Exception of Trees

The most restrictive position from the point of view of the tenant is where there is an 'exception of trees' in the grant, for now the tenant for life or years is deprived of even this 'special' property and the lessor free to enter and take the trees for themselves, make contracts for the sale of standing trees, or grant to another a profit of trees. In such cases, the lessor is said to have simply 'the property', rather than 'the general property' in the trees,[74] or even their 'ownership'.[75] However, this should again not be taken to mean they have a right to the possession of the trees themselves. Like lessors having 'the general property', lessors with 'the property' or 'ownership' cannot themselves camp out in the trees. The doctrine of accession still means that the trees form part of the land, and the right to possession of the land is, albeit temporarily, vested in the lessee. The right of the lessor is instead to enter and cut and take the trees, which would be unlawful had they only 'the general property'. In this respect, 'the property' in the trees, though having no specific name, is akin to a profit of trees, and it is notable that in *Bettison v Langton*, Robert Walker LJ described analogous sporting rights reserved to the lord of the manor as 'properly classified as profits'.[76] In this respect, it is pertinent to note that it is perfectly possible for lessors to have easements over land they have leased to another. Moreover, as will be seen below, the right behaves similarly to profits in terms of extinction and suspension.[77]

We should finally note that in the case of an 'exception of trees' (and *a fortori* a grant where the tenant is impeachable for waste) there is no severance or detachment of the lessor's right from the reversion: it does not become a free-standing right, akin to a profit in gross. In *Liford's Case*,[78] a freeholder granted a lease of land to the plaintiffs for their joint lives, 'excepting the timber trees'. The lessor entailed his reversion in favour of his son, who authorised the defendant to enter the land to show trees to a potential buyer. The plaintiff lessees sued the defendant in trespass, arguing that the exception of trees had severed the lessor's right from the reversion, which had not therefore passed to the son but to those entitled under his will. Coke CJ held that, notwithstanding the exception, the right to the trees remained 'parcel of the inheritance of the land'. Consequently, had the lessor died intestate and there had been no prior conveyance of the reversion, 'the trees' would have gone to the heir, not the executors. In the case itself, however, 'the trees' went with the reversion into the son's hands. 'Timber trees', said Coke CJ, could not 'be felled with a goose quill'.[79] In other

[74] *Liford's Case* (n 71) 48b.

[75] 'The lessor has the general ownership, right, and inheritance': *Douglas* (n 36) 750 (Denman CJ).

[76] *Bettison* (n 33) 62. Admittedly, in the same sentence he speaks of the 'ownership' of trees and minerals being vested in the lord, but this cannot literally be true; they too can only be profits.

[77] Text to n 113.

[78] *Liford's Case* (n 71).

[79] ibid 50a.

words, the lessor's right was appurtenant to his estate, passing automatically with the reversion.[80] At no point had it become a right in gross.

VIII. STANDING TREES AS CHATTELS

We saw that the doctrine of accession meant that standing trees form part of the land, and that there can be no separate rights to their possession until felled. We also saw that there can be a profit of trees, and interests equivalent to the same when 'excepted and reserved' in leases for life or years. However, it is important to stress that such profits and analogous rights give no right to possession of the trees themselves, only to enter and take them. The rights do not treat the trees themselves as present goods. Nevertheless, there are some cases concerning contracts for the sale of standing trees which appear to contradict this. Moreover, in *Beatty v Mathewson*, Duff J spoke of standing trees as 'chattels'. Both propositions, however, are doubtful.

A. Contracts for the Sale of Standing Trees

As noted, once physically severed from the land, trees become goods and so are capable of being subject to personal property rights. Contracts for the sale of goods are nowadays governed by statute, the Sale of Goods Act 1979, re-enacting (with amendments) the Sale of Goods Act 1893, which consolidated the common law. Both statutes distinguish a 'sale', a contract by which the property in the goods is immediately transferred from seller to buyer, from 'an agreement to sell', a contract where the transfer of the property in the goods is to take place at some point in the future.[81] Under the statutory regime, and previously at common law, property in goods passes when the parties intend it to pass.[82] However, this is only possible where the goods are 'specific' or 'ascertained'.[83] Until that point, property cannot pass, no matter what the parties intend. As Lord Mustill said in *Re Goldcorp*, 'It makes no difference what the parties intended if what they intend is impossible.'[84] What his lordship there said about unascertained gold bars applies *a fortiori* to standing trees, which are neither specific nor ascertained goods; indeed, they are not even goods at all.

[80] It is trite law that the benefit of profits (and easements) appurtenant to an estate pass on a conveyance of such estate without the need for express words: J Williams, *Rights of Common and Other Prescriptive Rights* (1880) 315; *Godwin v Schweppes* [1902] 1 Ch 926, 932 (Joyce J).

[81] Sale of Goods Act 1979, ss 2(3) and 2(4).

[82] ibid, s 17.

[83] ibid, s 16.

[84] *Re Goldcorp* [1995] 1 AC 74, 90, citing C Blackburn, *The Effect of the Contract of Sale* (1845) 122–123.

The point is illustrated by the Scottish case of *Morison v Lockhart*,[85] a decision of the Inner House of the Court of Session.[86] A life tenant of land contracted to sell standing timber, the purchaser to cut the trees. Before the cut was complete, the vendor died. His successor was held entitled to refuse the purchaser entry to cut any more, the latter's argument that title to the trees passed by dint of the contract being rejected as an impossibility. The contract was not a sale, but an agreement to sell. Lord Johnston said:

> Growing timber cannot be sold so as to transfer the property as it stands, for as long as it is growing it is *pars soli*, and can only be transferred with the land on which it is growing. … While growing it may be 'goods' in the sense of the Act, about which a contract of sale may be made, but it does not follow that a sale is effected ….[87]

Lord Kinnear said that trees could not 'be conveyed so long as they are still growing, excepting as part of the land, however effectually they may be sold and delivered when they are cut down and turned into corporeal moveables'.[88]

As Lord Johnston noted, though trees may be considered 'goods' even while standing, it is only in the context of describing the contract as one to sell (future) goods. Questions have arisen south of the border regarding the enforcement of such contracts, for if they were for the sale of 'lands, tenements or hereditaments, or any interest in or concerning them', they were by section 4 of the Statute of Frauds 1677 only enforceable where there was a sufficient written memorandum.

Unsurprisingly, most cases held that contracts for the sale of standing trees were agreements for the sale of (future) goods and so not caught by the section. Thus, in *Smith v Surman*,[89] the holder of a fee simple title to land agreed to sell the trees presently standing, the trees to be cut by the vendor. The court held the contract to be outwith the statute. Bayley J said that 'the true construction of the bargain is, that it is a contract for the future sale of the timber when it should be in a state fit for delivery'.[90] Littledale J said:

> [T]he contract in this case was not a contract for the sale of lands, tenements, or hereditaments, or any interest in or concerning the same within the meaning of the fourth section. Those words in that section relate to contracts (for the sale of the fee-simple, or of some less interest than the fee), which give the vendee a right to

[85] *Morison v Lockhart* (1912) SC 1017.

[86] The Sale of Goods Act 1979, and its predecessor, the Sale of Goods Act 1893, apply, with limited exceptions, equally between England and Wales and Scotland. Indeed, the main impetus for the legislation was the desire of Scottish merchants for a uniform sales law between the different nations: A Rodger, 'The Codification of Commercial Law in Victorian Britain' (1991) 80 *Proceedings of the British Academy* 149.

[87] *Morison* (n 85) 1023.

[88] ibid 1028. The decision was endorsed by the English Court of Appeal in *Kursell v Timber Operators and Contractors* [1927] 1 KB 298.

[89] *Smith v Surman* (1829) 9 B & C 561.

[90] ibid 568.

> the use of the land for a specific period. If in this case the contract had been for the sale of the trees, with a specific liberty to the vendee to enter the land to cut them, I think it would not have given him an interest in the land within the meaning of the statute. The object of a party who sells timber is, not to give the vendee any interest in his land, but to pass to him an interest in the trees, *when they become goods and chattels*.[91]

To the same effect is *Marshall v Green*.[92] An oral contract was made for the sale of 22 growing trees to be cut and taken away as soon as possible by the purchaser. It was argued by the vendor, in resisting an enforcement claim, that *Smith v Surman* was distinguishable because here the purchaser was to cut the trees. This meant that he was 'to have the property in the trees while standing, and the licence given him to go on the land becomes irrevocable, because coupled with his interest in the growing timber', which therefore amounted to an interest in land.[93] The argument was rejected. Lord Coleridge CJ said it was 'obvious' that a sale of trees to be taken away immediately 'was not a sale of an interest in land, but merely of so much timber',[94] while Brett LJ held that the contract was only for the purchase of trees, not of an interest in land in addition.[95]

Critical of *Marshall v Green*, however, is *Lavery v Pursell*.[96] A contract was entered into for the sale of the materials from a building to be demolished by the purchaser within two months of the making of the contract. In an unreserved judgment, Chitty J held it was a contract for the sale of an interest in land and therefore unenforceable for want of writing. But what interest was it that was contracted to be sold? Chitty J said it was the building itself:

> The thing sold, as it stands at the moment, is a hereditament. It is said that there is no interest in a hereditament, but then that is answered, if I am right, in saying that the standing house is a hereditament. Then it is said that there is no interest in the soil. That is true in this sense, and in this sense only, that there is no permanent interest. But in this contract, and in fact in every contract of this kind, there must be, and is here, a right to go in and hold for the purpose of pulling down; and that again seems to be an interest in the hereditament or tenement.[97]

That cannot be right. When we think, as we must, in terms of rights rather than physical things, such a statement is nonsensical. It is trite law that we do not contract to sell goods but property rights thereto.[98] Equally, we do not contract

[91] ibid 573 (emphasis added).

[92] *Marshall v Green* (1875) 1 CPD 35.

[93] ibid 37 (Cave QC). This seems to be based on the difficult case of *Webb v Paternoster* (1619) Popham 151.

[94] ibid 40.

[95] ibid 42.

[96] *Lavery v Pursell* (1888) 39 Ch D 508.

[97] ibid 514.

[98] 'A contract of sale of goods is a contract by which the seller transfers or agrees to transfer the property in goods to the buyer for a money consideration, called the price': Sale of Goods Act 1979, s 2(1).

to sell land or houses, but titles, freehold or leasehold, thereto.[99] The word 'hereditament' means inheritable, as opposed to uninheritable,[100] and we inherit rights, not things. The question Chitty J should have asked was whether the right contracted for was a profit, to which section 4 would have applied, or the sale of future goods, to which it would not.[101]

More worryingly, Chitty J thought that *Marshall v Green* was wrongly decided in that it held that standing trees could be made chattels by agreement of the parties:

> Now the Court appears to have considered that there was no interest in the land. I agree that it was a point … that required a good deal of attention, whether a standing tree is a chattel or can be made by any acts of the parties a chattel. It is a hereditament at the time when the contract is made. It is just as much a hereditament in point of law as a house which is standing on the land and just as much so as the mines which are underneath. I only speak now as a real property lawyer. I am bound of course by the English law to say that a tree is not a chattel.[102]

This, however, is a misrepresentation of *Marshall v Green*. As we have seen, what the court in fact decided was that the contract was for the sale of future goods.[103] At no point did it hold that standing trees could be made chattels by agreement of the parties. Unfortunately, Chitty J is not the only person to make this mistake.

B. The Judgment of Duff J in *Beatty v Mathewson*

In *Beatty v Mathewson*,[104] the facts of which are given below,[105] Duff J thought it 'indisputable that growing timber may be so granted as to vest it *in sitû* in the grantee as a chattel'.[106] He cited three cases as authority, *Herlakenden's Case*, an anonymous decision from 1593, and *Stukeley v Butler*, saying that it was too late to dispute this fact 'notwithstanding the vigorous criticism by Chitty J in *Lavery v Pursell*'. However, the authorities do not bear him out,[107] and his comment on *Marshall v Green* shows he is making the same mistake as Chitty J.

[99] The modern rule for such contracts, contained in s 2 of the Law of Property (Miscellaneous Provisions) Act 1989, speaks of contracts 'for the sale or other disposition of an interest in land'.

[100] 'Whatsoever may be inherited, be it corporeal or incorporeal, real, personal, or mixed, is an hereditament': W Sheppard, *The Touchstone of Common Assurances* (1648) 91.

[101] Precisely this question was asked in the very similar decisions of *Stratford v Mole & Lea* [1941] 24 TC 20 and *Mills v Stokman* (1967) 116 CLR 61; the answer in both was that it was a profit.

[102] *Lavery* (n 96) 516.

[103] Above, text to nn 92–93.

[104] *Beatty v Mathewson* (1908) 40 SCR 557.

[105] Text to n 120.

[106] *Beatty* (n 104) 569.

[107] He also relied on *Shepherd's Touchstone of Common Assurances* and *Williams on Executors*, but these do nothing more than reproduce *verbatim* what is said in the cases.

i. Herlakenden's Case

In *Herlakenden's Case*,[108] the Earl of Oxford held a fee simple title to Colme Park in Essex. He granted a 21-year lease of a 380-acre parcel to three tenants in common, 'excepting the trees'. He then conveyed 'the trees' to the same three tenants, who later assigned their lease to Bragge, who in turn assigned to Ivy. In the meantime, the lessees separately sold 'the trees' to Herlakenden. When Herlakenden entered, cut down, and took away 1,000 trees, he was unsuccessfully sued by Ivy in trespass.

Ivy's argument seems to have been that the grant by the Earl to his tenants of 'the trees' gave them no right at all, that 'the wood' was thereby 'united again to the land', and the right consequently destroyed. The argument of Herlakenden, by contrast, was that 'the wood' remained as an interest distinct and severed from the land. Not surprisingly, Ivy's argument was rejected. If correct, it would have meant that the lessees who had bought 'the trees' in fact bought nothing. It would have been:

> a prejudice to him, that during the term he could not fell them, but should be punished in waste, and after the term should lose them; and it would be against reason that the lessor should against his own grant have them again.[109]

It is difficult to see anything in the case supporting Duff J's statement that standing trees can be severed from the land and turned into chattels. The language of severance refers only to the landlord's right to cut the trees, which, when granted to the tenants, would amount, as we have seen,[110] to a profit in gross. Duff J can only have been reading the references to 'the trees' and 'the woods' as being to the physical things themselves, rather than the right to take them.

ii. Anonymous Decision of 1593

The second case relied on by Duff J is a sparsely reported decision of 1593.[111] The full report reads as follows:

> In a waste the case was, that a lessee for years purchased trees growing upon the land, and had liberty to cut them within eighty years, and after the said lessee purchased the inheritance of the land and devised it to his wife for life, the remainder to the plaintiff in fee, and made his wife executrix, and died, who after married with the defendant, who cuts the trees, whereupon the action is brought. And by opinion of all the Court the action was maintainable, for although the trees were once chattels, yet by the purchase of the inheritance they were united to the land: and judgment was given for the plaintiff accordingly.

[108] *Herlakenden's Case* (1589) 4 Co Rep 62a.
[109] ibid 63b.
[110] Above, text to n 33 and n 61.
[111] *Anon* (1593) Owen 49.

We need more facts, but what seems to have happened is that a freeholder granted a lease of land for years with either an exception of trees or with impeachment for waste. The landlord then granted a profit of trees to the lessee for a period of 80 years. The lessee then bought the reversion and later made a will of his freehold in favour of his wife for life, remainder to the plaintiff, naming his wife as executor. After the lessee/now freeholder's death, his widow married the defendant. When the defendant later cut down some trees, he was successfully sued by the plaintiff remainderman. The fact that the lessee bought up the reversion meant that his 80-year profit was extinguished, meaning that his wife had no such independent right. As a mere life tenant, she was liable for waste should she cut timber[112] and so could not licence the defendant to cut the trees. What Duff J seems to rely on is the statement that 'the trees were once chattels'. However, this is simply a reflection of the fact that profits for years were chattels real. Nowhere does the court say that the physical trees themselves were chattels.

iii. Stukeley v Butler

The final case is *Stukeley v Butler*.[113] The Earl of Sussex was seised of the manor of Cleave, comprising a house 'and 100 acres usually occupied with it, and 700 more, and certain woods called Blagrave, Pitchil, Erridge, Bore, and Readwood'. He granted a lease of the manor to Robert Butler, his wife, and son, the defendant in the action, for their joint lives. The lease excepted 'all timber trees'. The Earl later 'bargained and sold' to Edward George by deed:

> all those things, the woods, underwoods, timber & trees, of his then standing, growing and existing in and on the whole of the manor of his of Cleave, in the aforesaid county of Somerset, viz in and on all those coppices of his, whether the wood called Erridge Wood, containing 24 acres, and in and on the whole of the wood called Borewood containing 10 acres and in and on the whole of the wood called Blagrave Wood, containing 6 acres, and also in and on the whole of the other wood called Pitchil Wood, containing 7 acres, together with all of the other woods and underwoods, timber & trees standing and existing on the estate and manor of Cleave which can with convenience be spared and felled without prejudice and loss to the state and maintenance … of the aforesaid manor of Cleave.

The Earl also covenanted to allow George and his assigns for a period of five years to fell and carry away the trees without the interruption of the lessor or any others, and to 'make sawing pits, and to square and cut the timber upon the ground during the said term'.

George later bargained and sold 'all the woods' to Prowse, who in turn bargained and sold to Robert Butler 'all the woods in Blagrave, Pitchil and

[112] Above, text to n 67.
[113] *Stukeley v Butler* (1617) Hob 168.

the seven hundred acres'. Prowse later bargained and sold the remainder of his woods to the Earl, who in turn bargained and sold his reversion and all his woods to Stukeley. On Robert Butler's death, he left his woods to his son. When the son felled trees in the Blagrave and Pitchil Woods and the seven hundred acres, Stukeley unsuccessfully sued him in trespass.

The case turned on the construction of the grant. To the son's reliance on the original grant of 'the trees' to George, Stukeley had two arguments. First, the grant did not include the seven hundred acres but was limited to the five woods named in the 'viz' clause, meaning that some at least of the felling was unlawful. This was rejected by Hobart CJ, who held the 'viz' clause to be void as repugnant to the general grant of woods.[114] Second, even if valid, the grant to George was limited to five years, which period had expired. This too was rejected, Hobart CJ holding that the five-year covenants merely added to the rights otherwise granted and did not cut down the terms of the grant itself.[115] The claim was therefore dismissed.

So far, then, the case says nothing about trees as chattels. However, in a passage relied upon by Duff J, Hobart CJ said:

> It is clear, that by the grant of the trees by a tenant in fee-simple, they are absolutely passed away from the grantor, and his heirs, and vested in the grantee, and go to the executors or administrators, being in understanding of law, divided as chattels from the free-hold ....[116]

Though this passage does seem to provide support for Duff J's statement that standing trees can be considered chattel interests, it must be treated with caution.

Hobart CJ is clearly speaking about the right to enter and cut the trees, not a right to possession of the trees themselves. After all, that was what Butler was relying on in his defence. Thus, when the judge speaks of 'the trees' being 'absolutely passed away from the grantor', he is describing a profit in gross. The mystery, however, is why such right is said to pass to the executors or administrators. The only explanation is that, at that point, it had not been established that profits in gross were realty rather than personalty. The decision where that is made plain, *Buckeridge v Ingram*,[117] dates from almost two centuries later, so it may be that in 1617, the point had not yet been established. Given that there is no livery of seisin with the grant of a profit, this is not an untenable position to take. Indeed, Holdsworth, describing the medieval land law, said that because a profit in gross was not annexed to the holding of any land, it was 'a personal as opposed to a praedial right'.[118] So it may be that at this time profits in gross were

[114] ibid 169–173.
[115] ibid 173–174.
[116] ibid 173.
[117] *Buckeridge* (n 45).
[118] WS Holdsworth, *An Historical Introduction to the Land Law* (1927) 95.

not considered realty, and so would indeed descend 'as chattels', in other words, as chattel interests. But either way, what Hobart CJ is clearly discussing is the profit of trees, not a right to possession of the trees themselves.

A final point relates to Duff J's reference to *Lavery v Pursell*. As we saw, Chitty J there said that *Marshall v Green* was wrong to hold that it was possible to legally sever standing trees by contract and turn them into chattels. Duff J's reference to Chitty J's criticism of that case indicates that he too read *Marshall v Green* as sanctioning this. However, as we have seen, this is a mistake. All the court there decided was that the contract was for the sale of future goods, not an interest in land. It did not decide that standing trees could be legally severed from the land and turned into chattels.

IX. FREEHOLD ESTATES IN TREES

We turn finally to the possibility of there being a freehold estate in standing trees, a 'treehold'. We will first examine the judgment of Duff J in *Beatty v Mathewson*, and then its treatment in later cases.

A. The Judgment of Duff J in *Beatty v Mathewson*

In *Beatty v Mathewson*, Duff J, in addition to his statement that standing trees can be made chattels, said that there can be 'an estate in fee simple in growing timber'.[119] The facts of the case were these. In 1872, Mathewson, holder of a fee simple title to land, sold to Beatty all the 'good merchantable pine growing or being upon the land, at the rate of 75 cents per thousand feet board measure, to be paid for when cut, with ten years to be allowed for taking off the timber'. Mathewson was to be allowed to cut and use any trees he needed for his own use on the land for farming purposes. In 1881, the parties signed another agreement, replacing the first, which, in consideration of a lump sum of $130, purported to:

> grant, bargain, sell and assign unto (Beatty) his heirs and assigns, all the pine, oak, birch, hemlock and other timber now standing, growing or being in or upon all and singular that certain parcel or tract of land and premises .... To have and to hold the same unto the said party of the second part his heirs and assigns forever, together with full power, liberty, right and authority for the said party of the second part, his servants, workmen and agents from time to time and at all reasonable times hereafter during the term of [ ] years to fell, cut down, grub up, saw, dress, hew and work up the said timber, and together with full and free ingress, egress and regress, for the said party of the second part his servants, workmen and agents with or without

[119] *Beatty* (n 104) 567.

> horses, oxen, waggons, carts, sleighs, trucks and teams to enter into and upon and over the said lands and premises for the purposes aforesaid, and also for the purpose of taking and carrying away the said timber with liberty also to make all such roads as may from time to time be necessary for getting out and removing the said timber, and for that purpose to cut, fell, hew and remove such trees, logs and brush as may be deemed necessary.

The agreement was drawn up on a printed form adapted from the short form of conveyance of titles to land, the word 'lands' being changed to 'timber' in the covenants and other printed parts of the document. The reason the 'term of [ ] years' provision was left blank was that the parties had not at that point agreed how long the right should last.

Beatty entered the land and cut timber until his death in 1893, and his executors authorised others to do so until 1905. Mathewson then sought an injunction against the executors preventing further cutting, a declaration that the right to take the timber had lapsed, and damages for trespass. The issue was purely one of construction, viz, whether the agreement was a contract for the sale of future goods or the grant of a perpetual right to enter and cut the trees, or at least a right to do so while there were trees still standing. The trial judge, Magee J, held that the contract merely granted a licence to remove the timber within a reasonable time, which time had elapsed. He therefore allowed the claim.[120]

His decision was upheld by a majority of the Ontario Court of Appeal, which rejected the argument that Beatty had been granted 'the legal estate in the trees and therefore the right to possession'.[121] The contract, despite its form, was nothing more than an agreement to sell.[122] Dissenting, Meredith JA held that what was described as 'an absolute sale and conveyance of lands', could not be converted into 'a sale and bill of sale of goods, or into a mere demise of lands for years' and that 'even if the sale had been one of goods only, the property in them passed under the deed' and that he was 'unable to perceive by what legal process it repassed to the plaintiff'.[123] However, Meredith JA was unspecific as to the interest in land contracted to be sold, though given that no right to possession of the land on which the trees were standing was granted, he can only have been thinking of a profit. As to how, in the alternative, property in the trees as goods could pass before physical severance was not explained.

A further appeal to the Supreme Court of Canada also failed.[124] The issue was again whether the document granted the purchaser 'an estate in inheritance in the trees' or was simply a contract for the sale of future goods. Iddington J,

[120] *Beatty v Mathewson* (1907) 15 Ont LR 557, 566–67.
[121] ibid 571.
[122] ibid.
[123] ibid 581.
[124] *Beatty* (n 104).

with whom Giroud J agreed, held that, though badly drafted and ambiguous, the document gave the purchaser no 'estate in inheritance' but was merely a sale of the then existing timber, to be cut and removed by the purchaser at some reasonable time. MacLennan J simply agreed with the reasoning of the majority of the Court of Appeal.

Davies and Duff JJ dissented. Davies J said that what was granted was not a mere right to cut trees but an estate of inheritance in the trees themselves; it was therefore impossible to imply a reasonable period in which the right was to be exercised. Duff J held that the words used by the parties had the effect of 'vesting in the grantee an estate in fee simple in the growing timber described', It could not be disputed, he said, that 'the owner of an estate of fee simple in land on which trees are growing may by an appropriate assurance vest in another an estate of inheritance in one or more of the trees'.[125] Exactly what this 'estate of inheritance' was, a freehold in the trees themselves or a profit, is however unclear.

Some clue can be derived from the counsel's reliance on *Wickham v Hawker*,[126] already encountered above,[127] which concerned a profit of hunting, the implication being that when speaking of 'an estate of inheritance', Duff J meant a profit in fee. Moreover, the sources relied on by Duff J for his proposition seem to support this. He first cited a passage from *Leake on Uses and Profits of Land*:

> A grant or an exception from a grant, of the trees growing in certain land, creates a property in the trees, separate from the property in the soil; but with the right of having them grow and subsist upon it. An estate of inheritance in a tree may thus be created.[128]

This is hardly authority for a fee simple in the trees themselves. The author is clearly speaking of a profit of trees, as the language of separation from the property in the soil and the right to have them grow and subsist upon it demonstrates.[129] Duff J also cited a passage from an American text, *Washburn on Real Property*:

> But if the owner of land grants the trees growing thereon to another and his heirs, with liberty to cut and carry them away at his pleasure, forever, the grantee acquires an estate in fee in the trees, with an interest in the soil sufficient for their growth, while the fee in the soil itself remains in the grantor.[130]

[125] ibid 567–68.
[126] *Wickham* (n 38).
[127] Text to n 38.
[128] SM Leake, *Law of Uses and Profits of Land* (1888) 30.
[129] Above, text to n 58.
[130] J Wurts, *Washburn's Treatise on the American Law of Real Property*, 6th edn (1902) 16.

Once again, the author is clearly talking about a profit, again indicated by the language of the right-holder having an 'interest in the soil sufficient for their growth'. This is not a fee simple estate in the trees themselves.

So far, then, Duff J's 'estate of inheritance' is nothing more than a freehold profit. However, he also placed reliance on a *dictum* in the already encountered *Liford's Case*,[131] where Coke CJ said:

> A man may have in inheritance in fee-simple in lands, as long as such a tree shall grow, 27 Hen 8, 29b because a man may have an inheritance in the tree itself. *Vide* 46 Ed 3, 1b in Trespass, 32 Hen 6, 6, 20 Hen 6, 22b, 5 Hen 4, 2.[132]

This might indicate that Duff J was thinking about a fee simple title to possession of the trees themselves, not a freehold profit. However, the passage must be treated with caution, for three reasons.

First, *Liford's Case* is authority for exactly the opposite of the notion that there can be a fee simple estate in the trees themselves. As we have seen, Coke CJ said that timber trees could not be 'felled with a goose quill'.[133] Second, though it is possible to have a fee simple determinable on the life of a tree,[134] to say that this is because it is possible to have an inheritance in the tree itself is a misstep. There are many other types of valid limitations, for example, 'as long as the Church of St Paul shall stand',[135] 'so long as B hath heirs',[136] and 'till C returns from Rome',[137] yet we would not say that the grantee had respectively an inheritance in St Pauls, B and his heirs, or C staying in Rome; the limitation merely marks the length of the estate.

Third, Coke's assertion that a person can have 'an inheritance in the tree itself' is not supported by the four yearbook cases he cites, which are equivocal at best. In the first,[138] a claim was brought in trespass 'for goods carried off, and for grass grazed and trees cut down'. The plaintiff argued that the case was all about personalty, but the defendant argued it was a mixed claim of personalty and realty, which had jurisdictional consequences. Although the final remarks do present the case as about personalty, they concern arguments of pleading, not substance.

The second[139] was a writ of trespass concerning grass. The report is unclear as to whether the grass was growing or already physically severed from the land.

[131] Above, text to n 58.
[132] *Liford's Case* (n 71).
[133] Above, text to n 80.
[134] C Sweet, *Challis's Law of Real Property*, 3rd edn (1911) 256, gives examples of limitations for 'as long as such a tree shall grow', 'during the time that such a tress shall grow', and 'as long as such a tree stands.
[135] *Walsingham's Case* (1573) 2 Plowd 547, 557.
[136] ibid.
[137] *Duke of Norfolk's Case* (1682) 3 Ch Ca 1, 46 (Serjeant Maynard).
[138] (1372) YB Hil 46 Edw III, fo 28b, pl 2.
[139] (1453) YB Mich 32 Hen VI, fo 6v, pl 18.

The defendant justified the trespass through a descent, which suggests that his argument was that he was entitled to the grass by inheritance. The report again focuses on a pleading point, but the implication may be that the defendant could argue he had inherited the grass but that he had pleaded that point incorrectly. In any case, what the defendant was probably relying on was a profit of pasture or herbage, so that the case says nothing about any 'severance' of the grass from the land having the effect of turning it into a chattel interest.

The third case[140] says nothing about trees being personalty and appears instead, as with the previous one, to concern a profit, this time of trees not pasture, while the fourth[141] is about trees being within the fee simple title inherited, the specific question concerning the rights of an underage heir in wardship against his guardian. It did not concern trees as personalty.

In sum, therefore, and despite Coke CJ's *dictum*, *Liford's Case* is not authority for the proposition that there can be a freehold interest in a standing tree; if anything, it is authority for the opposite. The best interpretation of Duff J's dissent in *Beatty v Mathewson* is that he simply construed the agreement as creating a perpetual profit in gross, not a fee simple title to the trees themselves, and it was that which justified him refusing to grant the injunction sought.

B. Subsequent Treatment of Duff J's Dissent in *Beatty v Mathewson*

Duff J's dissent has been approved on several occasions. All, however, can be explained on orthodox grounds and none are authority for there being a freehold title to possess standing trees.

The first case is *Eastern Construction Co v National Trust Co*,[142] a decision of the Privy Council on appeal from the Supreme Court of Canada,[143] wherein Duff J himself had reiterated his thinking in *Beatty*. A lease of land by the Crown contained a reservation of all pine trees. A third party entered and cut down the trees, which acts were later ratified by the Crown. The lessee sued the third party in trover and detinue, actions concerned with interference with the right to possession of goods. The claim failed on the ground, following Duff J's analysis, described by Lord Atkinson as 'able and convincing', that 'the property in the pine trees growing on these locations remained in the Crown'.[144] The result can be explained, however, on orthodox reasoning. As we have seen, in the case of a reservation of trees by a landlord, when physically severed from the

[140] (1442) YB Hil 20 Hen VI, fo 22v, pl 20.

[141] (1410) YB Hil 5 Hen IV, fo 2v, pl 7. Coke's reference is not so specific as to make it clear that this is the case to which he was referring, though it does at least concern trees.

[142] *Eastern Construction Co v National Trust Co* [1914] AC 197.

[143] *Sub nom, National Trust Co v Miller* (1912) 3 DLR 69.

[144] *Eastern Construction Co* (n 142) [208].

land, the best right to their possession vests in the landlord, not the tenant,[145] meaning that the tenant can bring neither trover nor detinue where the landlord licenses the interference. There was thus no need for Lord Atkinson to rely on anything said by Duff J in *Beatty v Mathewson*. It is certainly not an endorsement of the idea that there can be a fee simple title to the trees themselves, as opposed to a profit in fee.

Duff J's dissent was also applied by the Ontario High Court in *Smith v Daly*,[146] which concerned a grant in fee simple with a reservation of 'merchantable timber'. When, some years later, a licensee of the grantor cut down trees, he was sued by the freeholder, who argued that the reservation either only applied to trees merchantable at the time of the grant or was void for uncertainty. Both arguments were rejected and the claim dismissed. Though Wells J approved the statement of Duff J in *Beatty* that there might be freehold estates in trees, this was again unnecessary for the decision; the reservation is better analysed as the grant of a freehold profit.

John Austin and Sons Ltd v Smith[147] was a decision of the Ontario Court of Appeal. It involved a sale of a fee simple title to land, 'saving and excepting and reserving thereout and therefrom all timber products'. When the purchaser later refused to allow the vendor to exercise the right, he was sued for an injunction. The purchaser, relying on a limitation statute, pleaded that they had been in continuous, uninterrupted, open and visible possession of the land from 1958 to 1974 and had therefore become its absolute owners. In the alternative, they argued that the grant was subject to an implied term that the vendor's rights be exercised within a reasonable time, which time had elapsed. The Court held that an 'estate' was reserved in the grant, which was 'a fee simple in the trees with soil sufficient for their growth', though the 'fee simple in the soil itself' had passed to the purchaser, and that such right had not been lost by inaction. Here, the right concerned was clearly a freehold profit of trees: as we have seen, the language of a right to 'the trees with soil sufficient for their growth' is exactly that used in the profit cases.[148] Indeed, in the final case in which Duff J's dictum was approved, *McDonnell Estate v Scott World Wide Inc*,[149] the Nova Scotia Court of Appeal expressly held that what was granted was a profit of trees.

X. CONCLUSION

The objection to any separate property right in standing trees is that once planted, the separate physical identities of trees are destroyed and that because

[145] Above, text to n 74.
[146] *Smith v Daly* [1949] 4 DLR 45.
[147] *John Austin and Sons Ltd v Smith* (1982) 132 DLR (3rd) 311.
[148] Above, text to n 58.
[149] *McDonnell Esteate v Scott World Wide Inc* (1997) 149 DLR (4th) 645.

they no longer have such separate identity, they cannot be the subject-matter of separate property rights. This is the doctrine of accession. By the same token, once felled, trees are capable of being the subject-matter of property rights separate from the land on which they formerly stood and such rights will be chattel interests. As to the position in the interim, though a contract to sell trees can be a contract for the sale of (future) goods, arguments for separate property rights to possession of the trees, either personal or real, cannot be sustained. Though there may be a profit of trees, which profit can exist for an equivalent period to a freehold title to land, there can be no separate right to possess the trees themselves while standing, nothing we might call a 'Treehold'. Cases which speak of a grant of property in 'the trees' are concerned with the grant of a profit, not a right to possession, real or personal, of the trees themselves.

More generally, this chapter has demonstrated the importance of two things in property law. First, a distinction must always be drawn between rights and physical things. When lawyers speak of land and trees, they sometimes mean the land or trees themselves, sometimes rights with respect to them. This only leads to confusion. Second, when speaking of rights, the nature of the right in question must always be made clear. There can be rights to possession of physical things, but also rights, such as profits, of a lesser nature. These need to be clearly distinguished. Simply speaking, for example, of 'a freehold of trees' obscures this important difference.

Part II

Morality of Property

4

Against Conventionalism

JEREMY WALDRON

I. INTRODUCTION

THIS IS A conference on property,[1] and the conventionalism mentioned in my title this evening is conventionalism about property – the suggestion that private property and property rights are mere matters of convention, legal constructions out of whole cloth that do not represent rights or principles grounded independently in morality or natural law.

The debate about conventionalism is in large measure a debate about the aspersions that conventionalists cast upon John Locke. Theorists of property, said Alan Ryan in his 1984 book *Property and Political Theory* 'rightly spend a lot of time in the company of Locke'.

> His *Two Treatises of Government*, provide, so he told his nephew [*– so Locke told Locke's nephew –*], the best account of property that he knew of. They defend the proposition that the sole purpose for which government exists is to defend the property of its subjects; and they give an account of how men came by that property which has been enormously influential.[2]

Private property, Locke said, existed in a state of nature on the basis of natural law; and the rights that people now have over man-made and natural resources (including land) are in their origin natural rights based on moral principles that respect self-ownership and the investment of individual labour.

> [T]hough the things of Nature are given in common, yet Man (by being Master of himself, and Proprietor of his own Person, and the actions or Labour of it) had still in himself the great foundation of property; and that which made up the great part of what he applied to the Support or Comfort of his being … was perfectly his own, and did not belong in common to others.[3]

Positive law did not create property rights; individual labour did. That was Locke's view. The mission of positive law was and is to uphold these

[1] Oxford Law Faculty: Modern Studies in Property Law Conference, 29–31 March 2022.

[2] A Ryan, *Property and Political Theory* (Oxford, Blackwell, 1984) 14.

[3] J Locke, *Two Treatises of Government* (P Laslett ed, London, Cambridge University Press, 1960) 316 (II, §44). Hereafter this is referred to as 'Locke, TT'.

independently justified rights and defend them against the incursions of burglars, state officials, and well-meaning majorities. It is to provide juridical framing for the economy in which natural property rights operate and circulate. Property is not set up by law. It is something law is tasked with defending. That is the anti-conventionalist position.

So: theorists of property spend time in the company of John Locke. I have certainly done hard time in this regard, much of it in the course of my doctorate on the right to private property at Oxford beginning in 1978 under the supervision of Dr Ryan as well as Professor Ronald Dworkin. I have published two books on Locke's political theory and a number of articles,[4] and I am convinced that Lockean ideas are of great importance in thinking about property.

In their book, *The Myth of Ownership*, my New York University colleagues Liam Murphy and Thomas Nagel say that time spent on these matters in the company of Locke is time wasted.[5] They say Locke's attempt to find a natural law basis for property, prior to and independent of positive law, is downright implausible. They say property is an artifact of positive law; it is a legal convention. They say time served in the company of Locke would have been better spent reading the works of philosophical conventionalists like Jeremy Bentham and David Hume. '[T]here is no such thing as natural property,' said Bentham, 'it is entirely the work of law.' He was echoing Hume: 'Tis very preposterous … to imagine that we can have any idea of property, without fully comprehending … its origin in the artifice and contrivance of men.'[6] Bentham is unforgiving in his conventionalism, pushing as deep as it can go. 'What is it,' he asks, 'that serves as a basis to law, upon which to begin operations, when it adopts objects which, under the name of property, it promises to protect?' Is not there at least a Lockean foundation? No there is not, says Bentham. Here is the most he thinks we can say on Locke's behalf:

> Have not men, in the primitive state, a natural expectation of enjoying certain things, – an expectation drawn from sources anterior to law? Yes. There have been from the beginning, and there always will be, circumstances in which a man may secure himself, by his own means, in the enjoyment of certain things. The savage who has killed a deer may hope to keep it for himself, so long as his cave is undiscovered; so long as he watches to defend it, and is stronger than his rivals.[7]

[4] J Waldron, *The Right to Private Property* (Oxford, Clarendon Press, 1988), hereafter 'RTTP'; *God, Locke, and Equality: Christian Foundations of John Locke's Political Thought* (Cambridge, Cambridge University Press, 2002); 'Locke, Tully and the Regulation of Property' (1984) 32 *Political Studies* 98; 'Two Worries About Mixing One's Labour' (1983) 33 *Philosophical Quarterly* 37; 'Locke's Account of Inheritance and Bequest' (1981) 19 *Journal of the History of Philosophy* 39.

[5] L Murphy and T Nagel, *The Myth of Ownership: Taxes and Justice* (Oxford, Oxford University Press, 2002).

[6] D Hume, *A Treatise Concerning Human Nature* (LA Selby-Bigg ed, Oxford, Clarendon Press, 1888) 491 (Bk III, pt. 2, sect. ii).

[7] J Bentham, 'Security and Equality' in CB Macpherson (ed), *Property: Mainstream and Critical Positions* (Toronto, University of Toronto Press, 1978) 52.

But, says Bentham, '[h]ow miserable and precarious is such a possession! A feeble and momentary expectation may result from time to time from circumstances purely physical; but a strong and permanent expectation can result only from law.'[8]

Hume's approach is slightly different from Bentham's. Property is not initially a matter of *legal* construction for Hume, but it is still a convention in the technical sense. People fight over resources and the fighting settles down into various equilibria of possession, defined by the holdings that each person can defend. Peace dividends become available when each person matches the others' willingness to refrain from attacking existing holdings. And so conventions emerge, respecting de facto possessions, putting them under the auspices of 'mine' and 'thine'. Hume's view is that law comes into the picture much later to firm up these conventions and underpin the long-term, interest-based reasoning that the relevant equilibria presuppose.[9] It is fascinating, but I will try not to make too much of the difference between Bentham and Hume in what follows. It is mainly a Benthamite account – property as initially a legal construction – that Murphy and Nagel have in mind.

Stay away from Locke, say Murphy and Nagel. Well, I am pretty promiscuous about the company I keep, and I have hung out too with Hume and Bentham.[10] And having experienced the higher pleasures of conventionalism along with the more dubious satisfactions of Lockean philosophy, I would like in this chapter to revisit the issue between them, and say a word or two in support of the anti-conventionalist case. Not that I do not feel the attractions of the conventionalist critique of Locke's childish fantasies. I do. And I acknowledge that Hume's theory has a number of pragmatic advantages (mainly epistemic), which I have set out at length elsewhere.[11] Still, after all these years – almost 40 years since my doctorate, 20 years since *The Myth of Ownership* – I find myself siding with John Locke and the principles of natural law, and against Murphy and Nagel.

Conventionalism can be a matter of degree. For example: languages are conventional systems, with signs and sounds correlated arbitrarily with determinate meanings. But there may be a few non-conventional elements – a strand of onomatopoeia here and there. Something similar is true of positive law and natural law. As we will see, they are often larded together. Certainly, conventionalism can apply in some areas and not others. Murphy and Nagel apply

[8] ibid.

[9] I follow the interpretation of Hume's theory in J Buchanan, *The Limits of Liberty: Between Anarchy and Leviathan* (Chicago, University of Chicago Press, 1975).

[10] J Waldron, 'The Advantages and Difficulties of the Humean Theory of Property' (1994) 11 *Social Philosophy and Policy* 85; 'To Bestow Stability upon Possession: Hume's Alternative to Locke', in J Penner and H Smith (eds), *Philosophical Foundations of Property Law* (Oxford, Oxford University Press, 2013) 1; 'Is Coleman Hobbes or Hume (or perhaps Locke)?' in B Bix (ed), *Analyzing Law: New Essays in Legal Theory* (Oxford, Clarendon Press, 1998) 117; 'Supply Without Burthen Revisited' (1997) 82 *Iowa Law Review* 1467.

[11] See the discussion in J Waldron, 'The Advantages and Difficulties of the Humean Theory of Property' (1994) 11 *Social Philosophy and Policy* 85.

their conventionalist approach to promise (and contract) as well as to property. (They think the case is substantially the same. I am not going to consider promising here, though I will note a few areas where the logics of the respective areas of law are quite different.) Bentham was pretty much an opponent of all talk of natural rights – a conventionalist about everything in this domain.[12] Modern day conventionalists, though, are more discriminating. They accept that the natural law view applies to some normative practices:

> [S]ome moral obligations or rights make sense all on their own; there is no need to appeal to a social practice or convention to make sense of them. The duties not to kill or hurt people without special justification, … the duty to care for children; the virtue of benevolence; the rights of freedom of movement and expression and conscience – all of these duties, rights, and virtues derive their plausibility directly from some clear human interest.[13]

That is Liam Murphy.[14] But Murphy says it is preposterous to think that property rights could be among these free-standing moral rights.

So, there is conventionalism and anti-conventionalism. What should we call the anti-conventionalist alternative – the position that property law *can* be understood as reflecting or reproducing certain law-independent demands of morality?[15] I am tempted to call it the 'natural law' position. I know that seems a bit arch, and I am embarrassed to use the phrase. It sounds old-fashioned and Catholic; if someone believes in the natural law of property, what is to stop them from pontificating about natural law on marriage, sexuality, and abortion?[16] Also, I do not want to give the impression that Lockean considerations about property are spooky or metaphysical (at least in their modern manifestations).[17] My embarrassment about the phrase 'natural law' might be a sign that Lockean ideas are too cloying, too rich. Better to invoke the austere, stainless-steel lines of legal convention than the sweet, soggy mysteries of natural law. When the issue is put this way, conventionalism seems like the grown-up view, counselling us to put aside childish things. But I am going to use 'natural law' anyway.

[12] See J Bentham, 'Anarchical Fallacies' in J Waldron (ed), *Nonsense Upon Stilts: Bentham, Burke and Marx on the Rights of Man* (New York, Metheuen, 1987) 46.

[13] L Murphy, 'The Artificial Morality of Private Law: The Persistence of an Illusion' (2020) 70 *University of Toronto Law Journal* 453, 457. I shall refer to this article repeatedly in what follows, using the abbreviation Murphy, *AMPL*. It is the clearest and most sustained account of the conventionalist position.

[14] ibid 479. Murphy also says: 'Some areas of law, such as, for example, some or all of the constitutional law of individual rights, simply pick up on what we hold to be independently cognizable moral rights. Here, we might say that, if the law is good, it will simply reflect morality.'

[15] ibid 455: sometimes he calls it 'libertarianism'; he also uses the phrase 'market moralism'.

[16] See N Bamforth and D Richards, *Patriarchal Religion, Sexuality and Gender: A Critique of New Natural Law* (Cambridge, Cambridge University Press, 2008).

[17] But, of course, there are theological elements in Locke's own property theory: see Locke (n 3) 204–5 (I, §86). See also Waldron, *God, Locke and Equality* (n 4) 151–87.

Whether you call it natural law or the Lockean view, my position is that a legal system should uphold property rights in response to certain moral concerns for the persons whose rights they are. These are rights that embody people's work, initiative and earnings; their exercise of freedom; and their responsibility for their own actions and projects. My view is that natural law considerations like these have been dismissed too quickly – indeed, dismissed *precipitously* without enough consideration about what a full-blooded conventionalism would have to involve.

Sometimes the natural law position is dismissed in a sort of *panic* in face of the complexity of modern property arrangements. Christopher Kutz says that '[t]here is simply no way to understand our complex system of divided interests and fractionated claims, much less to justify the economic systems that depend upon them, except on an instrumental, conventionalist basis.'[18] I will consider the complexity argument for conventionalism, such as it is, in section VIII below. But let me anticipate a couple of points. The mere fact that some complex property interest cannot *wholly* be characterised in terms of natural law does not mean that natural law considerations play no role in understanding and defending it. It may still play a crucial role in establishing the moral infrastructure on which the complexities are built. Also, natural law is associated with the doctrine of *determinatio*, referring to human choices of detail and technicality in the constructions we build on a natural law basis. *Determinatio*, says Aquinas, is a mode similar to 'that whereby, in the arts, general forms are particularized as to details: thus the craftsman needs to determine the general form of a house to some particular shape'.[19] Or as Locke puts it, 'The Obligations of the Law of Nature, cease not in Society, but only in many Cases are drawn closer, and have by Humane Laws known Penalties attached to them, to enforce their observation.'[20] There are always technical layers to add to the principles that natural law establishes when we implement those principles in a real-world legal system. This is true even in the areas where (as we have seen) Murphy concedes that conventionalism does not apply: in the law of homicide for example. We all acknowledge a natural law principle against killing; but an awful lot of complex and technical work has to be done to implement it as part of a criminal code; there have to be degrees of homicide, definitions, defences, and penalties, for example. That is why, as John Finnis says, '"No one may kill …" is legally so defective a formulation.'[21] But my point is that the need for such technicality does not transform the prohibition on murder into a mere convention.

18 C Kutz, 'Torture, Necessity and Existential Politics' (2005) 95 *California Law Review* 235, 258–9.

19 Thomas Aquinas, *Summa Theologiae*, I-11, Q. 95, a. 2.

20 Locke (n 3) 375–76 (II, §135).

21 J Finnis, *Natural Law and Natural Rights* (Oxford, Clarendon Press, 1980) 283. See also the discussion in J Waldron, 'Torture, Suicide, and Determinatio (the 2010 Natural Law Lecture)' (2010) 55 *American Journal of Jurisprudence* 1.

II. LAW ON BOTH SIDES

This suggests there might be some common ground between the two perspectives we are considering. Let us begin with what is said on both sides about the role of positive law. Conventionalists say that property rights require law for their security. Listen to Bentham, for example, on the fragility of the naturalistic bond: 'A feeble and momentary expectation may result from time to time from circumstances purely physical; but a strong and permanent expectation can result only from law.'[22] Well, this is something that both positions share. Locke too observed that 'in the state of nature, the enjoyment of the property [one] has … is very unsafe, very insecure',[23] and that positive law is the remedy. Both sides accept that legal institutions are a stabilising force for a society's property arrangements.

If there is a difference, I suppose it is that the Lockean does not think that the insecurity positive law is supposed to relieve discredits or blocks out the moral considerations that law-making is supposed to respond to. Bentham thinks it does.

The conventionalist point may be that so-called natural property rights simply cannot do their work in the absence of positive law. But what sort of work is this supposed to be?

Maybe they cannot operate as a flourishing framework for a fully operational economy. But it is a mistake to think that this type of social viability is required for the natural law position. We must not have too demanding a sense of what the natural law position requires. True, some natural law philosophers imagine a sort of *sequence*: once upon a time there were property rights; they endured for a considerable time in a state of nature and helped define a flourishing economy; but as time passed, respect for the rights became precarious; and legal rules and institutions had to be brought in to reinforce them. But that sequencing may be presented as a matter of logic or genealogy, ie, in the order of normative argument, rather than as a literal matter of epochs, history or prehistory.

In my view, the natural law position has never required that natural law principles can by themselves constitute a viable social order in the absence of positive law. What on earth would that mean? The question is not whether natural rights could have worked in an epoch bereft of positive law. The question is whether natural rights to property can do their *moral* work – the work of informing, influencing and constraining positive law and state policy in various ways – without presupposing positive law as the basis of their moral presence. Their function is to determine the principles to which positive law is to be responsive and which it is supposed to reinforce and protect. And that is the account that the conventionalist is committed to deny. The conventionalist undertakes to

[22] Bentham (n 7) 52.
[23] Locke (n 3) 368 (II, §123).

show that it makes no sense for positive law to be held responsive to the sort of principles that an account like Locke's specifies in its natural law presentation.

III. MORALITY ON BOTH SIDES

I think we can say that there is room for morality and moral considerations on both sides of this debate as well. It may seem that the natural law side claims a monopoly on the role of moral considerations in our thinking about property. Legal property rights, they say, ought to reflect the importance of moral rights, natural rights, the respect that morality requires for the honest acquisitions of property-holders, and so on. But it would be wrong to infer from this that moral considerations will not also feature on the conventionalist side, and it is no discredit to the conventionalist *qua* conventionalist that moral considerations play a part on his side too.

Sometimes the conventionalist obscures this by saying things like 'Property is *merely* a legal convention.' *Merely* as opposed to what? Merely a convention as opposed to a moral idea? Or *purely* a legal convention – *purely*, uncontaminated by what? By moral considerations? But conventionalists do not have to say that the conventions we set up are random or arbitrary. We set up the conventions we do for reasons, and those reasons reflect what is important to us. Maybe David Hume's account comes as close as imaginable to the sort of arbitrariness connoted by the idea of a 'mere' convention. Humean property conventions are not imagined as products of intentional design. They emerge as coordinative equilibria; they are not constructed.[24] However, as we shall see, they still end up looking like property rights, looking as though they were responsive to natural law considerations. Intentionally or not, Hume's conventions are riveted on the idea of defensible possession – which has a sort of Lockean shape.

For Bentham, property rights *are* understood as designed – and I am sure this is so for Murphy and Nagel too. In the simple Benthamite model, the relevant considerations guiding such design are consequences and in particular utility. Our designing a system of rules regarding access to and exchange of resources answers to utilitarian or welfarist concerns. Now, these are surely moral considerations (impoverished, no doubt, but moral none the less.) And, as I said, it is no part of the conventionalist account to eschew such moral support.

So: Murphy, Nagel, and other conventionalists need not commit themselves to the view that property is a morality-free zone. Indeed, Murphy's moralism about property goes well beyond this. He says, quite fairly, that 'we must not confuse conventionalism with utilitarianism, let alone with the idea that economic efficiency is the only relevant value for institutional design'.[25] Maybe other values and principles are relevant too. '[T]he values that the practices can

[24] See Buchanan (n 9).
[25] Murphy (n 13) 460.

achieve system-wide can be as lofty ... as you like.'[26] Their aims 'can include social justice'. And Murphy adds, as a sort of hostage to fortune (which we will definitely want to explore), that they may even include 'values more closely connected to the subject matter of the practices'.

So what, then? There is no difference between the conventionalist and the natural law view? We have a definitional problem here – one that should perhaps be felt more acutely by conventionalists than they let on. Is it possible to draw a clear distinction between: (a) the moral considerations that support a given kind of property convention but still allow us to call it a mere convention; and (b) those moral considerations which reveal, when used, that those who use them are not really conventionalists at all? It looks like this has to be a difference between two kinds of moral consideration that can enter into the design and constraint of a property system. The term 'natural law' suggests objectivity. But the contrast between (a) and (b) is not a contrast between subjective and objective moral considerations. Objectivity can be on the conventionalist side as well. The conventionalist can say that their conventions are justified by objective considerations of general utility and social justice. On the other hand, Murphy also says that 'conventional rules ... cannot be understood as reflecting corresponding *real* moral rights or duties that people have, for none exist'.[27] I am not sure what this means. Maybe it is about rights (as a matter of form and content) rather than moral reality (as a matter of metaphysics). Maybe Murphy is suggesting that there are no real *rights-based* reasons relating to property.[28] Or maybe he wants to exclude only a particular kind of rights-based reason – namely, moral reasons that link *this* object to *this* person given *this* action (productive labour, for example). For he says the

> moral reasons ... people have to respect others' property are not reasons ... directed to particular owners; they are not reasons grounded in the rights or even the interests of particular owners. The reasons – to sustain the valuable practice and not freeride on it – run to society at large, to the benefits of the institutional system as a whole.[29]

In other words, Murphy seems to be saying that the non-conventionalist view – the natural law view – must be organised around the idea of rights-based or special-rights-based considerations. A special rights-based reason has to do with rights that vest only pursuant to a condition or contingency, like the rights arising out of a promise (contingent on a promise having been given and received)

[26] ibid.

[27] Murphy (n 13) 458 (my emphasis). He goes on: 'Rather, it is that the effective operation of the practice as a whole does good – for society as a whole – and that is the main reason why, generally speaking, the rules should be followed, since non-compliance with the rules will tend to undermine the practice.'

[28] For the distinction between rights-based and non-rights-based considerations, see R Dworkin, *Taking Rights Seriously* (London, Duckworth, 1977) 90–6 and 169–76. See also JL Mackie, 'Can There be a Right-based Moral Theory?' in J Waldron (ed), *Theories of Rights* (Oxford, Oxford University Press, 1984) 168, and Waldron (n 4) ch 3.

[29] Murphy (n 13) 458.

or rights of property (contingent on acts of acquisition or transfer in one's favour).[30] Any other sort of consideration – oriented, for example, to the interests of society, or even the interests of individuals considered in general – is fair game for the conventionalist to use.

Murphy does say that the conventionalist position can *indirectly* generate what look like rights-based moral considerations; they generate indirect arguments that are more person-focused in character. He acknowledges moral arguments based on expectations, for instance.[31] He says that in the Humean story,

> [m]oral motivations, based in recognition of the utility of the practices, can kick in once the practice is up and running; eventually, conventional morality may come to treat the rules of the practices as moral norms.[32]

And such conventionally-generated rights may be highly deserving of moral respect: consider Bentham's strictures on the importance of respecting established expectations; what law has created and encouraged, law must uphold.[33] But Murphy's idea seems to be that – important though these expectations are in themselves – they cannot be what gets the system up and running in the first place. That is what the conventions do, in response to moral considerations of a goal-based rather than a special-rights-based character.

But what if we still seem to see in the conventional arrangements – in the ideas that they track and to which they are responsive – the independent influence of apparently natural law ideas of the Lockean kind? Conventionalists tell us, for example, that we set up these conventions in the way we do because it is really important to guarantee to the individual the fruits of their labour. Now that is not just regular welfarist rationalisation of a convention – that is something *like* a natural law account. Listen to Bentham, for example: '[T]he laws provide for subsistence indirectly, by protecting men while they labour, and by making them sure of the fruits of their labour.'[34] Even in the midst of the tribute he pays to the work of positive law, Bentham gives voice to Lockean ideas:

> Law does not say to man, Labour, and I will reward you; but it says: Labour, and I will assure to you the enjoyment of the fruits of your labour – that natural and sufficient recompense which without me you cannot preserve; I will insure it by arresting the hand which may seek to ravish it from you.[35]

I hear in that passage the influence of threads of natural law ideas. The least convincing part of the conventionalist case is when its proponents say, 'No ideas of this kind can possibly enter into our moral thinking about conventions.

[30] See HLA Hart, 'Are There Any Natural Rights?' in J Waldron (ed), *Theories of Rights* (Oxford, Oxford University Press, 1984) 85 and also Waldron (n 4) ch 4.

[31] Murphy (n 13) 459.

[32] ibid 479.

[33] Bentham (n 7) 57.

[34] ibid 44.

[35] ibid 50.

No such ideas play any role in making the case for setting up conventions in one way rather than another.' There is something similar in Hume, who talks about

> a convention enter'd into by all the members of a society to bestow stability on the possession of … external goods, and leave everyone in the peaceable enjoyment of *what he may acquire by his fortune and industry*. … I observe that it will be for my interest to leave another in the possession of his goods, provided he will act in the same manner with regard to me.[36]

Again, it all sounds very Lockean. And I want to say, against the conventionalists, that *that* is what it takes to be a natural law theorist of property – that you think that strands of at least something like Lockean theory play an important and necessary role in justifying the legal constructions we set up.

If the pure conventionalist theory were true, then one would not expect legal rules of property to be shaped necessarily in a Lockean way. They might have the most bizarre and counterintuitive shapes. But – surprise, surprise! – that is not how it turns out. Murphy acknowledges this point in his suggestion that in a conventionalist theory, the reasons supporting the convention can be 'as closely tailored to the surface phenomena of ownership … as you like'.[37] Well, we need to ask how much of that can be true before we have to say that conventionalism has more or less abandoned the field to its opponent. I mean: if the alleged convention involves the construction and assignment of individual property rights – something which almost all legal systems do – and if those constructions and assignments are motivated by individual-respecting moral considerations, then the anti-Lockean character of the resulting scheme is certainly undermined.[38]

Bentham goes even further along these lines. Though law may encourage expectations of various kinds, *some* legal structures, he says, find it more difficult than others to get a grip on the human imagination. Though he emphasises law's capacity to govern and manipulate expectation, he does not think this capacity is unlimited. There are certain laws, he says, which

> lie under a sort of natural incapacity of being made known of the people: they refuse to take hold of the memory. In vain would instruction force them upon the

[36] Hume (n 6) 489 (Bk III, pt. 2, sect. ii) (emphasis added).

[37] Murphy (n 13) 460.

[38] Consider Hanoch Dagan and Avihay Dorfman's suggestion that property is not a 'convention simplicter', in the sense of serving 'only as a solution to a recurring coordination problem'. (see their article 'Interpersonal Human Rights' (2017) 51 *Cornell International Law Journal* 361 379–80.) Property, they say, plays 'a crucial role … in people's self-authorship and their ability to relate as equals'. This role implies that any conventions involved are quite different in character 'from other, garden-variety conventions'. By enacting or developing a convention of this kind, society empowers people 'to become full agents' and to engage with others in relationships of mutual recognition and respect. 'Given the human condition, in which people's embodiment and development "involve dependent, interdependent, and mutually enriching relationships with others," any polity committed to respecting people's dignity or normative agency – that is, to human rights – is morally obligated to uphold (or establish) such a convention.'

> memory: finding no reason to give them support, they presently drop out, unless where by accident the idea of their singularity and absurdity should give them footing in a susceptible mind.[39]

His point seems to be that law ignores at its peril the natural economy of 'human feelings, the only true standards of right and wrong in the business of legislation'[40] and that in the manipulation of expectations law should work in tandem with the structure of affections and inclinations which we find already in the human mind.[41] Conventions that mimic Lockean ideas may work in this way. Those that seem arbitrary by Lockean lights may not.

I have been trying to show the conventionalist in the light of a natural lawyer *malgré lui*. Hume returns the compliment:

> Examine the writers on the laws of nature; and you will always find, that, whatever principles they set out with, they are sure to terminate here at last, and to assign, as the ultimate reason for every rule which they establish, the convenience and necessities of mankind. A concession thus extorted, in opposition to systems, has more authority than if it had been made in prosecution of them.[42]

The natural law theorist ends up sounding like a utilitarian, while the conventionalist ends up sounding like a natural lawyer. Maybe this shows that Richard Epstein is right when he says that we have exaggerated the divergence between the two streams of thought.[43] Or maybe it shows that the attempt to distinguish sharply between conventionalist and non-conventionalist theories of property is a non-starter.

IV. STRANDS AND FRAGMENTS

We scholars tend to exaggerate the importance of theoretical coherence. For us, it is tempting to think that, if natural law theory works at all, it has to apply itself to legal questions as a comprehensive and well-worked-out totality – as though Thomas Aquinas were to come back on earth among us with the whole *Summa Theologica* open and ready to determine all outstanding questions of property. In the real world, however, that is not how justification works. What happens is that various reasons, various considerations, are adduced to support a practice and, whether or not they are fully-interconnected, if enough of them

[39] J Bentham, 'Supply without Burthen or Escheat Vice Taxation', in W Stark (ed), *Jeremy Bentham's Economic Writings* (London, Allen & Unwin, 1952) vol 1, 306.

[40] ibid.

[41] This phrasing is taken from J Waldron, 'Supply Without Burthen Revisited' (1997) 82 Iowa Law Review 1479–80.

[42] D Hume, 'An Enquiry Concerning the Principles of Morals', in LA Selby-Bigg (ed), *Enquiries Concerning Human Understanding and Concerning the Principles of Morals* (Oxford, Clarendon Press, 1902) 195.

[43] See, eg, R Epstein, 'From Natural Law to Social Welfare: Theoretical Principles and Practical Applications' (2015) 100 *Iowa Law Review* 1743.

have a natural law flavour we say that that is a natural law justification. This, at any rate, is how I want to proceed.

Each such strand of justification – connected to or isolated from the others – represents a natural law consideration. And the burden of the conventionalist position is not only that there is no fully-worked-out natural law theory that can justify everything about property, but that there are no (or can be no) important strands or fragments of natural law justification that bear on the central issues. The burden of argument in other words is asymmetrical. Conventionalists undertake to extirpate natural law considerations entirely from the field, because their position is that there are no such considerations and it is nonsense to bring them up, let alone undertake to piece them all together. For their part, natural lawyers commit only to show that there are significant gaps in the conventionalist account that can be filled only by the natural law considerations they adduce (though some of course, like Locke, purport to show much more than this).

How fragmentary can the natural law account afford to be? In a way that was what we were considering in the previous section, where we wondered whether it was possible to mark the point at which a morally-motivated conventionalism might slide over to become a rudimentary natural law account. Some strands may be too fragmentary or inconclusive. Probably we should say, for example, that the considerations about property mentioned in HLA Hart's 'minimum content of natural law' – such as that 'if crops are to grow, land must be secure from indiscriminate entry'[44] – are not quite enough, for each of them could as well mark the need for a convention as intimate the importance of a natural law consideration. But emphasis on the moral importance for individual autonomy of persons' being endowed with holdings that they can take themselves to have earned – this is certainly an instance of the sort of strand of natural law justification that I have in mind. And it remains so, even though it is not presented as part of a fully-worked-out theory.

V. AGAINST LOCKE

Conventionalists sometimes get very annoyed when a natural lawyer has the effrontery to offer a full-on theoretical argument. So, for example, a considerable amount of the vehemence that the conventionalist directs at the natural law position is directed at John Locke himself. Liam Murphy seems outraged that the substance of Locke's theory continues to be taken seriously in some quarters. He (Murphy) says that Locke's position is 'well known to be extremely implausible'.[45] He says it 'makes no sense',[46] that it is a 'clear failure' and 'one

[44] HLA Hart, *The Concept of Law*, 3rd edn (L Green ed, Oxford, Oxford University Press, 2012), 196.
[45] Murphy (n 13) 462.
[46] ibid.

of the most unfortunate philosophical ideas in the history of the West'.[47] 'We can almost consign naturalistic accounts of property rights to the dustbin of history.'[48]

Now, if it is widely accepted that Locke's natural law theory of property is wrong, then we have to ask: might the natural law *approach* to property be right even though some particular natural law theory of property (like Locke's) is wrong? Robert Nozick, when he was explicating the structure of a Lockean account, took pains not to specify the content of the Lockean-structured conception.[49] He implied that Locke's theory of mixing one's labour was at best one account of justice-in-acquisition among many. And he was interested in what a number of such theories had in common. For consider: the natural law position is not necessarily given to us all at once, or once for all. The natural lawyer says it is something worth investigating; it is worthwhile trying to find out the best moral justification for property and property rights. Whereas the conventionalist says this is a fool's errand.

Murphy says that Locke's is 'the only naturalistic theory we have going'.[50] That is not quite true. First occupancy is another theory, not organised around labour in the way that Locke's theory is – Locke saw it as a competitor – and it develops its sense of entitlement in a different way. Maybe first occupancy is more libertarian in its justification, for it rests on the point that the first occupant who takes possession of a resource does so, *ex hypothesi*, without pushing anyone else aside, whereas he is the one who must be pushed aside by second and subsequent occupiers.[51] Certainly first occupancy theory had different practical implications in Locke's day, making it much less easy to displace indigenous titles in America than on a labour/cultivation account.[52]

VI. INTERMEDIATE RIGHTS: OUR DISTANCE FROM ACQUISITION

There is one line of argument open to the conventionalist – and pursued in part by Murphy – that I think is quite difficult for the Lockean natural law theorist to refute. Difficult, but (as we shall see) not impossible. It goes like this.

[47] ibid 463–64.

[48] ibid 465.

[49] R Nozick, *Anarchy, State and Utopia* (New York, Basic Books, 1974) 230: 'I am as well aware as anyone of how sketchy my discussion of the entitlement conception of justice in holdings has been. But I no more believe we need to have formulated a complete alternative theory in order to reject Rawls' undeniably great advance over utilitarianism, than Rawls needed a complete alternative theory before he could reject utilitarianism. What more does one need … in order to begin progressing toward a better theory, than a sketch of a plausible alternative view …?' I shall refer to this work as Nozick, ASU.

[50] Murphy (n 13) 464.

[51] See Waldron (n 4) 285–56.

[52] See J Tully, 'Rediscovering America: the Two Treatises and Aboriginal Rights', in J Tully (ed), *An Approach to Political Philosophy: Locke in Context* (Cambridge, Cambridge University Press, 1993) 165–66.

Even if something like Locke's labour theory of property in Chapter V of the *Second Treatise* is accepted, there are challenging issues about how far his account can help us with a natural-law understanding of property rights *today*. Though Murphy finds it ridiculous, the Lockean account seems on its strongest ground when it consecrates the investment of labour in a resource – land or object – by the first person who took it into human possession at the dawn of time. That person says,

> I worked on this – worked hard – and it never belonged to anyone else; my labor made it what it is – a farmstead not just a piece of barren land. So the mixing of my labor with this resource demands respect, and respect is what positive law is required to give it, based on the natural law principles set out in John Locke's *Second Treatise*.

Or, as John Simmons (a modern day Lockean) puts it,

> If I am the first settler of a vast uninhabited territory (in another solar system, say), and I build a home and cultivate the land needed to comfortably support me, surely the settlers coming after would wrong me (violate my property rights) if they simply seized my land and home, with ample and equally attractive land and resources available to them.[53]

Unfortunately, whatever case of this kind we develop, it has next to no application to *modern* rights of property, almost none of which represent rights to things taken initially from nature by the present-day property-holder. If the anti-conventionalist position is Lockean in character, it must face up to the point that the Lockean account sanctifies mostly rights of initial acquisition that only existed centuries ago.[54] So there is the problem. The anti-conventionalist position looks at its most plausible when law is responding to the case that can be made regarding rights of initial acquisition. But modern property rights do not fit that description.

Perhaps indigenous property is an exception, assuming one can offer a Lockean or first-occupancy basis for property rights of indigenous peoples.[55] It may work as an exception especially when the property rights in question are rights deemed to be held by *a whole people* over many generations, rather than by persons (passed hand-to-hand from one individual to another). Perhaps also rights of intellectual property fall into this category: they have been recently 'acquired' by the investment of labour by the author who now claims the benefit of them.[56] But most latter-day property rights present themselves as, at best,

[53] AJ Simmons, 'Historical Rights and Fair Shares' (1995) 14 *Law and Philosophy* 149, 152–53.

[54] Maybe Lockean principles cover some of the rights of accession within a conventional system that Hume talks about in the second phase of his theory of property: see Hume (n 6) 509 (Bk III, pt. 2, sect. iii).

[55] See J Waldron's discussion in 'Indigeneity? First Peoples and Last Occupancy' (2003) 1 *New Zealand Journal of Public and International Law* 55.

[56] See, eg, W Gordon, 'A Property Right in Self-Expression: Equality and Individualism in the Natural Law of Intellectual Property' (1993) 102 *Yale Law Journal* 1533, 1568 and M Chatterjee, 'Lockean Copyright versus Lockean Property' (2020) 12 *Journal of Legal Analysis* 136.

intermediate links in a long chain of transfers, very distant from both the fact and the morality of initial acquisition. I claim to be entitled to this piece of land – *as a matter of natural right?* – because I bought it from someone who bought it from someone who inherited it from someone who bought it from someone … and so on down a long chain of what Robert Nozick would call justice-in-transfer.[57] Give me a break, says the conventionalist.[58]

Notice how different this is, if we turn from property to promise. The promissory anti-conventionalist can say of a promise given today that it has moral force now, and that respect for such moral force is capable of informing the construction of a set of legal rules today regarding contract. In the realm of promises given and received today, the anti-conventionalist has a manifestly plausible foothold. Not so with property.

The conventionalist will say: whatever natural law may do to vindicate the position of a Lockean farmer at the dawn of time, modern systems of property *have* to be treated as mere conventions, unaffected by that sort of consideration. That is one reason conventionalists say the Lockean stuff is irrelevant. The conventionalist will say too that Locke himself recognised this, by essentially sidelining the state of nature story about the emergence of natural property rights and arguing that by the time you get to modern society, even in the late seventeenth century, property rights are surely just the product of positive law.[59]

So, for the natural lawyer, the question is this: can we develop a sense of the moral importance of property rights that present themselves *in media res* in a long chain of transfer and yet still capture the constraining force of a focused rights-based morality. Murphy says that 'the fact of transfers over the millennia makes it quite impossible for any naturalistic theory of property rights to tell us who owns what now'.[60] But the point is not so much the epistemic one that, after millennia, the naturalistic account cannot tell us who owns what; it is rather that the power of the naturalistic considerations is focused only on acquisition, whatever the state of our subsequent knowledge.

Looking back now at the doctoral dissertation that I wrote about property in the 1980s, I find that I actually devoted a few pages to this issue, but without any determinate conclusion.[61] Do rights get weakened or transformed as they pass from hand to hand down the ages? If property rights are transferred for consideration, maybe the interplay of individual earnings in particular deals helps to conserve the moral force of the holdings; but this will work less well with bequest etc. In *Anarchy, State and Utopia*, Robert Nozick entertained the

[57] Nozick (n 49) 151.

[58] This issue about the sheer length of the chain of transfer – the distance now from initial acquisition – is treated separately here from the issue of historic injustice. I shall address the historic injustice theme in section VII.

[59] Locke (n 3) II, §§38 and 45. But see also the dispute between me and James Tully about how to interpret this: is this genuine conventionalism on Locke's part or just *determinatio*? J Waldron, 'Locke, Tully and the Regulation of Property' (1984) 32 *Political Studies* 98.

[60] Murphy (n 13) 477.

[61] Waldron (n 4) 259–62.

possibility (which he attributed in part to Hayek) that patterns of earning or benefit to society may be discernible in the distribution of recent entitlements. If most transfers are done for reasons, then there will be a tendency for the value of holdings to align with people's actions benefiting others, so that such benefits can be cited as natural law reasons for upholding the resulting property rights.[62]

Or, even without the benefit of such an economic theory, we might simply focus on the elements of natural law morality represented by current holdings here and now, in reference to their immediate history and their immediate significance to those who hold them. So, for example, a piece of land may have been held by individuals over 50 generations since it was first taken into human ownership – passed from hand to hand by sale, purchase, gift, bequest, and inheritance – and it may be destined to continue being transferred from hand to hand over many generations to come. But right now *here we are* in the middle of this chain of past and future entitlements – remote from the title's Lockean origins – confronting the ownership of it by an individual here and now. And the question arises: is there any element of natural law in respect of *this holding* which would enable us to challenge the designation of it as purely a matter of convention?

Well, suppose the individual property-owner scrimped and saved to put themselves in a position to purchase the holding and has devoted all their energies in the years since to its improvement. And suppose they enjoy it on that basis, incorporating it into their present projects and purposes as something they have earned and is entitled to use for their benefit. It may have the sort of moral significance for the individual holder that Margaret Radin describes in her article 'Property and Personhood', being incorporated into their projects and sense of self in a way that reflects their initiative and their achievement in acquiring it.[63] On the basis of considerations like these, they resist expropriation and demand that those who design the system of tax-and-transfer take into account as an independent constraint the moral status of their relation to the land. The considerations she adduces are not exactly Lockean, distant as they are from Locke's initial acquisition; but they are counterparts of Lockean natural law ideas, *in media res* so to speak. They have a neo-Lockean 'vibe'.

As a matter of fact, concerns of this kind, articulated in this way, are probably much more familiar to ordinary people who stand up for their property rights than the arcane detail of Locke's theory of justice-in-initial-acquisition (however familiar the latter may be to the 17 or 18 scholars in the world who are interested). Perhaps Murphy and Nagel will say that the sentiments here are too loose and confused to count as genuine instances of natural law. Here as elsewhere, I have no investment in any particular meaning for the phrase 'natural law'. What we do seem to have are moral considerations which bolster the claims

[62] Nozick (n 49) 159.
[63] M Radin, 'Property and Personhood' (1982) 34 *Stanford Law Review* 957.

individuals may make about their holdings and their rights over them, and which preclude their being characterised in purely conventional terms.

Most likely Murphy and Nagel will seek to describe these sentiments as just the psychological shadow of our conventions. They will not deny that those who inhabit a system of property are likely to find themselves stuck with proprietorial intuitions. Conventionally established property rights tend to take on a moral life of their own, as people invest their affections – in a Benthamite way – in and around the legal structures. But – Murphy and Nagel will say – that does not show that the conventionalism is false. It is a matter of priority or the order of argument: the conventionalist says that our moral intuitions are built up in the shadow of our legal conventions, not vice versa. *However*, if the property-owner resists that characterisation of their moral sentiments, even when the conventionalist position is fully explained to them, I think we have to say that it is at least an open question whether we should treat this as constituting a natural law account. Eventually we have to take what people say seriously. The conventionalist should not want their position to degenerate into a mere dogma where anything said against their view is treated as yet more evidence of the power of the relevant conventions.

VII. HISTORIC INJUSTICE

Not only is the chain of property rights long – with an immense distance between present-day holdings and the dawn-of-time acquisitions that Lockean natural law speaks so highly of – but it is also dirty, contaminated with historic injustice of various sorts. Indigenous peoples were robbed of their land; property rights were stolen under the auspices of law by Anglo settlers displacing Mexican small-holders in California; people are defrauded every day by the thousands of schemes that human ingenuity can devise; not to mention class exploitation; and the long-term influence of our comprehensive failure to implement the social justice safeguards that natural law requires – a Lockean proviso, for example, or a principle of charity.[64] Chains of entitlement riddled with injustice like this can hardly preserve the moral standing of the individual property rights that they pass from hand to hand, even assuming that such passage makes sense. Once again, Liam Murphy sums up the case against natural law:

> Current, legally protected holdings, anywhere in the world, cannot possibly reflect natural ownership rights as that theory explains them. Assuming that fraud and force entered into actual history pretty much as soon as acquisition began, and assuming that whatever natural theory of rightful transfer one favours will not bless all of the legal transfers that have happened through history, we will have no basis for assuming that existing legal property rights bear any useful relation to moral property rights.

[64] For Lockean provisos, see Locke (n 3) 288 (II, §27) and Nozick (n 49) 174–82. For a Lockean principle of charity, see Locke (n 3) 170 (II, §42) and Waldron (n 4) 146.

> So what do we now own? Not only do we need a theory of transfer adequate to assess the legitimacy of all that has gone on since the first acquisitions, but we also need a theory of rectification of enormous complexity. What do we say, for example, about a fortune acquired by an investor who made use of capital acquired in good faith at the end of a chain of fifty other good faith transfers all subsequent, however, to an ancient petty theft?[65]

He will say: surely this shows that natural law ideas cannot be taken seriously. Existing property rights can hardly be taken to represent the bona fide application of moral principles.

It is an important point. But it fails to explain why we take gross historic injustice seriously in cases where some sort of redress *is* possible. When indigenous rights advocates talk about historic injustice, they are not just dismissed as being under a misconception concerning the true nature of property. Or rather, they used to be dismissed in that way – with Anglo conventionalism sponsoring a rather nihilistic story about *res nullius* (on the Australian model, for example). But now we say that if redress is possible, it should be attempted, even if its impact is largely symbolic. Why? Because the past existence of injustice *matters*, in a way that it could not possibly matter if conventionalism were correct. Our outrage at historic injustice and our paltry and haphazard attempts to rectify it bear witness in a backhanded way to the living power of natural law.

But hang on! Can *Waldron* say this – given his work on the supersession of historic injustice? (Historic injustice is superseded when changing circumstances mean that the original (violated) property rights would have had to be changed anyway to adapt to new populations for example.)[66] Yes, I can, even being aware of the impact of what I have called 'the supersession thesis' in diminishing the compelling normative power of some historic injustice claims. The supersession thesis is not a concession to conventionalism. It is rather a counter-intuitive element in a complex natural law theory, tracing the normative response of natural law principles to changing circumstances. One would never embark on supersession reasoning unless one took natural law ideas seriously.

Robert Nozick acknowledges that the rectification of injustice embroils the historical entitlement theory in great difficulties, and he even speculates that an entitlement theorist might have to have recourse to *Rawlsian* ideas to get out of those difficulties. Maybe things like the Difference Principle can be viewed as 'rough rules of thumb meant to approximate the general results of applying the principle of rectification of injustice', given that 'those from the least well-off group in the society have the highest probabilities of being (the descendants of) victims of the most serious injustice …'.[67] This readiness to adapt to the

[65] Murphy (n 13) 464.

[66] See J Waldron, 'Superseding Historic Injustice' (1992) 103 *Ethics* 4 and 'Settlement, Return and the Supersession Thesis' (2004) 5 *Theoretical Inquiries in Law* (Tel Aviv) 237.

[67] Nozick (n 49) 231.

ways of the enemy may sound congenial to the conventionalist position. But Nozick does not say that historic injustice has left such a mess that natural law can no longer provide any guidance. He does not just scramble for the quite different logic of a conventionalist solution. Instead, he thinks it through to see what natural law theory provides as a second- or third-best. His thought is that the application of Rawlsian principles may be the best way of doing justice to natural law principles in circumstances of endemic fraud, expropriation, and so on.

VIII. COMPLEXITY

My arguments have been rather laborious. But the case for conventionalism about property builds itself up in layers and it has to be rebutted point by point, layer by layer. The significance of legal complexity is one such layer. Indeed, much of what I have been saying is about how we deal with complexity in social and legal theory.

It would be bad enough if we were just dealing with a long sequence of property rights passed from hand to hand over the centuries. But as property is iterated in this way, the transfers become more complex: individual holdings become encumbered with liens and mortgages; property is split into layers of interests – leaseholds, life interests, etc as a result of complex testamentary arrangements. Can natural law really account for this? We saw Chris Kutz earlier denying that it can.[68] Even if we thought simple Lockean rights were natural rights and even if we could cobble together an independent moral account of the force of natural rights centuries downstream from initial acquisition, it might still seem that conventionalism in some shape or form is unavoidable when we try to give an account of complex property interests in and for the modern world. The bells and whistles here are surely the work of positive law – the original work of law – for only legal construction can account for such complexity. Complexity is a persuasive consideration for conventionalists to invoke. Because we figure that conventional structures can be as complex and counter-intuitive as we – their creators – care to make them, we conclude that of course complexity is probably better explained in a conventionalist theory than in a natural law morality.[69] Natural law morality is supposed to deal in the rigid simplicities of rights and deontological principles.

In fact, however, those positions may well be reversed. Actually-existing natural law deontology is renowned for its complex casuistry – ever hear of the

[68] See above, at the end of section I (text accompanying n 18).

[69] Murphy (n 13) 479, says: 'As societies get more complex, details are added to the legal orders of property and contract that do not have any kind of presence in the non-legal practice.'

doctrine of double effect? And that is partly what I was saying about supersession at the end of the previous section: supersession shows how complicated natural law can be. And, on the other side, some aspects of Humean conventionalism may require simplicity – the straightforward equilibria of defensible possession that are supposed to emerge from a Humean state of anarchy, for example. These conventionalist elements cannot do the work they are supposed to do if they are too arcane or too complex for people to *see*.

Even if this is not the case, there are many ways in which a natural lawyer can account for complexity.

(i) There is *determinatio*, which we have already mentioned[70] and which natural law has always accommodated.
(ii) There is the moral complexity of natural law itself, often involving the introduction of new principles; think, for example, about the difference that Locke thinks is made to the application of the spoilage proviso by the consent-based introduction of money.
(iii) There are ways of building conventional structures upon natural law foundations, which is not a way of discrediting the natural law element, but just a way of establishing its infrastructural significance.

What I want to emphasise is this: the mere fact that the natural-law position does not itself explain some complex property interest does not mean that natural law considerations play no role. They may still play an important role in establishing the infrastructure of a complex property interest even though they cannot deal with high level superstructure.

Unless we have explored each of these possibilities with regard to the complexity of each of these alleged 'obviously' conventional outcomes, we are not in a position to infer pure conventionality – mere conventionality – from complexity. For example, unless we explore John Finnis's suggestion about the connection between bankruptcy and distributive justice,[71] we should not be saying, as Murphy says, that

> [n]o one thinks that the complex structure of bankruptcy law … simply reflects natural moral requirements on citizens. Bankruptcy law requires moral justification, of course, but that takes the form of a complex weighing of considerations, where the particular rules may not at all reveal on their surface the moral reasoning that led to their enactment. So there is no natural moral order of bankruptcy ….[72]

Natural law has manifold resources with which to frame and model the complexity that conventionalism prides itself on explaining.

[70] See above section I, text accompanying nn 20–21.
[71] See Finnis (n 21) 188–93.
[72] Murphy (n 13) 479.

IX. CONCLUDING THOUGHTS (ON TAX ETC)

Liam Murphy and Thomas Nagel do not defend conventionalism about property for its own sake. They defend it also because they want to discredit certain ways of arguing about taxation. They want to discredit the view that my income is *mine* and that that moral entitlement should be respected in public determinations of tax rates etc. They acknowledge

> the question whether a general presumption has to be overcome against taxation and in favor of leaving resources in the private hands of those who have created or acquired them – a presumption … in favor of allowing people to do what they want with the resources that they have acquired through participation in a free market economy.[73]

They say that '[i]f there were such a presumption, or prima facie case against, it would mean that the case for supporting various projects and aims out of tax revenue would have to be that much stronger.'[74] Responding to this possibility, Murphy and Nagel want the conventionality of property rights to pre-empt all talk of such a presumption. Private property, they say, 'is a legal convention, defined in part by the tax system; therefore, the tax system cannot be evaluated by looking at its impact on private property, conceived as something that has independent existence and validity'.[75] They say that

> the modern economy in which we earn our salaries, own our homes, bank accounts, retirement savings, and personal possessions, and in which we can use our resources to consume or invest, would be impossible without the framework provided by government supported by taxes. This doesn't mean that taxes are beyond evaluation – only that the target of evaluation must be the system of property rights that they make possible. We cannot start by taking as given, and neither in need of justification nor subject to critical evaluation, some initial allocation of possessions – what people originally own, what is theirs, prior to government interference.[76]

But the fact that the property system could not operate without surrounding structures of tax and so on does not show that property rights are conventional, or that any strand of natural law reasoning in this regard must be derivative. We ought to evaluate tax systems by reference to all sorts of things, and it would be very odd if natural law intuitions relative to property were to be precluded from playing any role at all. Murphy and Nagel believe that there is an array of considerations that are relevant morally and politically to the determination of tax rates – *that* is not just an arbitrary convention. But they maintain, for

[73] Murphy and Nagel (n 5) 5.

[74] ibid 5.

[75] ibid 8.

[76] idem. Saying that an initial allocation is taken 'as given, and neither in need of justification nor subject to critical evaluation' (ibid 8) is a *frightful misrepresentation* of the natural law view. The natural law theory *is* a justificatory theory involving critical evaluation. Anything it takes as 'given' is presented as the upshot of moral argument.

some reason, that the rights of individual property-owners are not among them. Among all the things that ought to be taken into account when setting tax rates, Lockean considerations – the strands of natural law that I have invoked – are uniquely inappropriate. The rights of individual property owners are derivative (among other things) from whatever we decide to do about taxation. But, say Murphy and Nagel, they have no role to play in determining that.

I doubt that I am alone in finding this implausible. Murphy says that 'it is clearly not appropriate, when reasoning about what a just set of legal and economic institutions would be, to give baseline moral significance to the status quo set' of property rights.[77] That is fair enough; maybe they are right that the status quo does not have *baseline* moral significance. But can they possibly be right that the moral considerations with which property rights are typically defended – fragmentary or full-blooded considerations, various kinds of natural-law idea that I have been talking about in this lecture – can they possibly be right that those considerations have no moral significance at all?

[77] Murphy (n 13) 483.

5

Expanding the Categories of Negative Easements – Time for Change?

SUSAN PASCOE*

I. INTRODUCTION

THE SUPREME COURT decision in *Fearn v Board of Trustees of the Tate Gallery*,[1] that the Tate Gallery was liable in private nuisance to the owners of neighbouring flats due to substantial interference with the claimants' ordinary use and enjoyment of their properties, also has significance for the law of negative easements. The reason is that the decision in *Fearn*, decided by a majority of three to two with the leading judgment delivered by Lord Leggatt, will apply only in fairly rare circumstances[2] where the defendant's use of land cannot be regarded as a common or ordinary use of the land and the visual intrusion on a neighbouring property is of sufficient duration and intensity to be actionable as a nuisance. The decision in *Fearn* will also not apply to a claimant's building where the design or construction of a building is abnormal or unusual.[3] The judgment therefore means that it is an opportune time to consider the criteria that should be used to expand the category of negative easements not only generally, but also specifically whether it should include a right to privacy by not being overlooked from neighbouring land in circumstances which arise outside the factual matrix of *Fearn*.

Lord Leggatt agreed with the Court of Appeal that liability in nuisance does not extend to 'overlooking',[4] but the activities complained of included that 'a very significant number of the roughly half a million people who visit the Tate's viewing gallery each year peer into the claimants' flats and take photographs of them',[5] which are sometimes posted on social media. The glass walls of the

* I am very grateful to Professor Alison Clarke for discussions on this topic and also for very helpful suggestions from participants in the MSPL conference. The usual disclaimers apply.

[1] *Fearn v Board of Trustees of the Tate Gallery* [2023] UKSC 4.

[2] ibid [103].

[3] ibid [76]–[80].

[4] ibid [90].

[5] ibid [92].

claimants' flats were not unusual, 'either in the context of modern high-rise blocks of flats generally or in the particular locality'.[6] On the issue of invasion of privacy, Lord Leggatt decided that applying the common law of nuisance to the activity would not require an extension of the law and that no new privacy laws are needed to deal with this complaint, since 'The concepts of invasion of privacy and damage to interests in property are not mutually exclusive.'[7] This is equally important for the law of negative easements where the 'amenity value of real property'[8] should be evaluated in a wider context.

There has always been an innate reluctance of the courts to recognise negative easements, because they give the owners of the dominant land the right to prevent the owners subject to the easement from engaging in otherwise permissible acts on their own property. Overcoming the common law's disinclination to recognise negative easements is analysed by reference to Dagan's *A Liberal Theory of Property*.[9] The law has traditionally acknowledged the following kinds of negative easements: the right to the flow of water through an artificial channel, so that the water cannot be blocked from entering the dominant land; the right to the servient land's support for buildings on the dominant land, so that the support structure cannot be removed; and the right to a flow of air and the flow of light through a defined channel or aperture, so that the servient owner cannot do or allow anything on their land that obstructs or substantially diminishes that flow of air or light.

The same effect could be achieved through the use of restrictive covenants, but historically these rights have been granted as easements, and it is clear that they can be acquired through prescription. Since restrictive covenants cannot be acquired by prescription, that may be why the law acknowledges only this limited class of negative easements.[10] *Gale on Easements* has suggested that it is thought that the class of negative easements is now closed, because only these rights appear to have been accepted as an easement.[11] By restraining the owners' freedom in the occupation and use of their property, negative easements are an anomaly in the law and the law is prudent about not extending them beyond the categories which are well known.[12]

Other negative easements would therefore be anomalous easements like the right to light.[13] They may be *ejusdem generis* the existing categories and likewise merit protection. The corollary of a right not to be overlooked could be considered to be the right to a view which would be the right not to have a view

[6] ibid [79].
[7] ibid [112].
[8] ibid.
[9] H Dagan, *A Liberal Theory of Property* (Cambridge, Cambridge University Press, 2021) 7.
[10] Law Commission, *Making Land Work: Easements, Covenants and Profits à Prendre* (Law Com No 327, 2011) [2.19] and fn 19.
[11] J Gaunt and P Morgan, *Gale on Easements*, 21st edn (London, Sweet and Maxwell, 2020) [1–62].
[12] *Hunter v Canary Wharf Ltd* [1997] AC 655, 726 (Lord Hope).
[13] ibid 709 (Lord Hoffmann), citing *Webb v Bird* (1861) 10 CB(NS) 268, 285 (Willes J).

blocked. Additional categories of negative easements that should be recognised are solar and wind easements which are analogous to the traditional common law easements of light and air. Solar easements will become important with the increasing significance of green energy necessitating rights to ensure adequate access to direct sunlight for solar energy systems. Express easements could set out the specifications and dimensions of the easement, possibly including specific vertical and horizontal angles that must remain open to sunlight, or maximum heights and widths of trees, structures and buildings close to the property to prevent shade which will inhibit solar production and could also specify the hours and months during which direct sunlight to a specified building or structure may not be obstructed. Numerous states in the US have passed statutes recognising and protecting solar easements.[14]

The Law Commission did not make any recommendation that allows the creation of easements that benefit solar panels.[15] Their view was that:

> It is not clear how the existing law on rights to light, which is founded on the sufficiency of light passing through windows and into the rooms beyond, but not upon photovoltaic surfaces, can accommodate solar panels. Consequently, we do not think that solar panels can benefit from rights to light as presently understood.[16]

The Law Commission was right to acknowledge that the acquisition of an easement by prescription takes 20 years, but noted that

> consultees appeared to be arguing for protection for solar panels to arise as soon as they are installed. The effect of this would be to give an owner a wholly novel right over another's land, restricting the use of a neighbour's land without first giving its owner any opportunity to avoid that happening.[17]

The Law Commission's suggested solution was that impact on solar panels should be factored into the circumstances in which planning permission should be granted.[18] It will, however, become increasingly important for the law of easements to evolve, since solar panels on roofs are likely to be one of the main sources of renewable energy in future and people who have invested money in roof panels should know that this investment has some legal protection.[19]

Wind easements are currently only endorsed by legislation in a few states in the US.[20] Wind easements will also increase in importance in England due to the ever-increasing need for new sources of energy. These easements protect the

[14] SC Bronin, 'Solar Rights in the United States' in RJ Heffron and GFM Little (eds), *Delivering Energy Policy in the EU and US* (Edinburgh, Edinburgh University Press, 2016) ch 16.

[15] Law Commission, *Rights to Light* (Law Com No 356, 2014) [2.83].

[16] ibid [2.79].

[17] ibid [2.79].

[18] ibid [2.82].

[19] ibid [2.77] quoting the contribution of the Ceredigion Green Party to the Consultation Paper.

[20] YR Lifshitz, 'Winds of Change: Drawing on Water Law Doctrines to Establish Wind Law' (2015) 23 *NYU Environmental Law Journal* 434.

property owner's ability to install a wind turbine without worrying about a tall building being constructed in the upwind direction that could block the wind. Such easements can ensure the viability of investment in the development of wind energy production and preserve the continuous flow of air.

If negative easements, such as solar or wind easements, are not created expressly, the difficulty with negative easements will arise with easements claimed by prescription where the owner of the servient land is having limitations imposed on the land without even being aware that the owner of the dominant land has acquired an easement. The Law Commission had considered whether to abolish prescription for negative easements only and decided in 2011 not to recommend its abolition for negative easements.[21] The Law Commission then provisionally proposed the abolition of prescription for rights to light in its Consultation Paper in 2013 on *Rights to Light*.[22] However, they considered the responses of consultees to the proposal and reached the conclusion that prescription should not be abolished as a means of acquiring rights to light.[23] There was considerably stronger support for retaining prescription than for abolishing it and 'it was clear that many consultees value not just rights to light themselves, but having a strong and effective mechanism by which they can arise'.[24] The Law Commission's recommendation of a statutory notice procedure[25] that would allow landowners to require their neighbours to tell them, within a specified time, if they intend to seek an injunction to protect their right to light, or to lose the potential for that remedy to be granted, and an updated version of the procedure that allows landowners to prevent their neighbours from acquiring rights to light by prescription, would go some way to meeting objections and could be applied to other negative easements as well.

II. APPLYING DAGAN'S ANALYSIS TO NEGATIVE EASEMENTS

Expanding the category of negative easements is analysed by examining Dagan's autonomy-based theory of property which is founded on three pillars of carefully delineated private authority, structural pluralism, and relational justice. He advocates judges of appellate cases using new cases and social developments as triggers for the ongoing refinement of the law, as opportunities for revisiting the normative viability of its current understandings and for paradigm shifts in the law in order to enable constructive change and reflexive internal critique.[26]

[21] Law Commission, *Making Land Work* (n 10) [3.81].
[22] Law Commission, *Rights to Light: A Consultation Paper* (Law Com No 210, 2013) [3.48].
[23] Law Commission, *Rights to Light* (n 15) [2.64].
[24] ibid [2.62].
[25] ibid [6.1].
[26] Dagan (n 9) 34–37.

A. Role for Individual Autonomy

An examination of individual autonomy, self-determination, and self-authorship, as envisaged by Dagan, may provide justification for proprietary rights to extend the categories of negative easements. Dagan argues that self-determination is absent from property theory today and, that also applies in circumstances where *Fearn* would not apply, for example, because the defendant's use of land is common or ordinary. Liberal property should be an empowering device in the service of people's self-determination and support for people's autonomy. The expansion of property necessarily limits non-owner's liberty and broadening the types of negative easements will inevitably limit owners of neighbouring property as well. Nevertheless, property's private authority is delineated, so that owners' interpersonal, horizontal power is necessary for their self-determination. Property empowers self-determining individuals to pursue their conception of the good, and this autonomy-enhancing *telos* legitimises property and shapes its legal contours.[27]

i. Application to Negative Easements?

There are difficulties applying Dagan's theory to determining the legal contours of negative easements. Although a liberal polity constructs its property law so as to serve the self-determination of owners while constantly remaining attentive to property's possible threat to the autonomy of others,[28] easements create particular difficulties due to the need to balance the rights of two neighbouring owners with conflicting interests. If a dominant owner is given the right not to be overlooked, a duty is necessarily imposed on the servient owner not to do or allow anything to be done that will interfere with that right. Dagan's principle governing how individuals must relate to each other is sometimes phrased that each individual must 'respect' each other's self-determination, but 'respect' could have variable meanings and sometimes refers to duties of 'accommodation'.[29] One person may be obliged to take some positive steps to help other people realise their aims as long as this does not too greatly diminish their own. An autonomy calculus needs to be conducted to evaluate the self-determination of the person being accommodated against the interests of the person doing the accommodating. An unqualified right to exclude others from one's property might be needed to protect the autonomy of a homeowner,

[27] This is reflective of a Razian account of autonomy – see A Nair, 'Property and Autonomy in the Marketplace: Freedom to Sell as Freedom of Exit' (2022) 33 *King's Law Journal* 34. For a contrast with the theory of Kant, see N Sage, 'Liberalism and Common Callings' (2022) 33 *King's Law Journal* 43. For a comparison with Rawls, see K Wells, 'Crucial Options: Dagan on Self-determination and Structural Pluralism' (2022) 33 *King's Law Journal* 53.

[28] MR Cohen, 'Property and Sovereignty' (1927) 13 *Cornell Law Quarterly* 8, 12–13 discussed in Dagan (n 9) 61–62.

[29] Sage (n 27) 45.

since a person's home is bound up with their sense of personhood. As Cohen has suggested, the interpersonal implications of the power that owners enjoy vis-à-vis others are not easily defensible because, potentially, property poses a normative threat to others.[30]

Such a strong emphasis on individual autonomy is too complex conceptually for negative easements. Sage has argued that Dagan should set aside his commitment to individual autonomy and instead develop further his conceptions of 'community' and 'structural pluralism', although as he admits, 'the resulting account would no longer be, at least in Dagan's sense of the term, a *Liberal* Theory'.[31] McFarlane, in critiquing Dagan's analysis, has raised concerns arising, inter alia, from the prioritising of the autonomy-enhancing aspects of property in relation to the continuity between property law and private law more generally, and questions whether Dagan's account recognises sufficiently the distinctiveness of property.[32] Applied to easements, it could be argued that the diversity of legal relations recognised by private law means that the autonomy-enhancing effects of the power to create negative easements are qualitative rather than quantitative, which can be problematic in this context.

Dagan's insistence on autonomy is due to the fact that the range of heterogeneous property types is to give each individual an extensive range of options to choose from when making their life plans. In evaluating negative easements, the constraint on self-determination of the owner of the servient tenement may seem relatively small compared to the sacrifice that would be required of the owner of the dominant land who may have daily and regular impositions of, for example, being overlooked, whereas the limitations imposed on the servient owner's ability to build is a negative obligation preventing extending the property in a way that would interfere with the dominant owner's property.

In the case of *Fearn*, depriving members of the public from the extension to the Tate's viewing gallery would seem a relatively minor inconvenience in the scheme of life. Lord Leggatt analysed the difficulties of reconciling the different public and private interests involved and resolved this by stating that, 'where significant considerations of public interest are raised', these are relevant, 'not in determining liability, but, where liability is established, in deciding whether to grant an injunction or to award damages'.[33] With easements, as with covenants, there are two autonomous owners with a right to self-determination. Lord Leggatt explained that there is no obligation on occupants where there is an actionable nuisance to take remedial steps, such as installing blinds, privacy film or net curtains, because that places the responsibility 'entirely on the victim rather than on the person who carries out the activity'.[34] The same principles

[30] Cohen (n 28) 12–14.
[31] Sage (n 27) 44.
[32] B McFarlane, 'Property: Duties, Diversity, and Limits' (2022) 33 *King's Law Journal* 23, 27.
[33] *Fearn* (n 1) [120].
[34] *Fearn* (n 1) [83].

should be applicable to negative easements in considering their validity ex ante, as opposed to ex post controls, which will be examined later.

ii. Historical Perspective – Lack of Individual Autonomy of Owner of Dominant Land

The legal system in England and Wales does not give people or homes a general right to natural light[35] or a natural right to prospect or privacy.[36] Foster has examined how, under early common law, access to light and air was looked upon as a natural right, 'incident to the ownership of land'.[37] By the end of the sixteenth century, however, English courts no longer classified light and air as natural rights, but as negative easements. Though the courts made little mention of the right to view during this period, it appears that view may also have constituted a natural right up until the time of *William Aldred's Case*[38] in 1610, when the court expressly held that an action in nuisance would not lie for the stopping of prospect. It was held that a right to a 'prospect' or good view could not exist as an easement, because it 'is a matter only of delight, and not of necessity, no action lies'.[39] This opinion was correctly dismissed in *Dalton v Angus*[40] as 'more quaint than satisfactory'. The court in *Dalton* cited as 'a much better reason'[41] that of Lord Hardwicke in *Attorney-General v Doughty*,[42] whose opinion was such a right should not be acquired by prescription and should only be created by actual agreement, because otherwise 'there could be no great towns'.

Nevertheless, Lord Hardwicke did raise quite clearly the possibility of individual views being protected by 'a particular right'.[43] He did not specify the nature of that right, but it is at least possible that he envisaged an easement. Poulsom contests the argument that easements of prospect would unduly hinder urban development, because public law can be rigorous and effective in protecting views in 'great towns' in England and Wales.[44] Nevertheless,

[35] Law Commission, *Rights to Light* (n 15) [2.62].

[36] Gaunt and Morgan (n 11) 1-64, citing *Tapling v Jones* (1865) 11 HLC 290, 305, considered in *Fearn* (n 1) [97]; *Fishmongers' Co v East India Co* (1752) Dick 163; *Potts v Smith* [1868) LR 6 Eq 311, [318]; *Campbell v Paddington Corp* [1911] 1 KB 869, 878, 879; *Hurdman v North Eastern Railway Co* (1878) 3 CPD 168, 174. See also *Victoria Park Racing and Recreation Grounds Co Ltd v Taylor* [1937] 58 CLR 479, 507, discussed in *Fearn* (n 1) [99].

[37] TJ Foster, 'Securing a Right to View: Broadening the Scope of Negative Easements' (1988) 6 *Pace Environmental Law Review* 269, 275.

[38] *William Aldred's Case* (1610) 9 Coke Reports 57b, 77 ER 816.

[39] ibid. During this same period, the English judiciary created the Doctrine of Ancient Lights, based on prescription of unobstructed flow of light and air onto property, provided the owner has enjoyed this right for a period of 20 years.

[40] *Dalton v Angus & Co* [1881] 6 App Cas 740, 824.

[41] ibid.

[42] *Attorney-General v Doughty* (1778) 2 Ves Sen 453, 454.

[43] ibid.

[44] MW Poulsom, 'Taking a View: The Protection of Prospects in England and Wales' [2018] *Conv* 133, 136–137.

Lord Leggatt in *Fearn*, having considered the decision in *Hunter v Canary Wharf Ltd*,[45] explained that the reason why no claim lies for interference with a view or prospect is that 'anyone may build what they like on their land, unless this violates an agreement not to do so or an acquired right to light or to a flow of air through a defined aperture'.[46] There was, nevertheless, a caveat to this that 'interference resulting from construction (or demolition) works will not be actionable … in so far as all reasonable and proper steps are taken to ensure that no undue inconvenience is caused to neighbours'.[47] This caveat can be particularly significant for the law of negative easements.

Historically, the objection has been that negative easements are insufficiently certain. In *Harris v De Pinna*,[48] Bowen LJ compared a claim to the passage of undefined air over the premises to an 'amenity of prospect, a subject-matter which is incapable of definition'.[49] As Poulsom highlights,[50] the strong belief that, with regard to easements, this is an inescapable feature of a view is much less evident in relation to covenants and public law. The difficulty is the preventative action needed to stop a negative easement arising and the extent of the burden on the servient owner. The same arguments that apply to rights of light and support are also relevant to other negative easements. There is inevitably a difference between only the neighbouring servient land being affected and a range of neighbouring properties. The further those tenements are from the potential dominant tenement, the less likely it is that their owners will appreciate, and guard against, the risk of an easement being claimed.[51]

Any property interests, including easements, need to be clearly defined, so that the servient owner is aware of the limitations of what they can do on their land. No right to privacy was established in *Browne v Flower*[52] in 1911 where Parker J was of the view that the law does not recognise 'any easement of prospect or privacy'.[53] Rights to a view and rights to privacy were notably treated as interchangeable by Parker J in *Browne*. Parker J was of the view that 'Either they have less privacy, or if they secure their privacy by curtains they have less light.'[54] This raises the issue of what steps a landowner can be expected to take to protect their privacy which was tackled in *Fearn*.

It is evident that policy decisions are underlying the restrictive nature of the current law. In *Hunter v Canary Wharf*,[55] Pill LJ regarded the analogy between a right to receive a television signal and the 'loss of prospect to be compelling.

[45] *Hunter* (n 12).
[46] *Fearn* (n 1) [36].
[47] ibid [37] referring to *Andreae v Selfridge & Co Ltd* [1938] Ch 1.
[48] *Harris v De Pinna* [1886] 33 Ch D 238.
[49] ibid 262.
[50] Poulsom (n 44) 135.
[51] ibid 137.
[52] *Browne v Flower* [1911] 1 Ch 219.
[53] ibid 225.
[54] ibid 227.
[55] *Hunter* (n 12).

The loss of a view, which may be of the greatest importance to many householders, is not actionable and neither is the mere presence of a building in the sight line to the television transmitter.'[56] The problems were explained well by Lord Hope that the radio and television signals:

> may come from various directions over a wide area as they cross the developer's property … Their passage from one point to another is invisible. It would be difficult, if not impossible, for the developer to become aware of their existence before he puts up the new building. If he were to be restricted by an easement from putting up a building which interfered with these signals, he might not be able to put up any substantial structures at all.[57]

The House of Lords differentiated a restriction, which has been constituted by express grant or by agreement in which case some flexibility in the recognised categories may be permitted from the acquisition of an easement by prescription. Their view was that:

> Where the easement is of a purely negative character, requiring no action to be taken by the other proprietor and effecting no change on the owner's property which might reveal its existence, it is important to keep to the recognised categories. A very strong case would require to be made out if they were to be extended.[58]

It would create immense difficulties if courts were now to take the same view in relation to broadband and mobile signals being blocked and one would hope for a more contemporary approach to reflect the realities of the age in which we live and the technical advances that have been made.

In analysing policy, Lord Leggatt did not seem concerned that there may be difficulties in deciding where to draw the line in resolving whether the objective test of nuisance had been met.[59] Likewise, the fear of the floodgates opening should not in appropriate cases fetter the law of easements. It is arguable that a restrictive policy to land rights should have no place in the twenty-first century and it is the parameters to this self-determination which will be critical. There was a significant distinction drawn by Lord Blackburn in *Dalton v Angus and Co*[60] between a right to light, which could only impose a burden on land very near the house and which should be protected when it had been enjoyed for 20 years, and a right of prospect, which would impose a burden on a very large and indefinite area and should not be allowed to be created except by actual agreement. Such a differentiation between express easements and those created by prescription is welcome, if it thereby facilitates the recognition by the law of negative easements, but there is still a need for the law to recognise negative easements created by prescription. A grant will not be presumed when the grantor

[56] ibid 666.
[57] ibid 727.
[58] ibid 726.
[59] *Fearn* (n 1) [106]–[108].
[60] *Dalton* (n 40) 824.

could not have reasonably prevented the enjoyment of the subject of the grant,[61] but this does not prevent easements arising by prescription as acknowledged in *Dalton*.

B. Structurally Pluralistic

Dagan's second pillar of a liberal property law is structural pluralism, which provides concrete support for innovative types of land rights. This theory of property recognises the profound heterogeneity of property types which causes difficulties for monistic, more traditional theories that look for the structural core of property, which Dagan considers to be misguided. As Dagan rightly points out, the internal life of property is structured through sophisticated governance mechanisms that facilitate various forms of interpersonal relationships which would not be possible without an enabling legal infrastructure which applies in, for example, easements, covenants, leaseholds, commonholds and trusts.[62]

This plurality of types enables property law to offer varying balances between the different values that property can serve – independence, personhood, community, and utility in diverse social settings and respecting a variety of resources. When the law's menu of property types is sufficiently rich for each major sphere of human action, it offers people a range of meaningful choices for resource governance and co-governance that supports self-determination. Dagan is of the view that a significant part of property law is not about vindicating the rights of autonomous excluders, but rather about creating governance institutions that manage potential conflicts of interest among individuals who are all stakeholders in one resource or in a given set of resources. These dramas of property law occur, literally, within property; they deal with the internal life of property rather than with its foreign affairs.[63] Dagan describes colourfully that property need not be confined

> to a tragic choice between the Hohfeldian Scylla of unprincipled multiplicity and the Blackstonian Charybdis of unacceptable uniformity. There is a principled midway position between these disappointing poles: the autonomy-based conception of property, which is structurally pluralistic.[64]

The balancing of interests is, as already explained, complex in relation to negative easements due to the need to deal with conflicts between adjacent landowners caused by the limiting effect of negative easements on the servient owner.

[61] *Fearn* (n 1) [39], [44]; Gaunt and Morgan (n 11) [1–63], citing *Chasemore v Richards* (1859) 7 HL Cas 349, 370 (Wightman J); *Dalton* ibid 776; *Chastey v Ackland* [1895] 2 Ch 389, 397 (Lopes LJ).

[62] Dagan (n 9) 6.

[63] ibid 82.

[64] ibid 88.

Property governance regimes will need to determine the fine balance between competing interests.

i. Numerus Clausus – Influence on Negative Easements?

Dagan's understanding of property's plurality and support for innovative types rejects the *numerus clausus* principle's canonical understanding.[65] It also requires a refinement of the *numerus clausus* principle so that, alongside this inventory of state-sponsored property types, property law will also include a residual property type that can be privately designed while properly ensuring the interest of third parties to not be subject to non-transparent arrangements which would rule out negative easements that would be too broad for being acquired by prescription.

For law to consolidate people's expectations in compliance with the prescriptions of both structural pluralism and the rule of law, it must recognise a necessarily limited number of categories of relationships and resources. The conventional understanding of the *numerus clausus* principle, however, goes further. It stands for the proposition that property rights exist only in a fixed number of forms, so that private arrangements can enjoy the status of property only if they are pigeonholed into the delimited menu of state-recognised property forms. But even the most sophisticated attempts to justify this dimension of the *numerus clausus* principle are not fully persuasive.[66]

Therefore, though law's traditional facilitation of standardised property types along structural pluralistic lines is laudable, Dagan's view is that a liberal property regime should reconsider the hostility of *numerus clausus* toward tailor-made property rights.[67] He is right that liberal property law is perfectly justified in proscribing idiosyncratic arrangements insofar as they entail negative external effects, both social (for example, segregation) and economic (for example, fragmentation), or as they impinge on individual rights (either those of the parties themselves or of third parties).[68] People should thus be able to create their own idiosyncratic frameworks of interpersonal interactions and not merely idiosyncratically adjust state-sponsored frameworks. This does not mean that property law must adopt a *numerus apertus* (open list) principle, allowing 'bizarre rights' to be registered or recorded on par with law's standardised types.[69]

As Dagan argues, in the liberal conception of property, the creation and modification of property types often is, or at least should be, triggered by

[65] ibid 11.

[66] ibid 101.

[67] ibid 149, discussing TW Merrill and HE Smith, 'Optimal Standardization in the Law of Property: The Numerus Clausus Principle' (2000) 110 *Yale Law Journal* 1, 26–34, 56–68.

[68] ibid 112.

[69] ibid.

challenges bearing on the desirability of the normative underpinnings of property types, their responsiveness to their social context, or their effectiveness in promoting their contextually examined normative goals.[70] Inherent dynamism, triggered in moments of property law's 'paradigm shifts', represents a perennial quest 'for better and best law' – a relentless 're-examination and reworking of the heritage'. Judges have a 'duty to justice and adjustment' which means the 'on-going production and improvement of rules'.[71] This is clearly lacking in the law of negative easements.

Nevertheless, *numerus clausus* may not be helpful in common law systems. There is no explicit recognition of the *numerus clausus* in common law, which naturally renders the status of the doctrine somewhat insecure.[72] Given basic differences between civil law systems and common law systems, it is not surprising that the *numerus clausus* is expressly recognised in the former but not the latter. In common law systems, there is no inherent reason why existing forms of property should not be subject to judicial revision and supplementation. Nevertheless, common law courts often behave toward property rights very much like civil law courts do. They treat previously recognised forms of property as a closed list which Merrill and Smith describe as a norm of judicial self-governance. Jurisprudentially speaking, the *numerus clausus* functions in the common law much like a canon of interpretation, albeit a canon that applies to common-law decision-making rather than statutory interpretation or like a strong default rule in the interpretation of property rights.[73] If one observes what lawyers and judges do, it is clear that the *numerus clausus* exerts a powerful hold on the system of property rights. The chances of persuading a court to create a new type of property in any particular case are too remote to be taken seriously.[74]

Nevertheless, a liberal approach to property seems to have been adopted by the Supreme Court in *Regency Villas Title Ltd v Diamond Resorts (Europe) Ltd* without reference to *numerus clausus*.[75] The recognition of rights to use indoor and outdoor recreational facilities as easements by the Supreme Court broke new ground by expanding the scope of easements. As Lord Briggs stated in *Regency Villas*, easements have acquired 'an independent jurisprudence of their own'[76] indicating that they are now independent of the Roman law of servitudes which gives them greater scope to form their own identity. Novel forms of easements were recognised to reflect changes in society and the case went further

[70] ibid 152.

[71] ibid 153 discussing KN Llewellyn, *The Common Law Tradition: Deciding Appeals* (Boston, Little, Brown and Co, 1960) 36, 38, 190–91, 217, 222–23; KN Llewellyn, 'The Normative, the Legal, and the Law-Jobs: The Problem of Juristic Method' (1940) 49 *Yale Law Journal* 1355, 1385.

[72] Merrill and Smith (n 67) 9.

[73] ibid 10–11.

[74] ibid 23.

[75] *Regency Villas Title Ltd v Diamond Resorts (Europe) Ltd* [2018] UKSC 57, [2019] AC 553.

[76] ibid [2].

than *Re Ellenborough Park*.[77] This represented an important shift in recognising the validity of new types of easements. Lord Briggs was clear 'that the common law should, as far as possible, accommodate itself to new types of property ownership and new ways of enjoying the use of land'.[78]

Restricting the rights of the owners of the servient land to a considerable extent is therefore not without precedent in the law of easements as shown in *Regency Villas*, where burdens of maintenance, which could only be voluntary, were placed on the owners of the servient land. Although *Regency Villas* concerned positive easements, such a broad-minded approach could arguably be extended to negative easements. It is extraordinary that the Supreme Court thought it important that freehold timeshare arrangements should be made to work when timeshare has nearly disappeared as a legal mechanism. It is therefore arguable, a fortiori, that the rights of a homeowner should be respected by law with room for manoeuvre to accommodate negative easements.

ii. *Influence of the Rule of Law*

One implication of the aspirational nature of liberal property is that the various property types are subject to ongoing normative re-evaluation and possible reconfiguration.[79] The question is whether that complies with the rule of law despite its multiplicity and dynamism. As Dagan states, Smith argues that it does not and that it cannot.[80] A structurally pluralistic conception of property, Smith claims, can hardly be distinguished from the bundle understanding of property and both irreparably undermine stability. Rejecting the dominion conception of property, Smith therefore suggests, might substitute rigidity with 'near-chaos'.[81] Only the presumption of exclusion, Smith concludes, can assure that we keep the bundles 'lumpy' and 'opaque' and avoid 'hard-to-predict ripple effects through the entire system'.[82] Dagan rejects Smith's criticisms by arguing that because property types are supposed to consolidate expectations and express ideal types of interpersonal relationships, an autonomy-based property regime supports, even requires, that our property types be relatively stable and internally coherent and adhere to the rule of law.[83] Extending the category of negative easements would, therefore, comply with the rule of law.

[77] *Re Ellenborough Park* [1956] Ch 131.
[78] *Regency Villas* (n 75) [76].
[79] Dagan (n 9) 159.
[80] HE Smith, 'Property Is Not Just a Bundle of Rights' (2011) 8 *Econ Journal Watch* 279, 287; HE Smith, 'Property as the Law of Things' (2012) 125 *Harvard Law Review* 1691, 1705–06 discussed by Dagan (n 9) 159.
[81] HE Smith, 'On the Economy of Concepts in Property' (2012) 160 *University of Pennsylvania Law Review* 2097, 2113 discussed by Dagan (n 9) 160.
[82] Smith ibid 2116.
[83] Dagan (n 9) 161.

iii. *ut res magis valeat quam pereat* in the Framework of Structural Pluralism

The validating principle *ut res magis valeat quam pereat*, which Dagan does not discuss, is now analysed within the framework of structural pluralism. This principle of validating construction means that, where possible, a construction should be preferred which results in the relevant claim being treated as valid rather than be void. The principle is well established as applied to the construction of contracts and subordinate legislation. As Lord Briggs stated in *Regency Villas*:

> the parties intended to confer upon the facilities grant the status of a property right in the nature of an easement, rather than a purely personal right … That being the manifest common intention, the court should apply the validation principle ('ut res magis valeat quam pereat') to give effect to it, if it properly can.[84]

This principle should be applied to negative easements, and it is helpful to ascertain how the Supreme Court, Privy Council and House of Lords have treated it in a few other property law cases. In *Enka Insaat ve Sanayi AS v OOO 'Insurance Company Chubb'*[85] in 2020, the Supreme Court supported application of the 'validation principle' to assist in preventing parties from circumventing their arbitration agreements. However, the Supreme Court declined to apply it in *Generics UK Ltd (t/a Mylan) v Warner-Lambert Co LLC*[86] (published interestingly on the same day as *Regency Villas* on 14 November 2018) in an intellectual property and patents case. Lord Briggs stated in *Generics UK Ltd*, 'in my opinion, validating construction will not usually have a significant place in modern patent law'.[87] The Privy Council quoted the validating principle approvingly in *Rolle Family and Co Ltd v Rolle*[88] in 2017 on the issue of escrow, though the case failed on other arguments and grounds.

The validating principle was implicit, though not explicit, in *Moncrieff v Jamieson*[89] in 2007 and *Lawrence v Fen Tigers Ltd*[90] in 2015. *Moncrieff* broke new ground with Lord Scott stating obiter that very extensive use of the servient land may be an easement as long as the servient owner retained possession and control,[91] although recent authority prefers the narrower reasonable use test.[92] A change in the historically cautious approach in not recognising easements that may not be sufficiently certain is evident in *Lawrence*.[93] In *Lawrence*,

[84] *Regency Villas* (n 75) [25].
[85] *Enka Insaat ve Sanayi AS v OOO 'Insurance Company Chubb'* [2020] UKSC 38, [2020] 1 WLR 4117 [95] (Lord Hamblen and Lord Leggatt), [127] (Lord Sales).
[86] *Generics UK Ltd (t/a Mylan) v Warner-Lambert Co LLC* [2018] UKSC 56, [2019] Bus LR 360.
[87] ibid [95].
[88] *Rolle Family & Co Ltd v Rolle* [2017] UKPC 35, [2018] AC 205.
[89] *Moncrieff v Jamieson* [2007] UKHL 42, [2007] 1 WLR 2620.
[90] *Lawrence v Fen Tigers* [2014] UKSC 13, [2014] AC 822.
[91] *Moncrieff* (n 89) [55].
[92] See, eg, *Virdi v Chana* [2008] EWHC 2901, [2008] NPC 130; *Kettel v Bloomfold Ltd* [2012] EWHC 1422, [2012] L & TR 30; *De La Cuona v Big Apple Marketing Ltd* [2017] EWHC 3783.
[93] *Lawrence* (n 90) was approved in *Fearn* (n 1) [18], [46], [109], [110], [119], [120], [129].

it was acknowledged that it may be possible to acquire by prescription an easement to carry on an activity which resulted in noise that would otherwise cause an actionable nuisance, provided that such noise nuisance had been emitted for 20 years, albeit not necessarily continuously.[94] Lord Neuberger was of the view that the right 'may be too indeterminate to be an easement, but it can still be the subject of a perfectly valid grant',[95] although he did not analyse what precise form that grant would take or what type of interest it would create. His view was that a right to emit noise could be an easement, describing it as 'the right to transmit sound waves over the servient land'.[96] As he acknowledged, the precise extent of a right to transmit sound waves obtained by prescription must be highly fact-sensitive, and may often depend not only on the amount and frequency of the noise emitted, but also on other factors including the character of the neighbourhood and the give and take.[97] Such judicial flexibility on the subject matter of a grant may allow the recognition of negative easements in appropriate circumstances.

C. Relational Justice

i. Complex Balancing of Horizontal, Interpersonal Interactions

The third pillar of liberal property, relational justice, is the dimension of justice that focuses on the terms of our interactions as private individuals rather than as citizens or as subjects of state institutions. The impact of interpersonal contacts on self-determination affirms and vindicates the claims of people to mutual respect for self-determination.[98] A genuinely liberal private law casts our horizontal, interpersonal relationships as interactions between free and equal individuals, respecting one another as the persons they actually are. This inevitably poses difficulties in relation to negative easements because, as discussed, of the conflicting interests of the owners of the dominant and servient lands.

Recognition of negative easements is also complex under Blackstone's conception of property as 'sole and despotic dominion'[99] as the regulative idea of private property with the right to exclude as the most defining feature of property law with the rival interests of two neighbouring owners. In Dagan's view, this renewed orthodoxy of property as a stronghold of interpersonal independence fails both descriptively and normatively, because the dominion understanding of property unduly disregards property's structural pluralism

[94] ibid.

[95] ibid [32]. See also Poulsom (n 44) 135.

[96] ibid [41].

[97] ibid [38] referring to *Cambridge Water Co v Eastern Counties Leather plc* [1994] 2 AC 264, 299 (Lord Goff), discussed in *Fearn* (n 1) [29]–[33].

[98] Dagan (n 9) 8.

[99] ibid 9, referring to W Blackstone, *Commentaries on the Laws of England*, Vol 2 1765–1769 (Chicago, University of Chicago, 1979).

and property's compliance with relational justice.[100] In relation to negative easements, Blackstone's conception of property is too blunt a tool to deal effectively with the nuanced approach needed to deal with the complexities inherent within negative easements.

The tensions generated between the owners of the dominant and servient lands are exacerbated by the servient owner being prevented from acting in an otherwise lawful way on their land. The existence of potential protective measures that could be taken by the owner of the dominant land to prevent privacy being invaded, such as installing net curtains, privacy film or solar blinds, which Lord Leggatt in *Fearn* made clear are not required as remedial steps in a nuisance claim,[101] should arguably not be a reason to refuse to recognise easements of privacy not to be overlooked ex ante applying the *Re Ellenborough Park*[102] criteria. These considerations in easements should apply to ex post and not ex ante controls.

Ex ante restrictive controls, in prioritising security and stability of land rights, are justified insofar as they limit the rights which can burden properties perpetually by controlling the freedom of landowners to create new land burdens that will bind successive owners, which might result in inefficient fragmentation. Stricter ex ante regulation of easements also minimises the dangers of idiosyncratic burdens on land. Nevertheless, negative easements may be of such importance to the enjoyment and security of the owner of the dominant land that, as Van der Walt has argued, the traditional ex ante strategies of preventing fragmentation are becoming increasingly more unsuitable and ex post strategies are more suitable to the dynamic economy of the twenty-first century.[103] In his view, both common law and civil law jurisdictions are gradually shifting away from 'an ex ante (common-law rule) preventing the creation of "atypical property arrangements" to ex post (statutory and judicial intervention) remedying the negative effects of such arrangements'.[104]

Prioritising the interests of the owner of the dominant land to claim negative easements may sit uncomfortably with notions of relational justice. Dagan argues that an autonomy-enhancing conception of property requires precisely the kind of accommodative structure that the dominion conception of property precludes.[105] This accommodative structure would surely require the owner of the dominant land to take mitigating steps to prevent a breach of privacy. It would be far too cumbersome to introduce a proportionality test into the ex ante recognition of easements. Van der Walt and van Staden suggest a proportionality test to be incorporated in balancing two prominent common

[100] ibid.

[101] *Fearn* (n 1) [81]–[88].

[102] *Re Ellenborough Park* (n 77).

[103] AJ van der Walt, 'The Continued Relevance of Servitudes' (2013) 3 *Property Law Review* 3, 21–22.

[104] ibid 22.

[105] Dagan (n 9) 127.

law principles, namely, that the servitude holder has all the rights necessary for the effective exercise of their servitude, and that the servitude must be exercised *civiliter modo*, so as to impose the least possible burden on the servient land.[106]

The extent to which restrictions can be imposed on the servient owner is a very important factor in analysing relational justice. Recognising, for example, a right to privacy by not being overlooked, will restrict development on the servient land, but the Supreme Court in *Regency Villas* in relation to recreational easements seemed unconcerned about the impositions on the servient owner on the facts of that case. Different considerations inevitably apply in restricting developments on the servient land. Easements are a governance property arrangement that should encourage the flourishing of the owners of the dominant tenement.[107] The rivalrous nature of property is highlighted in particular by negative easements and balancing the interests of the owners of the dominant and servient tenements, and this may be too complex an issue for governance property. There are overlaps between Dagan's liberal theory of property and Alexander's analysis of governance property that aims at achieving certain values, including autonomy, aggregate welfare, and the Aristotelian idea of human flourishing. Human flourishing is a pluralistic moral value comprising multiple values, including individual autonomy and freedom, social welfare, community and sharing, and personhood and self-realisation.[108]

There are also similarities with the analysis by Blandy, Bright and Nield of enduring property relationships in land which has particular resonance in the context of negative easements due to the need to avoid conflicts in using land in order for the negative easements to benefit the dominant land.[109] The authors apply to property relationships the key idea from relational contract theory that parties to contracts are 'embedded in complex relations',[110] which is particularly pertinent to negative easements and Dagan's notions of relational justice. The continuing nature of the relationship is an important feature, affecting the way in which the governing norms are articulated at the outset, and accommodating the possibility that these may need to evolve and be adjusted over time to reflect the dynamics of the relationship between right-holders.[111] As the relationship

[106] AJ van der Walt and S van Staden, '"Progressive" Judicial Interpretation of Servitudes and Ancillary Servitude Entitlements – *Jersey Lane Properties (Pty) Ltd t/a Fairlawn Boutique Hotel & Spa v Hodgson*' (2016) 79 *Journal of Contemporary Roman-Dutch Law* 671, 675–76; discussed in S Pascoe, 'Re-evaluating Recreational Easements – New Norms for the Twenty-First Century?' in B McFarlane and S Agnew (eds), *Modern Studies in Property Law*, vol 10 (Oxford, Hart Publishing, 2019) 167, 181.

[107] See GS Alexander, 'Governance Property' (2012) 160 *University of Pennsylvania Law Review* 1853.

[108] ibid 1875. See further R Walsh, 'Property, Human Flourishing and St Thomas Aquinas: Assessing a Contemporary Revival' (2018) 31 *Canadian Journal of Law and Jurisprudence* 197.

[109] S Blandy, S Bright and S Nield, 'The Dynamics of Enduring Property Relationships in Land' (2018) 81 *MLR* 85, 85–86.

[110] ibid 87, citing R Macneil, 'Relational Contract Theory: Unanswered Questions' (2000) 94 *Northwestern University Law Review* 877, 881.

[111] ibid 88.

is sustained through time, there may be a degree of 'give and take, live and let live'[112] which was stressed numerous times by Lord Leggatt in *Fearn*. This approach is needed to accommodate changes in the use of land, in the identity of the rights-holders, in external regulatory and economic forces, as well as in the parties' preferences for rigidity or flux.[113] Applying this to negative easements, in a dispute between neighbouring owners, it may be necessary to resolve not only the disputed property relationship, but also the personal relationship between the parties.[114]

ii. Effect of Human Rights on Relational Justice?

In Dagan's view, the autonomy-based foundation of property also implies that liberal property is a human right that bounds the power of judges and legislators and provides standing against governments and private parties.[115] Relational justice rejects the conventional division between public and private law. Dagan argues that property's horizontal dimension governing our interactions with others must inevitably require the recognition of some core mandatory norms of interpersonal human rights.[116] This involves the reinterpretation of the human right to property as one that is operative horizontally and not only vertically, and is undermined not only by failing to protect property rights but also by failing to recognise such rights.[117] Lord Leggatt in *Fearn* was correct that 'There is no need or justification for invoking human rights law when the common law has already developed tried and tested principles which determine when liability arises for the type of legal wrong of which the claimants complain.'[118] Likewise, the common law should recognise the validity of negative easements without recourse to Article 8, which is not appropriate in this situation, because allowing an interplay of the common law of easements with Article 8 would significantly overcomplicate the law of easements.[119]

iii. Freehold Covenants?

Within the realms of relational justice, it also needs to be considered what other areas of law a landowner should be using to assert their claims. Gray and Gray set out 'the historic view' that 'common law recognised, for instance, no such right as a prescriptive (or any other) easement to preserve a good view over an

[112] *Fearn* (n 1) [28], [34], [63], [91], [124].
[113] Macneil (n 110) 88.
[114] ibid 89 and discussed also by Pascoe (n 106) 178.
[115] Dagan (n 9) 11.
[116] ibid 176.
[117] ibid 246.
[118] *Fearn* (n 1) [113]. See also D Nolan, 'Nuisance and Privacy' (2021) 137 *LQR* 1, 3–4.
[119] Compare the approach taken in *McDonald v McDonald* [2016] UKSC 28, [2017] AC 273 [43] in relation to landlords and tenants.

adjacent landscape' and state explicitly that 'such a right may be acquired only [by] a restrictive covenant which precludes the owner of neighbouring land from building [so] as to obstruct the view which it is desired to protect'.[120]

While protecting views using easements appears to be limited and uncertain, the same cannot be said of protection using covenants. In analysing whether rights differ in their content depending on whether they are negative easements or restrictive covenants, if the claimants in *Fearn* had the benefit of a restrictive covenant, they would have been in a much stronger position than if they had a negative easement. A restrictive covenant would impose specific restrictions and obligations on the owners of the Tate Gallery not to overlook the flat owners whereas a negative easement would be more imprecise in being able to determine the scope and parameters of the right of the flat owners to prevent the Tate from engaging in certain activities.

Having excluded the possibility of an easement of prospect in *Phipps v Pears*,[121] Lord Denning's view was that freehold covenants need to be used to protect the view from one's property. Underpinning the decision is that the right could not be acquired by prescription and could not pass under section 62 of the Law of Property Act 1925, because the right was not known to the law. There is an underlying tension in relation to prescription imposing rights on landowners of which they may have not been aware and the concern that they should be created expressly. The difficulty is that, in many cases, the possibility of freehold covenants may be unrealistic, because a landowner cannot anticipate what developments there will be in the future and many landowners will not want to enter agreements with their neighbours restricting their activity on their own land. Nevertheless, most buyers of new build houses and flats enter covenants restricting activity on their land and the same applies to the vast majority of units in estate developments since the late nineteenth century.

Freehold covenants also have the significant advantage over easements of the jurisdiction under section 84 Law of Property Act 1925 to discharge or modify covenants, which is used very extensively. It is notable that the Supreme Court in the landmark case of *Alexander Devine Children's Cancer Trust v Housing Solutions Ltd*,[122] when analysing the public interest ground in section 84,[123] demonstrated Dagan's pluralistic approach to determining land rights in balancing the interests of those provided with affordable housing with those of terminally ill children in a hospice. The court dismissed the appeal and refused the application for the restrictive covenants to be modified due to the cynical

[120] K Gray and SF Gray, *Elements of Land Law*, 5th edn (Oxford, Oxford University Press, 2009) 615 and see Poulsom (n 44) 138–139.

[121] *Phipps v Pears* [1965] 1 QB 76.

[122] *Alexander Devine Children's Cancer Trust v Housing Solutions Ltd* [2020] UKSC 45, [2020] 1 WLR 4783. See further T Sutton, 'LPA 1925 s.84 and cynical breaches: Alexander Devine Children's Cancer Trust v Housing Solutions Ltd' [2021] *Conv* 213.

[123] Law of Property Act 1925, s 84(1)(aa) and (1A)(b).

and deliberate breach of covenant by the developers with a view to making a profit. The decision thereby protected the right of the children's hospice not to have their grounds overlooked. Covenants can be very effective devices in these particular contexts, preventing neighbours spoiling views or overlooking property.

There were specific covenants in *Gilbert v Spoor*[124] and *Davies v Dennis*[125] that enabled views to be protected, but there are inherent limitations of covenants,[126] such as the requirements that the burden of a freehold restrictive covenant can only run in equity and that a covenant requiring steps to be taken, if construed as positive, will not run at all. Unlike easements, covenants in England and Wales are not legal interests in land under the Law of Property Act 1925, or interests which override under the Land Registration Act 2002.[127] Freehold covenants are therefore not a panacea, and the law of easements needs to fill the void in suitable cases.

It has been acknowledged that a right to a view may be created by express grant or covenant and that 'the enforcement by a court of a covenant not to build so as to obstruct a view has been described as an extension in equity of the doctrine of negative easements'.[128] This is a clear and powerful indication that equity prefers to extend the law using the medium of covenants rather than extending the scope of negative easements. Nevertheless, the effects of limitations with covenants can be seen in other cases. One of the underlying problems in *Regency Villas* was non-enforceability of positive freehold covenants which was a factor in leading the Supreme Court to recognise recreational and sporting easements. There are, however, significant difficulties giving a freehold owner a right to use physical facilities (recreational or otherwise) which require regular management and maintenance when there is no satisfactory legal mechanism for enforcing duties to manage and maintain them which highlights the need for reform of the law of freehold covenants.

iv. Planning Permission as a Tool for Relational Justice?

Reconciling the conflicts between public and private interests is brought to the fore with consideration of whether planning permission and planning laws are sufficient to protect landowners from invasions of privacy. It is clear that they are not, because planning permission was given, for example, in *Fearn*,[129]

[124] *Gilbert v Spoor* [1983] Ch 27.

[125] *Davies v Dennis* [2010] 1 P & CR DG13 at D33.

[126] Poulsom (n 44) 139.

[127] ibid 142.

[128] See Foster (n 37) 277 fn 70 citing CJ Gale, *A Treatise on the Law of Easements* 305, 9th edn (London, Sweet and Maxwell, 1916).

[129] *Fearn* (n 1).

Gilbert[130] and *Davies*.[131] As Lord Leggatt stated explicitly in *Fearn*, 'the planning system does not have as its object preventing or compensating violations of private rights in the use of land. Its purpose is to control the development of land in the public interest'.[132] It can also be problematic that not every development requires planning permission. If planning guidance can define privacy principles, that may facilitate the recognition of easements of privacy not to be overlooked.[133] The guidance could state that a right not to be overlooked could not arise from a property exceeding a particular distance, calculated by reference to size, nature and locality of the dominant property.[134] An alternative could be statutory restrictions on building above a certain height within a certain distance of another's land, defined by geometric principles, just as the Party Wall etc. Act 1996 defines works on or close to boundaries. Rights capable of prescriptive acquisition might be restricted to those which confer 'practical benefits of substantial value or advantage',[135] or which increases significantly (for example more than *x* %) the value of the property.[136] The Law Commission identified the difficulty of calculating the amenity value of light which would also apply to a right not to be overlooked and in particular, the absence of a 'one size fits all' approach.[137]

However, in the National Planning Policy Framework published by the Ministry of Housing, Communities and Local Government in July 2021, there is no reference to or acknowledgment of privacy concerns, so this is clearly not forthcoming in the near future. A grant of planning permission does not authorise the infringement of private rights to light. Guidance in the Framework states, 'when considering applications for housing, authorities should take a flexible approach in applying policies or guidance relating to daylight and sunlight, where they would otherwise inhibit making efficient use of a site'.[138] Building Regulations prohibit putting transparent windows in a new or altered building within a specified distance of neighbouring buildings. It would be considered contrary to the public interest to allow a building that would invade the privacy of others, such as providing a view into a public lavatory or changing rooms in shops, theatres, or sports facilities. Private property should be considered in the same way.

130 *Gilbert* (n 124).
131 *Davies* (n 125).
132 *Fearn* (n 1) [109].
133 Poulsom (n 44) 143 in relation to protecting a view.
134 ibid.
135 ibid, using wording from the Law of Property Act 1925, s 84(1A)(a).
136 ibid.
137 Law Commission, *Rights to Light* (n 15) [8.84]–[8.86], discussed in ibid.
138 Ministry of Housing, Communities and Local Government, *National Planning Policy Framework* (2021) para 125(c).

III. CONCLUDING REMARKS

The governing norms in contextual property relationships need to be adjusted to broaden the parameters of negative easements to reflect the realities of twenty-first century living to include not only the right to privacy by not being overlooked and the right to a view in pertinent cases, but also to recognise solar and wind easements, rights to receive broadband and mobile signals and other negative easements as further technological advances are made. There are numerous complexities, especially in relation to prescription as has been demonstrated, and the factual matrix will inevitably be important in determining whether there is an easement, but a planning process is needed that is specifically alert to protecting these kinds of rights. As has been demonstrated, even applying Dagan's theory of liberal property to negative easements is fraught with difficulties. However, as Dagan is keen to emphasise, an understanding of property's plurality would provide opportunities for the expansion of the law through support for innovative types of easements.

Following a structurally pluralistic architecture, land law needs to pay close attention to the governance regimes. All types of land rights that affect the interests of neighbouring owners face the challenge of shaping the governance regime that is needed to facilitate co-operation.[139] Rules of governance dealing with the *inter se* rights of such owners need to be treated as an integral part of land law.[140] Dagan's theory of liberal property can be used in the critical assessment of specific property regimes and in establishing suitably contextualised schemes as is done here with negative easements. Where a landowner is claiming, for example, an easement of privacy not to be overlooked in circumstances not covered by the criteria governing nuisance in *Fearn*, protective measures to mitigate the invasion would need to be evaluated, but should not prevent a right arising. Such mitigating steps would inevitably be much more complicated with other types of negative easements, thus potentially strengthening the arguments for their validity, which would represent an important milestone in the development of land law.

[139] H Dagan, 'Liberal Property: Clarifications and Refinements' [2022] *King's Law Journal* 3, 21.
[140] See ibid 22.

6

'More in Hope than in Expectation': The Legal Limits of Disinheriting Adult Children

HEATHER CONWAY*

I. INTRODUCTION

IN AUGUST 2021, the actor Daniel Craig announced that he would not be giving his children a substantial inheritance.[1] Preferring to spend his money or give most of it away, Craig joins a list of high-profile figures such as Nigella Lawson, Sting and Bill Gates who view this decision as an exercise in good parenting by incentivising their children to work hard and vast sums of inherited wealth doing them 'no favours'. Of course, such sentiments are laudable when the children in question have had the lifetime advantages of growing up in a wealthy family and can still trade on a famous parent's name and connections after their demise.[2] However, disinheriting children is not within the exclusive realms of the rich and famous, even if the underlying reasons differ and there is significantly less wealth to pass on.

Recent decades have seen a shift in the passing of wealth between generations. Increased life expectancies mean that adult children are inheriting from their parents at a later age,[3] while the latter are consuming more of their own

* I am grateful to both MSPL delegates at Oxford and the independent reviewer for their helpful comments.

[1] Craig apparently views inheriting vast sums of money as 'distasteful' – see C Bateman, 'James Bond star Daniel Craig says he will not leave children substantial inheritance as he finds practice 'distasteful' (Sky News, 18 August 2021) news.sky.com/story/james-bond-star-daniel-craig-says-he-will-not-leave-children-substantial-inheritance-as-he-finds-practice-distasteful-12384357 (accessed August 2022).

[2] See, eg, I Brassington, 'On Rights of Inheritance and Bequest' (2019) 23 *The Journal of Ethics* 119, 120.

[3] Adult child beneficiaries may already be in their 50s or 60s when this occurs – see, eg, B Willenbacher, 'Individualism and Traditionalism in Inheritance Law in Germany, France, England, and the United States' (2003) 28 *Journal of Family History* 208, 222.

capital as they live for longer with rising living costs[4] and high care fees when this becomes a necessity.[5] For many members of the so-called baby-boomer generation, SKI-ing (or 'spending the kids' inheritance') has become a lifestyle choice as they travel and enjoy life to the full rather than saving money to pass on to their adult children.[6] In these circumstances, any sense of parental 'spending guilt' may be tempered by wealth transmission that has already taken place and reduces any assumed obligation to maintain on death, such as investment in their children's education and financial support for key life events (eg, help with buying a home).[7]

This chapter, however, focuses on situations in which a parent – for whatever reason – makes a very conscious decision to leave their adult child(ren) nothing.[8] At the negative end of the emotional spectrum, there may have been a long-term estrangement or falling out, or parental disapproval of a child's lifestyle choices.[9] Cutting off children can also be a punitive measure, for some sort of slight or misconduct (whether real or perceived).[10] Less censorious reasons include shifting family patterns and financial responsibilities where recoupling creates priorities towards a new spouse or partner.[11] Alternatively, a parent may feel that adult children have already benefitted from substantial lifetime gifts,[12] or it might be a simple case of wanting to pass wealth elsewhere (eg, to a charity).[13] Whatever the explanation, those affected may decide to challenge their exclusion from a validly executed will.

As is well-known, both the Inheritance (Provision for Family and Dependants) Act 1975 in England and Wales and its 1979 counterpart in Northern Ireland[14] allow a child of the deceased to challenge a validly executed will on the basis

[4] Soaring, at the time of writing, because of the effects of the coronavirus pandemic and the global financial tremors caused by Russia's invasion of Ukraine.

[5] A report published in March 2021 suggested average costs of around £35,000 per year – see LaingBuisson 'Care Homes For Older People UK Market Report 31ed' (Report, March 2021), available at www.laingbuisson.com/wp-content/uploads/2019/09/Care_Homes_for_Older_People_32ed_CONTENTS.pdf (accessed August 2022).

[6] Though the desire to spend is balanced against a pragmatic attitude of conserving wealth to maintain a reasonable standard of living in later life and leaving something to pass on – see K Rowlingson, '"Living Poor to Die Rich"? Or "Spending the Kids' Inheritance"? Attitudes to Assessing Inheritance in Later Life' (2006) 35 *Journal of Social Policy* 175. A research project involving the same author and funded by the Joseph Rowntree Trust found that around a quarter of the 2,000+ participants interviewed would limit their spending in order to pass wealth to their children – see K Rowlingson and S McKay, *Attitudes to Inheritance in Britain* (Bristol, Policy Press, 2005).

[7] JH Langbein, 'The Twentieth-Century Revolution in Family Wealth Transmission' (1987–1988) 86 *Michigan Law Review* 722, 723.

[8] Rather than simply dissipating any potential inheritance through parental spending habits.

[9] Both these things were apparent in *Ilott v The Blue Cross* [2017] UKSC 17 while estrangement was also a key factor in *Re Creeny* [1984] NI 397.

[10] As in *Re McGarrell* [1983] 8 NIJB where the deceased – who excluded his only daughter from his will – had spent the last year of his life in residential care against his wishes.

[11] As in *Ames v Jones* [2016] 8 WLUK 256 and *Re H (Deceased)* [2020] EWHC 1134 (Fam).

[12] *Miles v Shearer* [2021] EWHC 1000 (Ch).

[13] As in *Ilott v The Blue Cross* [2017] UKSC 17 though a desire for charitable giving was not the primary motivation!

[14] Inheritance (Provision for Family and Dependants) (NI) Order 1979).

that it failed to make 'reasonable financial provision'[15] for that particular individual – defined as what is needed for their 'maintenance'.[16] The chapter considers the extent to which the law respects and facilitates the autonomous choices of the testator[17] or retrospectively imposes different legal obligations based on presumptive notions of parental responsibility and other justificatory bases through the medium of family provision. It begins by setting the contextual backdrop to these contests before moving to the well-known case of *Ilott v The Blue Cross*.[18] Utilising the 2017 Supreme Court ruling as a staging post in the contemporary debate around passing wealth to adult children in these three jurisdictions,[19] the chapter goes on to explore the legal limits of disinheriting adult children and how this aligns with prevailing social norms. In doing so, it analyses the post-*Ilott* case law, and associated judicial trends. Finally, the chapter concludes by examining where the inter-generational transfer of assets currently lies on the continuum between *entitlement* and *privilege*, and considers options for modifying the current legal approach.

II. TESTAMENTARY FREEDOM, FAMILY OBLIGATION AND THE PARENT-CHILD RELATIONSHIP

While the underlying reasons are complex and multi-faceted, a decision to exclude adult children from the distributive contents of a will speaks to one of the core tenets of common law succession regimes: parents are not legally obliged to provide for their children[20] on death. Any concept of parental 'disinheritance' is therefore as innately flawed as the SKI acronym, since testamentary freedom[21] allows a testator to decide the post-mortem fate of their wealth and pass it to persons of the testator's choosing.[22]

[15] The basis of all claims under the relevant legislation – 1975 Act, s 1(1); 1979 Order, Art 3(1).

[16] For all categories of applicant (other than a surviving spouse or registered civil partner), reasonable financial provision is limited to 'maintenance': 1975 Act, s 1(2)(b); 1979 Order, Art 2(2). The concept of 'maintenance' is not defined in the statute and is discussed in the case law – see n 52 and accompanying text.

[17] The term 'testator' is gender neutral throughout this chapter, unless context or the facts of a particular case indicate otherwise.

[18] *Ilott v The Blue Cross* [2017] UKSC 17. The case was previously listed as *Ilott v Mitson*.

[19] Though the discussion resonates beyond England, Wales and Northern Ireland since the family provision system exists, in various guises, throughout most of the common law world. Similar systems (and substantively similar contemporary debates) can be found in Australia, New Zealand and Canada; for an illustration in the former, see S Villios and N Williams, 'Family Provision Law, Adult Children and the Age of Entitlement' (2018) 39 *Adelaide Law Review* 249.

[20] Or anyone else.

[21] Defined by Leslie as the 'right to distribute property upon death solely according to the dictates of one's own desires, unfettered by the constraints of society's moral code or the claims of others' – M Leslie, 'The Myth of Testamentary Freedom' (1996) 38 *Arizona Law Review* 235, 235.

[22] However, absolute testamentary freedom has always been something of a legal myth – see, eg, A Guest, 'Family Provision and the Legitima Portio' (1957) 73 *LQR* 74, 81–82 (it is 'misleading to regard English law as backed by centuries of testamentary freedom').

Family provision seeks to balance the autonomy of the testator with a legally constructed notion of responsibility to certain family and dependants, thus bringing into conflict the twin ideals underpinning the inheritance system: freedom of testation and familial obligation. Of course, more detailed analysis reveals that the two are not inherently incompatible since the core ideal of providing financial support for family members was a key feature in the genesis of testamentary freedom; as Atherton explains, making a will was always tempered by familial and social norms, since post-mortem distribution 'was not to exist in the abstract' but was located 'in a framework of moral responsibility, duty and obligation'.[23] Family provision claims are a paradigmatic illustration of the tensions between testamentary freedom and family obligation. Which one ultimately prevails is easy to predict where infants or minor children, and disabled or 'otherwise dependent'[24] adults, receive nothing under a dead parent's will; courts have little tolerance for the testator's actions in these circumstances.[25] Yet the same does not hold true for an adult son or daughter with earning capacity – the so-called 'able-bodied adult child' to use the phrase so beloved of succession law commentaries in the past. The position of an adult son or daughter who is economically self-sufficient (or, at least, has earning potential), and who was not financially dependent on a deceased parent before death (even if in financial need) – for present purposes, what we might class as an 'independent' adult child – is much more precarious.[26]

Writing in the early 1920s, Kenny described 'family transmission of property' as a 'natural duty of parents and a natural right of descendants'.[27] A century later, social attitudes surveys still lend credence to this idea, suggesting that children are regarded as the natural recipients of parental bounty, after the individual in question has provided for a surviving spouse or partner.[28]

[23] R Atherton, 'The Concept of Moral Duty in the Law of Family Provision – A Gloss or Critical Understanding' (2000) 6 *Australian Journal of Legal History* 5, 23–24.

[24] To borrow the descriptor in S Grattan, *Succession Law in Northern Ireland* (Belfast, SLS Legal Publications (NI), 1996) 197.

[25] Claims on behalf of infants and minors are virtually guaranteed to succeed in these circumstances (see *In Re Patton* [1986] 3 NIJB 35 and *Re R (Deceased)* [2021] EWHC 936 (Ch)), while those involving disabled or otherwise dependent adults are likely to trigger an award (see, eg, *Re Debenham (Deceased)* [1986] Fam Law 101).

[26] One assumes that this was the category of child that featured in the thoughts of the celebrities and high-profile figures mentioned in the opening paragraph.

[27] M Kenny, 'Is Inheritance a Right?' (1923–1924) 5 *Loyola Law Journal* 183, 184.

[28] See, eg, J Finch and J Mason, *Passing On: Kinship and Inheritance in England* (Abingdon, Routledge, 2000); G Douglas, H Woodward, A Humphrey and L Mills, 'Enduring Love – Attitudes to Family and Inheritance Law in England and Wales' (2011) 38 *Journal of Law & Society* 245. Research carried out by the present author over a decade ago, which interviewed older people in Northern Ireland, revealed a very strong sense of parental obligation towards adult children, and leaving them 'what was left', even if participants disliked the notion of allowing challenges to a will – H Conway and L Glennon, '"*To Give Or Not To Give?*": *The Transmission of Wealth on Death by Older Persons* (Report for the Changing Ageing Partnership, School of Law, Queen's University Belfast, September 2010). More recent research published by Legal and General in November 2021

Wills often reflect this;[29] and any deviation through parental disinheritance breaches some sort of assumed moral code.[30] Yet, it would be wrong to think that the family provision system subscribes to any notion of inheritance as a natural right for independent adult children who are excluded from a dead parent's estate. As a general rule, the law does not impose an obligation to maintain independent adult offspring. And while it would be wrong to suggest that freedom of testation reigns supreme, and that independent adult children have no chance of succeeding in family provision claims, case law suggests that such applicants are very much on the privilege side of the entitlement-privilege continuum when parental wealth is channelled elsewhere.

III. THE LEGAL LANDSCAPE UP TO AND INCLUDING *ILOTT*

Claims by 'independent' adult children have always been one of the most contentious aspects of the modern family provision system.[31] The lack of guidance in both the 1975 Act and 1979 Order is partly to blame. Each claim is assessed on two interrelated judicial questions: (1) did the will (or intestacy) make reasonable financial provision for the claimant (the threshold question); and (2) if not, what reasonable financial provision should be made (the quantum issue)?[32] However, the legislation simply limits such claims to maintenance and specifically directs courts to look at the 'manner in which the applicant was being, or … might expect to be, educated or trained'[33] (something that will be irrelevant for the majority of such applicants) alongside the general factors applicable in all family provision claims.[34] These include the financial resources

shows that 60% of participants left assets to their children, though the figure does not distinguish between young and adult children – Legal & General, 'Planning for the future' (November 2021) www.legalandgeneral.com/insurance/over-50-life-insurance/wills/planning-for-future/ (accessed August 2022).

[29] Though Kennedy queries whether such attitudes are a 'true reflection of the testator's wishes, or … what he feels is expected of him' – V Kennedy, 'Not the Beginning of the End: The Tension Between Pure Testamentary Freedom and Self-Imposed Moral Restrictions, A Case for Formalising Limitations' [2020] *Conv* 214, 219.

[30] This includes an unequal distribution of estate assets where the parent has more than one child. Even though a parent may be acting with the best of intentions (eg, helping a child who is not as financially secure as their siblings, or rewarding a child who looked after their parent(s) in later years), inheritance inequalities are often viewed as favouritism and as posthumous signs of who the parent loved more – see H Conway, '"Where There's a Will": Law and Emotion in Sibling Inheritance Disputes' in H Conway and J Stannard (eds), *The Emotional Dynamics of Law and Legal Discourse* (Oxford, Hart Publishing, 2016). However, equal division can also be a source of contention if one child feels that this is manifestly unjust – see, eg, *Noble v Morrison* [2019] NICh 8 discussed at nn 101–103 and accompanying text.

[31] The term 'modern' refers to the system established under the 1975 Act and 1979 Order respectively.

[32] Affirmed by the Supreme Court in *Ilott v The Blue Cross* [2017] UKSC 17, [23].

[33] 1975 Act, s 3(3) and 1979 Order, Art 5(3). While the legislation refers to 'applicant', the term 'claimant' often appears in judgments; the two are used interchangeably here.

[34] Specific factors apply to each category of applicant and are directly referable to the relationship in question (1975 Act ss 3(2)–(4) and 1979 Order, Arts 5(2)–(4)).

and future needs of the applicant and any beneficiaries of the estate, the size of the estate, and 'any obligations and responsibilities which the deceased had towards any applicant … or towards any beneficiary'.[35] Beyond the legislation, other issues have created additional confusion, including the absence of a pre-existing financial tie between the parties, and no clear sense of what obligations (if any) exist between parents and their independent adult children. With infants and minors, there is a clear element of financial dependency that transcends the death of a parent. However, the same is not true for independent adult children who are (or should be) capable of providing for themselves and were not financially reliant on their now deceased parent.[36]

Against this uncertain contextual backdrop, it is hardly surprising that much judicial time and effort has been expended on trying to formulate workable and coherent principles to augment the statutory framework for determining family provision claims by independent adult children. Initially, these were treated quite favourably by English courts[37] – a trend that persisted in Northern Ireland for many years, where courts tended to be much more sympathetic towards such applications under the 1979 Order.[38] However, as far back as *Re Coventry*,[39] we had a line of authority that signalled a more cautious approach to claims under the 1975 Act.

Neither time nor present subject-matter affords the luxury of analysing these cases in detail.[40] Suffice to say that independent adult children had varying degrees of success when seeking to challenge a will, and would have been ill-advised to see a family provision claim as an immutable means of undoing what they undoubtedly perceived as the unjust and unfair actions of a now deceased parent. The cases seemed to confirm that a son or daughter with earning capacity would face an uphill struggle to claim successfully under the 1975 Act, even if the applicant was in dire financial circumstances. As Peart and Borkowski remarked in 2000, English courts adopted a 'parsimonious' approach to these claims.[41] However, the same courts were also guilty of introducing an additional legal threshold for claims by independent adult children,

[35] 1975 Act, s 3(1); 1979 Order, Art 5(1).

[36] Likewise, with other categories of applicant under the 1975 Act or 1979 Order the rights and responsibilities arising in spousal relationships, claims by infant children, financial dependants, and unmarried cohabitants are more readily identifiable and, therefore, much less contested.

[37] See, eg, *Re Christie* [1979] Ch 168.

[38] In all three reported cases involving independent adult children pre-*Ilott*, the applicant succeeded – see *Re McGarrell* [1983] 8 NIJB, *Re Creeny* [1984] NI 397 and *McKernan* v *McKernan* [2007] NICh 6.

[39] *Re Coventry* [1979] 2 WLR 853, [1980] Ch 461.

[40] For an overview, see H Conway, 'Do Parents Always Know Best: Posthumous Provision and Adult Children' in W Barr (ed), *Modern Studies in Property Law: Volume 8* (Oxford, Hart Publishing, 2015) 118.

[41] N Peart and A Borkowski, 'Provision for Adult Children on Death- The Lesson from New Zealand' (2000) 12 *Child and Family Law Quarterly* 333, 333. However, this was not a universal approach – see, eg, *Espinosa v Bourke* [1999] 1 FLR 747.

despite this additional threshold having no legislative basis. As well as a need for maintenance, such applicants had to establish that the deceased owed them some sort of 'moral obligation' or the existence of 'special circumstance(s)' over and above the filial tie.[42]

Against this backdrop, the stage was set for a clear statement of principle by an appellate court on the direct subject of independent adult children. This opportunity finally arrived in the *Ilott* litigation, with its long and protracted legal history. The facts are well-known, and need only be rehearsed briefly.[43] Following a period of estrangement lasting almost 30 years, Melita Jackson left a net estate of some £486,000 to a number of animal charities and nothing to her only daughter Heather Ilott. Aged 44 at the time of her mother's death, Heather was clearly in financial need: she had not worked since the birth of her first child in 1984 and her husband worked part-time. The couple were living with three of their five children in a three-bedroom property rented from a Housing Association, and the family were dependent on state benefits to meet basic living expenses.

At earlier stages in the *Ilott* litigation, it is safe to say that the pendulum had swung more towards the independent adult child (not quite reaching 'entitlement' but certainly away from the 'privilege' narrative), based on the two Court of Appeal rulings in particular. The first of these, on the threshold question,[44] strengthened the idea of this category of applicant being able to make a successful financial provision claim despite not having been financially dependent on their parent (even for many years). When the matter returned to the Court of Appeal on the issue of quantum[45] and Heather Ilott was awarded £143,000 to purchase her home with a further £20,000 to draw upon if needed,[46] it seemed to indicate a more generous standard of treatment for independent adult children while questioning what steps a testator could actually take to disinherit an adult child.

When the charities appealed this award, *Ilott* became the first family provision case to reach the highest appellate court in the UK. The fact that this was only on the issue of quantum is unfortunate, though more on this later.

[42] See, eg, *Re Jennings* [1994] Ch 286 and *Re Abram (Deceased)* [1996] 2 FLR 379. Relevant factors might include the provision of care (at a personal cost) by the applicant to the deceased, or situations where the applicant is incapable of earning a living due to physical or mental disability.

[43] For a more detailed analysis of the *Ilott* saga, see B Sloan, '*Ilott v The Blue Cross* (2017): Testing the Limits of Testamentary Freedom' in B Sloan (ed), *Landmark Cases in Succession Law* (Oxford, Hart Publishing, 2019) 301. See also H Conway, 'Testamentary Freedom, Family Obligation and the *Ilott* Legacy' [2017] *Conv* 372.

[44] *Ilott v Mitson* [2011] EWCA Civ 346, [2012] 2 FLR 170.

[45] *Ilott v Mitson* [2015] EWCA Civ 797.

[46] Arden LJ was especially influenced by Heather's very limited financial resources, noting that they were at 'such a basic level that they outweigh[ed] the importance that would normally be attached to the fact that [Heather was] an adult child who had been living independently for so many years': ibid [45].

The Supreme Court did take the opportunity to set out some core principles, which can be inelegantly summarised as follows:

- Testamentary freedom is important in cases involving contested wills: 'English law recognises the freedom of individuals to dispose of their assets by will … in whatever manner they wish'.[47]
- Conduct has always been a relevant factor in family provision cases,[48] but it is not usually a decisive one.[49] While family provision claims should focus on whether reasonable financial provision has been made for a particular claimant, the reasonableness or otherwise of the testator's actions in excluding a particular individual can be taken into account,[50] though a family provision claim will not succeed just because the deceased may have acted unreasonably or spitefully. However, awards should not become 'rewards for good behaviour on the part of the claimant or penalties for bad on the part of the deceased'.[51]
- Maintenance means just that; it 'cannot extend to any or every thing which it would be desirable for the claimant to have' and must 'import provision to meet the everyday expenses of living'.[52]
- Nominated beneficiaries (such as the charities in *Ilott*) do not have to justify their selection nor do they have to demonstrate some sort of financial need, even though their needs will be highly relevant.

On the thorny question of an independent adult child establishing a moral obligation on the part of a parent in order to succeed, Lord Hughes (who delivered the leading judgment) made the following observation:

> There is no requirement for a moral claim as a sine qua non for all applications under the 1975 Act, and Oliver J (in the case of *Re Coventry)*[[53]] did not impose one.

[47] *Ilott* (n 18) [1].

[48] Courts are required to look at the 'conduct of the applicant or any other person' under s 3(1)(g) of the 1975 Act and Art 5(1)(g) of the 1979 Order.

[49] For a case in which conduct *was* a decisive factor, see *Wright v Waters* [2014] EWHC 3614 (Ch). The deceased's 64-year-old, wheelchair-bound daughter failed to establish that reasonable financial provision had not been made for her when she was excluded from her mother's will. Despite living in necessitous circumstances, and no other beneficiary having a particular need for the estate, the court held that the daughter's conduct a decade earlier in refusing to return investment monies that her mother had given her, and in writing letters disowning her mother and wishing her dead, outweighed all other factors.

[50] According to the Supreme Court, this could be factored into conduct under s 3(1)(g) of the 1975 Act (Art 5(1)(g) of the 1979 Order), or perhaps the deceased's obligations and responsibilities towards the applicant under s 3(1)(d) (Art 5(1)(d)). It is more difficult to see how this fits into the latter category.

[51] *Ilott* (n 18) [17].

[52] ibid [14]. This affirms the fairly restrictive interpretation in previous case law – see, eg, the comments of Browne-Wilkinson J (as he then was) in *In Re Dennis (Deceased)* [1981] 2 All ER 140, 146 describing it as 'payments which … enable the applicant … to discharge the cost of his daily living at whatever standing of living is appropriate to him'.

[53] [1979] 2 WLR 853, [1980] Ch 461. This judgment is taken as the starting point for the moral obligation threshold in adult child cases.

> He meant no more, but no less, than that in the case of a claimant adult son well capable of living independently, something more than the qualifying relationship is needed to found a claim, and that in the case before him the additional something could only be a moral claim. That will be true of a number of cases. Clearly, the presence or absence of a moral claim will often be at the centre of the decision under the 1975 Act.

In short, independent adult children are very unlikely to succeed simply because they are the child of the deceased; some other significant factor is needed, and will usually be argued.

The Supreme Court ruling signalled something of a return to orthodoxy after the commotion caused by the Court of Appeal judgments, and was seen by many (current author included) as tempering expectations somewhat.[54] Will-makers (and those advising them) were assured that personal choices were a weighty factor, and that the inherent limitations of the maintenance threshold would curb any temptation towards judicial excess where reasonable financial provision had not been made. However, the judgment also reasserted the basic premise that claims under the 1975 Act (and the 1979 Order) are fact-specific: one ruling cannot act as a template for another, or a predictor of success.

Of course, *Ilott* itself is somewhat unusual in terms of the value of the estate, the mother's choice of charities as principal beneficiaries, the long and enduring family estrangement, and the fact that the final appeal was on the issue of quantum only. The Supreme Court decision will always be tainted with a sense of 'what if', given that leave to appeal the threshold question was refused earlier in the litigation. And while the final award was significantly reduced, Heather Ilott still ended up with a one-tenth share of her mother's estate, despite having no expectation to inherit anything. This was largely on the basis of financial need and some mild judicial disregard for the mother's actions in cutting her daughter out of her life (though there was clearly 'fault' on both sides). Moreover, there was no clear statement of principle for independent adult children claims, or formulation of guidance to assist lower courts.[55] As Kerridge concedes, *Ilott* was a 'serious disappointment' for anyone 'hoping for significant clarification' of such claims under the 1975 Act.[56] In her supplemental judgement, Lady Hale expressed dissatisfaction with the current state of the law, noting that it gives judges 'virtually no help in deciding how to evaluate [applications by adult children] or balance them with other claims on the estate',[57] and the lack of factors

[54] Conway (n 43).

[55] Such complaints are not exclusive to this jurisdiction, with a lack of 'higher court leadership' also noted in adult child cases in Australia – Villios and Williams (n 19) 258. Perhaps this is a little unfair: difficulties in challenging the exercise of judicial discretion in lower courts, and costs, are obvious barriers to appellate claims – as well as the emotional impact of the litigation. All of this makes the Supreme Court ruling in *Ilott* seem more of a missed opportunity.

[56] R Kerridge, 'Family Provision in England and Wales' in KGC Reid, MJ de Waal and Re Zimmerman (eds), *Comparative Succession Law, Volume III: Mandatory Family Protection* (Oxford, Oxford University Press, 2020) 384, 401.

[57] *Ilott* (n 18) [58].

for guiding 'whether an adult child is deserving or undeserving of reasonable maintenance'.[58] Such criticisms make the Supreme Court's reluctance to seize some sort of opportunity here seem a little more curious.

IV. INDEPENDENT ADULT CHILDREN IN THE POST-*ILOTT* ERA

In some ways, the Supreme Court ruling in *Ilott* has done little to discourage claims by independent adult children, even if the resultant awards may be more modest. A lot of uncertainty remains, and the fact that post-*Ilott* applications have met with varying degrees of success is unsurprising.

One might venture to suggest that there have been more 'hard-line' statements in some of the judicial reflections on individual claims, as the following analysis reveals. For convenience, the cases are subdivided into two broad categories: those where the deceased's will excluded independent adult children in favour of other categories of beneficiary, and those where it favoured other adult children at the notional expense of their siblings.

A. Other Nominated Beneficiaries

One of the first post-*Ilott* cases – and one with more than a passing factual resemblance – was *Re Nahajec (Deceased)*.[59] The deceased's will left an estate worth almost £270,000 to a close friend; his daughter, who was born in 1985, was the only child from his second marriage and claimed under the 1975 Act.[60] The father-daughter relationship had been marked by periods of estrangement: the father had cut himself off from his family when he separated from the claimant's mother in 1996 until the daughter contacted him in 2007; they were on good terms until 2009 when the father disapproved of his daughter's boyfriend and ceased contact with her until his death in 2015 despite his daughter's repeated attempts to reconcile. Having executed his final will, the deceased also left a note explaining his decision to leave nothing to his children, stating that he had 'not seen or heard from any of [them] in the last 18 years', that he believed they had 'no interest in me or my welfare' and were 'to my knowledge, sufficiently independent of means not to require any provision from me'.[61]

The daughter was living alone in rented accommodation and had payday loan debts of £6,600; she worked as a part-time retail assistant on a zero-hours contract and also at a veterinary surgery where she was only paid for

[58] ibid [66].

[59] *Re Nahajec (Deceased)* [2017] 7 WLUK 399 (18 Jul 2017, County Court (Leeds)).

[60] The deceased's son from his first marriage (who was unable to work because of ill-health and a disability) had also claimed under the 1975 Act; this had been settled by a payment of £22,000. His other son from his first marriage had not made any claim.

[61] *Re Nahajec (Deceased)* (n 59) [4].

nine hours per week but worked over 20 in the hope of becoming a qualified veterinary nurse. In assessing her claim, HHJ Saffman acknowledged that the court's task was not to ask whether the deceased had acted unreasonably but whether the will – looked at objectively – produced an unreasonable result. Working through the general statutory factors, particular attention was paid to sections 3(1)(a), (c) and (g) of the 1975 Act.[62] The daughter was clearly in financial need and was living a 'rather frugal existence';[63] she also genuinely believed that becoming a veterinary nurse would put her on a much more stable financial footing.[64] The defendant, as sole beneficiary of the estate, had some resources but was not well off. Turning to category (g), the court likened the daughter's application to a moral claim on the estate, and placed the blame for any estrangement on the father as a 'stubborn and intransigent and insensitive … man who found it hard to forgive people who disagreed with him'[65] and had rebuffed his daughter's numerous attempts to reconcile. There was also an important reference to the letter that had accompanied the deceased's will, and its specific reference to his children being of sufficiently independent means not to require any provision from him; looking at the daughter's financial circumstances, it was 'difficult to see how this description could sensibly be applied to her'.[66]

The court also paid particular attention to the manner in which the daughter was being or might expect to be educated or trained under section 3(3) of the 1975 Act.[67] This is a comparatively rare instance of the category specific factor influencing an independent adult child claim, though entirely appropriate on the facts, given the daughter's reasonable and realistic aspiration to train as a veterinary nurse. However, section 3(3) did not ultimately assist in this case as HHJ Saffman explained:

> The subsection requires the court to have regard to the manner in which the applicant was being or in which *he might expect* (my emphasis) to be educated or trained. At the time of the deceased's death the applicant was not being trained and there is no cogent evidence that she might have expected her father to meet the cost of education and training at any future date. It seems to me that the way in which this particular subsection is drafted requires the court to have regard to the manner in which the claimant herself might have expected to be educated or trained. It is not a question of whether it would have been reasonable for a deceased person to contribute towards a claimant's education or training, the question appears to be whether the claimant expected it from the deceased person.[68]

[62] The equivalent provisions are Arts 5(1)(a), (c) and (g) of the 1979 Order.
[63] *Re Nahajec (Deceased)* (n 59) [35].
[64] The daughter had inherited £16,000 on her mother's death in 2013 but had used this to set herself up in rented accommodation and pay off some debts.
[65] *Re Nahajec (Deceased)* (n 59) [59].
[66] ibid [60].
[67] The equivalent provision is Art 5(3) of the 1979 Order.
[68] *Re Nahajec (Deceased)* (n 59) [102].

On the facts, the daughter clearly did not expect this from her father though her desire to become a veterinary nurse was relevant under section 3(1)(g). Assessing this, and the other section 3(1) factors, HHJ Saffman reached a final figure of £30,000 which represented 11.3 per cent of the estate. Although significantly less than the £59,000 sought by the daughter, this would allow her to clear her debts[69] and work towards her qualification.

Estrangement and a sense of apportioning blame were also apparent in *Rochford v Rochford*[70] where an adult daughter who had endured a difficult relationship with her father was left £25,000 in his will with the bulk of the estate (some £193,000) going to the deceased's sister. Despite not being an example of parental disinheritance, and the fact that the daughter was not an independent adult child (she suffered from a physical disability, had limited income and had been unable to work since she was 36), the case is notable not simply for the fact that the court increased the daughter's inheritance by an additional £85,000.[71] In considering section 3(1)(g) of the 1975 Act (any other matter including conduct),[72] the court took the view that the daughter had a moral claim on the estate because she had made every reasonable effort to keep in touch with her father, even when he rejected her.

Other decisions have seen a will favour a surviving spouse over children, something that chimes with the ethos of family provision regimes where the former have preferential status.[73] *Miles v Shearer*[74] shows how a testator's stated – and entirely justified – reasons for excluding their adult children can be a significant factor. Two adult daughters, then aged 39 and 40, applied for reasonable financial provision from their father's £2.2 million estate of which his second wife was the principal beneficiary. The girls' parents had funded their private education, gap years and university courses; more importantly, the deceased had gifted the first claimant £177,000 and the second claimant £185,000 to invest in property, when he sold a property in London in 2008. At the same time he told both daughters that they would receive no further financial assistance from him, setting out his reasons in a letter that painted a less than flattering picture:

> Last night you mentioned money a number of times … I really do not want there to be any surprises/disappointments on this subject. But the fact that you mention it so often means that it may already be a subject of friction, or that it could become a subject of friction in the future.

[69] A sum that merely allowed the daughter to do this was deemed to be too low.

[70] *Rochford v Rochford* [2021] 2 WLUK 699.

[71] In reaching this decision, the court was swayed by various things, including the fact that the deceased's sister had refused to engage in mediation (based on what she believed was the strength of her claim) and the fact that the same individual was financially secure (she owned her own home, had state and private pensions, and no dependants). However, the court's assertion that any inheritance the sister received in this case was a 'windfall' is hard to reconcile with the Supreme Court's rejection of that idea when discussing the charitable beneficiaries in *Ilott*.

[72] The equivalent provision is Art 5(1)(g) of the 1979 Order.

[73] As evidenced by the fact that reasonable financial provision for surviving spouses is not limited to maintenance – see n 16.

[74] *Miles v Shearer* [2021] EWHC 1000 (Ch).

> First, your mother has half of my money (including my pensions). So I have less to spend/invest/waste/pass on.
>
> Second, [my wife] and I intend to live for a long time and we intend to spend all of our money … It would be wrong for you to have any expectations, and … there is not likely to be very much to pass on.
>
> … …
>
> Fifth, over the last 35 years or so I have spent a great deal of money providing the family lifestyle … I have also provided substantial deposits for both [of you] … I am delighted that you are now earning a decent salary and well done to you for that. But from now on you are on your own financially. I would not approve of it any other way.
>
> You can expect the odd present (probably a lot smaller than you might think appropriate) and my love, company, advice and support etc. I hope that you will take this in the right way and we can put this subject to rest.[75]

In refusing the application, the court noted that both claimants had funded their own lifestyles since 2008. Focusing in particular on the deceased's obligations and responsibilities towards his daughters under section 3(1)(d) of the 1975 Act,[76] Sir Julian Flaux C began by stating that there was 'no legal obligation on a parent to maintain an adult child' and that this particular factor was 'concerned with obligations and responsibilities which the deceased had immediately before death, not in the past'.[77] Both daughters might have enjoyed an affluent standard of lifestyle until their parents' divorce, but could not have expected this to continue indefinitely – and the deceased had no financial obligation towards them immediately prior to his death. Following substantial gifts in 2008, the deceased had made it repeatedly clear that his daughters could not expect any further financial assistance from him; this 'disclaimer of responsibility militate[d] against his having any obligations or responsibilities towards [them] … at the time of his death'.[78]

In a ruling that also seems instinctively correct, *Shapton v Seviour*[79] reaffirmed the lack of any legal obligation towards maintaining adult children, while not holding back in its criticism of the claimant in this particular action. The deceased's will left his entire estate to his second wife; she suffered from Motor Neurone Disease and the couple's home (which formed the bulk of the £268,000 estate, the rest being insurance policies worth some £51,000) had been specially adapted to meet her needs. The deceased's daughter from his first marriage brought a family provision claim, seeking an award of £75,000.[80]

[75] ibid [25].
[76] The equivalent provision is Art 5(1)(d) of the 1979 Order.
[77] Miles (n 74) 102.
[78] ibid [111].
[79] *Shapton v Seviour* [2020] WTLR 1047.
[80] The deceased also had a son from his first marriage, while his wife had two adult children from another relationship. None of them contested the estate distribution, though the court described the current relationship between the surviving spouse and step-daughter as 'frankly toxic' – ibid [10].

In dismissing her claim as 'absolutely hopeless',[81] Deputy Master Lloyd pointed to the modest size of the estate (most of which was tied up in the home) and to the fact that the deceased's wife would 'need every penny [of the cash assets] to live out her remaining years in dignity and comfort'.[82] The daughter and her husband were both employed and living in a £240,000 house; simply wanting a larger home was 'never on the cards in this application' and the couple's credit card debts of around £20,000 were 'self-inflicted'.[83] In a final rebuke, the Deputy Master dismissed the daughter's apparent belief that 'she was entitled as of right to one quarter of her father's estate. She clearly [was] not'.[84]

The previous two cases contrast significantly with *Re H (Deceased)*[85] where a 50-year-old daughter who received nothing under her father's will was awarded almost £139,000 from a net estate of £554,000. The deceased had left everything to his elderly and disabled wife who had extensive health problems and was worried about funding her care home costs; the couple's daughter had severe mental health issues that left her unable to work (she relied on state benefits to support herself and her two minor children), and had been estranged from her parents for years.[86] In deciding that reasonable financial provision had not been made, Cohen J cited the claimant's 'severe and debilitating mental illness which [made] her unable to support herself and her … children'; there was no doubt that she was 'in a position of real need'.[87] On the issue of quantum, the judge acknowledged that the priority was to ensure that the wife, as sole beneficiary of the estate, could meet her care home costs for the rest of her life. However, despite having been estranged from her parents and essentially financially independent of them for 20 years, the daughter was awarded around a quarter of her father's estate to meet her current financial needs, assist her recovery and possibly enable her to return to work.[88] Though laudable, the outcome is difficult to reconcile with *Shapton* – both in terms of the needs of the deceased's surviving spouse, and the generous sum awarded here. The fact that the daughter blamed her parents for her illness may have been a factor.

B. Unequal Treatment of Children

A parent's decision to leave adult children different amounts of their estate, or to exclude one while benefitting the others, flies in the face of the so-called

[81] ibid [13].
[82] ibid [15].
[83] ibid [17].
[84] ibid [19].
[85] *Re H (Deceased)* [2020] EWHC 1134 (Fam).
[86] The couple's adult son, who had also received nothing, did not contest the will.
[87] *Re H (Deceased)* (n 85) [44]–[45].
[88] The sum included ongoing therapy costs and purchase of white goods etc but a claim for housing was refused. The judgment is also interesting for allowing a sum to partially discharge legal costs under a conditional fee arrangement.

equality norm: ie that parents treat all their children equally on death.[89] Several post-*Ilott* judgments have dealt with family provision claims instigated in these circumstances.

The issue facing the court in *Ball v Ball*[90] was whether three claimants, who had been cut out of their mother's will after making allegations of sexual abuse against their father (and were estranged from their family as a result) could establish lack of reasonable financial provision.[91] The deceased's other eight children were all beneficiaries under her will, which left a small estate of under £200,000. Rejecting the application, the court noted that the claimants were in a very similar financial position to the beneficiaries – they were 'all getting by' but nothing more, and the modest estate and numerous beneficiaries meant that making a financial award in the claimants' favour would not make a significant difference anyway.[92] Moreover, it was held that the father's abuse did not constitute a moral obligation on the mother to compensate the claimants under her will as she did not 'authorise, instigate or encourage' the abuse.[93]

Less traumatic, though still harmful for all involved, is *Re Mohammed (Deceased)*,[94] where the mother left a net estate worth close to £400,000 to her elder daughter, and nothing to her younger daughter who brought a family provision claim.[95] The claimant had been estranged from her mother for a decade, though the underlying reasons were unclear: the judgment mentioned the mother's disapproval of her daughter's attitudes to motherhood (the claimant had two children) and the claimant having briefly relocated to Trinidad in 2009 to be near her now deceased father. Aged 52, unable to work because of underlying health reasons[96] and reliant on universal credit payments as her main source of income, the daughter sought £128,000 to meet her current and future financial needs which she based on an annual figure of £10,000. Large sections of the judgment focused on the claimant's financial circumstances and outgoings, though the court found that she had made a 'conscious attempt … to understate her income and overstate her outgoings'[97] – including telling the

[89] It has been suggested that unequal treatment is more socially acceptable for inter vivos transfers, which are attuned to specific needs: see C Sappideen, 'Families and Intergenerational Transfers: Changing Intergenerational Transfers: Changing the Old Order' (2008) 31 *University of New South Wales Law Journal* 738.

[90] *Ball v Ball* [2017] EWHC 1750 (Ch).

[91] The claimants reported their allegations to the police; the father subsequently pleaded guilty to the majority of charges against him.

[92] Though financially pragmatic, one might question this reasoning on the basis that some sort of award would nevertheless have helped them monetarily, and – perhaps more importantly – might have assuaged (publicly) some of the negative emotions they may have felt after being ostracised by their family for revealing the father's abuse *and* being disinherited as a result.

[93] *Ball* (n 90).

[94] *Re Mohammed (Deceased)* [2021] EWHC 2532 (Ch); [2021] 7 WLUK 742.

[95] The deceased had three children, and left nothing to her son as well. The reasons were not stated in the judgment, and there was no reference to a family provision claim by the son.

[96] The claimant had been a practising lawyer. No independent evidence was submitted in respect of the ongoing health issues.

[97] *Re Mohammed (Deceased)* (n 94) [110].

court that she had spent and gifted to her daughters a £45,000 inheritance from her paternal grandmother.

Deputy Master Glover found that the claimant had not established a lack of reasonable financial provision. In assessing the general factors, emphasis was placed on the daughter's financial needs under section 3(1)(a) of the 1979 Act,[98] the fact that she was not living with a monthly deficit and had sufficient resources to meet both her outgoings and to 'provide a safety net for unforeseen expenditure or "life's little luxuries"'.[99] This was unlikely to change in the foreseeable future. Looking at any physical or mental disability of any applicant under section 3(1)(f),[100] it was possible that the claimant here was suffering from one or both these things, though there was no independent medical evidence to this effect. However, her needs as presented to the court could be met from her own resources and did not give rise to any maintenance requirement that should be met from her mother's estate.

Finally, and for the sake of completeness, it is worth noting that *Noble v Morrison*[101] is, to date, the only post-*Ilott* reported judgment involving independent adult children in Northern Ireland. The case is not one of parental disinheritance. Instead, an adult daughter successfully challenged an equal estate division under her father's will, claiming a much larger share than her two siblings – a succession law example of the sardonic saying that 'no good deed goes unpunished'. Like the English cases discussed immediately above, the core *Ilott* principles were distilled and applied in *Noble*. So far, so unremarkable, though in working through the general statutory factors McBride J seemed to adopt the old Animal Farm analogy of 'all animals being equal' when she noted that one or more of these factors may have magnetic importance.[102] What is more striking about *Noble* was the provision of housing to satisfy a maintenance claim, and how this was achieved. This was the major feature of the judgment, not just because the absolute transfer of a home to the claimant is a relatively rare occurrence; it is something that is extremely rare for an adult child.[103]

C. Lessons Learned?

There are obvious dangers in relying solely on reported cases involving independent adult children. In practice, a large number of these claims (even palpably weak ones) will settle or compromise before a final hearing, with the estate

[98] The equivalent provision is Art 5(1)(a) of the 1979 Order.
[99] *Re Mohammed (Deceased)* (n 94) [138].
[100] The equivalent provision is Art 5(1)(f) of the 1979 Order.
[101] *Noble v Morrison* [2019] NICh 8.
[102] Similar views were expressed by King J at an earlier stage in the *Ilott* litigation.
[103] H Conway and S Grattan, 'Family Provision: A New Approach to an Old Dilemma' [2021] *Trusts and Estates Law & Tax Journal*.

making a 'nuisance payment' to avoid the expense and uncertainty of a full trial.[104] However, the cases discussed here are a useful snapshot of how courts approach what most people would probably still view as 'non-conventional' estate distributions, even if there is little in terms of principle or pronouncement on the inheritance 'entitlements' of independent adult children.[105] It is difficult to reconcile the outcomes in any meaningful way, and an air of unpredictability still lingers. Yet, while each case turns on its own facts, some points can be made with a certain degree of conviction.

The mere existence of the parent-child relationship will not suffice in itself; there is no concept of family patrimony that triggers an entitlement. On a more nuanced view, being in financial need is not always enough for an independent adult child to succeed,[106] though impecunious circumstances can be a significant factor.[107] The composition and size of the estate, and the other demands being made on it, are relevant considerations, while parental rejection of a child's repeated attempts to reconcile may influence the final outcome. Within the factual matrix, certain things can trigger some sort of moral obligation for a deceased parent to maintain their otherwise independent adult offspring, though how influential this is moving forward remains to be seen – and there is no sense of imparting a moral obligation on the basis of a mere filial tie between deceased and applicant. If an adult child is self-reliant, then no provision can be deemed reasonable financial provision; and courts certainly will not look favourably on financially secure children who are seeking a (larger) slice of the financial pie to fund an affluent lifestyle or climb the higher rungs of the housing ladder.

V. LOCATING ADULT CHILDREN ON THE 'ENTITLEMENT VERSUS PRIVILEGE CONTINUUM'

Finch and Mason's seminal work views inheritance as a 'process that *constitutes* families, not simply reflects them'[108] since an individual (through identifying

[104] This seems to be the position in Northern Ireland, at least – and I am grateful to Sheena Grattan BL for confirming this.

[105] In his analysis of post-*Ilott* cases involving independent adult children, Ross argues that they 'do not indicate that the floodgates have opened or are likely to do so', and submits that most of these cases would have been decided in the same way before *Ilott* – S Ross, 'Inheritance (Provision for Family and Dependants) Act 1975 and Claims by Adult Children' (2021) 19 *Trust Quarterly Review*.

[106] Lord Hughes in *Ilott* described it as 'a necessary but not a sufficient condition for an order' (*Ilott* (n 19) [19]).

[107] Both *Ilott* and *Re H (Deceased)* seem to equate need to some sort of notional entitlement, as does *Lomax v Greenslade* [2018] EWHC 2623 (Ch) although *Ilott* is not cited in the judgment. In *Lomax*, the deceased's 1997 will left his entire estate – the bulk of which comprised a London property valued at almost £700,000 – to a Ms Greenslade. His three adult children challenged the will; all three were struggling financially, though for very different reasons. An order that Ms Greenslade (who was already financially secure) should receive £69,000 from the estate, with the balance being divided equally between the deceased's three children, was upheld on appeal.

[108] Finch and Mason (n 28) 2.

those who will inherit their assets) can define their most 'intimate kin'.[109] While this might suggest a movement away from traditional kinship patterns and distributive trends in wills, the social attitudes surveys mentioned earlier[110] suggest that adult children are still viewed as the natural recipients of at least some portion of inherited wealth. Even without a concept of forced heirship under a common law legal system, an independent son or daughter – for the majority of will-makers – sits further along the 'entitlement' end of the parental inheritance continuum that is presented here.

What is reflected in the attitudinal, however, is not necessarily reflected in the testamentary intent of all parents; deliberate disinheritance can and does occur. The rich and famous mentioned at the beginning of this chapter may be comfortable in making such public pronouncements – not least because their independent adult children are unlikely to find themselves seriously disadvantaged or in any sort of (serious) financial peril as a result. For other 'ordinary' testators, however, the consequences of their actions are likely to be more keenly felt – both financially and emotionally – by a disinherited adult child. And this is where the discretionary regime of family provision comes into play.

As Douglas explains, any resultant family provision application calls into question

> … the claim of the child, based on his or her individual needs, to be supported beyond the death of the deceased. Such 'children' challenge the usual assumption in English law that, once they reach adulthood, financial responsibility (as distinct from the tie of affection) towards one's children terminates.[111]

In squaring the testator's testamentary freedom with the extent to which the law should recognise some sort of legal obligation towards the applicant in proceedings by independent adult children under the 1975 Act (and the 1979 Order), judges are not using the family provision jurisdiction to effectuate a normative – if not a legal – requirement that parents should benefit their adult children. Instead, the post-*Ilott* case law suggests that they are (for the most part) prioritising freedom of choice while leaving sufficient room for judicial manoeuvre where the statutory tests show that reasonable financial provision was not made; and the underlying rationales, post-*Ilott*, are couched firmly within the statutory checklist of applicable factors and maintenance thresholds, with less scope for judicial moralising or posing the erroneous question of whether the testator acted unreasonably (which is not the basis of the legislation).

From a legal perspective, inheriting parental wealth does not constitute some sort of loosely defined natural right for independent adult children, regardless of prevailing socio-cultural attitudes. As a legal mechanism, a discretionary family provision system nudges these claims firmly towards the privilege end

[109] ibid 10.
[110] See n 28.
[111] G Douglas, 'Family Provision and Family Practices – The Discretionary Regime of the Inheritance Act of England and Wales' (2014) 4 *Oñati Socio-Legal Series* 222, 225.

of inheritance continuum where no inheritance can be guaranteed: applicants should not simply succeed because they are the son or daughter of the deceased, something that courts in post-*Ilott* cases have largely reinforced. The bigger question seems to be how to graduate the scale between no award, and some measure of financial provision based on individual circumstances.

VI. CONCLUSION

Claims by independent adult children stand at the intersection of a number of complex factors: family relations, great expectations, financial need and often family strife. Two basic observations can be made. First, a somewhat schizophrenic attitude prevails. On the one hand, we have a fixation on testamentary freedom; on the other, there is widespread public support for ensuring that adult children are provided for when necessary. Second, with no agreed sense of what, if anything, a parent owes an independent adult child, courts must determine such applications without the benefit of a normative template.[112] In her supplemental judgment in *Ilott*, Lady Hale observed that the case raised 'some profound questions about the nature of family obligations … and the relationship between the freedom of property owners to dispose of their property as they see fit and their duty to fulfil their family obligations' which were '[not] answered by the legislation which we have to apply'.[113] Seven years later, these answers seem as elusive as ever.

So, normatively speaking, where could we go from here? Working within the existing legislative framework, one solution might be to limit adult child claims to those in financial need.[114] Though superficially attractive, one wonders if such a restrictive approach is the correct way to distinguish between what Lady Hale described as 'deserving' and 'underserving' claims.[115] Another option would be to upscale the category specific criteria under the 1975 Act,[116] something that Lady Hale seemed to lobby for in *Ilott*.[117] Additional factors might include things like the provision of care for a parent by an adult child applicant

112 And no special factors beyond education or training needs.

113 *Ilott* (n 18) [49].

114 As in the Canadian province of Manitoba – see The Dependants Relief Act, SM 1989–90, c 42, CCSM c D37, s 2(1).

115 An adult child who had 'fallen on hard times' could make a family provision claim, but so could the 'lame ducks' and prodigals who did not work hard or make their own way in life – something that might be more contentious. See generally S Grattan, 'Of Lame Ducks, Black Sheep and Family Bonding' (2000) 51 *Northern Ireland Legal Quarterly* 198.

116 Despite the unrestricted eligibility of adult child applicants, the current statutory emphasis on training or educational needs will only be relevant in a small number of cases.

117 Though it is worth noting that, in 2011, the Law Commission decided against any legislative reform that would give adult children a greater success rate under the 1975 Act – Law Commission of England Wales, *Intestacy and Family Provision Claims on Death* (Law Com No 331, 2011), [6.1]–[6.26].

or the latter's contribution to a family business (to strengthen individual claims), and the prior receipt of significant lifetime gifts or financial support from the deceased parent (to justify a particular exercise of testamentary freedom). Similar options have been mooted elsewhere;[118] and while preferable to straying down a highly subjective path of 'fairness' and 'justice' as alternative yardsticks,[119] there is always a danger that new statutory criteria might problematise things further.[120] The elusive search continues for a discretion that is more circumscribed by principle and can be 'exercised in a way that is predictable',[121] despite the widely divergent factual circumstances presented by individual cases. One suspects, however, that independent adult children seeking significant sums from a dead parent's estate should do so in varying degrees of hope rather than in expectation.

[118] Most notably, by various law reform bodies across Australia – see Villios and Williams (n 19) 272–74.

[119] Lady Hale in *Ilott* suggested that it might be 'unfair to cut children out of wills because of the contribution they had made to enriching the lives of their parents' (*Ilott* (n 18) [54]), something that would be virtually impossible to include (or assess) within a legislative framework.

[120] It is interesting that none of the cases discussed in this chapter involved a claim based on the provision of care for a parent. The difficulties of evaluating this have been noted elsewhere – see, eg, B Sloan, 'Testamentary Freedom and Caring Adult Offspring in England & Wales and Ireland' in K Boele-Woelki, J Miles and JM Scherpe (eds), *The Future of Family Property in Europe* (Cambridge, Intersentia, 2011). Sappideen argues that rewarding care with an estate payment conflicts with 'the role of social exchange within family relationships … where assistance is not measured in monetary terms but is given through love and affection' – Sappideen (n 89) 762.

[121] Kerridge (n 56) 141.

Part III

Leases and Co-Housing

7

Leases and the Nature of Co-ownership

NATALIE MROCKOVA AND LUKE ROSTILL*

I. INTRODUCTION

WHEN TWO PARTIES wish to co-occupy a piece of land as co-lessees, two sets of requirements must be satisfied. First, the requirements of a valid lease. Second, the requirements imposed by the law of co-ownership. This chapter aims to examine two questions that arise as a result of the overlap of these two sets of rules: what is the nature of, and the relationship between, unity of possession (a requirement of co-ownership) and exclusive possession (a requirement of leases) in cases involving a co-owned lease (Key Question 1)? And in what circumstances can two or more parties be equitable tenants in common in respect of a lease, and what is the legal effect of this co-ownership arrangement both internally and externally (Key Question 2)? However, before we deal with these controversial and largely unresolved issues, the remainder of this section will first set out some elementary propositions concerning the nature of leases and co-ownership, for these are the bedrock of the ensuing analysis. Section II will then examine Key Question 1. Section III will explore how Key Question 2 has been, and should be, answered. Section IV will conclude.

The following rules about leases are well settled in English law. First, a lease typically arises out of a contract between the landlord and the tenant(s).[1] The tenant ordinarily acquires a term of years,[2] which is a type of legal estate

* We wish to thank all those who commented on an earlier version of this chapter at the MSPL conference, as well as an anonymous reviewer, for the very useful and insightful feedback that we received.

[1] *Hammersmith and Fulham LBC v Monk* [1992] 1 AC 478 (HL) 483 (Lord Bridge), 491–93 (Lord Browne-Wilkinson); *Prudential Assurance v London Residuary Body* [1992] 2 AC 386 (HL) 390 (Lord Templeman). See also S Bridge, E Cooke and M Dixon (eds), *Megarry & Wade: The Law of Real Property*, 9th edn (London, Sweet & Maxwell, 2019) 16-001, 16-006.

[2] A lease will give rise to a term of years only if: (1) the grantor has the capacity to grant a legal estate (*Bruton v London & Quadrant Housing Trust* [2000] 1 AC 406 (HL)); and (2) the formality requirements for the creation of a legal estate are satisfied: Law of Property Act 1925

in land.[3] Consequently, the lease has been described as 'a hybrid, part contract, part property'.[4] It is certainly the case that many contractual rules apply to leases, including the doctrines of repudiation[5] and frustration,[6] and their terms are determined by the regular contractual rules of construction[7] and implication.[8] In this chapter, we are concerned only with leases that give rise to a term of years and, henceforth, we will treat the terms 'lease' and 'term of years' as interchangeable.[9]

Second, as Lord Templeman explained in *Street v Mountford*,[10] '[t]o constitute a tenancy the occupier must be granted exclusive possession for a fixed or periodic term'.[11] Whether an occupation agreement creates a lease often turns on whether the requirement of exclusive possession is satisfied. As a result, it is crucial to determine the exact meaning of exclusive possession. It is clear from the case law that exclusive possession is *not* to be equated with actual occupation. The main focus is on the legal entitlements of the grantee, rather than on which rights have actually been exercised in practice. Lord Templeman made this plain in *Street*: '[t]he tenant possessing exclusive possession is', for a time and subject to certain restrictions, 'able to exercise the rights of an owner of land' – most importantly, the right to control entry and to 'keep out strangers and keep out the landlord'.[12]

Third, when determining whether exclusive possession has been granted in any given case, it is necessary to focus on the substance of the arrangement rather than the label that the parties have used to describe the arrangement. After a series of cases involving shams (in the broad sense of this term),[13] in which landlords sought to avoid statutory regulation by labelling occupation agreements as 'licences' or otherwise disguising the nature of the agreement, the

(hereinafter 'LPA 1925') ss 52, 54. Originally, a lease created only personal rights, but it has been recognised for a long time that a lease may create a proprietary interest: 'a legal estate in leaseholds was created by the Statute of Gloucester 1278 and the Act of 1529 21 Hen. VIII, c.15': *Street v Mountford* [1985] AC 809 (HL) 814 (Lord Templeman).

[3] LPA 1925, ss 1(1)(b), 205(1)(xxvii).

[4] *Linden Gardens Trust Ltd v Lenesta Sludge Disposal Ltd* [1994] 1 AC 85 (HL) 108 (Lord Browne-Wilkinson).

[5] *Hussein v Mehlman* [1992] 2 EGLR 287.

[6] *National Carriers Ltd v Panalpina (Northern) Ltd* [1981] AC 675 (HL).

[7] *Javad v Aqil* [1991] 1 WLR 1007 (CA).

[8] *Liverpool City Council v Irwin* [1977] AC 239 (HL).

[9] We are, therefore, excluding so-called '*Bruton* leases' from our discussion.

[10] *Street v Mountford* [1985] AC 809 (HL).

[11] ibid 818. Lord Templeman may have thought that rent was also a necessary element of a lease, but it is not: see *Ashburn Anstalt v Arnold* [1989] Ch 1 (CA); LPA 1925, s 205(1)(xxvii).

[12] Ibid 816 (Lord Templeman). See also *National Car Parks Ltd v The Trinity Development Co (Banbury) Ltd* [2001] EWCA Civ 1686, [2002] 2 P & CR 18, [12] (Arden LJ); *Watts v Stewart* [2016] EWCA Civ 1247, [2018] Ch 423, [31]. And for a more extensive discussion, see N Mrockova, 'The Meaning of Exclusive Possession' [2021] *Conv* 183.

[13] The term 'sham' is sometimes used in a narrow way and differentiated from 'pretence' and 'mislabelling': see S Bright, 'Avoiding Tenancy Legislation: Sham and Contracting Out Revisited' [2002] *CLJ* 146, especially 150–60.

House of Lords in *Street* emphasised that the court must identify the true nature of the transaction between the parties. Lord Templeman explained that

> [i]f the agreement satisfied all the requirements of a tenancy, then the agreement produced a tenancy and the parties cannot alter the effect of the agreement by insisting that they only created a licence. The manufacture of a five-pronged implement for manual digging results in a fork even if the manufacturer ... insists that he intended to make and has made a spade.[14]

Conceptually, this is not difficult to comprehend, but in practice it is sometimes hard to know how much weight to give to the account of the parties' rights set out in the written instrument and when to look beyond it.[15]

The legal position is relatively straightforward where a lease is held by a single person. This chapter, however, focuses on more complex cases involving shared occupation and where it may be reasonably contended that the occupiers are co-owners of a lease. Where a lease is allegedly held by more than one person, it is not entirely clear how to determine whether the parties have exclusive possession. Difficult questions arise as to the precise meaning of exclusive possession (a requirement of a lease) and unity of possession (a requirement of valid co-ownership) and how these relate to one another. These issues are crucial for our understanding of the nature of co-ownership of a lease by two or more parties, but they are not widely discussed in the case law or fully investigated in the academic literature. These are some of the reasons why we wish to address, in section II of this chapter, Key Question 1.

As with the law of leases, many aspects of the law of co-ownership are clear and settled. First, there are two principal forms of co-ownership in English law: the joint tenancy and the tenancy in common.[16] Where an interest is co-owned by joint tenants, they, together, hold the entire interest and they do not each hold a separate interest.[17] In contrast, where an interest is co-owned by tenants in common,[18] each co-owner is entitled to a share and this entitlement is itself a transferable interest. As Lewison LJ explained in *Procter v Procter*, 'in the case of a tenancy in common, the co-owners hold the title in undivided shares .... [E]ach tenant in common has his own separate and distinct interest which he

[14] *Street* (n 10) 819.

[15] See, eg, *Antoniades v Villiers* [1990] 1 AC 417 (HL) where it was held that the purported right of the 'licensor' to use the rooms together with the 'licensees' and to permit others to do so was a pretence, as it was not genuinely intended. Whether a purported right actually has been exercised is clearly not the only relevant factor. See also *Aslan v Murphy* [1990] 1 WLR 766 (CA).

[16] Two other forms of co-ownership have been recognised: tenancies by entireties and coparcenary. The former was abolished by the Law of Property Act 1925, s 37, Sch 1, Pt VI; and the latter, which arose where an entailed interest descended to female heirs jointly, has virtually disappeared as a result of the 1925 reforms.

[17] *Wright v Gibbons* (1949) 78 CLR 313 (HCA) 329 (Dixon J); *Hammersmith and Fulham LBC v Monk* [1992] 1 AC 478 (HL) 492 (Lord Browne-Wilkinson). Each joint tenant does hold a separate right, as against the others, not to be excluded: see section II.B below.

[18] Contrast the view that land may be 'co-owned' where each 'co-owner' holds a separate estate in respect of the same land and there is no estate or interest that is held by the co-owners *together*: see, eg, R Smith, *Plural Ownership* (Oxford, OUP, 2005) 25–26.

can assign either to a third party or to his co-owner.'[19] A necessary element of both a joint tenancy and a tenancy in common is unity of possession,[20] and it is widely accepted that a joint tenancy, but not a tenancy in common, also requires unity of interest, time, and title.[21]

Second, while historically, a legal estate or interest in land could be held by co-owners as joint tenants or tenants in common, this was modified by the 1925 legislation. Section 1(6) of the Law of Property Act 1925 ('LPA 1925') provides that a legal estate or interest in land 'is not capable of subsisting or of being created in an undivided share'.[22] In the modern law, therefore, there is only one form of co-ownership in respect of legal estates and interests: the joint tenancy.

Third, where a legal estate is held by joint tenants, the estate is held on trust.[23] The trust might be created expressly or imposed by law. It is a noticeable feature of the 1925 Act that it imposes a trust on joint tenants where no trust was intended. For example, if X conveys a fee simple estate to A and B to hold outright as joint tenants, A and B will, as a result of section 36(1), hold the estate on trust for themselves.[24] Similarly, if X purports to convey a fee simple to A and B to hold in 'undivided shares', as a result of section 34(1), it 'shall … operate as if the land had been expressed to be conveyed' to A and B 'as joint tenants in trust' for themselves.[25] Crucially, where a legal estate is held on trust, the beneficiaries' interests can be overreached, which means a purchaser of the estate can take it free from the equitable interests of the beneficiaries. This sheds light on a central objective of the changes brought about to the law of co-ownership by the 1925 legislation. As Lord Oliver explained in *City of London Building Society v Flegg*, '[t]he whole philosophy of the Act in relation to undivided shares was that a purchaser of the legal estate … should not be concerned with the beneficial interests of the tenants in common'.[26]

One issue that is not well settled but crucial for our enquiry is in what circumstances two or more parties can be equitable tenants in common in respect of a lease. It is also not clear what the legal effect of this co-ownership

[19] *Procter v Procter* [2021] Ch 395 (CA) [21].

[20] Bl Comm II, 182. See also *Higgs v Leshel Maryas Investment Co Ltd* [2009] UKPC 47 [50]; Smith (n 18) 22. Unity of possession is discussed further in section II.B, below.

[21] See, eg, *AG Securities v Vaughan* [1990] 1 AC 417 (HL) 472 (Lord Oliver), 474 (Lord Jauncey); EH Burn and J Cartwright, *Cheshire and Burn's Modern Law of Real Property*, 18th edn (Oxford, OUP, 2011) 494–95; *Megarry and Wade* (n 1) 12-002–12-008. We consider this further in section II.B, below.

[22] For the meaning of 'legal estate' in s 1(6), see ss 1(4), 205(1)(x).

[23] The trust will count as a 'trust of land' within the meaning of section 1 of the Trusts of Land and Appointment of Trustees Act 1996 ('TOLATA 1996').

[24] *Cunningham-Reid v Public Trustee* [1944] KB 602 (CA); *Goodman v Gallant* [1986] Fam 106 (CA) 110 (Slade LJ); *City of London BS v Flegg* [1988] AC 54 (HL) 77–78 (Lord Oliver); *Crawley BC v Ure* [1996] QB 13 (CA) 24 (Glidewell LJ); *Stack v Dowden* [2007] UKHL 17, [2007] 2 AC 432, [55] (Baroness Hale). See also: Law Commission, *Transfer of Land: Trusts of Land* (LC 181 1989) paras 1.2, 3.1. For a contrary view, see AYS Georgiou, '*Marr v Collie*: The Ballooning of the Common Intention Constructive Trust' (2019) 82 *MLR* 145, 156.

[25] *Re Landi* [1939] Ch 828 (CA) 835–36 (Sir Wilfrid Greene MR).

[26] *City of London Building Society v Flegg* [1988] AC 54 (HL) 77.

arrangement is both internally (as among the lessees) and externally (as against the landlord and the rest of the world). We will examine these issues, which are the subject matter of Key Question 2, in section III.

II. KEY QUESTION 1: EXCLUSIVE POSSESSION AND UNITY OF POSSESSION IN CO-OWNED LEASES

We saw in section I that co-ownership of a lease involves the intersection of the rules on leases (requiring exclusive possession) and on valid co-ownership (requiring unity of possession). The purpose of this section is to elucidate the interaction of these rules by examining and clarifying the nature of, and the relationship between, exclusive possession and unity of possession in the context of co-owned leases. Section II.A examines the meaning of exclusive possession in this context. Section II.B then explores the meaning of unity of possession in the context of both forms of co-ownership (joint tenancies and tenancies in common) of leases. It offers a new analytical framework that sheds light on the meaning of unity of possession by differentiating between the position of co-owners at law and in equity. Finally, section II.C examines how the two concepts – exclusive possession and unity of possession – interact and relate to each other in the context of co-owned leases.

A. Meaning of Exclusive Possession in the Context of Co-owned Leases

Exclusive possession is a pre-condition for having a lease and a source of extensive powers of a tenant.[27] In the context of co-owned leases, this has two significant features. First, the putative co-lessees must show that they – *together* – are entitled to control entry and exclude the world in general, including the landlord. Co-lessees do not each hold separate rights to exclude; they have a *joint* right. This was emphasised by Sir George Waller in *AG Securities v Vaughan* when he said that the focus is on whether 'as a group they have exclusive possession'.[28] This approach was approved by Lord Bingham and Lord Jauncey in the House of Lords,[29] and in subsequent cases.[30]

Second, exclusive possession is a concept that focuses on the *external* effect of the entitlements that the co-lessees hold together. In other words, the co-occupiers who jointly enjoy exclusive possession hold a right to exclude against the world at large – the landlord, trespassers, etc – but the rules concerning exclusive possession do not *fully* determine or spell out the position of the

[27] See section I (text to n 11) for further details.
[28] *AG Securities v Vaughan* [1990] 1 AC 417, 433 (CA, dissenting).
[29] ibid 446 (Lord Bingham) 473–4 (Lord Jauncey).
[30] See, eg, *Mikeover v Brady* [1989] 3 All ER 618 (CA) 625 (Slade LJ).

co-lessees vis-à-vis each other. That relationship is largely governed by different principles, which are discussed in the next sub-section.

B. Meaning of Unity of Possession in the Context of Co-owned Leases

We saw in section I that any form of co-ownership – joint tenancy or tenancy in common – must satisfy unity of possession to be validly created. Unlike exclusive possession, unity of possession is primarily about the *internal arrangements* – the rights, powers, and obligations – of co-owners vis-à-vis each other. Unfortunately, the cases and existing literature provide only very limited discussion of what unity of possession means.

In the words of Roger Smith: '[t]he essence of unity of possession is that each co-owner is entitled to possession of all the property: not just part of it.'[31] That is useful in clarifying that co-ownership of an estate in a single piece of land (with unity of possession) is to be differentiated from parallel estates in two separate plots of land (with no unity of possession). Smith further stipulates that when establishing unity of possession one should 'not concentrate overly on physical occupation [but rather] the nature of the rights of the co-owner'.[32] Although useful on one level, these statements tell us very little about the meaning of 'possession' in this context, and fail to explain the relationship with the 'exclusive possession' that is required for a lease. The remainder of this subsection deals with the former enquiry; subsection II.C then deals with the latter.

We will suggest that, unlike exclusive possession which has a fixed meaning, unity of possession is a flexible concept which adapts to the nature of the right being co-owned.[33] Consequently, we will identify and briefly examine the nature of unity of possession in the context of co-owned leases with respect to four instances of co-ownership – distinguishing co-ownership at law from co-ownership in equity, and joint tenancies from tenancies in common:

	Joint tenancy	Tenancy in common
At law	1. ABC co-own a leasehold estate as joint tenants.	[available pre-1926] 2. ABC co-own a leasehold estate as tenants in common.
In equity	3. ABC co-own an equitable interest, as joints tenants, under a trust of a leasehold estate.	4. ABC co-own an equitable interest, as tenants in common, under a trust of a leasehold estate.

[31] Smith (n 18) 22.
[32] ibid.
[33] Contrast, for example, co-ownership of a freehold estate with co-ownership of an easement or a profit à prendre: unity of possession in respect of a fee simple differs significantly from unity of possession in respect of an easement or profit. For further discussion, see n 70 below.

In the first place, it is necessary to differentiate between *unity of possession at law and in equity*. At law, unity of possession relates to a legal estate (in the leasehold context, this means the term of years). In equity, unity of possession does not relate to a legal estate directly. Since co-ownership of legal estates in land is now managed through the mechanism of a trust,[34] unity of possession in equity relates, in this context, to an equitable interest held under a trust of the co-owned legal estate. The position at law is relatively well-discussed in the cases and we will draw on those discussions to illustrate what unity of possession at law means. The nature of unity of possession in equity is much less well-understood.

In the second place, it is necessary to consider what *unity of possession looks like in joint tenancies* – where it is merely one of four unities that must be present – compared to in *tenancies in common* – where it is the only unity that is required. As we will see, a major difficulty with the existing discussions of unity of possession in the context of joint tenancies is that, as one of several requirements, it is not always clear whether a particular implication or conclusion arises from a lack of unity of possession or one of the other unities. Tenancies in common, on the other hand, only require unity of possession and allow individuals to hold in undivided shares, meaning that each co-owner has certain powers to deal with their undivided share in the co-owned property without the need to agree or co-ordinate with the others.[35]

When combined, these two sets of options – law vs equity, joint tenancy vs tenancy in common – create four possible forms of co-owning in the context of leases. The remainder of this section briefly examines these four possibilities. Section III will then build on this basic examination when considering whether a tenancy in common in equity remains available following the enactment of the LPA 1925.

	Joint tenancy	Tenancy in common
At law	1. ABC co-own a leasehold estate as joint tenants.	[available pre-1926] 2. ABC co-own a leasehold estate as tenants in common.
In equity	3. ABC co-own an equitable interest, as joint tenants, under a trust of a leasehold estate.	4. ABC co-own an equitable interest, as tenants in common, under a trust of a leasehold estate.

There are several important cases that deal with *legal joint tenancies*. Unfortunately, many decided cases examine the four unities together, which obscures the meaning of unity of possession, and pay no, or only limited,

[34] See section I (text to n 23).

[35] This is discussed further below: see text to n 60. See also sections I and III.B for discussion of the meaning of 'undivided share'.

attention to the meaning of unity of possession per se. For example, Lord Bridge in *Hammersmith and Fulham LBC v Monk*[36] stated that:

> all positive dealings with a joint tenancy require the concurrence of all joint tenants if they are to be effective. Thus, a single joint tenant cannot exercise a break clause in a lease, surrender the term, make a disclaimer, exercise an option to renew the term or apply for relief from forfeiture.[37]

His Lordship did not explain which, if any, of these consequences are caused by the lack of unity of possession, nor shed any light on how unity of possession can be lost in these cases. Similarly, in *Hounslow LBC v Pilling*[38] the Court of Appeal refused to accept that a notice given by one joint tenant with a view to exercising a break clause could be effective to bring an end to a legal joint tenancy. However, no explanation was given as to whether this was a consequence of unity of possession or some other factor.[39]

In some cases, the discussion is more clearly separated, but the meaning of unity of possession is not fully explored. For example, in *Wiseman v Simpson* Ralph Gibson LJ stated that '[a]s joint tenants each has the [legal] right to occupy and neither can lawfully exclude the other.'[40] In *AG Securities*, Sir George Waller offered further thoughts in his dissenting judgment in the Court of Appeal, stating that unity of possession 'must be possession of the whole. Each occupant was given the right to use the flat and so it could be said that there was unity of right to use the flat'.[41] In the House of Lords, Lord Jauncey and Lord Oliver followed Sir George on this point, but their Lordships simply asserted that there was no unity of possession on the facts without providing a detailed explanation.[42] As a result, the modern cases offer only limited assistance when ascertaining the meaning of unity of possession where a lease is co-owned by joint tenants.

There are, however, several older cases that shed some light on what it means to say that, where a legal estate is held by joint tenants, each joint tenant is entitled to 'possession of the whole'.[43] These cases support the proposition that, where a legal estate is co-owned by joint tenants, it is not tortious for one of the joint tenants to have the sole occupation of, or to otherwise solely enjoy, the land, but it *is* tortious for one of the joint tenants to oust (ie exclude) the other(s) from the land. In *Smales v Dale*, for instance, the Court

[36] *Hammersmith and Fulham LBC v Monk* [1992] 1 AC 478 (HL).

[37] ibid 490.

[38] *Hounslow LBC v Pilling* [1993] 1 WLR 1242 (CA).

[39] Some commentators maintain, plausibly, that the consequences discussed in this paragraph are aspects of unity of interest: see, eg, *Megarry and Wade* (n 1) 12-006.

[40] *Wiseman v Simpson* [1988] 1 WLR 35 (CA) 42.

[41] *AG Securities* (n 28) 436.

[42] ibid 472 (Lord Oliver), 474 (Lord Jauncey). See Smith (n 18) 24.

[43] See, eg, *Smales v Dale* (1614) Hob 120, 80 ER 269; *Fisher v Wigg* (1700) 1 Salk 391, 392; 91 ER 339, 340 (Holt CJ); *Ford v Lord Grey* (1703) 6 Modern 44, 87 ER 807. See also 4 Bacon Abr 516 (7th edn).

of King's Bench, according to Hobart's report, opined that the 'possession' of one co-owner is 'over all lawful' and 'therefore … a joint-tenant, or tenant in common, can never be disseised by his fellow, but by an actual ouster'.[44] In a New Zealand case, *McCormick v McCormick*,[45] in which a husband and wife held a legal estate in certain land as joint tenants, Salmond J considered several eighteenth- and nineteenth-century English cases and averred that, where one joint tenant, A, had had the sole use of the land, the other joint tenant, B, was entitled to receive compensation from A if A 'has actually excluded [B] and wrongfully prevented him from having the use of the common property'.[46] Where one joint tenant acquires the fruits of the land, such as profits and rents, this does not, without more, amount to an ouster and is not tortious,[47] but they may be required to account for what they have acquired.[48]

Building on both the older and modern cases, the meaning of unity of possession where a leasehold estate is co-owned by joint tenants appears to refer to a situation where each legal joint tenant has, as against the other joint tenant(s), a right to occupy the whole. More precisely, each legal joint tenant has, as against the other joint tenant(s): (a) a right not to be excluded – or 'ousted' – from the land; and (b) a liberty to access the land, to acquire the profits, and to occupy or otherwise make use of it. Each joint tenant, therefore, owes their co-tenants a duty not to exclude them from the land.[49]

When ascertaining the meaning of unity of possession with regard to a *legal tenancy in common*, we must look at the pre-1926 case law because, as we saw in section I, legal estates in land can no longer be held under a tenancy in common, following the enactment of the LPA 1925. Nevertheless, an examination of the rules that were in place before 1926 provides a crucial insight into the mechanics of co-ownership – and the meaning of unity of possession – in this context. It also provides a useful point of comparison between legal and equitable co-ownership.

The case law shows that the presence of unity of possession where a legal lease was held by co-lessees as tenants in common had several important features: each co-lessee was entitled to occupy the land; each co-lessee could have lawfully dealt with a greater or smaller part of the land than the other co-lessees so long as they did not oust the others; and if a co-lessee received and kept more of the

[44] *Smales v Dale* (1614) Hob 120, 80 ER 269.

[45] *McCormick v McCormick* [1921] NZLR 384.

[46] ibid 385. See also *Harrison v Walker* [1919] 2 KB 453 (KB) 458 (McCardie J).

[47] Co Litt 200b; *Willion v Berkley* (1561) 1 Plow 223, 247; 75 ER 339, 378 (Anthony Brown J): 'if there are two join-tenants, and the one takes all the profits of the land, the common law permits it'.

[48] Before 1926, a joint tenant was able to bring an action of account under the statute 4 & 5 Anne c. 16 where: (i) his co-tenant received a monetary payment (eg rent) or something else from a third party that the co-owners were entitled to by virtue of their co-ownership; and (ii) the co-tenant had received and kept more than her proper share. See *Wheeler v Horne* (1740) Willes 208, 125 ER 1135; *Henderson v Eason* (1851) 17 QB Rep 701. In the modern law, a joint tenant of a legal estate is a trustee and a requirement to account for rents and profits is imposed by the law of trusts: *Re Landi* [1939] Ch 828 (CA); E Cooke, 'Equitable Accounting' [1995] *Conv* 391, 397–98.

[49] Where, however, there is a trust of land, the common law position will be subject to the statutory scheme created by TOLATA 1996.

fruits than they were entitled to, they may have been required to account to the others. We will now consider each element in turn.

First, each legal tenant in common had a right vis-à-vis the other co-owners to occupy the land.[50] This does not mean that the occupation had to be concurrent or equal.[51] It must not, however, have amounted to an ouster.[52] This is illustrated by the House of Lords' decision in *Jacobs v Seward*.[53] In that case, A and B co-owned a lease with respect to three fields as legal tenants in common. B put a lock on the gate and cut the grass which he turned into hay and removed from the field. A sued B for trespass, but the court held that no tort was committed. Lord Hatherley LC explained that '[s]o long as a tenant in common is only exercising lawfully the rights he has as tenant in common, no action can lie against him by his co-tenant.'[54] It appears, therefore, that where one legal tenant in common relied on their shared rights by solely occupying the land, this did not contravene unity of possession. However, His Lordship added that B would have committed a wrong against A in 'cases in which something has been done which has destroyed the common property, or where there has been a direct and positive exclusion of the co-tenant in common from the common property, he seeking to exercise his rights therein, and being denied the exercise of such rights'.[55] So, the mere fact that one legal tenant in common was in sole occupation of co-owned land did not contravene unity of possession, but destroying part of the land or preventing the other co-lessees from entering or occupying the land amounted to a wrong and contravened unity of possession.[56]

Second, where a legal tenant in common acquired the fruits of the land, such as rents and profits, they may have been required to account to their co-tenants.[57] As is the case with respect to joint tenants, however, it was not wrongful for a legal tenant in common to acquire the rents or profits.[58] A legal tenant in common, therefore, had a liberty to acquire the fruits of the land, but if they did so, they were liable, in certain circumstances, to account to their co-tenants.

While the core elements of unity of possession among legal joint tenants and legal tenants in common were the same, it is important to recognise that

[50] See Smith (n 18) 22, 28, 120, 131.

[51] *M'Mahon v Burchell* (1846) 2 Ph 127, 41 ER 889; 1 Coop T Cott 457, 47 ER 944; *Jones v Jones* [1977] 1 WLR 438 (CA) 441–42(Lord Denning MR).

[52] *Goodtitle v Tombs* (1770) 3 Wils KB 118, 95 ER 965; *Jacobs v Seward* (1872) LR 5 HL 464 (HL); *Luke v Luke* (1936) 36 SR NSW 310 (NSWSC); *Jones v Jones* [1977] 1 WLR 438 (CA) 441–42 (Lord Denning MR).

[53] *Jacobs v Seward* (1872) LR 5 HL 464 (HL).

[54] ibid 474.

[55] ibid. See also *Wilkinson v Haygarth* (1847) 12 QB 837 (QB).

[56] Compare *Baker v Barclay's Bank* [1955] 1 WLR 822, 827 (Devlin J). See also *Re Kostiuk* (2002) 215 DLR 78.

[57] A tenant in common was liable to account under the statute 4 & 5 Anne, c 16 in certain circumstances: see n 48 above and the cases cited there. See also *Bull v Bull* [1955] 1 QB 234 (CA) 237 (Lord Denning MR).

[58] *Martyn v Knowllys* (1799) 8 Term Rep 145, 101 ER 1313; *Jacobs v Seward* (1872) LR 5 HL 464 (HL); *Kennedy v De Trafford* [1897] AC 180 (HL) 186–87 (Lord Herschell), 190–91 (Lord Macnaghten).

the fact that legal tenants in common, but not joint tenants, held 'undivided shares' affected the entitlements that flowed from unity of possession.[59] Each legal tenant in common could deal with their undivided share independently of the other co-lessees.[60] Importantly in this context, unity of possession was not disturbed by such individual dealings. Instead, the co-holding structure remained in place while the identity of the holders of the individual undivided shares – and thus the identity of the holders of a right to occupation and the bearers of the duty not to oust – changed.

	Joint tenancy	**Tenancy in common**
At law	1. ABC co-own a leasehold estate as joint tenants	[available pre-1926] 2. ABC co-own a leasehold estate as tenants in common
In equity	3. ABC co-own an equitable interest, as joint tenants, under a trust of a leasehold estate	4. ABC co-own an equitable interest, as tenants in common, under a trust of a leasehold estate

The meaning of *unity of possession in equity* is much more problematic and is generally not fully or accurately explored in the cases or academic literature.[61] On one view, the rights of co-lessees (joint tenants and tenants in common) at law and in equity are similar, or even the same. Lord Denning MR stated in *Bull v Bull*: '[s]uch being the rights of legal tenants in common, I think that the rights of equitable owners in common are the same, save only for such differences as are necessarily consequent on the interest being equitable and not legal.'[62] Similarly, Graham Barnsley argued that 'the fact that one or more of the equitable co-owners were also trustees at law [ie legal co-owners] afforded them no superior right of possession'.[63] He continued by saying that '[t]he right [of equitable co-owners to occupy the land] is enjoyed qua beneficiary. He is entitled by reason of his interest in the land, i.e., by virtue of his equitable joint tenancy or tenancy in common.'[64] And he concluded by adding that '[t]he fact

[59] Contrast DG Barnsley, 'Co-owners' Rights to Occupy Trust Land' [1998] *CLJ* 123, 127: 'The incidents flowing from this unity of possession were the same, whether the co-owners were joint tenants or tenants in common.'

[60] This can lead to the fragmentation of the title. A desire to avoid this is one of the main reasons why the LPA 1925 abolished legal tenancies in common: see section III.C.

[61] Note that a statutory regime for dealing with occupation and 'compensation' for occupation under trusts of land, which is not considered in detail here, was introduced by TOLATA 1996 (see especially ss 12–15).

[62] *Bull* (n 57) 237.

[63] Barnsley (n 59) 128. Note that Barnsley's contentions are at times difficult to reconcile – in some parts of his argument he recognises that the rights are not the same (because, for instance, the rights of equitable co-owners under a trust do not bind people in general), while elsewhere he appears to claim that they are identical.

[64] ibid 131–32. The contention that, in the common law (as opposed to under TOLATA), a beneficiary of a trust of land has, qua beneficiary, a right to occupy should be distinguished from the

that [co-owners] happen to be beneficiaries under a trust of land and that the legal estate is vested in others on trust for them is quite immaterial.' However, we believe that this account is, at best, misleading and, at worse, simply false.

As we have seen, co-ownership of a legal estate nowadays gives rise to a trust.[65] Unity of possession in equity, therefore, attaches *not* to a legal estate (the leasehold estate in our context) but rather to the equitable interest in respect of the estate that is held on trust.[66] It is important to recognise that, where an equitable interest under a trust is co-owned, the rights and obligations of the co-owners inter se are not the same as where a legal estate is co-owned. This takes us back to the qualification articulated by Lord Denning in *Bull v Bull*, which was mentioned earlier: 'save only for such differences as are necessarily consequent on the interest being equitable and not legal'.[67] We know that there are significant differences between equitable rights under a trust and legal estates in land.[68] For instance, an equitable interest under a trust does not comprise a right to exclusive possession vis-à-vis the world at large.[69] The position of equitable co-owners is in *this* respect (though not others) similar to that of those who co-hold an easement: if A and B co-own a freehold estate in Blackacre and co-hold an easement (eg a right of way) over Greenacre, what they co-hold in respect of a Greenacre is a *non-possessory* right – that is to say, they do not co-hold a right to exclusive possession of Greenacre.[70] It cannot be correct, therefore, to say that the rights of those who co-own a legal estate are the same as those that emanate from co-ownership of an equitable interest under a trust.

The discussion above also suggests that unity of possession does not have a fixed meaning in all cases of co-ownership or co-holding; on the contrary,

narrower claim that the existence and extent of the occupation rights of beneficiaries under the common law depends upon the purpose of the trust: see, eg, Smith (n 18) 121.

[65] See section I.

[66] M Grant, 'Co-ownership: What Could be Simpler?' [1987] *CLP* 159, 163. For this reason, Grant describes this form of co-ownership as a mode of indirect co-ownership.

[67] See n 62 above and text thereto.

[68] See, eg, *Schalit v Joseph Nadler Ltd* [1933] 2 KB 79 (DC); *Akers v Samba Financial Group* [2017] UKSC 6, [2017] AC 424. There are several prominent theories of the precise nature of an equitable interest under a trust. It is not possible for us to adjudicate on the merits of these here, but any defensible theory must allow that there are differences between a legal estate and an equitable interest under a trust.

[69] *Leigh & Sillivan Ltd v Aliakmon Shipping Co Ltd* [1986] AC 785 (HL); *Parker-Tweedale v Dunbar Bank Plc (No 1)* [1991] Ch 12 (CA); *MCC Proceeds v Lehman Bros* [1998] 4 All ER 675 (CA); *Roberts v Gill & Co* [2010] UKSC 22, [2011] 1 AC 24, [45]–[62] (Lord Collins JSC). For further discussion, see, eg, J Edelman, 'Two Fundamental Questions for the Law of Trusts' (2013) 129 *LQR* 66; W Swadling, 'In Defence of Formalism' in A Robertson and J Goudkamp (eds), *Form and Substance in the Law of Obligations* (Oxford, Hart Publishing, 2019) 103–110; B McFarlane and A Televantos, 'Third Party Effects in Private Law: Form and Function' in P Miller and J Oberdick (eds), *Oxford Studies in Private Law Theory, Volume 1* (Oxford, OUP, 2020) 112–14.

[70] It is a basic and uncontested feature of easements that they are, in this sense of the term, 'non-possessory' (see, eg, J Gaunt QC and The Hon. Mr Justice Morgan (eds), *Gale on the Law of Easements*, 21st edn (London, Sweet & Maxwell, 2020) 1-01, 1-03) and, therefore, unity of possession in respect of an easement *cannot* entail that each co-owner has a right to possession.

it is context-specific. In the same way that unity of possession in respect of an easement pertains to mere limited rights of enjoyment and not to a right to exclusive possession, the unity of possession that exists where those who co-hold an equitable interest under a trust of a leasehold estate also has a meaning and effect that differs from unity of possession in respect of a legal estate.[71]

C. Relationship between Exclusive Possession and Unity of Possession

So far in this section, we have seen that exclusive possession in the law of leases refers to the lessee's (or co-lessees') right to exclude the world at large, including the landlord. We have also observed that unity of possession is a source of internal rights and duties among co-owners (including co-lessees) and that the exact content and scope of these depends on whether the co-owners hold as joint tenants or tenants in common, and whether they hold the leasehold estate directly (and so co-own at law) or whether they only have an equitable interest under a trust of land (and thus co-own in equity). This final part of section II looks at the relationship between the two concepts – exclusive possession and unity of possession – and the importance of correctly understanding their relationship and interaction.

A limited understanding of how the two concepts interact has led to incomplete, misleading, and at times outright wrong analyses of the rules. For example, Sir George Waller in *AG Securities* discussed unity of possession in connection with a landlord's rights to enter the land,[72] but a landlord's ability to enter affects exclusive possession, not unity of possession.[73] Similarly, Lord Oliver and Lord Jauncey in the House of Lords concluded that there was no exclusive possession and appear to assume that it simply followed from this that there was no unity of possession.[74] This is problematic because, as we have seen, unity of possession and exclusive possession are not the same.

Some academic analyses are also not in line with our understanding of how the two concepts interact. Susan Bright, for example, writes that 'unity of possession is not simply to do with de facto occupation, it is to do with the legal right to exclude non-owners from the property.'[75] But while it is true that both exclusive possession and unity of possession focus on the parties' *legal* entitlements rather than the facts on the ground, it is crucial to distinguish: (a) the entitlements that the co-lessees, together, hold against the landlord and the rest of the world, which is what exclusive possession is concerned with;

[71] It is not possible to provide a comprehensive analysis of unity of possession in this chapter, but some of the implications of the fact that the effect of unity of possession depends on the nature of the right that is co-owned are further explored in sections II.C and III.C.

[72] *AG Securities* (n 28) 436.

[73] See sections II.A and II.B above.

[74] See *AG Securities* (n 28) above and text thereto.

[75] S Bright '*Street v Mountford* Revisited' in S Bright (ed), *Landlord and Tenant Law: Past, Present and Future* (Oxford, Hart Publishing, 2006) 34–35.

from (b) the entitlements that each co-lessee has as against the other co-lessees, which is what unity of possession is primarily about. Similarly, Peter Sparkes states that '[u]nity of possession might be equated with a joint right of exclusive possession.'[76] But this cannot be right either. Although they overlap and coexist in the context of the co-ownership of leases, they are not identical, and the degree of their overlap depends on the right to which they are applied. In a case where a legal lease is co-owned, the co-lessees' joint right to exclude the world at large is distinct from, and therefore must not be equated with, the rights that each co-lessee has, individually, against the others. Exclusive possession and unity of possession are even further differentiated in cases of non-possessory rights, such as co-ownership of equitable interests under a trust of land or co-ownership of an easement, because there can be no exclusive possession in such cases at all.

So, is there a better way for analysing the relationship of exclusive possession and unity of possession in the context of co-owned leases? First, it is clear that there is an overlap between unity of possession and exclusive possession in some instances (eg a legal joint tenancy of a lease[77]) but not in others. Making broad statements about the overlap of the two concepts without specifying that this is only true of a legal joint tenancy of a lease is unhelpful.[78] As a result, it is best to always be aware of the nature and source of the relevant rights. When dealing with co-lessees' rights to exclude (and other related rights that affect third parties) one has to consider exclusive possession. On the other hand, when dealing with internal arrangements between the co-lessees – their rights and obligations inter se – it is necessary to focus on unity of possession and the mode of co-ownership (and, thus, on whether unity of possession is the only requirement, as in a tenancy in common, or whether it is supported by other unities, as in a joint tenancy). This is particularly important given that unity of possession is a flexible concept that adapts to the nature of the right or interest to which it is applied. If we separate the two concepts, it becomes much easier to understand both what needs to be shown and the implications of co-ownership in particular contexts.

III. KEY QUESTION 2: EQUITABLE TENANCIES IN COMMON IN THE LEASEHOLD CONTEXT

Our aim in this section is to address Key Question 2 and, thus, to identify the circumstances in which two or more parties may be equitable tenants in common

[76] P Sparkes, 'Co-tenants, Joint Tenants and Tenants in Common' (1989) 18 *Anglo-American LR* 151, 152.

[77] A similar point may be made in relation to a legal joint tenancy of a freehold estate.

[78] Smith also makes this mistake when he talks about unity of possession as meaning that each co-owner 'own the whole thing together, or … have rights to the whole (recognized by the right to possess the whole and by survivorship on death)': Smith (n 18) 28.

under a trust of a leasehold estate, and the legal effect of such an arrangement both internally (as among the co-tenants) and externally (as against the landlord and the rest of the world). We saw in section II that the precise legal effects of a co-ownership arrangement depend not only upon which specific form of co-ownership (joint tenancy or tenancy in common) is present, but on the type of interest that is co-owned. These points are connected, not least because, as we have already pointed out,[79] a tenancy in common can exist in respect of an equitable interest but not in respect of a legal estate or interest in land. For our purposes, it is particularly important to distinguish co-ownership of a leasehold estate from co-ownership of an equitable interest under a trust of a lease. As we saw in section II.B, a lease and an equitable interest under a trust have different incidents, and consequently the legal effects – both internally (ie, among the co-lessees inter se) and externally (ie, vis-à-vis the landlord and the rest of the world) – of co-owning the former and co-owning the latter are not the same.

In what follows, we will first explore whether it is possible for parties to hold an equitable interest as tenants in common in the leasehold context and, if it is, the circumstances in which such an arrangement will be present. We find it puzzling that, in the existing case law, the creation of an equitable tenancy in common in respect of a lease by virtue of section 34(2) of the Law of Property Act 1925 has rarely been considered, and seems never to have been successfully applied,[80] in the context of shared occupation where it is at least arguable that the parties intended to create a tenancy in common in respect of a lease. The courts have often taken a bifurcated approach: either a lease is granted to the occupiers *as joint tenants*, which will be the case only if the four unities are present, *or* the occupiers are *mere licensees*. In some cases, the courts have also recognised a third option – that co-occupiers hold parallel leases over distinct parts of the land (for example, separate leases in respect of different rooms).[81] But the courts have largely overlooked another important possibility: that the co-lessees are equitable tenants in common. We are not the first to point this out. Smith, for instance, has observed that in *AG Securities v Vaughan* the question as to whether the four occupiers were equitable tenants in common 'was not considered by the House of Lords'.[82] Similarly, Bright has noted that in *Mikeover v Brady*, the Court of Appeal did not consider whether the occupiers could be equitable tenants in common.[83] In the remainder of this section, we seek to build on these insights. In section III.A, we consider whether an equitable tenancy in common has been recognised by the courts in the leasehold context

[79] Text to n 22.

[80] As we will see, an equitable tenancy in common was found in *Malayan Credit v Jack Chia-MPH Ltd*, but not through the application of s 34(2): see n 84 below and text thereto.

[81] In such circumstances there is no unity of possession and, therefore, there cannot be a co-owned lease: see Smith (n 18) 23–26.

[82] Smith (n 18) 24. See also Sparkes (n 76).

[83] Bright, 'Protecting Multiple Occupancy' (1992) 142 *NLJ* 575.

and how such an arrangement may arise. In section III.B, we investigate, through examining the scope of section 34(2) of 1925 Act, whether an equitable tenancy in common could arise in a case such as *Mikeover*. In section III.C we analyse the legal consequences of such an arrangement for the occupiers, the landlord, and third parties. In section III.D, we briefly reflect on the desirability of the current rules.

A. Recognition of a Tenancy in Common in Equity in the Context of Co-owned Leases

It is clear that, in the modern law, a tenancy in common may arise in equity in the leasehold context. This is illustrated by *Malayan Credit v Jack Chia-MPH Ltd*,[84] in which a legal lease was granted to two companies, A and B, as joint tenants. The Privy Council held that that A and B were tenants in common in equity in unequal shares. As is clear from the discussion in section II.B, an equitable tenancy in common in this context means a tenancy in common in respect of an equitable interest under a trust. Given this, the Privy Council must be regarded as having decided that A and B held the legal lease as joint tenants on trust for themselves and that they therefore (also) co-owned an equitable interest, which they held as tenants in common in unequal shares.

While *Malayan Credit* concerned the law of Singapore, it can hardly be doubted that, in England and Wales too, parties may hold an equitable interest in respect of a lease as tenants in common.[85] This is demonstrated by the fact that if A and B hold a lease as joint tenants on trust for themselves (as a result of, for instance, the operation section 36(1) LPA 1925),[86] A and B may severe the equitable joint tenancy and thereby create an equitable tenancy in common.[87]

How may two or more persons acquire an equitable interest as tenants in common under a trust of a lease? There are various circumstances in which such a trust will arise. An obvious example is where a trust of a lease for tenants in common is *expressly* created, as for example where X assigns a lease to A and B to hold on trust for C and D as tenants in common,[88] or where X grants a lease to A and B to hold on trust for themselves as tenants in common. A further example, and one that is particularly significant for our purposes, concerns section 34(2) of the 1925 Act. Under this provision, an equitable tenancy in

[84] *Malayan Credit v Jack Chia-MPH Ltd* [1986] AC 549 (PC).

[85] See *Cunningham-Reid v Public Trustee* [1944] KB 602 (CA), discussed below: text to n 105.

[86] This is discussed in section I: see text to n 23.

[87] See, eg, LPA 1925, s 36(2).

[88] *Re Selous* [1901] 1 Ch 921 (Ch) (decided before the enactment of the LPA 1925, but there is no good reason to think that such a trust could not be created today).

common in respect of a lease may arise in the absence of a declaration of trust. It states:

> Where ... land is expressed to be conveyed to any persons in undivided shares and those persons are of full age, the conveyance shall (notwithstanding anything to the contrary in this Act) operate as if the land had been expressed to be conveyed to the grantees, or, if there are more than four grantees, to the four first named in the conveyance, as joint tenants in trust for the persons interested in the land.

As we have said, the courts have only rarely considered whether section 34(2) may be invoked where two or more parties claim to be co-owners of a lease. We believe that this is to be regretted and that some cases should have been decided differently if the courts had given due consideration to the provision. With a view to supporting this contention, we will first consider the *applicability* of section 34(2) and then turn to its *effect*.

B. Applicability of Section 34(2)

In *Mikeover v Brady*, the Court of Appeal's view was that, while the occupation agreement purported to confer on A and B a 'joint right of exclusive occupation', it did not grant a lease to them as joint tenants because, according to the terms, each was to owe a *separate* rental obligation and, therefore, there was no unity of interest.[89] No consideration was given to section 34(2) or to the possibility that the occupiers may have had a tenancy in common in equity. In our view, this was a mistake. To explain why, it is necessary to examine section 34(2)'s scope of application.

The provision applies only where 'land is expressed to be conveyed to any persons in undivided shares'. Let us begin with the meaning of 'convey'. Section 205(1)(ii) of the 1925 Act states that '[i]n this Act unless the context otherwise requires', '"[c]onveyance" includes a ... lease, ... release and every other assurance of property or an interest therein by any instrument' and '"convey" has a corresponding meaning'.[90] In *Rye v Rye*, the House of Lords held that a disposition can count as an 'conveyance' within the meaning of section 205(1)(ii), and within the ordinary meaning of the term, only if it involves an instrument in writing.[91] It seems that this is applicable in the context of section 34(2), though the position is not settled.[92]

[89] *Mikeover* (n 30).

[90] LPA 1925, s 205(1)(ii).

[91] *Rye v Rye* [1962] AC 496 (HL). While writing is necessary, it may not always be sufficient: where, under ss 52 and 54 of the Law of Property Act 1925, a deed is required, it is arguable that there is no 'conveyance' unless there is a deed, see *Borman v Griffith* [1930] 1 Ch 493 (Ch) 498–99 (Maughan J). One may argue that, conversely, where these provisions permit an oral grant of a lease, this should count as a 'conveyance', at least for the purposes of section 34(2).

[92] See *Rye* (n 91).

How should the term 'undivided shares' in section 34(2) be interpreted? It cannot be doubted that a conveyance to persons as tenants in common counts as a conveyance 'in undivided shares'.[93] This is because, as Lewison LJ explained in *Procter v Procter*,[94] 'in the case of a tenancy in common, the co-owners hold the title in undivided shares'.[95] It is also clear that a conveyance to parties as joint tenants does *not* amount to a conveyance 'in undivided shares'.[96]

Section 34(2) applies only if land is *expressed* to be conveyed to persons in undivided shares. Clearly, a conveyance 'to A and B in undivided shares' would fall within the subsection (assuming that A and B are of full age). In light of the discussion in the previous paragraph, it seems a conveyance to 'A and B as tenants in common' would also be covered. But is it necessary for the conveyance to actually state that A and B are to hold 'in undivided shares' or as 'tenants in common', or is it sufficient that the conveyance includes statements or terms that indicate that A and B are to so hold? Some commentators have claimed that the former, narrower reading is correct.[97] The better view, however, is that the broad interpretation should be preferred. This is for three reasons. First, the broad interpretation is in line with the views of Sir Benjamin Cherry, the principal drafter of the 1925 legislation. In his lectures on the 1925 legislation, Cherry opined that, by virtue of section 34, 'a conveyance *which would otherwise have created* undivided shares will operate as if the land had been conveyed to the grantees, or if more than four to the four first named, as joint tenants upon trust'.[98] He added that '[a]ccording to the definition of a "conveyance", it will include a declaration of trust in favour of persons in undivided shares.'[99] Second, the broad interpretation aligns with, and more fully secures, the purpose of the provision, which, as Cherry indicated, is to ensure that where parties attempt to create, by a conveyance, a legal tenancy in common in respect of land, it takes effect as though the estate had been conveyed to the disponees

[93] See, eg, *Goodman v Gallant* [1986] Fam 106 (CA) 110 (Slade LJ). It has been suggested that the term 'undivided shares' does not refer only to a tenancy in common, but also includes, for instance, coparceny: 'Concurrent Interests in Land' (1944) 9 *Conv* 37, 72, 181, at 185. This is not something that it is necessary for us to explore in this chapter – what matters, for our purposes, is that a conveyance to persons as tenants in common falls within s 34(2).

[94] *Procter v Procter* [2021] Ch 395 (CA).

[95] ibid [21].

[96] *Cf* (1944) 9 *Conv* 181, 183, concluding that 'the *probable* interpretation of the Act is that for the purposes of the property legislation the expression "undivided shares" excludes joint tenancy'. When one considers ss 1(6), 34, and 36 together, while also keeping in mind the aims of the legislation, it seems obvious that a conveyance to joint tenants does not count as a conveyance 'in undivided shares'.

[97] eg, (1944) 9 *Conv* 37, at 38–46.

[98] B Cherry, *The New Property Acts* (Solicitors' Law Stationery Society Ltd, 1926) 26 (emphasis added).

[99] ibid. *Cf* C Harpum 'Overreaching, Trustees' Powers and the Reform of the 1925 Legislation' [1990] *CLJ* 277, 298–302.

as joint tenants.[100] Third, the broad interpretation is consistent with the position, which was already well established in the case law prior to the enactment of the legislation, that an intention to create a tenancy in common may be found where, in the words of Lord Hatherley LC, there is 'anything which in the slightest degree indicates an intention to divide the property'.[101]

If our interpretation of the scope of application of section 34(2) is correct, it is certainly arguable that the sub-section should have been applied in *Mikeover v Brady*. Since the agreement, which consisted of two written documents, purported by its express terms to: (i) confer on A and B, together, a right of exclusive possession in respect of a flat for six months; and (ii) impose an obligation on each of them to pay £86.66 per month, this seems to be a case in which the grantor attempted to grant a lease, in writing, to A and B as tenants in common in equal shares. This analysis is in line with the decision in *Re North*, where a testator devised his title to land to A and B on condition that they 'pay in equal shares' ten shillings per week to the testator's wife and the court held that, since the condition imposed separate obligations on A and B, the testator had expressed an intention to transfer the title to them as tenants in common.[102] Putting all this together, *Mikeover v Brady* may be regarded as a case in which 'land' was 'expressed to be conveyed' to two parties, who were of full age, 'in undivided shares' and thus as a case in which section 34(2) was applicable. If this is right, the next question is: what is the effect of the sub-section?

C. Effect of Section 34(2) in the Current Law

If the discussion in section III.B is correct, it is important to now consider the legal effect of section 34(2). The provision can make co-occupiers, who would otherwise be mere licensees, into co-lessees and thereby significantly affect their legal relations inter se and vis-à-vis the rest of the world. But how, precisely, are its effects to be understood? Where section 34(2) applies, the conveyance is to 'operate as if the land had been expressed to be conveyed to the grantees … as joint tenants in trust for the persons interested in the land'. What does this mean? In particular, if the conveyance operates 'as if the land had been expressed to be conveyed' to the disponees 'as joint tenants', does this mean that the *standard rules on joint tenancies apply*, with the result that, where an estate is vested in two or more parties by the provision, the four unities must be present? Our primary aim in this sub-section is to show that an affirmative answer to this

[100] See Sir A Underhill, *A Concise Explanation of Lord Birkenhead's Act (the Law of Property Act 1922) in Plain Language* (Butterworth & Co, 1922) 99–102; AF Topham, *The Law of Property Acts, 1925* (Solicitors' Law Stationary Society Ltd, 1926) 27–28.

[101] *Robertson v Fraser* (1871) LR 6 Ch App 696, 699. See also *Re North* (n 102) below and text thereto.

[102] *Re North* [1952] Ch 397 (Ch). See also these pre-1925 cases: *Kew v Rouse* (1685) 1 Vern 353; *Robertson v Fraser* (1871) LR 6 Ch App 696, 699 (Lord Hatherley LC).

question is supported by the existing case law and to analyse the main ramifications of this for the legal position of the co-tenants as against each other, the landlord, and the rest of the world. We will then briefly comment on the appropriateness of the law's current approach.

The case law supports the proposition that, when a joint tenancy of a legal estate is imposed by section 34(2), the four unities will be present in respect of the legal estate. In *AG Securities v Vaughan*, the House of Lords held that in order for two or more persons to be joint tenants of a lease, the four unities must be present.[103] In *Mikeover v Brady*, Slade LJ said: '[i]t is … well settled that four unities must be present for the creation of a joint tenancy, namely the unities of possession, interest, title and time.'[104] In these cases, the courts did not draw a distinction between joint tenancies imposed by section 34(2) and joint tenancies created in other ways, though one should not place great weight on this for, as we have seen, no consideration was given to section 34(2) in these cases.

A more significant case, for our purposes, is *Cunningham-Reid v Public Trustee*,[105] which provides some support for the proposition that, where A and B hold a lease as joint tenants by virtue of section 34(2), A and B will have one and the same 'interest'. In *Cunningham-Reid*, the grantor, X, granted a seven-year lease of a floor of a building to two parties, A and B, at a yearly rent of £230. A and B jointly and severally covenanted for the payment of the rent. They also covenanted that the premises would be used only as the offices and committee rooms of the St Marylebone Conservative and Constitutional Union. A and B paid the rent in equal shares until B's death; thereafter, A paid the rent. A sought a contribution to the rent from B's executors but they refused. A submitted that it could be inferred from the covenant regarding the use of the premises that the lease was granted to A and B as tenants in common and that, consequently, prior to B's death, A and B were tenants in common in equity. This was presumably based on section 34(2) of the LPA 1925.[106] The Court of Appeal rejected A's submission and held that A and B were joint tenants at law and in equity and that, following B's death, A alone held the lease in accordance with the principle of survivorship and, therefore, B's executors were not under an obligation to contribute to the rent.

Luxmoore LJ, with whom Lord Green MR and MacKinnon LJ agreed, averred that, prior to B's death, either A or B could have been sued on the covenant because 'under the lease a legal joint tenancy is created, whereby [A and B] became joint tenants'.[107] His Lordship went on to consider the position in equity and concluded that A and B were equitable joint tenants. His Lordship

[103] *AG Securities* (n 28).

[104] *Mikeover* (n 30) 625.

[105] *Cunningham-Reid v Public Trustee* [1944] KB 602 (CA).

[106] A's counsel referred in argument to ss 34–36 of the 1925 Act and noted that these provisions, by themselves, did not determine whether A and B were, in equity, tenants in common or joint tenants: [1944] KB 602 (CA) 603.

[107] ibid 604.

pointed out, though, that *if* they had been tenants in common in equity, then 'the claim for contribution ought properly to have succeeded'. This suggests that Luxmoore LJ accepted that *if* section 34(2) had operated to vest the estate in A and B as joint tenants on trust for themselves as tenants in common, A and B would have owed the landlord a joint obligation to pay the full rent and, in consequence, if one of them had paid the full amount, he would have had a claim for contribution against the other. How does this support the contention that unity of interest must be present where section 34(2) creates a joint tenancy in respect of a lease? The answer is that, in the leasehold context, unity of interest is regarded as entailing joint obligations.[108] In other words, unity of interest will be present in respect of two putative tenants only if the tenancy obligations, including any obligation to pay rent, are owed jointly. Of course, on the facts of *Cunningham-Reid* it was obvious that the parties were under a joint rental obligation. But Luxmoore LJ's analysis suggests that, if a legal lease is held by joint tenants, the tenants' obligations will necessarily be joint, even where the legal joint tenancy is created by section 34(2).

The existing case law provides some support, then, for the view that where a joint tenancy is imposed by section 34(2) the four unities must be present. What are the ramifications of this, and of section 34(2) more generally? If the provision had been applied in *Mikeover*, A and B would have obtained a lease as joint tenants and held it on trust for themselves as tenants in common in equal shares. This is significant in and of itself, for, as we have seen, the actual decision was that no lease was granted at all and that the occupiers were mere licensees.

Three further aspects of the parties' legal position deserve to be noted. First, A and B in *Mikeover* – and others in a similar position – would owe the landlord a joint legal obligation to pay the full rent (£173.32),[109] but if one of them paid the whole sum, he or she could recover a contribution from the other.[110] The amount of the contribution would reflect the size of each party's share of the equitable interest;[111] on the facts, 50 per cent. Second, A and B would jointly hold a right to exclusive possession.[112] Consequently, they would each be under a duty not to oust the other from the land, and at the same time they would hold, together, a right to exclude the world in general – including the landlord – from the land.[113] Third, the trust of the lease would now count as a trust of land

108 *Somma v Hazlehurst* [1978] 1 WLR 1014 (CA), especially 1026 (Cumming-Bruce LJ); *AG Securities* (n 28); *Mikeover* (n 30).

109 This is a point made by Bright (n 75) 36.

110 *Bonner v Tottenham and Edmonton Permanent Investment BS* [1899] 1 QB 161 (CA); *Chalmers v Guthrie* (1923) 156 LT 382; *Cunningham-Reid* (n 105). See also sections II.A and II.B above.

111 *Cunningham-Reid* (n 105). Compare the rule that, where a trustee has an equitable right of indemnity against several beneficiaries absolutely entitled, 'they will be liable in proportion to their beneficial interests': L Tucker (ed), *Lewin on Trusts*, 20th edn (London, Sweet & Maxwell, 2022) 19-058; see also *Matthews v Ruggles Brise* [1911] 1 Ch 194 (Ch); *JW Broomhead (Vic) Pty Ltd (in liq) v JW Broomhead Pty Ltd* [1985] VR 891 (VSC); *Balkin v Peck* (1998) 43 NSWLR 706 (NSWCA).

112 See sections II.B and II.C above.

113 See the discussion in section II above.

within the meaning of section 1 of TOLATA 1996 and, consequently, the trust would be subject to the rules established by that Act.[114]

It is a significant fact about section 34(2), as it has been interpreted in the case law, that, so far as the legal estate is concerned, it imposes unity of interest in spite of the parties' intentions. In *Mikeover*,[115] for instance, the agreement, if the analysis above is correct, was that A and B would hold a lease as tenants in common in equal shares and would thus have separate rental obligations. But under section 34(2), they would have been (statutorily) *forced* to acquire a lease as joint tenants and, as they would thus have held one and the same 'interest', they would have been under a joint obligation to the landlord to pay the full sum.[116] There is a marked contrast between such an outcome and the approach of the courts. In *Somma v Hazelhurst*,[117] for instance, Cumming-Bruce LJ, having observed that it was 'impossible to reconstruct the separate obligations into one joint obligation without doing violence to the obvious intentions of the parties', refused to 'redraw the terms of the agreements to make each grantee jointly and severally liable' for the full rent, as this would have involved 'rewriting' the agreement.[118] As there was no discussion of the point, it is impossible to know whether Cumming-Bruce LJ would have regarded the imposition of a trust and the concomitant creation of a tenancy in common in equity as a satisfactory response to the 'violence' occasioned to the parties' intentions. His Lordship may have pointed out, correctly, that the imposition of a trust would not affect the position of the co-tenants vis-à-vis the landlord. But it would affect the rights of the co-tenants inter se. In many cases, it may not make a difference, in practice, whether A and B owe separate obligations to the landlord to pay, say, 30 per cent and 70 per cent of the total rent respectively, or whether they owe a joint obligation to the landlord to pay the full sum with the ability to recover a contribution (of 30 per cent or 70 per cent) from their co-lessee. In some cases, though, it will matter – for example, where one co-lessee disappears or becomes insolvent.

The foregoing analysis shows that there are important differences between: (i) A and B co-owning a leasehold estate as tenants in common, a form of holding that was taken away by the 1925 reforms; and (ii) the creation of a tenancy

[114] One complex issue, which it is not possible for us to examine here, concerns the precise content and scope of the duties that co-lessees owe in their capacity as trustees where they hold a lease as joint tenant on trust: see, eg, *Procter v Procter* [2022] EWHC 1202 (Ch); *Pile v Pile* [2022] EWHC 2036 (Ch).

[115] *Mikeover* (n 30).

[116] *Cf* R Smith, *Property Law*, 10th edn (Harlow, Pearson Education Ltd, 2020) 397: 'The normal consequence of a tenancy in common is that the co-owners hold as joint tenants on a trust of land, enabling the tenancy in common to exist in equity. Unfortunately, this analysis may not fit cases such as *Mikeover*, as a legal joint tenancy is not intended (it would require joint liability for rent).'

[117] *Somma* (n 108). In *Street v Mountdford*, Lord Templeman disapproved of the decision in *Somma v Hazelhurst* on the ground that the court had failed to recognise that the putative transaction was a sham: *Street* (n 10) 825.

[118] *Somma* (n 108) 1026.

in common in equity under a trust of a lease. Hence, it is misleading to think, as Maugham J thought in *Re Warren*,[119] that 'in substance the beneficial interests of the undivided owners in regard to enjoyment … have not been altered [by the 1925 legislation]'.[120] As we saw in section II, the rights of those who co-own an equitable interest under a trust are not, in substance, the same as the rights of those who co-own a legal estate. In the leasehold context, for instance, if A and B co-own a legal estate, they are entitled, together, to exclusive possession vis-à-vis the world in general; but if A and B hold merely an equitable interest under a trust of a term of years, and do not also co-own the legal estate, they may have a right to occupation vis-à-vis the trustee(s), but will have no right to keep out the world in general.

D. Exploratory Reflections on the Merits of the Current State of the Law

Having considered the current position in some detail in section III.C, we turn briefly to the question of whether the existing law concerning co-ownership in the leasehold context amounts to the best approach. There are at least two important issues here: whether the effect of section 34(2) has been correctly understood by the courts, and whether the general scheme introduced by the 1925 legislation, including the policy of not allowing legal tenancies in common, is appropriate in today's world, particularly in the leasehold context.

In connection with the first issue, it might be argued that, even if all four unities, including unity of interest, generally must be present where a joint tenancy is intentionally created, this rule, on a proper interpretation of the legislation, should not apply where a joint tenancy is imposed by section 34(2). This gives rise to questions about which aspects of a joint tenancy are conceptually essential,[121] about the nature and source of a lessee's obligations, and about what the purposes of section 34(2), and other relevant provisions of the legislation, are.[122] It seems that the provisions that: (i) abolished legal tenancies in common in respect of land; and (ii) facilitate the creation of tenancies in common in equity under a trust of a legal estate had two main objectives. First, to make it simpler and cheaper for co-owned land to be managed and for disputes among co-owners to be resolved, and, in particular, to avoid the huge costs and complexity brought about by the old partition actions.[123] A second and related

[119] *Re Warren* [1932] 1 Ch 42 (Ch).

[120] ibid 47. *Cf Re Landi* [1939] Ch 828 (CA) 835 (Sir Wilfrid Greene MR): 'The whole position of land held in undivided shares was, of course, entirely altered by the recent property legislation.'

[121] For discussion, see Smith (n 18) 26–30, 43–46, 83.

[122] For discussion, see JS Anderson, *Lawyers and the Making of English Land Law 1832–1940* (Oxford, OUP, 1992) 286–90.

[123] Committee on the Transfer of Land in England and Wales (the Scott Committee), *Fourth Report of the Acquisition and Valuation of Land Committee on the Transfer of Land in England and Wales* (1919, Cmd 424) para 24(c), App IV, Part 1, para (vi) (Sir Benjamin Cherry). See also (1922) 155 HCD (5th series) cols 390–91 (Sir Leslie Scott); Underhill (n 100) 99–100; Topham (n 100) 27–28.

objective was to make it easier to investigate title to co-owned land by preventing the legal estate from being divided among a large number of co-owners with distinct shares. Instead, the legal estate must be vested in no more than four joint tenants. In the words of Sir Arthur Underhill, who was an influential member of the committee that proposed the relevant reforms, legal tenancies in common caused great 'detriment to the proper management of land' and 'difficulty with regard to its sale, as not only must the parties be unanimous, but the title of each of them has to be deduced'.[124] This suggests that unity of title and at least some central incidents of unity of interest are required in order for the statutory provisions to fulfil their objectives.

The purposes of the statutory scheme are relevant to the second issue too. It can hardly be disputed that, as Bright has said, 'the co-ownership rules have not been developed thoughtfully with reference to short term leases' and 'the language of joint tenancies … does not really fit with rack rent leases where the true value of the lease to the occupier is the right to shelter rather than a monetary interest'.[125] The growth of owner-occupation in the twentieth century made the imposition of a trust for sale increasingly inappropriate, and this is part of the explanation as to why trusts for sale were replaced with trusts of land by TOLATA.[126] But the problems caused by the 1925 legislation in the leasehold context have not been addressed. And they have persisted against the background of a shifting legal landscape – one may wonder, for instance, whether in the modern world of registered conveyancing, the objections to the recognition of legal tenancies in common in respect of land are as weighty as they were in 1925. For all these reasons, it may now be appropriate to seriously consider the possibility of radically re-shaping the law of co-ownership and to revisit and revaluate the choices that were made around 100 years ago.

IV. CONCLUSION

This chapter has sought to address two questions that arise out of the interaction of the requirements of a lease and the requirements of co-ownership: Key Question 1, which concerns the nature of, and relationship between, unity of possession and exclusive possession; and Key Question 2, which relates to the circumstances in which a tenancy in common in equity will arise under a trust of a lease and the legal effects of such an arrangement.

[124] A Underhill, 'The Line of Least Resistance', App 1 to the Scott Committee's report (n 123) 30. See also (1922) 155 HCD (5th series) cols 390–91 (Sir Leslie Scott); Underhill (n 100) 99–100; Topham (n 100) 27–28; *City of London BS* (n 24) 88 (Lord Oliver).

[125] Bright (n 75) 36. See also Bright (n 83); Sparkes (n 76), especially 156–64.

[126] Law Commission (n 14) para 1.3 (especially at [3.17]).

The discussion of Key Question 1 has revealed that exclusive possession in the context of co-owned leases must be determined by looking at the co-lessees together and that it focuses on the external effect of a lease, namely the co-lessees' right to exclude all others. Unity of possession, on the other hand, is primarily concerned with the internal arrangements among the co-lessees – the rights and obligations that the co-lessees hold vis-à-vis each other. Unlike exclusive possession which has a fixed meaning, the meaning of unity of possession depends on the interest that is being co-held (eg, a leasehold estate, or an equitable interest under a trust of a leasehold estate) and the form of co-ownership (joint tenancy or tenancy in common). We argued that unity of possession at law (ie, relating to the leasehold estate) is relatively well understood and involves rights to occupy and not to be ousted. On the other hand, unity of possession in equity (ie relating to an equitable interest under a trust of a leasehold estate) may be much more limited and gives rise, in any case, to rights that differ from those held by legal co-lessees. Finally, we concluded that the relationship between exclusive possession and unity of possession is often misunderstood, leading to faulty reasoning and the misapplication of the rules. We suggested that – despite the overlap in some cases (eg, joint tenancy of a lease) – it is best to always analyse co-ownership of leases and the relevant rights by focusing on the source of those rights: if a case concerns the relationship between co-lessees and the rest of the world (eg, the landlord and strangers) the analysis must focus on exclusive possession; if a case concerns the rights or obligations of co-lessees inter se, the analyses must focus on unity of possession in a tenancy in common and all four unities in a joint tenancy. These findings improve our understanding of the concepts and their interaction, and clarify how courts can and should approach the issues that arise in this context.

The discussion of Key Question 2 built upon our analysis of the issues raised by Key Question 1 and, in particular, the point that the precise legal effects of a co-ownership arrangement depend upon which kind of interest is co-owned. Therefore, it is important in the leasehold context to distinguish co-ownership of a lease (leasehold estate) from co-ownership of an equitable interest under a trust of a lease. We explained that, while it is undoubtedly the case that co-lessees may co-own an equitable interest under a trust of a lease, the courts have, curiously, discussed this possibility only rarely, and have failed to consider section 32(4) of the LPA 1925 in circumstances where it was relevant. We argued that section 32(4) should have been applied in *Mikeover v Brady* and should be considered in similar cases in the future. We then analysed the legal effects of section 32(4) in the leasehold context. Our analysis shows: (i) that, if section 32(4) had been applied in *Mikeover*, a leasehold estate would have vested in the occupiers as joint tenants and they would thus have been co-lessees, not licensees; (ii) that the statute, as it has been interpreted in the case law, would have imposed a joint tenancy with the four unities, despite the contrary intentions of the parties; and (iii) that, as a result, the co-lessees would have owed a joint obligation to pay the full rent to the landlord, notwithstanding that separate obligations had been intended. Our analysis also considered the interaction, where a co-owned lease is held on trust for tenants in common, of the legal joint tenancy and the tenancy in common in equity, and some of the consequences of this for the parties. Finally, we briefly considered the appropriateness of the law's current approach to co-ownership in the leasehold context and suggested that the time is ripe to investigate whether this area needs to be reformed.

8

Legal Structures and Restrictions on Alienation in Cohousing: A Comparative Analysis of English and French Law

FABIANA BETTINI

I. INTRODUCTION

COMMUNITY-LED HOUSING EMERGED in the last few decades across the world as a response to the shortage of affordable housing and to the isolation and environmental impact generated by modern city living. Although taking a variety of forms, community-led housing projects are invariably characterised by a strong sense of community and a distinctive ethos. Residents are heavily involved in their housing project, from its design and realisation to its day-to-day management, and they usually share a vision and a set of values, such as solidarity, mutual cooperation, inclusion, intergenerational participation, and environmental sustainability. The overall aim of community-led housing is to create friendly, environmentally responsible and inclusive living environments.[1]

This chapter focuses on cohousing which, known since the 1960s, has recently re-appeared and significantly spread across many countries. Cohousing can be defined as a form of small-scale, community-led housing with common spaces and shared facilities. Cohousing members decide to set up a project because they share a vision and certain values, and these represent the pillars around which cohousing is organised.[2] The ethos of cohousing is first of all reflected in

[1] IL Tummers, 'Introduction to the Special Issue: Towards a Long-Term Perspective of Self-Managed Collaborative Housing Initiatives' (2015) 8(1) *Urban Research & Practice* 1.

[2] For an illustration of how cohousing sites may be organised, see K McCamant and C Durrett, *Cohousing. A Contemporary Approach to Housing Ourselves* (Berkeley, Ten Speed Press, 1998); see also K McCamant and C Durrett, *Creating Cohousing. Building Sustainable Communities* (Gabriola Island, New Society Publishers, 2011).

its physical layout. While members privately occupy their individual dwellings, common spaces and shared facilities play the most fundamental role. Compared to traditional forms of multi-owned housing, such as blocks of flats and condominiums, co-housing includes individual dwellings which are smaller in size but with more extensive common spaces and shared facilities. These may be, for example, a common kitchen and dining room, a laundry room, meeting rooms or guest rooms, and outdoor common spaces such as a garden or a playground for children.[3] Moreover, common spaces and shared facilities are usually located at the centre of the cohousing site, with private dwellings surrounding them. Cohousing may also feature central pedestrian walkways or village greens, while cars are often placed at the outskirts. The physical layout of a cohousing project can therefore encourage social contacts among its members and create a strong neighbourhood atmosphere.

Second, the active role played by cohousing members perfectly embodies the ethos of cohousing. Members are actively involved in the realisation of their cohousing project and, once this is accomplished, their participation is essential in its daily management. In particular, adult members collectively take care of the common spaces and shared facilities by volunteering work, such as repairs and cleaning, and by sharing the costs relating to their use and maintenance. Also, it is frequent in cohousing that adult members take turns in preparing communal meals, which are then eaten by all members together one or more days per week. As to decisions concerning the cohousing management, these are taken at community meetings, where all adult members are expected to participate, and highly democratic decision-making processes such as consensus are usually adopted.

Finally, members of a cohousing group are normally self-selected based on informal discussions before the cohousing project is realised, or even before it is conceived, and what drives this self-selection is that future cohousing members share the same vision and values about their living environment. At the same time, the vision and the values of a cohousing group – which are often encapsulated in a document or Charter – offer guidance for the admission of new members in case original members need or want to leave. In sum, cohousing has a distinctive ethos and specific organisational features when compared to traditional forms of multi-owned housing such as blocks of flats and condominiums.

Despite its specificities, though, cohousing seems to have 'no meaning in law'.[4] It is hard to define cohousing in legal terms and there is usually no dedicated legal structure available in any given country. However, in order to set up and manage cohousing, groups need to consider many legal aspects and lay

[3] Depending on the values and aims of the specific cohousing project, other services may also be available, such as bike or car-sharing, co-working, and ethical food buying options.

[4] S Blandy, 'Collective Property: Owning and Sharing Residential Space' in N Hopkins (ed), *Modern Studies in Property Law*, Vol 7 (Oxford, Hart Publishing, 2013) 152.

down their own rules. Usually, a cohousing group establishes rules to govern the ordinary life of cohousing. These concern the allocation of rights to cohousing members over their individual dwellings and over the common parts and shared facilities of cohousing, but also the allocation of costs among cohousing members in relation to the use, maintenance, and repair of these common parts and shared facilities. Similarly, cohousing rules regulate decision-making processes and the allocation of voting rights among cohousing members.

All these rules are put in place to ensure that the cohousing is well set up and able to run. Other rules may be adopted to deal with critical events which, although less common, could affect the normal functioning of cohousing quite seriously, or even threaten its very existence. For example, if a cohousing member challenges the apportionment of costs and refuses to pay their share, or if they do not fulfil their community commitments, such as cleaning and cooking, rules may establish what sanctions are imposed and how the cohousing group should decide on these matters. A particularly important issue concerns the situation where a cohousing member wishes to leave and sell their individual dwelling, or where they default on the mortgage and the bank seeks to realise its security by selling the property. In cases like these, where original members are replaced by new ones as a result of a spontaneous or forced sale, rules may regulate the resale of individual dwellings and guide the admission of new members. In sum, a cohousing group sets its own rules regarding this broad range of legal aspects and potentially critical events, thus ensuring that cohousing functions well and that its vision and values are upheld.

Against this background, the chapter considers cohousing in two legal systems, England and France. These systems belong to different legal traditions – common law and civil law respectively – and they present marked differences in the way they conceive ownership and property rights. Therefore, they offer an interesting perspective on the way cohousing is approached and on how its treatment can vary across legal systems. In both England and France, cohousing is a well-established form of community-led housing but, despite this and its distinctive features, it has attracted the attention of the lawmaker only to a limited extent. In England there is no legal definition of cohousing and no legal structures are specifically dedicated to it; in France a reform has defined *habitat participatif* – the French version of cohousing – and introduced new legal structures for it, but the use of these new structures is, however, not compulsory.[5] The lack of dedicated or compulsory legal structures for cohousing in the two legal systems has two practical implications. On the one hand, cohousing groups both in England and in France enjoy a great deal of flexibility in choosing the legal structures which are most appropriate to pursue the aims and reflect the values of their cohousing projects. On the other hand, though, cohousing groups may resort to existing legal structures to set up and

[5] See section II below for more details about the recent French reform on *habitat participatif* and its implications.

run their projects, and these structures may not be entirely suitable to translate into effective legal rules the ethos and specific features of cohousing.[6]

In light of this, the chapter compares cohousing legal structures in England and France and assesses the extent to which these structures are capable of supporting cohousing in both legal systems. In section II, the chapter explores the notion of cohousing and *habitat participatif* in English and French law, respectively, and it compares the legal structures available and most commonly used by groups in these jurisdictions. The chapter observes that the legal structures typically relied upon in the two legal systems for cohousing and *habitat participatif* are very different: in England, the widespread tendency is to resort to a mix of resident-owned freehold and long leases, while in France the traditional condominium-style regime, the *copropriété des immeubles*, continues to dominate the scene despite the introduction of new legal structures dedicated to *habitat participatif*. In section III, the chapter assesses whether and to what extent the legal structures thus identified can support the vision and values which typically underlie cohousing. To do this, the analysis focuses on the specific issue of restricting the right of cohousing members to resell their private individual dwellings. This is a particularly relevant issue because, when one of the original cohousing members wishes or needs to leave, new members may not share the vision and values of the cohousing group and may not be willing to abide by the cohousing rules. Therefore, a cohousing group may wish to establish rules which, by restricting alienation, help maintain a certain degree of control over who joins the cohousing community and ultimately help ensure that the cohousing continues to work well over time.

Drawing on this analysis, and comparing the responses given by English and French law, the chapter argues that the approach taken in the two legal systems as to the validity and enforceability of restrictions on alienation in the cohousing context is different. This difference depends not only on the different legal structures used for cohousing but also on the different conception of ownership and property rights which is prevalent in the two legal systems. The comparative analysis allows us to appreciate that English law, thanks to the lease, is flexible enough to accommodate the specific features and values of cohousing while, by contrast, in French law the traditional conception of ownership makes those restrictions appear as intolerable interferences into the owner's right.

[6] The legal structures used for cohousing vary according to the stage of the cohousing project. Legal structures used at the initial stages (to get funding, buy the land, secure permits, construct the building) may be, and normally are, different from those used after the cohousing project is accomplished and members can move in. It is these latter structures which normally govern the allocation of rights over individual dwellings and shared facilities, and which organise community living. Therefore, this chapter will mainly be concerned with structures of the latter type.

II. LEGAL STRUCTURES FOR COHOUSING IN ENGLISH AND FRENCH LAW

A. Cohousing in England: Notion and Legal Structures

Since the end of the 1990s the cohousing movement has regained momentum in the UK, though the numbers of new-built cohousing sites should not be exaggerated.[7] According to UK Cohousing, there are currently 19 established cohousing groups, and more than 60 are developing or forming.[8] Cohousing is defined as intentional communities created and run by their residents, in which each household has a private home, but residents come together to manage their community, share activities, and eat together.[9] Cohousing in England falls within the broader category of community-led housing,[10] though it remains distinct from other forms such as co-operative housing[11] and Community Land Trusts.[12]

Unlike France,[13] no legal reforms have been undertaken in England to introduce a dedicated legal structure for either cohousing or community-led housing more generally. The result is that cohousing in England is not associated with one specific legal structure, but a broad range of legal structures is available and cohousing groups can choose among them based on the vision and values they want to pursue.[14] In practice, a corporate vehicle is always needed to set up cohousing in England,[15] and the majority of established cohousing groups have resorted to a private company limited by guarantee

[7] M Field, 'Introduction: How Far Has Cohousing in the UK Come?' in S Bunker et al (eds), *Cohousing in Britain* (London, D&D Publications 2011) 5, 9.

[8] Information about the spread of cohousing across the UK and a directory of UK cohousing groups are available at cohousing.org.uk/cohousing-in-the-uk-and-worldwide/.

[9] The definition of UK cohousing is available at: cohousing.org.uk/about-cohousing/.

[10] There is a website dedicated to community-led housing and cohousing features in it: see www.communityledhomes.org.uk/types-of-community-led-housing.

[11] Co-operatives are defined as not-for-profit and democratic organisations run for and by their members: www.communityledhomes.org.uk/what-housing-co-operative. The CCH is the Confederation of Cooperative Housing. On their website, there is information about setting up a housing cooperative, including model rules to be used: www.cch.coop/registered-model-rules/.

[12] CLTs are not-for-profit, membership-based entities which hold and manage land in trust for the benefit of a given community. For a comparative analysis of CLTs, see F Bettini, 'Long Leases and Affordable Housing: A Comparative Analysis of French and English Law' in B McFarlane and S Agnew (eds), *Modern Studies in Property Law*, Vol 10 (Oxford, Hart Publishing, 2018) 225.

[13] See section II.B below.

[14] In making this choice, cohousing groups may be assisted by solicitors specialised in community-led housing. An example is Wrigleys Solicitors, which supported some well-known cohousing groups in England. For more information on their work, see www.wrigleys.co.uk/charities-and-social-economy/community-led-housing/cohousing/.

[15] One explanation for using a corporate vehicle is that co-ownership is not a viable option for setting up cohousing in England, as there cannot be more than four legal co-owners of a proprietary interest in land in English law: see Law of Property Act 1925, s 34. Therefore, unless the cohousing group is very small, a corporate vehicle will be needed to take on the freehold of the entire cohousing site. On this point, see also Blandy (n 4) 155, fn 16.

(hereinafter CLG).[16] Other structures could also be used, such as a company limited by shares, a cooperative society, a community benefit society, a community interest company, or a mutual home-ownership society, but these legal structures are rarely chosen in practice.[17]

As the CLG is the legal structure most commonly relied upon by English cohousing groups, the present subsection focuses on the CLG and discusses how it is employed in the context of English cohousing. Regulated under the Companies Act 2006,[18] the CLG is normally used to achieve not-for-profit purposes.[19] In the cohousing context, the CLG acquires and holds the freehold title to the cohousing site, including the common parts and the shared facilities of the building, grants long leases of individual dwellings to cohousing members, and decides how the building is managed. Since the corporate body is invariably membership-based, all the original members of the cohousing group are also members of the corporate body; new residents become cohousing members when they take on the lease of their dwelling or when, independently of that, they apply for membership.[20] This ensures that cohousing members not only have a property right in their private dwellings as leaseholders, but they also have decision-making powers as members of the corporate body which owns the freehold of the cohousing site, including all the common parts and shared facilities of the building.

The Articles of Association (hereinafter 'the Articles') are one of the key documents of English cohousing, as they set out the objectives for which a cohousing is established and contain rules about how cohousing is organised and run. The primary objective of a cohousing company is to acquire and provide housing and communal facilities for the benefit of the company's members through the sale of individual leasehold dwelling units,[21] and the maintenance and management of common areas and facilities. However, the objectives of a cohousing can be further specified outside the Articles themselves. Often,

[16] The most well-known examples of cohousing groups which opted for this legal structure are Cambridge Cohousing K1, Forgebank Cohousing Lancaster, Cannock Mill Cohousing, On the Brink Cohousing, The Open House Project, Copper Lane Cohousing, and Laughton Lodge. More information about these cohousing groups can be found on their respective websites.

[17] Examples of cohousing groups which have adopted a company limited by shares are Springhill Cohousing, Lansdown Cohousing, and Sladbrook Cohousing (and all companies have the same directors). For more information, see: www.therightplace.net/coco/public/properties.html (Springhill Cohousing), www.coflats.net/ (Sladbrook Cohousing). An example of cohousing group formed as a co-operative society is The Postlip Community: www.postliphall.org.uk/about-us.html. The Threshold Centre Cohousing Community, though originally incorporated as a company limited by shares (under a different name), is now a community interest company: see www.thresholdcentre.org.uk/. Lilac Cohousing is the only known example of a cohousing group which adopted the mutual home-ownership society structure: see www.lilac.coop/ for more information about this project.

[18] Companies Act 2006, s 3(3).

[19] PL Davies, S Worthington, and C Hare, *Gower's Principles of Modern Company Law* (London, Sweet & Maxwell, 2021) 9.

[20] See text preceding and to n 22 for a further discussion of this point.

[21] The 'sale of a lease' refers to what is technically an assignment of the leasehold interest. This will be analysed in detail in section III below.

cohousing groups state their vision and draw up a Charter of Values which lay down the objectives and values of their cohousing and can contain a list of the key rights and commitments of cohousing members. The vision and the Charter of Values can be referred to in the Articles and must all be accepted by prospective cohousing members (either at the moment of signing the lease or as part of their application to join the group). The Articles also establish rules about membership, meetings, directors, and voting rights. In terms of membership, there may be different categories of cohousing members: persons holding a lease of an individual residential dwelling ('leaseholders'), who become members automatically by signing the lease, and persons who are not leaseholders but reside in the property and use its communal facilities ('residents'), who have to apply for membership. In any case, both leaseholders and residents must first be approved by the company to join the group. It may sometimes be permitted that membership is granted to any other person who is committed to and supports the vision and values of the cohousing group.[22] The CLG is also flexible when it comes to rules about voting rights and decision-making. For example, voting rights may be allocated based on a number of criteria (eg, one vote per person, ten votes per household) and decisions at meeting are taken by consensus, unless the latter cannot be achieved or special majorities are required for more sensitive issues.[23]

While the Articles regulate all these aspects, the cohousing's main objective – providing housing for the benefit of its members – is achieved by way of granting residential long leases of the individual dwellings to the company's members. The lease is therefore the other key document of English cohousing.[24] First, very much like in traditional blocks of flats, leases of cohousing dwellings may be granted for a very long term (eg, 99 years, and up to 999 years), normally in exchange for the payment of an initial capital sum ('premium') and at a symbolic ground rent ('a peppercorn'). As leaseholders, cohousing members

[22] Membership can also terminate. In particular, leaseholders cease to be members if they cease to hold a lease of the property or if they die, while residents may cease to be members if they resign or die. When a member dies and their unit is inherited, there are procedures in place to ensure that the heir complies with the cohousing rules (signing the lease, including the charter of values, and becoming a new member of the cohousing company) if they want to stay. Otherwise, if the heir does not share the cohousing values, they can sell it to the cohousing group, assuming the cohousing is able to buy it back. A different issue would be whether these procedures are valid and enforceable in case they are challenged before courts by an heir who would like to live in the cohousing but would not want to abide by its rules. This aspect, though, is not analysed in this chapter. It should also be mentioned that, apart from the hypothesis of termination of membership mentioned earlier, a procedure to expel members could also be foreseen for cases where a member's conduct conflicts with the objectives and values of the company, or in case of breach of any of the company's Articles.

[23] The consensus model on which cohousing groups often rely is provided by Seeds for Change Lancaster Co-operative. See www.seedsforchange.org.uk/ for how consensus decision making works in detail.

[24] It should be noted that no model lease is provided by UK Cohousing. Lease agreements are tailored to the specific needs of a cohousing group, which usually seeks legal advice for drafting this key document.

have a property interest in their individual dwelling for the time being, and they have the right to dispose of it by means of assignment, mortgage, rent, and inheritance, unless – as we shall see below – specific terms in the lease restrict their rights.[25] In addition to this, leaseholders (and members of the company) enjoy the right to use the common spaces and shared facilities owned by the cohousing company. The company, as freeholder, is entitled to the reversion once the term of the lease expires. Since cohousing residents are members of the CLG that holds the freehold of the cohousing site, the cohousing group can set the terms of the lease in a way which reflects their vision and values. When entering the lease, both the company and the leaseholders promise to comply with certain covenants. The cohousing company shall normally only ensure the quiet enjoyment of the property by the leaseholders and that the property is kept in a good state of repair.[26] On the part of the leaseholders, covenants ensure that the cohousing values and rules are abided by. In particular, cohousing members promise in the lease to observe the cohousing rules, such as those regarding the allocation of charges and voting rights, and to respect cohousing policies, such as those about food, communal meals, and community work. It is also possible to include in the lease covenants against assignment, whereby the cohousing group exercise control over the resale of private individual dwellings by cohousing members. Furthermore, a cohousing lease may contain a forfeiture provision establishing that, in case of breach of covenant by one cohousing member, the company can exercise the right of re-entry and terminate the lease.[27] Therefore, the 'CLG plus lease' structure offers enough flexibility to cohousing groups and is well suited to capture the organisational features and ethos of cohousing.

Finally, it should be mentioned that, besides using a legal structure combining a corporate body (such as a CLG) and long residential leases, cohousing groups may opt for an entirely different legal structure, the commonhold, which closely resembles the French *copropriété des immeubles*.[28] Introduced by the Commonhold and Leasehold Reform Act 2002 ('CLRA 2002'), commonhold enables freehold ownership of flats or houses by commonhold unit holders while the commonhold association – of which all unit holders are entitled to be members – owns freehold title to the common parts and shared facilities. Compared to the CLG and leasehold structure, the commonhold presents the advantage of transferring to cohousing members the freehold of their individual dwellings. However, the flexibility of the cohousing group would be limited in several respects if they were to choose commonhold as their legal structure.

[25] This is the case for covenants against assignment: see section III.A for a detailed examination of this issue.

[26] These covenants may be expressly contained in the lease, but, even if not, they will be implied on the part of the landlord: see, eg, E Walsh, *A Guide to Landlord and Tenant Law* (London, Routledge, 2018) 39ff.

[27] The use of these covenants in the cohousing context will be the subject of specific analysis in section III.A.

[28] See section II.B below for a detailed analysis of *copropriété* in the context of French *habitat participatif*.

Indeed, the Commonhold Regulations 2004 prescribe standardised documents to be used as both Articles of Association and Commonhold Community Statement (CCS), and this affects the flexibility of cohousing groups to shape their own rules.[29] Moreover, on the specific aspect of controlling resale of individual dwellings, the CLRA 2002 provides that 'a commonhold community statement may not prevent or restrict the transfer of a commonhold unit'.[30] This is one of the reasons why the commonhold structure is seldom used in traditional blocks of flats and why it has been of limited significance in the cohousing context as well.[31]

B. Cohousing in France: Notion and Legal Structures

The cohousing model described above is known in France as *habitat participatif*. In the last few decades, such housing projects have proliferated and there are now hundreds of them.[32] The term *habitat participatif* does not perfectly correspond to the English term cohousing, but it is instead used as an umbrella term to indicate a wider range of forms which go from older forms of *habitat groupé* and *habitat autogéré*[33] to more recent *habitat participatif* projects. However, the common goal of all these forms is to place groups of residents at the heart of the conception, realisation, and management of their housing, and to provide a valuable alternative to both the private real estate market and public housing initiatives.[34] Moreover, like in England, *habitat participatif* remains conceptually distinct from *coopératives d'habitants*[35] and Community Land Trust.[36]

[29] For an exhaustive analysis of commonhold, see, eg, D Clarke, L Crabb, and N Roberts, *Clarke on Commonhold: Law, Practice and Precedents* (Bristol, Jordan Publishing, 2004).

[30] CLRA 2002, ss 15 and 20.

[31] So far, only one cohousing group has adopted a commonhold structure. However, the Law Commission has published a proposal for reform to reinvigorate commonhold, and, if legislation is passed, this may increase the chances that commonhold will be used by cohousing groups in the longer term. For the Law Commission's proposal, see Law Commission, *Reinvigorating Commonhold: The Alternative to Leasehold Ownership* (Law Com No 394, 2020). Another possible reason for the limited use of commonhold in both traditional blocks of flats and cohousing is that long leases of commonhold units are not allowed: see CLRA 2002, s 17, and Commonhold Regulations 2004, reg 11, which both restrict leasing to a term of seven years. The term is also non-renewable unless certain specified circumstances are met.

[32] The mapping of existing *habitat participatif* projects, at the different stages of their completion, is available at www.habitatparticipatif-france.fr/?HPFRecherche.

[33] The expressions *habitat groupé* and *habitat autogéré* were used during the 1970s-1980s to indicate squatters or self-managed groups occupying housing spaces. For further details, see C Devaux, *L'habitat participatif. De l'initiative habitante à l'action publique* (Rennes, PUR, 2015) 42–45.

[34] This definition is contained in the *Livre Blanc de l'Habitat Participatif* (Strasbourg, 2011) 1.

[35] The *cooperatives d'habitants* are defined as little and close-knit communities of individuals which are based on trust and cooperation: see Y Maury (ed), *Les coopératives d'habitants. Méthodes, pratiques et formes d'un autre habitat populaire* (Bruxelles, Bruylant, 2012). *Habicoop* is the French federation of *cooperatives d'habitants* and it has a dedicated website, which can be accessed here: www.habicoop.fr/.

[36] The CLT in France adopts the same model explained in n 12 above. The CLT France is formed as a network and their new website is currently under construction: see communitylandtrust.fr/. For more information about how the CLT model has been implemented in France, see Bettini (n 12).

In 2014, the *habitat participatif* was formally recognised by statute. The *Loi* ALUR defines it as a 'citizens-based initiative that allows individuals to associate, if necessary with legal entities, in order to participate in the conception and design of their individual dwellings and shared facilities, to construct or acquire one or more buildings and, where possible, to ensure their management'.[37] The statutory definition further emphasises that the *habitat participatif* promotes 'the construction and the supply of housing, as well as the development of collective spaces, under a logic of sharing and solidarity between residents'.[38] So, very much like English cohousing, the core of *habitat participatif* is to promote values such as sharing and solidarity among members of the community, but also mutual cooperation, environmental sustainability, social diversity, and intergenerational participation.[39]

Compared to England, the situation in France looks rather different in terms of the legal structures which are available and used for *habitat participatif*. The structure most commonly used in France is a condominium-type structure, the *copropriété des immeubles*, which in many respects resembles the English commonhold. The *copropriété* was introduced by statute in 1965 as a type of tenure which applies to all co-owned buildings,[40] and therefore its scope of application is not limited to *habitat participatif*. The distinctive feature of the *copropriété* is that it allows members to have exclusive ownership of their individual dwellings while, at the same time, common parts and shared facilities of the building are owned in common.[41] Therefore, *copropriété* is suitable to capture the basic organisational feature of *habitat participatif*, where members privately occupy their individual dwellings and share common parts and facilities. The *copropriété* structure applies either as a result of an express choice of prospective co-owners or by operation of law, when the first individual dwelling is sold off by the developer and the building becomes thenceforth co-owned. In the context of *habitat participatif*, groups can choose to set up their project either as a *copropriété* or by using a company. Even in this latter case, though,

[37] *Loi* n°2014-366 du 24 mars 2014 (Loi ALUR), Art 47. The definition now features in Art L200-1 *Code de la Construction et de l'habitation*.

[38] ibid. The *Loi* ALUR also introduced two legal structures specifically designed for *habitat participatif*. These legal structures will be discussed below and compared to the *copropriété* structure.

[39] Though not contained in the definition itself, these values are mentioned in the *habitat participatif* network website as the main values around which these projects are built: see www.habitatparticipatif-france.fr/?HPFDefinition.

[40] *Loi* 65-557 of 10 Juillet 1965. Given the prominence of individual ownership in the French Civil Code, and its hostility towards all forms of co-ownership, which were considered remnants of the feudal past, *copropriété* was introduced by statute only in 1938. This statute was then replaced by the *Loi* 65-557 of 10 Juillet 1965, which provides a comprehensive regulation of the increasingly important phenomenon of multi-owned properties: F Terré and P Simler, *Droit Civil. Les biens* (Paris, Dalloz, 2018) 502–06.

[41] Terré and Simler (n 40) 526–27. C Atias, 'Copropriété des immeubles bâtis' in *Répertoire de Droit Immobilier*, (Dalloz, 2015) 7 points out that the *copropriété* is a widespread type of tenure within the real estate market, because it satisfies the aspirations of people toward individual ownership while cutting down costs and diluting responsibilities.

groups remain free to switch to *copropriété* later on, or *copropriété* applies by operation of law where ownership of the individual dwellings is transferred by the *habitat participatif* company to its members.[42]

The *copropriété* is organised around the *règlement*, a detailed document where all property-related and organisational aspects of a co-owned building are regulated. The *règlement* is therefore the key document of *habitat participatif*. The *règlement* is an agreement between co-owners[43] which, in the context of *habitat participatif*, the members themselves are in charge of preparing.[44] While the *règlement* can reflect the aims and values of a particular *habitat participatif* project, this is only true to a limited extent. Indeed, the law prescribes that a *règlement* must contain certain mandatory provisions, and often goes as far as imposing their content, significantly affecting the freedom of *habitat participatif* groups to lay down their own rules.[45] First of all, the *règlement* must carefully identify the individual dwellings, their size and their value, as well as the share of undivided ownership of common parts and shared facilities pertaining to each dwelling.[46] Second, the *règlement* must specify how co-owners exercise their rights over the individual dwellings and over the common parts and shared facilities of the building.[47] In particular, the law prescribes that each co-owner has exclusive rights to use, enjoy, and dispose of their individual dwellings, like any other individual owner, provided only that they respect the *destination de l'immeuble* (that is, the purpose of the building) and do not undermine the rights of other co-owners.[48] Along the same lines, the law mandates that contractual restrictions on co-owners' right to alienate their dwelling are not allowed, unless they can be justified with regard to the *destination de l'immeuble*. Importantly, it is up to the *règlement* itself to specify what the *destination de l'immeuble* is

[42] The relation between companies and *copropriété* in the context of *habitat participatif* is discussed in more detail below: see text to n 54, n 55 and following n 55.

[43] *Loi* 65-557 (n 40) prescribes that each *copropriété* must have a *règlement*, and this could also be imposed by a decision of the judge in case co-owners do not provide one. As a result, scholars have questioned whether the *règlement* can be defined as an agreement *tout court* or its nature is more regulatory than contractual: see Terré and Simler (n 40) 538–39.

[44] In traditional co-owned buildings, it is normally the developer who prepares the *règlement*, and not the co-owners themselves. In any case, it is common to seek legal advice from solicitors and notaries to draft the *règlement*, which is a very complex document.

[45] Article 43, *Loi* 65-557 (n 40). Mandatory provisions are Arts 1, 1-1, 6 to 37, 41-1 to 42 and 46 of the same statute. Provisions which contradict those articles are to be considered as 'not written' and can be challenged before courts.

[46] The share of undivided ownership of common parts and shared facilities is allocated proportionally to the value of each private dwelling, the latter being measured in relation to the value of all individual dwellings which are present in a given building at the time the *copropriété* is established: see Art 5, *Loi* 65-557 (n 40).

[47] Arts 8 and 10, *Loi* 65-557 (n 40).

[48] At the same time, though, the law prohibits the sale (or any other act of disposition) of the co-owner's share of the common parts, each co-owner being only entitled to use and enjoy the common parts and shared facilities in common with other co-owners. Common parts can be disposed of only pursuant to a decision of the general assembly of co-owners (with various majorities required by the law for the different acts).

in practice. At a minimum, the *règlement* must say whether a building is residential, commercial, or mixed-use, but, in the context of *habitat participatif*, groups may want to stress that their building is also meant to pursue their vision and values.[49] Finally, the *règlement* must regulate the allocation of service charges relating to common parts and shared facilities among co-owners, as well as determine the allocation of voting rights and the majorities required for voting in the general assembly. In these respects, the law prescribes specific criteria of allocation of voting rights and mandatory voting majorities for the various matters, with co-owners having only little ability to change them. In light of all this, when the *copropriété* structure is used to set up *habitat participatif* projects, members have limited freedom to modify the *règlement* in order to reflect the values and specificities of their housing project.

Completely different from *copropriété*, other legal structures may be and have been used to set up *habitat participatif* projects in France, and notably limited liability companies such as the *Société Civile Immobilière d'Attribution* (SCIA)[50] or the *Société Civile Coopérative de Construction* (SCCC).[51] Compared to *copropriété*, these companies give more flexibility to groups both at the early stages of developing the project and later on, with regard to the allocation of rights over the individual dwellings and the transferability of such rights. Normally, the company owns the land and the building, including the common parts and shared facilities, while members – who are also shareholders – only have a right to enjoy their dwellings which does not have any proprietary effect. Compared to the *copropriété* structure, these companies do not allow their members to acquire ownership of their dwellings, and therefore it is unlikely they can obtain a mortgage loan to support the purchase.[52] For this reason, where companies such as the SCIA or SCCC are used for *habitat participatif*, they are meant to dissolve once the project is accomplished and individual dwellings are transferred to members. In this case, *habitat participatif* projects fall back to be regulated by the *copropriété* structure.[53]

Besides these limited liability companies, the *Loi ALUR* has introduced two legal structures specifically designed for setting up *habitat participatif*, namely

[49] In order to specify what their guiding values and commitments are, *habitat participatif* members might also draw up a charter of values, and reference it in the *règlement*, but it is unclear whether the Charter would be binding either on co-owners themselves or on their successors in title.

[50] The SCIA is a particular type of *société de construction immobilière* (SCI) which is governed by Arts L 212-1ff of the *Code de la Construction et de l'Habitation*.

[51] The SCCC is governed by Arts L 213-1 ff, L 212-2, L 212-6, and L 214-1 to L 214-9 of the *Code de la Construction et de l'Habitation*.

[52] A Lebatteux-Simon, 'Les alternatives à la copropriété', *Revue Loyers et Copropriété* n.1, Janvier 2015, étude 1, 4.

[53] Sometimes, however, groups may not wish to dissolve the company, so this becomes their permanent legal structure. One example of a project where the SCCC survived is the *habitat autogeré* project *La Petite Maison*, in Rennes: see www.hg-rennes.org. However, there is no data available to show how many *habitat participatif* projects have been set up via one of these companies and whether it later dissolved so as to make the *copropriété* structure applicable again.

the *coopérative d'habitants* and the *société d'habitation et d'autopromotion* (SAA).[54] Although these structures are likely to become commonly used in the future, not least because the legislator has encouraged existing projects to convert their structure into the new ones, they will not completely replace the *copropriété* structure. First, the *cooperative d'habitants* cannot grant its members a right of ownership over the dwellings but only a right to use and enjoy them which does not have proprietary effects.[55] Therefore, where *habitat participatif* residents wish to become owners of their dwelling, the *cooperative d'habitants* is of no avail. Second, under the new SAA structure, which is a refined version of the above-mentioned SCIA, members may be granted either a non-proprietary right of enjoyment or a right of ownership over the dwellings. In this latter case, though, the law provides that the SAA will be wound up as soon as the first member resigns from the *société* and requests to be granted ownership of the individual dwelling, with the result that the *copropriété* structure will become applicable again as a matter of law. In sum, even though these structures are more flexible in several respects, *copropriété* is the only real option available to *habitat participatif* groups if members wish to obtain ownership over their individual dwellings. In conclusion, despite the *Loi* ALUR having introduced specific legal structures for *habitat participatif*, the *copropriété* remains the most commonly used structure for cohousing in France. For this reason, the focus of this chapter will be on the *copropriété* structure in French law.

III. RESTRICTIONS ON ALIENATION IN COHOUSING: ENGLISH AND FRENCH LAW COMPARED

After explaining the meaning of cohousing in England and France, and the legal structures which are available in the two legal systems, section III focuses on one of the most crucial issues of cohousing: the resale of individual dwellings by cohousing members and the possibility to prevent, limit, or regulate this power of resale. As explained in the introductory section, cohousing is built around a set of specific values and rests upon the commitment of its members to community living. Therefore, a cohousing group may establish rules which, to various extent, restrict the ability of existing members (leaseholders in England and co-owners in France) to resell their individual dwellings. This allows original cohousing members to check that new members share the same cohousing vision and values and that they wish to abide by its rules, otherwise the normal

[54] Arts L 200-1 to 201-13, and Arts L 202-1 to 202-11, *Code de la Construction et de l'Habitation*. The two structures are cumulatively known as *sociétés d'habitat participatif*.

[55] The members' right to use and enjoy the dwellings stems from their acquiring and owning shares in the *coopérative*. The *coopérative* remains the only owner of the dwellings. The *contract coopératif* entered into by the *coopérative* and its members specifies the terms of the right conferred over the dwellings (eg, start date, length, payment due): see *Code de la Construction et de l'Habitation*, Arts L 201-2 and L 201-8.

functioning of cohousing could be undermined or its very existence threatened in the long term. As a result, the ability of a cohousing group to validly establish and enforce such restrictions on alienation is key. This section explores how English and French law respond to the issue of whether such restrictions on alienation are valid and enforceable, and this assessment will be made against the legal structures which are used for cohousing in the two legal systems and which have been examined in section II (ie, the 'CLG plus lease' structure in England and the *copropriété* structure in France). The chapter argues that the response given in English and French law to such restrictions on alienation is strictly dependent not only on the types of legal structure used for cohousing in the two legal systems, but also linked to the conception of ownership and property rights which is prevalent within the two jurisdictions.

A. Covenants against Assignment in English Cohousing

In the context of English cohousing, the validity and enforceability of restrictions on alienation is assessed against the 'CLG plus lease' structure analysed in section II.A.

In English cohousing, the lease is the key document where the obligations of cohousing members are laid down, and therefore it is in the lease that cohousing members can agree to put restrictions on their right to dispose in the form of covenants against assignment. At common law, a leaseholder is normally free to assign the lease to a third party,[56] the right to assign being 'incident to the estate'.[57] However, restrictions on assignment are permitted and commonly practiced in leases, either because they are imposed by statute or because the landlord and tenant may agree to introduce covenants against assignment in their lease. Indeed, the lease has a hybrid nature, 'part contract, part property',[58] meaning in this context that while a leaseholder has an estate in land which they are free to assign, it is possible to include in the lease contractual promises which bind the parties (and their future assignees).[59] Therefore, it is possible for

[56] The right of a leaseholder to dispose is not limited to assigning the lease, as they may also, eg, sub-lease, charge the lease, or part with possession. These rights are not irrelevant in the cohousing context, because their exercise by cohousing leaseholders could affect the normal way in which the cohousing community functions. However, the analysis in this chapter will be limited to covenants against assignment.

[57] *Church v Brown* (1808) 15 Ves 258, 264 (per Lord Eldon LC). In the same vein, the Law Commission more recently stated that 'a basic incident of the tenant's rights of property is that he should be able to dispose of property by assignment': see Law Commission, *Covenants Restricting Dispositions, Alterations and Change of User* (Law Com No 141, 1985) para 4.6.

[58] *Linden Gardens Trust v Lenesta Sludge Disposals Ltd* [1994] 1 AC 85, 108 (Lord Browne-Wilkinson). The hybrid nature of the lease is explored in S Bridge, 'Leases – Contract, Property and Status' in L Tee (ed), *Land Law: Issues, Debates, Policy* (Portland, Willan Publishing, 2002) 98, 113ff.

[59] Bright argues that modern leases are 'contract for possession plus' because they have come to contain many other promises beyond the grant of land to a tenant: see S Bright, 'Street v Mountford

a cohousing company and its members to include in the lease restrictions on the right of cohousing members to alienate their individual dwellings.

In English law, covenants against assignment may be absolute or qualified. Absolute covenants prohibit any form of alienation. This type of covenant is more common in short-term residential leases, where the landlord seeks to retain complete control over who occupies the premises, while they are rarer in long residential leases. Indeed, 'a lease containing such a prohibition is, by definition, unmarketable and hence in principle unmortgageable'.[60] For this reason, long leases granted by the cohousing company to its members do not usually contain absolute covenants against assignment. Alternatively, covenants against assignment may be qualified, meaning that they do not prohibit alienation *tout court* but permit it only with the prior consent of the landlord, which shall not be unreasonably withheld.[61] The landlord and tenant may also agree upon specifying conditions as part of the landlord's giving consent, and normally these conditions also need to satisfy the reasonableness test.[62] In the context of cohousing, qualified covenants against assignment are common practice. Such covenants subject the alienation of individual dwellings by cohousing members to the company's prior written consent and may further specify conditions for the company's giving consent. For example, a cohousing lease may provide as a condition that the assignee of the lease is a person who is eligible to become a member of the cohousing company, and that this person enters into a deed of covenant with the company whereby they undertake to abide by the cohousing values and rules.[63] So, qualified restrictions on assignment are in principle valid in the context of English cohousing, the only controversial point being whether the company's refusal of consent and the conditions for giving consent are reasonable.

Given that the relevant legislation does not contain a definition of reasonableness, the courts themselves have identified and developed a number of guiding

Revisited' in S Bright (ed), *Landlord and Tenant Law: Past, Present and Future* (Oxford, Hard Publishing, 2006) 31.

[60] S Whittaker, 'Tenant's Covenants – assignment and subletting – assignment of whole' in *Encyclopaedia of Forms and Precedents, Leasehold Flat Schemes (Long Leases)*, (2014) 25(3)A [593]. In 1985, the Law Commission expressed dissatisfaction with absolute covenants, stating in its report that: 'When he [the tenant] is prohibited or restricted from so doing [assigning the lease] [...] an inroad is made on what would otherwise be his common law right. [...] Therefore, it is the landlord's freedom to impose such a prohibition or restriction which has to be justified': Law Com (n 57).

[61] If the provision against assignment contained in the lease expressly mentions that 'the consent of the landlord shall not be unreasonably withheld', the covenant is considered to be 'fully qualified'. Absent such an express term, though, a term to this effect will nowadays be statutorily implied per s 19(1)(a), Landlord and Tenant Act 1927. Therefore, apart from certain tenancies which remain excluded (see s 19(4)), qualified covenants are always 'fully qualified' by operation of statute.

[62] S Bright, *Landlord and Tenant Law in Context* (Oxford, Hart Publishing, 2007) 525.

[63] An example of such covenants can be found in the lease adopted by the Lancaster Cohousing (on file with the author).

principles to ascertain whether the landlord's consent is reasonably withheld.[64] In particular, a landlord can reasonably withhold consent to protect themselves from having their premises used or occupied in an undesirable way or by an undesirable tenant or assignee.[65] Moreover, a landlord is not entitled to refuse consent on grounds that are totally extraneous to the relationship of landlord and tenant with regard to the subject matter of the lease.[66] Therefore, consent can be reasonably withheld if this is necessary to protect the landlord's contractual rights from being prejudiced by the proposed assignment. For example, a landlord's refusal could be justified where a proposed assignee is unlikely to be able to pay the rent and perform the obligations imposed by the lease. In contrast, it is likely that a refusal based on purely personal characteristics of a proposed assignee would be regarded as unreasonable.[67] Moreover, the landlord cannot refuse consent on grounds of disability, gender reassignment, pregnancy and maternity, race, religion or belief, sex or sexual orientation.[68] Finally, it is worth mentioning that the reasonableness of the landlord's refusal to consent in each case is a question of fact which depends upon all the circumstances.[69] Therefore, if the cohousing company refused their consent to an assignment on the ground that the proposed assignee did not comply with the conditions set in the covenants (eg, they are not eligible to become a member and/or they do not enter into a deed and promise to abide by the cohousing rules), a court would assess the company's refusal by applying the reasonableness test. In all likelihood, a court would judge such refusal reasonable by looking at the nature of the cohousing project and the relationship between the cohousing company and its members. Indeed, given that acceptance of the values and rules of cohousing is vital to its continuing existence, assignees who do not commit to such values and rules may be reasonably prevented from joining the cohousing.

Therefore, in case the company's refusal to give consent is deemed reasonable, the proposed assignee will not be able to enter the cohousing community. It should be mentioned though that the company does not usually refuse consent to a proposed assignee indefinitely but gives the cohousing member the possibility to effectively assign their interest in the dwelling and leave the cohousing. To achieve this balance of interests, the cohousing lease may specify the procedure to be followed where a proposed assignee is refused by the cohousing company. In particular, the cohousing lease may provide that, if the cohousing company does not approve of the assignee within an agreed period of time, the company

[64] See *International Drilling Fluids Ltd v Louisville Investments (Uxbridge) Ltd* [1986] Ch 513, 519–21 (Balcombe LJ), approved by the House of Lords in *Ashworth Frazer Ltd v Gloucester City Council* [2001] UKHL 59, [61], [70] (per Lord Bingham).

[65] *International Drilling Fluids* (n 64) 519–20.

[66] See *Houlder Brothers & Co Ltd v Gibbs* [1925] Ch 575; *International Drilling Fluids* (n 64) 520.

[67] See A Whittaker, 'Examples of What is Reasonable and Unreasonable in Grant of Consent to Lease Disposal' in *Encyclopaedia of Forms and Precedents, Landlord and Tenant (Residential Tenancies)*, 23(1) 863.

[68] Equality Act 2010, s 38(2)–(3).

[69] *International Drilling Fluids* (n 64) 521.

will have the option of purchasing the leasehold property, directly or through a nominee of their own.[70]

Two final points should be discussed regarding the enforceability of covenants against assignment and the remedies available in case an assignment is made in breach. Normally, an assignment in breach of covenant entitles the freeholder to damages or, in case the lease includes a forfeiture provision, to a right of re-entry.[71] Cohousing leases usually contain such a forfeiture clause, which authorises the cohousing company to re-enter the premises provided that appropriate notice is given.[72] It is also possible that, when giving notice, a cohousing company would nominate a person who is regarded as an acceptable assignee and allow the cohousing member to assign as an alternative to forfeiture. However, if no such forfeiture provision is included in the lease, the law provides that an assignment in breach of covenant is not void in and of itself,[73] and this may appear to render the provision of covenants against assignment pointless from the perspective of the cohousing company. However, some clarifications are in order. First, where the assignment concerns registered land, the cohousing company may prevent registration of an assignment in breach of covenant by entering a restriction on the Land Registry.[74] Second, it is unlikely that a cohousing member will be able to find anyone who is willing to purchase in breach of covenant. The reason for this lies in the rules about the enforceability of leasehold covenants. As regards the position of the leaseholder, the burden of leasehold covenants will pass on assignment of the lease and bind the assignee,[75] except where those covenants are 'expressed to be personal to any person'.[76] This means that the cohousing company will

[70] An example of this can be found in the lease adopted by the Lancaster Cohousing (on file with the author). Leases used in cohousing may sometimes also feature resale price restrictions. In particular, the lease may require that the leaseholder and the company must agree upon a selling price, the matter being referred to a valuer in case an agreement is not reached. The amount so determined could be binding upon the parties for a certain period, and the leaseholder could promise not to transfer the lease for an amount exceeding the agreed one during the nomination period.

[71] L Crabb and J Seitler, *Leases. Covenants and Consents*, 2nd edn (London, Sweet & Maxwell, 2008) 4–5. Other remedies could also be available to the landlord. In particular, it seems possible for the landlord to seek an injunction for breach of (a negative) covenant in circumstances where damages are not an adequate remedy and the lease does not contain a proviso for forfeiture or re-entry.

[72] Forfeiture is also subject to the leaseholder's right to apply for relief from forfeiture: LPA 1925, s 146. The protection for leaseholders is further strengthened in case of forfeiture of a long lease of dwellings: see Commonhold and Leasehold Reform Act 2002, s 168. On this point, see E Walsh, *A Guide to Landlord and Tenant Law* (London, Routledge, 2018) 131–35.

[73] *Property & Bloodstock Ltd v Emerton* [1968] Ch 94, 119 (Danckwerts LJ).

[74] See LRA 2002, s 40.

[75] See Landlord and Tenant (Covenants) Act 1995, s 3(1). The Act is applicable to leases granted on or after that date, and it will therefore apply to cohousing leases as they have usually been entered into after 2000. The benefit of a leasehold covenant will also pass to any assignee of the reversion, who will therefore have a remedy against the leaseholder in possession, but this is less relevant as it is unlikely that the cohousing company, given the nature of these projects, will assign their freehold to someone else.

[76] See Landlord and Tenant (Covenants) Act 1995, s 3(6)(a). In *First Penthouse v Channel Hotels and Properties* [2003] EWHC 2713 (Ch), at [49], Lightman J clarified that 'the formula [expressed

be able to enforce the terms of the lease against any successors in title of the original cohousing member. As a result, although the lease is not unmarketable, potential purchasers may feel discouraged from acquiring an interest in the cohousing dwelling.

In summary, while absolute covenants are virtually never used in long residential leases, qualified covenants against assignment are common practice and their validity and enforceability in English law is unquestionable. In the cohousing context, provided that a cohousing company does not refuse consent based on purely personal characteristics of the assignee or on discriminatory grounds, it is likely that English courts would find it reasonable to prevent assignment to a person who does not commit to respect the values and rules of cohousing. Also, in the unlikely event in which an assignment in breach of covenant occurs, the company will be able to enforce the covenant against the assignee as successor in title to the original cohousing member, unless the covenant is personal, and the company should also be able to re-enter the premises if a forfeiture clause is contained in the cohousing lease.

B. Restrictions on Alienation of Individual Dwellings in the French *Habitat Participatif*

In the context of French *habitat participatif*, the validity and enforceability of restrictions on alienation of individual dwellings is tested against the *copropriété* structure.

As explained in section II.B above, *copropriété* relies on a mix of individual and collective ownership, and the French legislator has predetermined the right balance between these elements via a complex set of (often mandatory) provisions. In principle, each co-owner has the most extensive rights to use, enjoy, and dispose of their private dwelling; in this respect, the legal position of a co-owner is not different from that of any other individual owner.[77] However, given the collective element of *copropriété*, some statutory rules are in place to mitigate the co-owner's unrestrained exercise of their rights.[78] Statutory law indeed provides that each co-owner is free to dispose of their individual dwelling, but can use and enjoy the property only in a way which does not undermine

to be personal] requires that the language of the tenancy, read in its context, expresses or otherwise conveys the intention that the covenant shall be personal in the sense that it is not to be annexed to the tenancy or reversion. There is no requirement as to how the intention is to be expressed: the tenancy does not have to spell it out in terms that the covenant is to be personal. The intention may be expressed explicitly or implicitly. The intention may be stated in terms or it may be deduced from the language used in its proper context.'

[77] See Art 544 of the French Civil Code: 'Ownership is the right to enjoy and dispose of things in the most absolute manner, provided that it is not exercised in a way prohibited by statutes or regulations.' This is also in line with Art 377 of the Code, according to which private individuals have the freedom to dispose of the property which they own.

[78] Atias (n 41) 10.

either the rights of other co-owners or *la destination de l'immeuble*.[79] Moreover, statutory law intervenes, again in attempt to balance the individual and collective elements of *copropriété*, to regulate the contractual freedom of co-owners to impose restrictions on the exercise of their property rights.[80] In particular, the statute provides that the *règlement* – which is in substance a contract into which co-owners enter – 'cannot impose any restriction on the rights of co-owners other that those justified by the *destination de l'immeuble*'.[81] Therefore, if in principle co-owners have contractual freedom to include in the *règlement* restrictions on the exercise of their property rights, including their right to dispose, these restrictions are subject to the *destination de l'immeuble* test. The notion of *destination de l'immeuble* then becomes the measure of the contractual freedom that co-owners enjoy in this area.[82] Therefore, in the context of *habitat participatif*, co-owners can exercise over their dwellings all the rights traditionally associated with ownership and, in particular, they have the right to dispose of the dwelling by way of alienation. Reinforcing this position, their ability to impose contractual restrictions on the resale of individual dwellings is curtailed by statutory law and limited to those restrictions which can be justified by the *destination de l'immeuble*.[83]

Similar to English law, different types of restrictions on the right of an owner to dispose of their property are known in French law and these can affect the right to dispose to different degrees.[84] Absolute restrictions completely paralyse the owner's right to dispose while other restrictions – which may be called 'qualified' in keeping with the English approach – restrict this right only partially or add conditions to its exercise. Contrary to English law, though, all these restrictions are traditionally met with distrust in French law because, since the *Code Napoleon* was introduced in 1804, the owner has been regarded as having an absolute and unfettered right of ownership over their property.[85] Although this sacralised vision of ownership has relaxed over time and contractual restrictions

[79] See Art 9, alinéa 1, *Loi* 65-557 (n 40).

[80] See Art 8, alinéa 2, *Loi* 65-557 (n 40). It should be mentioned that it is possible for the *règlement* to impose such restrictions only where it is agreed by all co-owners before the *copropriété* is set up, as this ensures that all co-owners have consented to the restrictions. Where, instead, the *règlement* is approved by a majority vote of the assembly or imposed by a court it cannot contain any restrictions on the right of co-owners to dispose of their individual dwellings.

[81] Art 8, alinéa 2, *Loi* 65-557 (n 40).

[82] F Jammes, 'La destination de l'immeuble mis en copropriété en France', *La Revue du Notariat*, vol 114, 2012, 223 observes that: '[a]ccording to Christian Larroumet, "the French legislator in 1965 did not want to sacrifice either the individual to the collective or the collective to the individual", and to strike this difficult balance it has introduced a regulatory concept within the law of *copropriété*, which is the *destination de l'immeuble*.'

[83] See text preceding and following n 95 for a further discussion of this point.

[84] It should be mentioned that the principles regarding restrictions on the owner's right to dispose are not contained in the *Loi* 65-557 (n 40) on *copropriété*. Instead, they are general principles of contract law which apply to all transfers of property, including the resale of *copropriété* units.

[85] F Danos, 'La diversité des restrictions conventionnelles au droit de disposer', *Revue des contrats* 1/2016, 187.

have been permitted, the right to dispose remains the most fundamental incident of ownership and owners should not completely strip themselves of it.[86] The protection of ownership therefore constitutes the benchmark for assessing the validity of any restrictions on the right to dispose.[87]

Absolute restrictions prohibit alienation *tout court*. Like English cohousing, in the context of French *habitat participatif* absolute restrictions against alienation are not used by *habitat participatif* groups. Were they included in the *règlement*, though, these provisions would likely be struck down by courts because the right to sell is considered such an essential prerogative of a co-owner's status that the *règlement* should and could not restrict it.[88] Similar to England, qualified restrictions against alienation are possible in France, though the range of what counts as a qualified restriction is broader in French law compared to English law. First of all, outside the context of *copropriété*,[89] it is possible to come across provisions against alienation which are valid and enforceable only if inalienability is: (i) limited in time; and (ii) justified by a 'serious and legitimate interest of one of the parties'.[90] While these rules have not been laid down with *copropriété* in mind, it is possible to imagine that *habitat participatif* groups may try to include in their *règlement* similar time-limited restrictions on their right to alienate and argue that such restrictions would be valid and enforceable based on 'a serious and legitimate interest'. For example, they may contend that a provision restricting alienation for the first three years after a co-owner has purchased their dwelling would be justified by the need to preserve the stability of the newly formed *habitat participatif* community. Whether or not this argument would convince a French judge to decide for the validity of a similar prohibition on alienation is not entirely clear.

Second, other types of qualified provisions against alienation limit the owner's right to dispose without blocking it altogether. They are common in French law, both within and outside the context of *copropriété*.[91] They can take the form of a right of pre-emption (*pacte de préférence* or *droit de préemption*) whereby, in case one co-owner wishes to leave and sell their dwelling, the other co-owners have the right to be offered the dwelling for sale with priority

[86] ibid.

[87] P Berlioz, 'La propriété, point de définition d'un régime unitaire', *Revue des Contrats* 1/2016, 152. See also Danos (n 85) observing that restrictions on the right to dispose are often subjected to a reinforced control by both ordinary courts and constitutional courts, given that these limitations must be of a reasonable extent.

[88] G Vigneron, 'Règlement de copropriété – Généralités – Champ d'application', *JurisClasseur Copropriété*, fasc 76, 2014, 89. See also J-N Beaulieu, 'Droits et obligations des copropriétaires – Aliénation de lot – Constitution de droits réels', JurisClasseur Copropriété, fasc 68–10, 2015, 14–16 noting that absolute restrictions do not pose particular problems because, by definition, they are void and have no effects, given the principle laid down in Art 544 of the French Civil Code.

[89] See Art 900-1 of the French Civil Code.

[90] ibid. See Berlioz (n 87) for a discussion of these inalienability provisions and, in particular, of the two requirements that they must be limited in time and justified by a serious and legitimate interest.

[91] This is suggested by Danos (n 85).

over any other person. Also, they could be drafted as a provision whereby the proposed buyer would be subject to the approval of the assembly of co-owners (*clause d'agrément*), and, in case of refusal, the assembly of co-owners would also have the duty to nominate their own buyer.[92] Similar to English cohousing, this type of qualified restrictions against alienation may be used in the context of *habitat participatif*. Their validity is however controversial. On the one hand, these provisions are treated more favourably than the qualified restrictions discussed above, and, in particular, they do not need to be limited in time to be valid.[93] On the other hand, the Cour de Cassation has systematically ruled against the validity of such provisions in the specific context of *copropriété* on the ground that they unduly undermine the right of co-owners to dispose of their property.[94] In this case, the Court considered such provisions as 'not written' and expunged them from the *règlement*. Therefore, if used in the *habitat participatif* context, it seems likely that a French court would rule against such qualified provisions against alienation unless they can be justified by the *destination de l'immeuble*.

Indeed, the notion of *destination de l'immeuble* may offer a valid foothold to *habitat participatif* groups to justify the inclusion of these restrictions in the *règlement*. While statutory law does not offer a definition of it, scholars and courts have clarified that the *destination de l'immeuble* does not refer to the purpose of the building in a narrow sense (eg, commercial, residential, mixed), but more broadly indicate 'the set of conditions for which the co-owner has bought the lot, considering all the provisions and contractual documents of the co-owned building, its structural characteristics, its status, as well as the social status of its occupants'.[95] Relying on this broader understanding of *destination de l'immeuble*, groups may stress in the *règlement* that their *habitat participatif* project is built around community facilities and values, which influence the structure and status of the building and ultimately constitute the reason why such a project has been set up and members bought their dwellings there. Based on this, a court might be willing to consider qualified restrictions valid.

[92] Danos (n 85) admits the *clause d'agrément* for certain types of companies, but it seems possible to use it in the context of *copropriété* as well.

[93] Cass 1re civ, 22 déc. 1959, JCP G 1960, II, 11494, case note by P Esmein; RTD civ 1960, at 323, obs J Carbonnier. But see Cass Civ 3e, 23 septembre 2009, n 08-18187, where the Cour de Cassation approved of a *pacte de preference* (between an owner and a municipality) restricting the owner's right to sell for 20 years and fixing a maximum resale price because it was justified by a serious and legitimate interest (ensuring housing affordability for that particular owner and in the long term).

[94] See, eg, Cass Civ 3e, 29 Mai 1979, n 78-11530. See also CA Toulouse, 10 Jan 2011, n 09-00802, *AJDI* 2011, 305 in relation to a provision of the *règlement* establishing a *droit de préemption* in favour of the other co-owner. In this case, the Court of Appeal said that 'the right of a co-owner to dispose of their dwelling is an essential prerogative which the *règlement* cannot restrict. […] providing that, in case of sale, the seller has to prefer the other co-owners, this [provision] has the effect of forcing the owner to sell to a buyer that they have not chosen and therefore it constitutes a restriction on their freedom to dispose of the property'.

[95] Versailles, 16 juillet 2009, Loyers et copr. 2010, n 49, obs Vigneron; Cass Civ 3e, 20 mai 2014, n 12-25.822.

For example, in the context of *copropriété*, the Cour de Cassation has recently invoked the *destination de l'immeuble* to rule in favour of the validity of a *pacte de préférence* on the ground that the *pacte*'s main purpose was to sustain and ensure the group's familial bond.[96] Notwithstanding decisions of this type, though, it is doubtful that a French court would respond positively to the argument that a broad understanding of *destination de l'immeuble* could be used in the specific context of *habitat participatif* to justify qualified restrictions on alienation.

A final point is in order in relation to the enforcement of restrictions on alienation contained in the *règlement* in the unlikely event a French court judges such restrictions valid. The approach taken by French law is different according to the type of restrictions considered. In the case of an absolute provision against alienation, the sale made in violation of the restriction would be declared void. Indeed, the solution is justified by the fact that the restriction directly and significantly affects the owner's right to dispose and makes the burdened property inalienable. Therefore, any attempt to sell property which cannot be legally sold would be of no effect.[97] Moreover, the provision against alienability is contained in the *règlement*, which is normally registered, and therefore the provision would be binding on the successors in title of the original co-owners.[98] As we said, however, this type of restriction is not commonly used by *habitat participatif* groups and, even if it were, would likely be considered invalid by French courts. A different approach is taken by French law as to the enforceability of 'qualified' restrictions against alienation, such as a *pacte de préférence*. When a sale occurs in violation of this type of restriction, the beneficiary of the *pacte* (ie the other co-owners in the context of *copropriété* and *habitat participatif*) would be able to obtain compensatory damages for breach of a contractual duty.[99] However, the possibility of declaring the sale void would depend on the position of the third-party purchaser. If the third party were in good faith – ie they were not aware of the existence of the pre-emptive agreement – the prohibition could not be used against them, despite the fact that the *règlement* was registered; if, however, the third party were in bad faith, the beneficiary of the

[96] Cass 3e civ, 30 juin 2009, n 07/21.146 and n 08-13.405, unpublished. On these decisions, see J-N Beaulieu (n 88) 24–25.

[97] Danos (n 85).

[98] Art 13, *Loi* 65-557 (n 40). All transactions relating to land (eg, transfers, gifts, creation of property rights, including the *réglement de copropriété*) should be recorded in the French *fichier immobilier*. Contrary to registration in the English Land Registry, though, registration in the French *fichier immobilier* does not affect the validity of title but serves an evidentiary and third-party enforceability function only. In particular, the *Loi* 65-557 (n 40) Art 13, prescribes that the *règlement de copropriété* is not enforceable against successors in title of the original co-owners if it has not been registered.

[99] Art 1123, alinéa 2, of the French Civil Code provides that 'where a contract is concluded with a third party in violation of an agreement containing a pre-emptive right, the beneficiary of the pre-emptive right may obtain compensation for damage suffered'.

pacte (that is, the other co-owners) could seek a declaration that the sale is void or to replace the third party with a person of their choice.[100]

In summary, absolute restrictions against alienation are rarely used in the context of *habitat participatif* and would likely be considered invalid by French courts. More common in *habitat participatif*, qualified restrictions against alienation would also likely be invalid, unless a French court was prepared to accept that they comply with the *destination de l'immeuble* as more broadly understood. Even if valid, though, qualified restrictions against alienation would pose an enforceability problem in French law in the case of a bona fide purchaser, and this may in practice strip French *habitat participatif* groups of their ability to control the entry of new members into the community.

IV. FINAL COMPARATIVE REFLECTIONS

The chapter has focused on the legal structures used for cohousing in two legal systems, England and France, and, against these structures, it has assessed the validity and enforceability of restrictions on alienation of private individual dwellings by cohousing members. As cohousing is built around a set of values and rests upon the commitment of its members to community living, it is crucial for the smooth functioning and the very existence of a cohousing group that there is some control over incoming members.

The analysis of English law has shown that cohousing is commonly set up by entrusting freehold ownership of the cohousing site to a membership-based corporate body, normally a CLG, which then grants a leasehold interest in the individual dwellings to its members. This structure shows great flexibility in terms of the freedom of cohousing members to impose restrictions on their right to dispose. Unlike French law, qualified covenants against assignment, which subject alienation to the consent of the landlord, are normally practiced in long residential leases, including leases used in cohousing. These covenants are agreed by the parties to the lease – in our case, the cohousing company and its members – and do not pose particular problems unless the consent of the landlord has been unreasonably withheld. This reasonableness test is, however, not framed by courts in terms of assessing the impact that the contractual freedom of the parties may have on the right to dispose, considered as one of the incidents of the leasehold estate. This assessment seems to have been made by the law ab initio, when admitting that, by virtue of its hybrid nature, a lease is a proprietary interest in land which does also allow covenants against assignment

100 Art 1123, alinéa 2, of the French Civil Code further states that: 'In the event the third party was aware of the existence of the agreement and that the beneficiary wanted to take advantage of it, the beneficiary may also seek annulment of the contract or request the court to replace the third-party purchaser.' This approach has been upheld by a decision of the Cour de Cassation, Chambre Mixte, 26 Mai 2006, in Bulletin 2006 MIXT, n 4, 13. See also Danos (n 85).

to be included among the terms of the lease. Instead, the principles guiding the reasonableness test are more directed at checking whether the landlord's refusal of giving consent pertains to the landlord-tenant relationship and the subject matter of the lease. As a result, the 'CLG plus lease' structure proves to be particularly suitable for cohousing as it is capable of capturing cohousing's most distinctive features and supporting its vision and values.

The position in French law is rather different. There, the traditional *copropriété* structure plays a key role in *habitat participatif*. Not only does *copropriété* apply in most cases but, very importantly, it is the only legal structure which allows *habitat participatif* members to acquire ownership of their individual dwellings, while at the same time ensuring that ownership of the shared facilities remain collective. However, this comes at a considerable cost in terms of flexibility, as the law governing *copropriété* limits the freedom of *habitat participatif* members to impose contractual restrictions on the right to dispose of their dwellings. Indeed, statutory law establishes that provisions restricting alienation can be validly included in the *règlement* only where they can be justified by the *destination de l'immeuble*, and French courts have adopted a rigid approach to such restrictions, systematically ruling against their validity on the ground that they constitute an excessive interference with the right of ownership. Because of this, the *copropriété* structure cannot guarantee that *habitat participatif* groups are able to control the entry of new members into the community.

In conclusion, in both legal systems the right to dispose is considered to be one of the main incidents of ownership and contractual restrictions on it are subject to court-controlled tests. However, given the hybrid nature of the lease, English law shows remarkable flexibility by allowing the inclusion of restrictions on the right to dispose in the lease while at the same time conferring on cohousing members all the benefits of a property right. In contrast, the French reluctance to permit restrictions which are seen as intolerable inroads into the owner's right to dispose, coupled with the absence of a flexible device such as the English lease, generates a legal framework which does not adequately sustain *habitat participatif* projects and their underlying values.

9

Can a Consumerist Model of Law Reform Solve the Problems of Leasehold Tenure?

HELEN CARR, CAROLINE HUNTER, CARL MAKIN AND GWILYM OWEN[1]

I. INTRODUCTION

DESPITE MORE THAN 50 years of reform,[2] leasehold as a tenure remains in crisis[3] and the English and Welsh governments have been forced to intervene yet again. The current programme of reform has been described as 'seminal',[4] and builds upon extensive consultation.[5] What is claimed to be transformative[6] is its consumer focus. In this chapter we interrogate the potential of a consumerist model of leasehold reform in the context of the persistent failure of legislative interventions. We start by demonstrating the need for a shift in the legal framing of leasehold, recalling long-term problems with the tenure as well as recent leasehold scandals emphasising the contested nature of leasehold reform. In the second part of the chapter, we expand upon the case for reform by providing granular evidence of the contemporary experience of leaseholders drawing on qualitative data collected by the authors during research into the sale and use of leasehold in Wales commissioned by the Welsh

[1] The authors are grateful to Dave Cowan, Sarah Nield and Lisa Whitehouse and the anonymous reviewer for their encouragement and constructive comments on earlier drafts of this chapter.

[2] S Blandy and D Robinson, 'Reforming Leasehold: Discursive Events and Outcomes, 1984–2000' (2001) 28(3) *Journal of Law and Society* 384.

[3] Propertymark, 'Leasehold: A Life Sentence?' (Propertymark, 2018) www.propertymark.co.uk/resource/leasehold-a-life-sentence.html (accessed 5 September 2022).

[4] By Robert Jenrick MP, then Secretary of State for Housing, Communities and Local Government in a written ministerial statement in 2021. See HC Deb 11 January 2021, vol 687, col 10WS.

[5] See for instance: Department for Communities and Local Government, 'Tackling Unfair Practices in the Leasehold Market: A Consultation Paper' (DCLG, July 2017).

[6] As described in the Queen's Speech briefing pack May 2022. See Prime Minister's Office, 'The Queen's Speech 2022' (Prime Minister's Office, 2022).

Government.[7] Our analysis is framed by the consumer-oriented requirements of informed choice, transparency, and fairness for leasehold purchasers. In the third part we suggest we are sceptical as to whether a consumerist framing can build a sufficiently powerful consensus to make meaningful inroads on the status-quo of property rights. Our scepticism is informed by the paradox at the heart of leasehold reform and draws on the history of consumer protections in property relationships and successful challenges to leaseholder rights in the courts. In the concluding part of the chapter, we draw our thoughts together on the prospects of the current reform project succeeding in light of the history of leasehold law failure and then, putting our scepticism about consumerism to one side, we speculate on the unpredictable consequences of a consumer rights driven paradigm of leasehold law reform.

II. WHY IS A 'SEMINAL' CHANGE IN LEASEHOLD LAW NECESSARY?

There are three reasons why a seminal change in leasehold law is necessary. First, not only has the extensive and longstanding dissatisfaction of leaseholders been inadequately addressed, but it has also recently intensified[8] and been effectively mobilised.[9] Second, leasehold homeownership is important, socially, economically, and politically. Third, numerous previous efforts at leasehold law reform have failed. More of the same does not appear to be a tenable political option particularly for a government seeking to revive commonhold *and* maintain leasehold as a viable option for homeownership.

A. Longstanding Problems

Residential leasehold has long provoked complaints of unfairness. As Lord Stonham put it in 1959

> From the beginning, the leasehold system has been harsh to tenants. In theory, of course, while the lease endures, the holder should enjoy similar rights to the freeholder. In practice, the status of the leaseholder has always been inferior.[10]

Leasehold enfranchisement has been on the political agenda since the 1880s when it was first proposed in Parliament as a means of avoiding prohibitive rent rises when leases expired and to improve the housing conditions of the

[7] H Carr, C Hunter, G Owen, C Makin and A Wallace, *Research into the Sale and Use of Leaseholds in Wales* (GSR report number 16/2021, Welsh Government, 2021).

[8] See for instance the Westminster Government's consultation on *Tackling Unfair Practices in the Leasehold Market* which received more than 6,000 responses. See Department for Communities and Local Government, *Tackling Unfair Practices in the Leasehold Market: Summary of Consultation Responses and Government Response* (DCLG, December 2017).

[9] The Leasehold Knowledge Partnership has had a major influence on government.

[10] HL Deb 28 July 1959, vol 218, cols 646–60.

working classes.[11] Limited changes were made but concern intensified as flatted home ownership increased after the second world war and particularly following the residential property price boom of the 1970s. Blandy and Robinson demonstrated in 2001 that leaseholders have simultaneously complained of freeholder exploitation and freeholder neglect since at least the middle of the twentieth century[12]

Legislation targeted two overlapping aspects of leaseholder dissatisfaction. First the time-limited nature of the lease was tackled via individual rights to enfranchise for leaseholders of houses, granted by the Leasehold Reform Act of 1967,[13] rights of pre-emption granted by the Landlord and Tenant Act 1987[14] and the grant of collective rights to enfranchise and individual rights to lease extension in the Leasehold Reform Housing and Urban Development Act of 1993.[15,16] These attempts to rebalance the power dynamic between freeholder and leaseholder had limited success in part because of the complexity and technicalities of the law and in part because of the costs and uncertainties inherent in enfranchisement/extension processes.[17]

The second target for law reform was to improve the fairness and effectiveness of the management of leasehold property. Rights to challenge unreasonable service charges and rights to challenge overly expensive and/or unnecessary major works were introduced in the Landlord and Tenant Act 1985[18] and slowly enhanced. But Blandy and Robinson note that 'poor maintenance, excessive service charges, limited consultation over works, defective leases, inadequate insurance arrangements, and leaseholders not knowing the identity of their freeholder have persisted despite the legislative reforms'.[19]

The most dramatic changes were promised by the Commonhold and Leasehold Reform Act 2002.[20] In addition to enhancing already existing protections for leaseholds, it provided for commonhold – a radical and coherent alternative to leasehold tenure. Commonhold enables owners to own their flat outright thus avoiding the problems of the wasting asset characteristic of the lease and the connected expense of extending the lease or enfranchising. There is no landlord – instead, owners have a stake in the building that includes their flat and make decisions together with other owners about shared areas.

[11] The Leasehold (Facilities or Purchase of Fee Simple) Bill 1884 was the first parliamentary Bill introduced to enable leasehold enfranchisement.

[12] Blandy and Robinson (n 2) 387.

[13] Leasehold Reform Act of 1967.

[14] Landlord and Tenant Act 1987.

[15] Leasehold Reform Housing and Urban Development Act of 1993.

[16] A useful table of legislative reform is provided in Blandy and Robinson (n 2) 388.

[17] See I Cole and D Robinson, 'Owners yet Tenants: The Position of Leaseholders in Flats in England and Wales' (2000) 15(4) *Housing Studies* 595, 597. Law Commission, *Leasehold Home Ownership: Buying Your Freehold or Extending Your Lease* (Law Com CP No 238, 2018).

[18] Landlord and Tenant Act 1985.

[19] Blandy and Robinson (n 2) 389.

[20] Commonhold and Leasehold Reform Act 2002.

No ground rent is payable. There is no risk of forfeiture (the right of a landlord to repossess the property following a breach of covenant by the lessee). A standard set of rules and regulations apply – avoiding the complexity of leases and giving owners greater clarity on rights and responsibilities. But 20 years from its enactment, its promise has not materialised. Only 20 commonhold schemes have been created to date,[21] 'a living testament to its failure in the marketplace'.[22] Drawing on earlier work of Baker[23] and Clarke,[24] James Brown suggests that a widespread ignorance of commonhold, the risk-averse nature of mortgage lending decisions and the complete lack of incentives for developers have all played roles in its failure.[25] For Xu, commonhold quickly became a 'laughingstock' and exists as 'one of the worst examples of carefully considered legislation having done more harm than good'.[26] For the purposes of the argument in this chapter, commonhold provides a further, and particularly prominent, example of legislative failure.

B. Recent Scandals

More recently an increase in the sale of leasehold houses has re-energised leaseholder dissatisfaction. Described by campaigners as 'fleecehold',[27] purchasers of leasehold houses have faced high and accelerated ground rents, making enfranchisement and lease extensions unaffordable, and excessive fees for permissions, for instance to erect conservatories. These practices have placed onerous financial barriers on the exercise of what should be normal practices of home ownership. It might have been expected that good legal advice would have protected purchasers from one-sided bargains. However, the National Leasehold Campaign (NLC) Conveyancing Satisfaction Survey, carried out in 2019, revealed that leaseholders had experienced poor conveyancing services.[28]

It is perhaps the 'cladding' or 'building safety' 'crisis' or 'scandal' that has generated the greatest collapse in leaseholder confidence. Fire safety and other inspections carried out following the Grenfell Tower fire of 14 June 2017 revealed that large numbers of residential and other buildings had been clad in

[21] L Xu, 'Commonhold Developments in Practice' in W Barr (ed), *Modern Studies in Property Law: Volume 8* (Oxford, Hart Publishing, 2015) 332.

[22] J Brown, 'English Commonhold: A Failed Experiment?' (2013) 3(2) *Property Law Review* 85.

[23] C Baker, 'First Major Commonhold Project – Lessons in Application' (2006) 10(3) *Landlord and Tenant Review* 70.

[24] D Clarke, 'Long Residential Leases: Future Directions' in S Bright (ed), *Landlord and Tenant Law: Past, Present and Future* (Oxford, Hart Publishing, 2006).

[25] Brown (n 22).

[26] Xu (n 21) 349.

[27] 'Fleecehold' refers to the practice of including onerous terms in the leases of leasehold property as well as onerous conditions being imposed on freehold property.

[28] The National Leaseholder Campaign (2019) Conveyancing Satisfaction Survey, available at nationalleaseholdcampaign.org/tag/survey/ (accessed 17 January 2023).

combustible materials which required remediation. Moreover, there was evidence of large-scale failure to comply with other building safety requirements.[29]

This has had profound consequences; home ownership, which generates (according to neoliberal social norms) a sense of achievement, autonomy, and security[30] became, for those leaseholders caught up in the cladding crisis, dysfunctional.[31]

Financial consequences were particularly severe. There was a real risk of very high bills for the costs of remediation, placing leaseholders' homes, livelihoods, and futures at risk.[32] This was compounded by increases in building insurance for affected buildings and the insistence of some mortgage lenders on external wall fire reviews (EWS1) for all buildings of whatever height. Not only are these costly for residents, the lack of available experts to carry out these reviews has effectively trapped leaseholders in their property.[33]

There is an important caveat here; we are not arguing that only leaseholders are impacted by these recent scandals. 'Fleecehold' is an issue for freeholders as well as leaseholders and freeholders have a particular problem as they lack the service charge protections enjoyed by leaseholders. Nor is the building safety crisis only experienced by leaseholders. It is also a crisis for those with enfranchised blocks and would be a problem in the unlikely event that one of the few commonhold blocks had building safety defects. However, leaseholders greatly outnumber others affected by the crisis and leasehold campaigners have effectively mobilised the scandals to demonstrate the unfairness of the tenure. In addition, the position of leaseholders is made more complex and more expensive because of the number of actors and relationships that are potentially involved – developers, freeholders, superior lessees etc. Our point is that these scandals have intensified leaseholder dissatisfaction to the extent that government has promised seminal change.

C. Why Leasehold Reform Matters

Seminal change would not be promised if leasehold did not matter, but it does. A significant proportion of residential property is leasehold. In 2019–2020 government statistics suggested that there were 4.6 million leasehold dwellings in England, 68 per cent of which were flats. This equates to 19 per cent of the

[29] J Preece, 'Living through the building safety crisis' (UK Collaborative Centre for Housing Evidence, 2021) housingevidence.ac.uk/publications/living-through-the-building-safety-crisis/ (accessed 5 September 2022).

[30] LF O'Mahony, *Conceptualising Home: Theories, Laws and Policies* (Oxford, Hart Publishing, 2007).

[31] See Preece (n 29).

[32] Many leaseholders also faced significant (and controversial) costs for interim first safety measures whilst awaiting remediation, such as waking watches.

[33] HCLG Select Committee, *Cladding: Progress of Remediation* (HC 2019–21, 172).

English housing stock.[34] In Wales leasehold ownership is estimated at around 16 per cent of all stock, approximately 235,000 properties.[35] UK Property Transaction statistics show there has been a generally rising year-on-year trend for residential leasehold transactions over the five years before 2019, with 99,420 transactions in the year ending April 2019.[36] While the figures are contested,[37] there is no doubt that a significant amount of wealth is invested in and generated by residential leasehold and that ensuring the integrity of the tenure is of critical importance economically.

Leasehold also contributes to the long-standing project of extending home-ownership. Home ownership has huge social, political, and economic significance. It matters to government because according to neoliberal rationalities it encourages independence, self-reliance, and freedom from the state.[38] Leasehold is pivotal here. Because leasehold property is often cheaper than freehold, it can provide more accessible home ownership. In addition, the leasehold form is critical to shared ownership, currently the primary means of widening access to home ownership.

Responsible property ownership has long been a significant motivation for leasehold reform. For Pointing and Bulos, the Leasehold (Facilities or Purchase of Fee Simple) Bill of 1884,[39] drafted in response to the housing crisis of the 1880s, was the product of

> A reforming consensus produced from a common belief that reform of the relations of property ownership and the encouragement by the state of responsible forms of ownership would solve the housing problem, and hence the political problem of 'outcast London'.[40]

Cole and Robinson's review of leasehold reform prior to 2000 notes how the 'rhetoric of property ownership [became] incorporated into the case to change the leasehold sector'.[41] A contemporary manifestation is found in Robert Jenrick's (then Housing Minister) statement to the House of Commons in January 2021, which highlighted the bureaucracy and expense associated with leasehold ownership.[42]

[34] MHCLG, 'Official Statistics: Leasehold dwellings, 2019 to 2020' (MHCLG, 8 July 2021) www.gov.uk/government/statistics/leasehold-dwellings-2019-to-2020/leasehold-dwellings-2019-to-2020 (accessed 5 September 2022).

[35] Carr, Hunter, Owen, Makin and Wallace (n 7) para 2.29.

[36] HMRC, 'UK Property Transaction Statistics – April 2019' (HMRC, April 2019) www.gov.uk/government/collections/property-transactions-in-the-uk (accessed 5 September 2022).

[37] Leasehold Knowledge Partnership suggests that there are far more leasehold properties than the data indicates. See Leasehold Knowledge Partnership, 'What's the probability that government leasehold statistics are still useless?' (LKP, 28 September 2017) www.leaseholdknowledge.com/probability-government-leasehold-statistics-still-useless/ (accessed 5 September 2022).

[38] See the explanation provided by D Cowan and M McDermont, *Regulating Social Housing: Governing Decline* (London, Routledge, 2006) 165.

[39] Leasehold (Facilities or Purchase of Fee Simple) Bill of 1884.

[40] JE Ponting and MA Bulos, 'Some Implications of Failed Issues of Social Reform: The Case of Leasehold Enfranchisement' (1984) 8(4) *International Journal of Urban and Regional Research* 467, 477.

[41] Cole and Robinson (n 17) 601.

[42] MHCLG, 'Government reforms make it easier and cheaper for leaseholders to buy their homes' (MHCLG, 7 January 2021) www.gov.uk/government/news/government-reforms-make-it-easier-and-cheaper-for-leaseholders-to-buy-their-homes (accessed 5 September 2022).

In each of these three examples the purpose of law reform is to enhance the quality of the property stake held by the leaseholder at the expense of the freeholder for significant social purposes.

D. The Failure of Previous Law Reform

The final reason that a 'seminal' change in leasehold law is required is because leasehold law reform is a catalogue of failure or at the very best constrained success. There are several reasons for this. Leasehold law reform has been largely reactive, responding to emergent scandals and effective campaigns. This has led to piecemeal reform leaving the law fragmented, complex and properly understood by only a very limited number of specialist lawyers.[43] This is most clearly seen in the context of enfranchisement. The Law Commission points out that the current enfranchisement regime 'is the product of over 50 Acts of Parliament, totalling over 450 pages. There are numerous anomalies and unintended consequences resulting from piecemeal changes over time. Certain terms in the legislation create much uncertainty, and scope for litigation'.[44]

Perhaps more significantly for the long-term stability of the tenure, leasehold law reform is highly contested. The interests of leaseholders and freeholders appear diametrically opposed and strong, often moral, arguments are mounted on each side. Pointing and Bulos suggest the origins of this fierce dualism lie in the emergence and subsequent failure of the Leasehold (Facilities or Purchase of Fee Simple) Bill of 1884. The Bill was designed to alleviate the scandalous high rents, overcrowding, insanitary conditions, jerry-building and exploitative landlordism that characterised the housing crisis of the 1880s and was 'based on the fear that a failure to solve the problem of working-class housing would threaten the political and social status quo'.[45] But the threat it posed to the landownership provoked a powerful response,

> Various propertied interests rallied round aristocratic landownership, and this process has been described as constituting a conservative consensus, or a reaction to the demand to reform the system of property ownership.[46]

For Pointing and Bulos the emergence of a conservative consensus had long-term consequences,

> which not only served to severely restrict the scope of prospective reform, but also crystallized the social forces opposed to reform, and in a sharper form as compared to the situation prevailing before the period of political crisis.[47]

[43] The fragmented provisions are contained for instance in the Landlord and Tenant Act 1985, the Landlord and Tenant Act 1987, the Commonhold and Leasehold Reform Act 2002 amongst others.

[44] Law Commission, *Leasehold Home Ownership: Buying Your Freehold or Extending Your Lease* (Law Com No 392, 2020) para 2.20.

[45] Pointing and Bulos (n 40) 477.

[46] ibid.

[47] ibid.

The dualism, and its moral overtones are visible in subsequent leasehold reform attempts. For instance, in parliamentary debates about the Landlord and Tenant Act 1954,[48] one of the earliest successful legislative interventions to protect leaseholders, Frank Soskice, the Labour MP for Sheffield Neepsend, articulated his party's view that lessees, particularly those from the working classes were vulnerable in the market.

> A house is not a thing which you can do without. If you have a family you have to have a house. To apply the expression "sanctity of contract" to a contract which, in effect, the landlord could impose upon the working man is a mere perversion of language. That is the problem.[49]

His purpose, to persuade the Conservative Government to extend the remit of the Act beyond security of tenure for lessees whose lease had expired, and include leasehold enfranchisement, failed and sanctity of contract prevailed. However, enfranchisement was again on the political agenda in 1967.[50] At that time there was a clear social problem that had to be addressed. Many long leases of working-class homes, particularly in the minefields of South Wales, were expiring and would revert to freeholders without compensation. Something needed to be done to avoid widespread injustice.[51] The government drew on notions of fairness and morality when they justified giving long leaseholders of houses a discounted right either to enfranchise or to a lease extension.[52]

For enfranchisement to succeed the government had to compromise. Rights applied only to owner-occupied, lower value houses. The justification was the need to minimise interference with freedom of contract. Nonetheless significant opposition remained. For instance, Lord Brook of Cumnor, for the opposition, argued that the Bill legalised theft.[53]

Cole and Robinson draw attention to similar contestations in their description of the bitterly fought battle between leaseholders and landowners during the passage of the 1993 Leasehold Reform, Housing and Urban Development Act,[54] even though it was a Conservative Government promoting reform.[55] They suggest that the amendments forced on the government by the House of Lords virtually emasculated the Act, increasing the costs and the complexities of enfranchisement.

If leasehold reform is to be viable and sustainable the dualism at its heart needs to be overcome. A consensus around reform needs to emerge which can counter the status quo of property ownership. The English and Welsh governments appear to have chosen to build a consensus around consumerism. This is

[48] Landlord and Tenant Act 1954.
[49] Speech of Frank Soskice MP. HC Deb 27 January 1954, vol 522, col 1775.
[50] This came in the form of the Leasehold Reform Act 1967.
[51] HL Deb 26 June 1967, vol 284, col 15.
[52] HC Deb 7 March 1967, vol 742, cols 1272–73.
[53] HL Deb 26 June 1967, vol 284, col 28.
[54] 1993 Act (n 15).
[55] Cole and Robinson (n 17) 600.

consistent with other governmental responses to the 'broken housing market'[56] including the Law Commission's projects on law reform, which it describes as making leasehold home ownership 'fit for purpose'.[57] We can glean something of what government means by consumerism from policy documentation. Promises of fairness and transparency have, in the last ten years, been repeatedly made to leaseholders. We see them in the White Paper *Fixing our Broken Housing Market* which indicated that action would be taken 'to promote transparency and fairness for the growing number of leaseholders'.[58] They appeared in the policy objectives given by the Westminster Government to the Law Commission – the promotion of transparency and fairness in the residential leasehold sector and the provision of a better deal for leaseholders as consumers. These objectives were repeated in 2021 by the then Secretary of State, who committed to 'fairness and transparency' to protect 'consumers … from abuse and poor service'.[59] The first piece of legislation delivered as part of the promised tranche of reforms, the Leasehold Reform (Ground Rent) Act 2022, caps rents on new long leaseholds to 'an annual rent of one peppercorn' provides a further example.[60] During the Report Stage of that Bill, Eddie Hughes MP (Minister for Housing) stated that providing a clear-cut date after which if a regulated lease is sold, there can be no monetary ground rent, makes things more transparent and easier for leaseholders.[61]

One of the most significant indicators of the consumer trajectory is the U-turn of the Competition and Markets Authority which, after some reluctance, agreed in 2019 to investigate the mis-selling of leasehold houses and potential unfair and/or onerous terms in leasehold property.[62] In its initial report published 28 February 2020,[63] it identified problems with high and accelerating ground rents, poor sales practices and high fees being charged for permissions, especially when there is no contractual basis for charging such a fee. In addition, the CMA expressed concerns that the checks and balances that ought to have protected homeowners from potentially harmful terms and practices, such as independent legal advice, had been ineffective. In September 2020 the CMA announced that it had opened cases in relation to possible breaches of consumer protection law in the residential leasehold sector. From that date onwards it has announced formal commitments from significant freeholders, including Taylor Wimpey, Aviva, and Persimmon as well as several housing associations to making changes to punitive ground rent terms and paying compensation to affected leaseholders.

[56] DCLG, *Fixing our Broken Housing Market* (Cm 9352, 2017) para 1.7.

[57] Law Commission, *Leasehold Home Ownership: Exercising the Right to Manage* (Law Com No 393, 2020).

[58] DCLG (n 56) para 4.36.

[59] Robert Jenrick MP, then Secretary of State. HC WS 11 January 2021, HCWS695.

[60] The programme of reform will be analysed by the authors in a separate article.

[61] HC Deb 24 January 2022, vol 707, col 807.

[62] The Competition and Markets Authority is an independent non-ministerial UK government department.

[63] Competition and Markets Authority, *Leasehold Housing: Update Report* (CMA, 2020).

Whilst the CMA is a powerful tool to mobilise on the side of leaseholders, we pay more careful attention to the form of consumerism proposed by the government and whether it is sufficiently robust a reform tool in the fourth section of this chapter. At this point and noting that the 2022 Queen's Speech included explicit reference to 'transforming the experience of leaseholders',[64] we turn to empirical evidence of the leaseholder experience in the contemporary property market.

III. A CONSUMERIST LENS ON LEASEHOLDER EXPERIENCE

In this section we draw on qualitative data collected by the authors during a project on the sale and use of leasehold in Wales supported by the Welsh Government. We provide a consumerist framing to our analysis as we discuss two aspects of the relationship between the landlord and the leaseholder which form the basis of the current regulatory logic affecting leasehold law: bargaining power and choice. We then discuss experiences of poor practice before concluding that these are indicative of a dysfunctional market which has eroded the confidence of leasehold purchasers.

A. Data Collection and Methodology

Data was collected between the end of 2019 and late spring 2020. The project design included a multi-method qualitative study consisting of an online qualitative questionnaire which received 129 responses, 27 in-depth qualitative interviews with leaseholders across Wales as well as two focus groups with 'professional' stakeholders, including solicitors involved in leasehold conveyancing and disputes and property agents. We draw primarily from our survey and qualitative leaseholder interview datasets.

B. Bargaining Power and Information Asymmetries

The modern freeholder-leaseholder relationship is characterised by an inequality of arms. On the one hand sits well-resourced, legally savvy, often multi-national developers and professional or institutional freeholders. For example, on 29 July 2017, the *Guardian* reported that one organisation, E&J Estates, was the freehold company collecting ground rents on over 40,000 properties from large-scale developments across the country.[65] Other developer-freeholder

[64] Queen's Speech 2022, see Prime Minister's Office (n 6).

[65] P Collinson, 'Leasehold tycoon: man whose firms control 40,000 UK homes' *The Guardian* (29 July 2017); www.theguardian.com/money/2017/jul/29/leasehold-tycoon-man-whose-firms-control-40000-uk-homes (accessed 24 January 2023).

companies such as Bellway, Taylor Wimpey and Barratt Developments have annual turnovers that stretch into the hundreds of millions of pounds. On the other hand, leaseholders are likely to be individual purchasers and will often be purchasing the property as their main residence. This complicates the seller-purchaser relationship and exposes leasehold purchasers to malpractice.[66]

Blandy reminds us that as leasehold provides people with homes, it is critical to individual feelings of ontological security. The legal abstractions of leasehold and freehold tenure forms often mask the immense psychological, cultural, and emotional importance of these structures to those who reside in leasehold properties.[67]

The prevalence of institutional or professional freeholders was clear within our dataset, where over 40 per cent of survey participants reported that their freeholder was a commercial organisation, and a further 13 per cent reported that their freeholder was a housing association.

Figure 1 Freeholder type – flat leaseholds

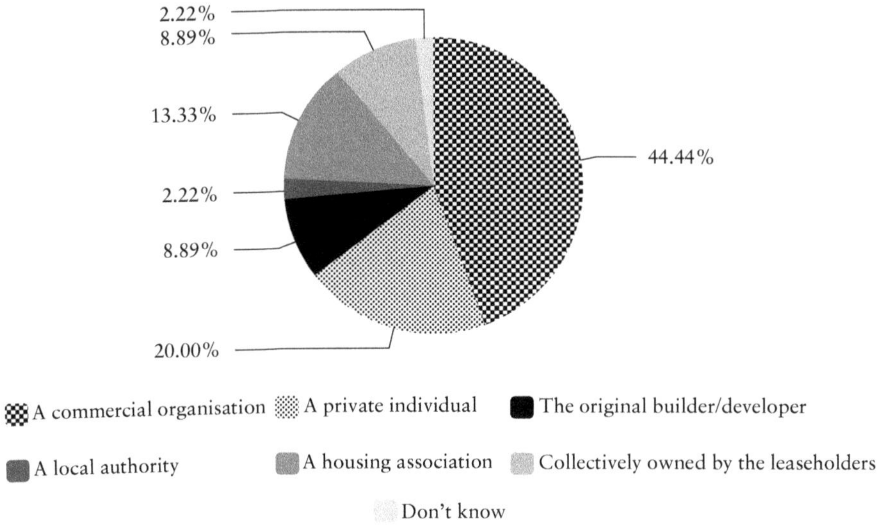

Inequality of bargaining power extends beyond financial resources and includes significant legal and informational asymmetries between leaseholders and freeholders at the point of purchase, particularly where the property is a new-build, and the freeholder is also the developer. The complicated pscyho-social implications

[66] S Blandy, 'Precarious Homes: The Sharing Continuum' in H Carr, B Edgworth and C Hunter (eds), *Law and the Precarious Home: Socio Legal Perspectives on the Home in Insecure Times* (Oxford, Hart Publishing, 2018).

[67] See L Fox, 'The Meaning of Home: a Chimerical Concept or a Legal Challenge?' (2002) 29 *Journal of law and Society* 580; and L Fox, *Conceptualising Home: Theories, Laws and Policies* (Oxford, Hart Publishing, 2007).

of informational imbalances are illustrated by the experience of a house leaseholder who purchased his home from a large national developer-freeholder:

> ... my ongoing complaint to them is why, when I put the reservation fee down why didn't they tell me at that stage or give me a document to say it was leasehold at that stage [...] that's when you've paid the £500 or £1000 [...]. They didn't supply that information to my solicitor until about ten days before exchange and by that time we were committed to buying the house because we'd obviously bought carpets and made other arrangements, including our kitchen and there was no way for us to pull out at that stage, so we went ahead.
>
> ***House leaseholder, Neath Port Talbot.***

Around half of the leaseholders (n=13) we interviewed raised concerns about the level of information and detail they were provided with at the outset. However, a more concerning finding was that although most leaseholders understood the fact that they were purchasing a leasehold interest in the property at the time of purchase, the majority did not understand what that would mean in terms of the day-to-day management and occupation of their property. As one leaseholder explained, the difference between the asset-based welfare ideal and the implications of leasehold interests can be unclear for purchasers:

> ... this again comes back to what did we know versus what did we not know. So we knew it was leasehold because it's an apartment and we were told most apartments are leasehold, it's not a big deal and it's just because it's a communal building, so this is like a terminology that's associated with it, but we didn't know what that actually meant.
>
> I thought that it was an asset just like my, my house was an asset that would rise in value all the time, that I would find security, I didn't know that that wasn't the case and [it] depreciates rather than appreciates, and so a leasehold property is something that you would buy because you can't afford a freehold, and that has shocked me tremendously.
>
> ***Flat leaseholder, Neath Port Talbot.***

Concerns relating to the knowledge and experience of consumers within the leasehold market were also expressed by the Competitions and Markets Authority in their 2020 update report. The CMA drew specific attention to the significance of the leasehold purchase within a consumer's life course, noting that for most consumers 'buying a house or flat will be their largest purchase and investment' and that because 'it is a relatively infrequent purchase consumers are unlikely to accumulate significant knowledge of the process or the salient characteristics of different forms of property ownership'.[68]

[68] CMA (n 63) para 33.

As the Law Commission points out, there is, at the heart of the relationship between landlord (freeholder or superior lessee) and leaseholder, a conflict of interests:

> The landlord may see leasehold solely as an investment opportunity or a way of generating income, while for leaseholders the property may be their home, as well as a capital investment.[69]

An additional point may be made here; there may be a conflict of interests between leaseholders who are owner occupiers of their leasehold properties and those who have bought leasehold properties as buy-to-let investments. Leaseholders who are resident in their properties may be more prepared to pay for improvements than those who do not live there.

These conflicts create substantial issues for the effective regulation of information asymmetries. Information requirements are often a hallmark of consumer empowerment regimes and involve imposing requirements on the commercial party with a stronger bargaining position to disclose information to the consumer (for example, emissions levels or energy ratings) to inform purchasing decisions. Such requirements have trickled into the regulation of leasehold, for example in the case of service charge demands,[70] and form part of the government's roadmap of reforms.[71] However, the potential for information requirements to remedy the issues experienced by leaseholders, particularly in terms of escalating costs, could be dampened by difficulty in accurately predicting the extent of future liability. Some leaseholders we interviewed had been provided with service charge projections in the case of new build leasehold developments that bore no correlation with the eventual charges. One participant described their experience of this process:

> I visited the marketing suite and they provided me with all kinds of glossy brochures on the interior, the equipment, listings of the properties still available, the price, the size, and they also provided me with something that I refer to as a work of fiction [...]. The document was titled the [...] Service Charge Proposal and it contained a very detailed description of the extent of services and their cost. [...] The document contained a statement that declared it was only an estimate, but the associated language was of a nature that injected a great deal of confidence into the proposal, because they said things like 'we have used our expertise in compiling this document' and 'we have considered the cost of other properties that we manage' and they manage tens of thousands of units in England and Wales.
>
> ***Flat leaseholder, Cardiff.***

[69] Law Commission (n 17) para 1.3.

[70] Under s 47 of the Landlord and Tenant Act 1987, service charges must be in writing. Furthermore, s 21B of the Landlord and Tenant Act 1985 provides that service charge demands must include the prescribed content.

[71] Queen's Speech 2022, see Prime Minister's Office (n 6).

The data highlights the difficulties in regulating information asymmetries in a market that has been historically premised on the principle of caveat emptor and within which there exists no obvious mechanism to obtain independent verification of estimates, and where there are broader doubts as to whether it is in fact possible to project costs with any reasonable degree of certainty. Building on the arguments made by Ann Stewart, the assumption that forms the basis of property law's reluctance to intervene in these delicate and complex relationships – 'two equal parties who know what they are doing' – is often simply false.[72] Leasehold purchasers find themselves in the middle of what Madden and Marcuse characterise as an arena of contestation where there is 'a conflict between housing as home and as real estate' and where 'housing is the subject of contestation between different ideologies, economic interests and political projects'.[73]

C. Choice

Market complexity coupled with information asymmetries has significant implications for consumer choice. This was recognised as early as the mid-1960s by the Molony Committee, commissioned by the Board of Trade to consider consumer protection. The committee concluded that in complex markets the consumer finds it beyond their power to make a wise and informed choice and is vulnerable to exploitation and deception.[74]

In the context of leasehold, the notion that even price is not a sufficient indicator of quality, and that consumers may be overwhelmed by the 'maze' of the purchase process was highlighted by the CMA in their investigation update report. They argued that the size of a leaseholder's investment is such that 'purchasers are capable of being blinded by the sums involved'.[75] Indeed, in the case of leasehold, the situation is complicated by the question of whether, even with the relevant information, the decision to purchase a leasehold interest amounts to a 'choice'. The notion of choice here is questioned on two primary grounds. The first is the centrality of 'ownership' as a symbol of security, success, and self-sufficiency in our neo-liberal society. As Carr pointed out in 2011:

> Private property – despite the financial crisis – remains the principal mechanism for delivering the wealth, self-reliance, and individual freedom that governments who have embraced neo-liberal rationalities promise their citizens.[76]

[72] A Stewart, 'Rethinking Housing Law: A Contribution to the Debate on Tenure' (1994) 9(2) *Housing Studies* 263.

[73] D Madden and P Marcuse, *In Defense of Housing: The Politics of Crisis* (London, Verso, 2016) 4.

[74] Board of Trade, *Final Report of the Committee on Consumer Protection* (Cmnd 1781, 1962) paras 42–43.

[75] CMA (n 63) para 34.

[76] H Carr, 'The Right to Buy, the Leaseholder and the Impoverishment of Ownership' (2011) 38 *Journal of Law and Society* 519, 519.

For Carr, a by-product of the Right to Buy and its extension of home ownership was that those who fail to chart a route through to home ownership are viewed as ineffective consumers potentially subject to processes of social exclusion such that 'the injustice of their position makes the stark realities of the neo-liberal/neo-conservative order patent'.[77]

Beyond the structural question of whether the potentially overwhelming nature of government driven property-owning hegemony acts to vitiate real choice for potential leaseholders, there is a broader question of whether there is truly scope for choice in the housing market.[78] Do leaseholders actively *choose* to purchase a leasehold interest, or is the nature of that interest either unavoidable or simply ancillary to the choice being made? The interviews we conducted asked each participant why they purchased that particular property, and whether they were specifically looking for a leasehold property at the time. Somewhat unsurprisingly, all 27 participants made clear that they were not specifically looking for a leasehold property.

As the chart below indicates, leasehold sales in Wales are skewed heavily towards the lower price quintiles. These figures were produced using Land Registry price paid data during our Welsh Government project.[79]

Figure 2 Proportion of all sales (%) by price and tenure

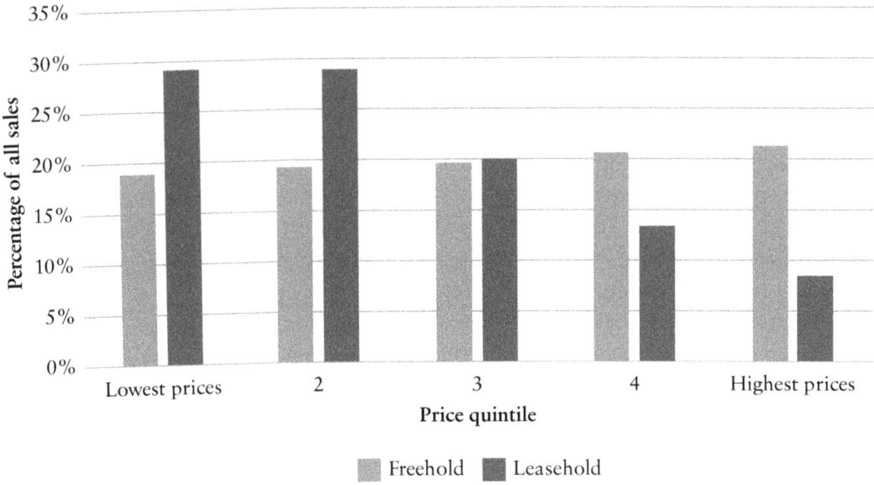

Source: Land Registry Price Paid Data (2018).

During the qualitative interviews, however, affordability did not appear to be the main reason for 'choosing' the tenure amongst many leaseholders.

[77] ibid 520.

[78] For a more detailed exploration of the problematic nature of choice in complex property law relationships, see L Whitehouse, 'The Home Owner: Citizen Or Consumer?' in S Bright and J Dewar (eds), *Land Law: Themes and Perspectives* (Oxford, OUP, 2008).

[79] Carr et al (n 7) 42.

For 44.4 per cent (n=12) of those leaseholders interviewed, the location of the property was key. Participants often cited proximity to family or friends, their workplace, or geographical features, such as beaches or a national park. Price was a primary or secondary reason for around 26 per cent (n=7) of participants and was commonly associated with factors forcing leaseholders to downsize, such as health or accessibility needs.

This data illustrates that the messiness of life leads individuals to opt for leasehold. A significant number of leaseholders moved into their property due to the location, sometimes where freehold tenure was not an option due to the concentration of apartments in the relevant area – for example, in dense urban areas such as Cardiff, or coastal areas where leasehold developments often constitute most of the new build stock. Other participants downsized after their children had left, and this was often coupled with retirement and the associated financial constraints that come with a reduction in income. One participant's story was a case in point of the messiness of circumstances that may lead to a decision to purchase a leasehold property. The participant was going through a relationship breakdown and wanted to maintain contact with his children. The only property that was affordable in the vicinity of the previous family home was a leasehold apartment. Here, the potential purchaser is balancing a plethora of personal, geographical, and fiscal factors when making a decision. The tenure form of the property is completely backgrounded, or entirely absent it would seem, from the 'choice' made by leaseholders.

It is notable that the government's response to its consultation on tackling unfair practices in the leasehold market supports our contention that leasehold is not a choice tenure, especially in the case of houses sold on leasehold.[80] This is to be contrasted with the government's position in relation to abolishing leasehold in favour of commonhold, where the notion of choice has been invoked as a reason to maintain a dual tenure system.[81] As noted by the Law Commission, the failure of commonhold in providing an alternative tenure form compounds the lack of choice faced by potential leaseholders.[82]

The data illustrates the complexity of decisions made by potential leaseholders during the purchase process. Not only are they having to navigate a maze of complex legal structures and processes, but the circumstances surrounding this decision and the socio-political context in which it takes place may be such that it is difficult to conceptualise that decision as a rational economic decision of an individual consumer engaging in a market activity. Whilst there is acknowledgment of the lack of choice within government, the answer appears to be a

[80] DCLG (n 8) para 35.

[81] Secretary of State for Housing, Communities and Local Government, *Government Response to the Housing, Communities and Local Government Select Committee Report on Leasehold Reform* (Cm 99, 2019) para 23.

[82] Law Commission, *Reinvigorating Commonhold: The Alternative to Leasehold Ownership* (Law Com No 394, 2020) para 1.30.

'reinvigoration' of commonhold, which seems optimistic given two decades of failed legislation and 60 years of failed endeavours. Behind this veil, it appears that the default policy position remains ambivalent on the issue of choice. Lord Shakleton's observation in 1967 remains apposite; it is reasonable to infer that a lot of people buy leasehold because they cannot find anything suitable on freehold terms.[83]

D. Poor Practices and Market Dysfunction

As this chapter has made clear, confidence in leasehold as a tenure has collapsed in recent years. The CMA noted several 'very serious' allegations of mis-selling made by leaseholders about the conduct of developers and sales staff.[84] The specific issues raised by the CMA were also present within our dataset. Several leaseholders who purchased new-build houses paid a reservation fee of between £500 and £1,000 only to later discover that the property was leasehold. Some leaseholders, such as our house leaseholder from Neath Port Talbot, only found out when it was practically impossible to withdraw from the process.

When leaseholders realised that the property was being sold on a leasehold basis, their concerns were often pacified by reassurances that their title was 'as good as freehold' or that they could easily and cheaply acquire the freehold later. As one leaseholder told us:

> When I first realised they said 'Oh don't worry about leasehold, it's the normal practice, you can buy it in a couple of years' time, it's X amount, it's not much money.' But since [the freehold] got sold to an overseas company, they're just pulling figures out of the sky … coming up with silly figures.
>
> ***House leaseholder, Bridgend.***

Poor practices were not limited to the sales process. As well as service charge issues covered above, leaseholders were concerned with permission fees and the impact that poor practices were having on their experience. Again, our findings align with the CMA investigation,[85] with some charges levied without basis in the lease document, or costs that seemed completely disproportionate to the permission being sought. One leaseholder told us about their experience as a member of a right to manage company where residents were having issues with fees levied by the freeholder in relation to pets:

> So you have to have permission to have a dog and they charge £250 for that. But it's not used to control the number of dogs on the site or anything, it's just to make money. We've discovered if you just ask for permission [the freeholder] charge[s] you £250 and that permission is only for two weeks […] they say we thought you had a

[83] HL Deb 26 June 1967, vol 284, col 17.
[84] CMA (n 63) para 44.
[85] CMA (n 63).

> visitor. You can have permission for the rest of the pet's life, but you're going to have to pay another £250.
>
> ***Flat leaseholder, Vale of Glamorgan.***

Several leaseholders mentioned regular fees levied for subletting, with examples of biannual renewal fees (eg, £40) on top of more substantial sums for new tenants (eg, £200). Leaseholders are entitled to challenge the reasonableness of a permission fees (administration charges) at the First Tier Tribunal (Property Chamber) under Schedule 11 of the Commonhold and Leasehold Reform Act 2002.[86] In *Proxima*, the Upper Tribunal stated, in obiter, that such costs ought to cover the reasonable administrative expenses of a landlord but should not be used as a source of profit.[87] Although many leaseholders queried or challenged the fees charged, particularly where provision for such charges was not made in the lease, it is notable that none of the participants intended to challenge fees at the Tribunal.

The data paints a picture of a dysfunctional tenure and a market within which consumer confidence has been utterly undermined. This complicates the use of traditional consumer mechanisms, such as information requirements or unfair terms regulation. The property law approach to specific issue dispute resolution fails to account for the relational nature of the tenure and the potentially life-limiting consequences that dysfunctionality within the market can have on leaseholders. As the house leaseholder from Bridgend who was told that leasehold was 'normal practice' noted:

> I had a report from the solicitor, the report on title said it was a perfectly good house, perfectly sellable, mortgageable; five years down the line it's not mortgageable and it's certainly not sellable.
>
> ***House leaseholder, Bridgend.***

IV. CONSUMERISM AND LEASEHOLD REFORM

Our data in section III demonstrates not only that leaseholders suffer significant problems, amplifying the case for reform, but also that notions of choice, transparency and fairness are complicated and elusive in the context of leasehold relationships. Whilst consumer-oriented reforms would improve the lot of leaseholders, our review of previous attempts at leasehold reform suggest they will be insufficient; the current relationship between leaseholders and freeholders offers too many opportunities for exploitation. Without something more substantial, the observation that Cole and Robinson made in the context of legislation in the 1990s will remain apposite and changes will offer 'some improvements to

[86] Commonhold and Leasehold Reform Act 2002, Sch 11.
[87] *Proxima GR Properties Ltd v McGhee* [2014] UKUT 59 (LC).

the situation of leaseholders but … not address fully the combination of factors responsible for their dissatisfaction'.[88]

In this section of the chapter our focus is not on whether being treated as consumers would be beneficial for leaseholders. Instead, we are concerned with something more fundamental. We argue that what is needed to stabilise leasehold as a tenure is more than conditional and contingent reforms. There needs to be a shift in the hierarchy of power between leaseholder and freeholder, a permanent change in the status quo of property rights. Drawing on Pointing and Bulos, we seek to answer an important question: can a sufficiently robust reforming consensus be built around a consumerist paradigm to achieve this necessary change in freeholder/leaseholder relationships? There are two features of the long history of leasehold reform that are pertinent here. The first is that the crystallisation of the social forces opposed to reform noted by Pointing and Bulos[89] has been strengthened by every subsequent reform effort. The second is the paradox at the heart of leasehold reform. Leasehold can only be reformed within the current property paradigm by increasing the property rights of leaseholders and decreasing the property rights of freeholders. This means that relying for instance on responsible property ownership as an argument for reform is problematic because responsible property ownership can also be deployed as a defence of the status quo. For example, Theresa Villiers MP criticised the abolition of ground rents in these terms,

> We are all united in wanting to stamp out abusive practices with ground rents, but is the defect of the hon. Gentleman's amendment not that it amounts effectively to a confiscation of existing property rights? That in itself has fairness issues, but it also deters future investment in our building stock. That future investment is needed, for example, if we are going to insulate against climate change and turn our buildings into more carbon neutral ones for the future.[90]

The powerful lobby for the status quo meant that whilst ground rents have been abolished for future leases, the reform has been constrained. The new legislation does nothing to remedy the problems of the recent spate of excessive and accelerating ground rents.

Taking these features of the current duality of the debate about leasehold reform into account, there are three reasons why we are sceptical of the potency of consumerism as a reforming consensus. The first is the very limited success of consumer interventions in property relationships, using as an example the limited effectiveness of the protections given to mortgagors. The second concerns the potency of property law as a tool for maintaining the status quo, supporting the conservative consensus, and constraining the impact of leasehold reform. Our third reason is less concerned with the power of the status quo.

[88] Cole and Robinson (n 17) 599.
[89] Pointing and Bulos (n 40).
[90] HC Deb 24 January 2022, vol 707, col 795.

It focuses on the problematic limitations of consumerism itself. Consumerism, which as Whitehouse notes, replaced citizenship as the conduit for rights as the role of the state shifted at the end of the twentieth century,[91] is not designed as a platform for radical reform of the status quo. Instead, it works within the market system seeking to address some of its more egregious harms. The question of whether consumerism packs a sufficiently powerful punch to disarm the powerful conservative forces of property is made more complex by the paradox at the heart of leasehold reform. What leasehold reform requires is that the importance of property rights is diminished for one form of property holder to strengthen the property rights of another.

A. The Limitations of Consumer Interventions into Property Relationships

Despite more general trends in consumer protections, in the UK almost all transactions concerning land were excluded from earlier consumer-oriented protections. The exceptionalism of transactions relating to land is a consistent theme noted in the literature.[92] Instead, land transactions are subject to the regime set out in the Law of Property Act 1925[93] as altered by the Law of Property (Miscellaneous Provisions) Act 1989.[94] Rather than a protective regime, the approach aims for certainty in dealings between two notionally equal players and sets the rules for fair play.

Even in areas where overtly 'consumerist' agendas have been pursued, such as mortgages, the stubbornness of property law's 'strict logic' has watered down regulatory efforts or opted for more comfortable paths that avoid the need to consider anything beyond economic concerns.[95] For Whitehouse, this has meant that property law continues to prioritise the economic interests of mortgagees over the difficult-to-quantify non-economic interests of the mortgagor. Property law not only ignores the potentially destructive personal impacts of repossession on mortgagors but fails in its wider role of holding mortgagees to account for unethical business practices.[96] To disrupt the status quo, any so-called 'consumer' reforms to leasehold must, as Whitehouse argues in the case of mortgages, 'offer a more proportionate and appropriate response to the differing levels of risk and resilience experienced by' leaseholders and freeholders.[97]

[91] L Whitehouse, 'The Home Owner: Citizen or Consumer?' in S Bright and J Dewar (eds), *Land Law: Themes and Perspectives* (Oxford, OUP, 2008).

[92] See, eg, L Whitehouse, 'The First Legal Mortgagor: A Consumer Without Adequate Protection?' (2015) 38 *Journal of Consumer Policy* 161.

[93] Law of Property Act 1925.

[94] Law of Property (Miscellaneous Provisions) Act 1989.

[95] L Whitehouse, 'Mortgage Possession at a Crossroads: Which Way Should We Turn?' [2019] *Conv* 227.

[96] ibid.

[97] ibid 249.

B. The Court, the Conservative Consensus and Leaseholder Rights

We have considered the contestation in Parliament about leasehold reform and how that contestation has strengthened the conservative consensus. That contestation is also played out in the courts where property law norms such as certainty in dealings, equality of bargaining power and good order further buttress the conservative consensus and have been successfully deployed to curtail leaseholder rights.[98]

To further the point made in the previous section, even within leasehold there are numerous examples of the courts intervening to curtail statutory leaseholder rights in ways that appear to frustrate parliamentary intentions. For instance, whilst the Commonhold and Leasehold Reform Act 2002[99] included provisions requiring that freeholders consulted with leaseholders on major works,[100] addressing a persistent complaint, the requirements were seriously weakened by the Supreme Court in *Daejan Investments Ltd v Benson*.[101] It decided that the correct legal test for dispensation from consultation requirements was whether the flat owners would suffer any relevant prejudice, and if so, what relevant prejudice, as a result of the landlord's failure to comply with the requirements. This was despite a lack of reference to prejudice in the words of the statute. Prior to the decision, breaches of the consultation requirements limited the amount that a freeholder could claim for works to a nominal sum, an incursion of the property rights of the freeholder. Subsequently leaseholders have been required to prove prejudice as well as breach before costs are reduced, changing what was a freestanding right designed to address information asymmetries and promote transparency, to one that is rebuttable.

Constraints on the interpretation of statutory rights are also illustrated by the caselaw on section 35 of the Landlord and Tenant Act 1987. The section gives parties to a lease the right to apply to the FTT for variation of the lease in particular circumstances. These include defects in the lease with respect to repair and insurance as well as defects in the computation of service charges.[102] In *Morgan v Fletcher*[103] the Upper Tribunal set out the limits to the provisions. To the surprise of leaseholders, it found that the rights are not there to remedy unfairness in service charge provision. The Tribunal can

[98] Property law academics have also played a part in maintaining the status quo. Writing in the context of proprietary estoppel, Dixon for instance characterises the hallmarks of a conventional property law approach: To this author, estoppel runs the risk of becoming an unprincipled doctrine, an ad hoc response to perceived unfairness: neither a Titian, a Howard Hodgkin, but a Jackson Pollock. All are beautiful to some, but I would suggest that land law needs form and shape. See M Dixon, 'Painting Proprietary Estoppel: Howard Hodgkin, Titian or Jackson Pollock?' [2022] *Conv* 30, 45.

[99] 1987 Act (n 14).

[100] Inserting s 20ZA into the Landlord and Tenant Act 1985.

[101] *Daejan Investments Ltd v Benson* [2013] UKSC 14.

[102] 2002 Act (n 20) s 35.

[103] *Morgan v Fletcher* [2009] UKUT 186 (LC).

only re-calculate the apportionment of service charges when the aggregate of the charges does not add up to 100 per cent. If the service charges add up to 100 per cent then the Tribunal's jurisdiction is ousted. This is particularly iniquitous when the landlord adds a further unit to the block and does not alter the previously settled apportionment. This leaves existing leaseholders in a position where they are subsidising the services provided to the new units. Again, we see the judiciary adopting a conservative approach to leaseholders' rights justifying their position because of the need to protect the integrity of the original bargain. It is difficult to see how new reforms providing for fairness and transparency would be more effective in promoting leaseholder rights than the current provisions.

The failures of the Right to Manage (RTM) usefully illustrate the long-term consequences for leaseholders of the conservatism of property law. The RTM was designed to provide a no-fault procedure short of enfranchisement for blocks of flats which for instance were inadequately managed by freeholders. As management of property is not supposed to be a profit-making activity it might have been supposed that freeholders would be glad to be rid of the burden. This has not been the case and freeholders have strongly resisted applications.[104]

There are also costs problems. The RTM company must pay the landlord's reasonable costs of the claim and must also pay the landlord's litigation costs if the landlord successfully challenges the claim in the Tribunal. What should have been a low-risk standard procedure, because of the interventions of the courts has been made high-risk, complex, expensive, and time-consuming.

What these examples illustrate is that a new reform consensus built around consumerism is unlikely to overcome the conservatism of property law any more than previous iterations of leaseholder reform projects have done.

C. The Limitations of Consumerism

In addition to the potency of property as a conservative consensus, there are practical limitations associated with the application of consumer logics to the leasehold relationship. Academic literature on consumerism for instance notes the problem of the information-saturated consumer,[105] and traditional consumer regulation mechanisms are more difficult to apply in the context of an on-going relationship like that of leaseholder and freeholder as opposed to the

[104] See Law Commission (n 44) para 214 for evidence of landlords' strict compliance with statutory procedures.

[105] L McShane and C Sabadoz, 'Rethinking the Concept of Consumer Empowerment: Recognizing Consumers as Citizens' (2015) 39(5) *International Journal of Consumer Studies* 544. T Harrison et al, 'The Internet, Information and Empowerment' (2006) 40(9) *European Journal of Marketing* 972.

more standard spot transaction. The programme of reform must take on board the fact that leasehold is not a homogenous tenure experienced in the same way by all lessees. The leaseholder/freeholder relationship is not as standard as most consumer/supplier relationships and power imbalances do not always follow predictable paths. Not infrequently, the tenant may be a corporate body and the freeholder a body of lessees. But our concern goes beyond these technical concerns.

As suggested earlier, consumerism, despite its progressive appearance, works within existing market frameworks. However, consumerist agendas also belie their potential to undermine due process and other key entitlements of citizenship.[106] Of particular concern is the potential for consumer agendas to lean towards and be captured by alternate forms of opaque self-regulation and potentially watered-down redress mechanisms. Although such moves are often accompanied by stern language and a flurry of activity, as Whitehouse explains in the case of the *Statement of Practice* published by the Council of Mortgage Lenders, they expose 'consumers' to unaccountable decision-making processes and lack teeth in the case of non-compliance.[107]

Consumerist agendas have often failed to live up to expectations. Without a significant disruption to the status quo of property law norms, it seems unlikely that the current reform package planned by central government will go far enough to unwind the dysfunctionality ingrained in leasehold.

V. CONCLUSION

Leasehold cannot be allowed to fail. Leaseholders are electorally important, particularly in urban centres, and having quite literally bought into the ideology of home ownership, there would be significant political consequences if as a result they became poorer and more constrained. Just as important any collapse in value of leasehold property would have serious economic consequences not just for individual leaseholders but more generally, and the social harm of a failed tenure cannot be underestimated. Marc Schelhase points to the systemic social harms which emanate from the privileging of 'ownership …' when the risk-reward balance tips unfavourably against a property owner.[108]

Yet the history of leasehold law reform shows how difficult it is for interventions to address the dissatisfaction of leaseholders. A reforming consensus is beginning to be built around consumerism. It is clear that, at least in policy circles, the property law principle of caveat emptor is losing favour, and the notion that both parties are bargaining from positions of equal strength is being

[106] Whitehouse (n 91).
[107] ibid.
[108] M Schelhase, 'Bringing the Harm Home: The Quest for Home Ownership and the Amplification of Social Harm' (2021) 26 *New Political Economy* 439.

debunked. The problem is whether that reform consensus will be sufficient to overcome the conservative consensus which supports the status quo of property. Our conclusion is that it will not. The status quo is very powerful and has become increasingly powerful with each iteration of leasehold reform. The history of consumerist interventions into property relationships is not propitious and the instincts and traditions of property law which have been successfully deployed to constrain past reform programmes will continue to have significant effects. Moreover, we are sceptical that the market-fixing approach of the current government is anything more than a further iteration of reactive policymaking; firefighting the collapse in confidence in the tenure brought about by a perfect storm of the building safety crisis, strong activist campaigns powered by social media, and extensive work by the Competition and Markets Authority to highlight the widespread nature of poor practice. Government is undoubtedly wary of the potential ripple effects that any market collapse would have on financial institutions and the buoyancy of the property market, as well as the ideological implications of upending the stability of property ownership.

We have another concern. Even if we are wrong, and a reform programme based on consumerism is sufficient to overcome the potency of the property status quo, the consequences we suggest are unpredictable. This is because the free and fair market, which is the goal of consumerist approaches, is unattainable in leasehold properties, so government is pursuing a chimera. We see at least two significant barriers to the exercise of free consumer choice, neither of which can be overcome in the contemporary economic paradigm. The first is the inadequacy of supply of affordable home ownership which renders notions of choice illusory, and the second the incompatibility of individual freedom and the collective nature of living in leasehold property. Further, we suggest that there may be an unexpected consequence of a consumerist approach; it offers a new dynamism to leasehold activism which might accentuate dissatisfaction and further destabilise the tenure. Leaseholders may well 'weaponise' their new status as consumers. Recently Harry Scoffin of the Leasehold Knowledge Partnership tweeted, in response to a letter in the *Financial Times*,[109] 'We, the consumers, will kill the market for leasehold flats. Sales already down 60% in 3 years. Then we will get our commonhold.'[110] This suggests that even if consumerism provided a sufficiently robust challenge to the status quo of property, it is unlikely to provide stability to leasehold, the outcome that government seeks.

[109] D Konstantinidis, 'Letter: Tower Block Developers' problems are Self-Inflicted' *Financial Times* (London, 27 May 2022) www.ft.com/content/ba185c53-2873-4d49-9c33-7d2c09a67e5c (accessed 6 September 2022).

[110] H Scoffin, 'We, the Consumers, Will Kill the Market for Leasehold Flats' (Twitter, 27 May 2022) twitter.com/HarryScoffin/status/1530128590809051137 (accessed 6 September 2022).

Part IV

Property and Equity

10

Proprietary Estoppel: Great Expectations and Detrimental Reliance

LORD SALES JSC*

I. INTRODUCTION

THE UK SUPREME Court has just handed down its important decision on proprietary estoppel in *Guest v Guest*.[1] This chapter is based on a lecture which was delivered prior to that. The Court was split 3:2, essentially along the dividing line foreshadowed in my title. Is the doctrine of proprietary estoppel about protection of the expectation interest, where the owner of property has encouraged the person who later relies on the doctrine to expect that the property will be conveyed to them? Or is it about the protection of that person's reliance interest, where they have suffered detriment by relying on that encouragement to act in a particular way?

Clearly, a view about the fundamental justification for legal protection in this area will have implications for the remedy which ought to be granted. Is there some half-way house available to mediate between these different justifications, so that one is more significant than the other in certain circumstances and vice-versa when the circumstances change? I have long been interested in this question, and in trying to identify when and according to what principle the law might tip between prioritising the protection of one or the other of these two interests. The judgments of Lord Briggs and Lord Leggatt are major contributions on this issue.

As always with common law doctrine, one has to approach these questions with one eye on the record of decided cases and one eye on the theoretical underpinning for the relevant legal principle to be distilled from the cases.

* This chapter is a revised version of the keynote lecture for the MSPL 2022 conference. I am grateful to Jake Thorold, my Judicial Assistant, for his excellent assistance in preparing the lecture and to Ben McFarlane and Bill Swadling for comments on an earlier version. The usual caveat applies.

[1] *Guest v Guest* [2022] UKSC 27.

Doctrine occupies both spaces and is drawn from both. Pure theory does not exist: courts in the common law tradition have to work from existing case law and doctrine, not least for reasons of the rule of law, in order to secure the stability and predictability which are important values in any legal system. On the other hand, mere reference to case law, without any idea of underlying theory and principle, cannot secure those values either. New cases arise, and to know what the law says about them requires reference to some unifying view of the applicable principles. This depends on an understanding of the theoretical, moral and practical justifications for those principles, which in turn reveals their extension and limits.[2]

This chapter is not an extended discussion of *Guest v Guest*. It is too early for that and it would not be appropriate for me to try to pass my own comment on the divisions of view between my colleagues. There is no doubt that the judgments provide considerable food for thought. This is an area where the common law will benefit from the usual processes of reflection and comment by the distinguished academic lawyers who work in this field, which in turn will feed back into legal argument and further judicial consideration and exploration. Benjamin Cardozo said of judging, 'The inscrutable force of professional opinion presses upon us like the atmosphere, though we are heedless of its weight.'[3] In the case of *Guest v Guest*, I think the academic and professional opinion which presses on judges in future cases will not be inscrutable, but highly articulated and thoughtful. That is greatly to be welcomed.

II. PROPRIETARY ESTOPPEL AS A DOCTRINE OF EQUITY

Proprietary estoppel in the guise authoritatively recognised by the House of Lords in *Thorner v Major*[4] is a core example of the courts' basic equitable jurisdiction to intervene in cases where the application of strict legal rules would produce a result sufficiently at odds with a party's reasonable expectations so as to 'shock the conscience of the court'. As Robert Walker LJ recognised in the important case of *Gillet v Holt*, 'the fundamental principle that equity is concerned to prevent unconscionable conduct permeates all the elements of the [proprietary estoppel] doctrine'.[5] Lord Briggs reiterates the same point in *Guest v Guest*: 'One of the principal functions of equity is to put right injustice to which the law is otherwise blind, by restraining the rigid application of legal rules where their implementation would be unconscionable.'[6]

As so often with equitable doctrines, the law finds itself in a state of tension between trying to be flexible to respond to the particular circumstances of the

[2] For discussion, see P Sales, 'The Common Law: Context and Method' (2019) 135 *LQR* 47.
[3] B Cardozo, *The Growth of the Law* (New Haven, Yale University Press, 1924) 61.
[4] *Thorner v Major* [2009] UKHL 18; [2009] 1 WLR 776.
[5] *Gillett v Holt* [2001] Ch 210, 225 (Robert Walker LJ).
[6] *Guest* (n 1) [4].

case before it, in all its moral and factual complexity, and trying to lay down clear rules for the future, which are predictable in their effect. Veer too far in the first direction, and law seems to turn on the length of the Chancellor's foot. Or, more accurately, on the instincts of the first instance judge who tries the case. If the outcome of the case turns on a very broad discretion in the judge, three things follow:

(1) It becomes difficult to mount an appeal. The usual approach for an appellate court where a highly discretionary standard is being applied is not to interfere with the conclusion of the first instance judge who has directed himself or herself correctly as to the discretionary test to be applied and has not reached a perverse or irrational conclusion overall. If those conditions are satisfied, an appellate court stands back and leaves the assessment of the trial judge in place. As Hoffmann LJ said in *Re Grayan Building Services Ltd*:[7] 'generally speaking, the vaguer the standard and the greater the number of factors which the court has to weigh up in deciding whether or not the standard [... has] been met, the more reluctant an appellate court will be to interfere with the trial judge's decision'. Related to this, it becomes more difficult for the superior courts to develop doctrine and general rules known and applicable throughout the legal system.

(2) In consequence, space opens up for a degree of capriciousness to enter the system. The same or similar cases can be decided in completely different ways by different judges, without there being any error of law. What is supposed to be the rule of law looks increasingly like the rule of men (or women).

(3) It becomes more difficult for the parties to predict how the law will react to what they do. This affects them at two points in time. First, when they interact with each other. If I behave in a particular way, will I have incurred obligations to the other person or will I have acquired rights against them? Second, when the day of reckoning arrives and I have to decide whether I go to law to assert a claim, with all the cost and stress that may involve, or whether I resist a claim made against me. Lack of clarity in the law and the possibility of victory or defeat turning on the roll of the dice of which judge you get can deter the risk adverse from vindicating their rights and encourage speculative litigation by the desperate or those with a disposition to gamble in the hope of victory.

These features of a strongly discretionary approach relying on a vague standard of 'unconscionability' with unspecified content pose particular problems when dealing with the allocation of property rights and the rules governing the acquisition and disposal of such rights. Property law is supposed to be a paradigm area for the application of fixed and clear rules, so that everyone can

[7] *Re Grayan Building Services Ltd (in liquidation)* [1995] Ch 241, 254.

know where they stand and what they own – not just the parties who have been dealing with each other, but also those looking to acquire property from them.

But veer too far in the opposite direction, to lay down firm and inflexible fixed rules in advance, and a different type of problem emerges. It is a well-known feature of legislating now for the future that the legislator cannot predict in advance every situation for which they might wish – had they foreseen it – to make provision by the rules they lay down. Two particular consequences flow from rigidity in the rules to be applied.

(1) A gap opens up between the rationale for having a rule and the rule itself, the more the rule is treated as governing in an inflexible way types of cases which are within the ambit of its formulation but outside the contemplation of the rule-maker. If the gap gets too wide, the moral authority of the law and public confidence in it is eroded. A different type of capriciousness emerges: the capriciousness arising from lack of foresight about how the rule will in fact operate, and the results it will in fact produce, in future, unanticipated cases. One might say there is a pathology associated with too much rule by law and too little rule by men (or women). Equity as a set of rules or principles grew out of the jurisdiction of the Lord Chancellor to modify the stringent application of the common law in order to do justice in the circumstances of the individual case. This is a reflection of Aristotelian thinking, using his concept of *epieikeia* (usually translated as equity) to supplement and work partial modification of legal rules at their point of application in order to ensure justice is done and that the application of a rule in the particular case is tied closely to the underlying justice-based rationale for having the rule in the first place.[8] In the early equity jurisprudence, this derivation was made clear, for instance in the *Earl of Oxford's* case.[9]

(2) Fixed rules may fail in their guidance function if the practical reality is that the people who are subject to the rules do not in fact look to them when dealing with each other, but instead rely more on general moral standards which they think will govern how others will behave in relation to them and which, in a vague way, they may expect the law broadly to reflect. The less the parties to a transaction which they regard as binding have been concerned to fashion their relationship by reference to the legal rules, the greater the justification for allowing a more flexible equitable standard to govern their case.

These points are, of course, very familiar across a wide range of legal contexts. There is an extensive literature on the choice between rules and standards as

[8] *Nicomachean Ethics*, V. 10. 1137b, 12–29; RA Wasserstrom, *The Judicial Decision: Toward a Theory of Legal Justification* (Stanford, CA, Stanford University Press, 1961) ch 10.

[9] *Earl of Oxford's* case (1615) 1 Ch Rep. 1, 6.

forms of legal ordering.[10] The choice reflects the tension between the guidance function of law and the function of law to produce just outcomes in particular cases. Proprietary estoppel is a case study in how these functions are balanced in a particular area and how the tension is resolved in a practical and concrete way in doctrine. That is one reason why the subject is so interesting.

Another is because, since land is such an important and valuable asset, it is an area in which ordinary, unsophisticated people, who have ordered their affairs without knowledge of the applicable legal rules, are drawn into litigation despite the huge expense. The courts therefore find themselves having to deal with cases where the pressure to do justice in the particular case is strong and where the law's guidance function has broken down to a significant degree. But do hard cases make bad law in this area? On the other hand, to what extent should justice in the individual case be compromised in the interests of providing guidance for other cases?

One hunded and fifty years on from the first Judicature Act, the resurgence of a doctrine like proprietary estoppel poses many questions for the modern relationship between equity and the common law. Reports of the demise of equity as a result of the supposed fusion brought about by the great procedural reforms in the 1850s and 1870s are exaggerated. One of the themes of this chapter is how equity overlays common law rules to mitigate the harshness that would result from those rules being applied rigidly in cases for which they are not well-adapted.

III. DETRIMENTAL RELIANCE AND THE PROPRIETARY ESTOPPEL EQUITY

I focus particularly on detrimental reliance in this context, which is an idea with a long history in our law of obligations. This idea has informed the balance which the courts have sought to strike between the competing imperatives of achieving justice on the one hand and, on the other, recognising the importance of adherence to prescribed formalities to promote legal certainty. One can also ask, is detrimental reliance now the essence of the doctrine, its be all and end all? Is the reliance interest the only interest of a claimant which is being protected? And what is the relationship between the grounds for equity's intervention and the remedy which should be given? Does the tension between rules and standards inform that question, or is there scope for a high degree of prescription as to the relief which might be ordered? These topics have had an impact in this area of the law over a long period. The judgments in *Guest v Guest* reflect the same themes being worked out.

[10] See, eg, F Schauer, *Playing by the Rules* (Oxford, Clarendon Press, 1991); L Alexander and E Sherwin, *The Rule of Rules: Morality, Rules & the Dilemmas of Law* (North Carolina, Duke University Press Books, 2001).

This chapter is concerned with the particular form of proprietary estoppel which was authoritatively recognised in *Thorner v Major*. That is, the cause of action arising where a person has acted to their detriment in reliance on a promise made by another in relation to land.[11] Three elements are required. First, there must be a promise made (or assurance given) by A to B that B has been or will be given an interest in property. Second, there has been reasonable reliance on that promise. Third, there must be an identifiable detriment to B if A resiles from the promise they have made. When these three features are present, an 'equity' will arise for the court to satisfy.

What is striking about this particular strand of proprietary estoppel, which Professor McFarlane and I called the 'promise-detriment' strand,[12] is that it creates a cause of action through which property rights can be created notwithstanding the absence of formalities. This feature means there is reason to question whether this strand of the doctrine should be considered a species of estoppel at all.

A particularly important aspect of this promise-detriment strand which can be overlooked is its backward-looking nature. Unlike a purely executory contract, proprietary estoppel does not impose duties or liabilities from the moment that the relevant promise is made. Rather, as Hoffmann LJ explained in *Walton v Walton*, the principle

> does not look forward into the future and guess what might happen. It looks backwards from the moment when the promise falls due to be performed and asks whether, in the circumstances which have actually happened, it would be unconscionable for the promise not to be kept.[13]

It would therefore be a mistake to understand proprietary estoppel as simply a variant of contract law, with detrimental reliance standing in place of consideration as the factor which obligates a person to keep a promise. Instead, the promise-detriment strand of proprietary estoppel constitutes a standalone doctrine targeted at the specific form of unconscionability that arises if a person, A, were wholly free to leave another person, B, to suffer a detriment as a result of B's reasonable reliance on A's promise. Although this doctrine has a complicated relationship with the strict requirements of contract law and in particular the ordinary formalities required for contracts relating to land, it must be analysed in its own right.

[11] *Thorner v Major* [2009] UKHL 18.

[12] B McFarlane and P Sales, 'Promises, Detriment, and Liability: Lessons from Proprietary Estoppel' (2015) 131 *LQR* 610. This strand of proprietary estoppel is distinct from two other strands. First, the acquiescence-based strand whereby a person, A, is estopped from asserting a right against another person, B, in circumstances where B has adopted a particular course of conduct in reliance on a mistaken belief as to their current rights and A knows that this belief is mistaken yet fails to correct B as to the true position. Second, the representation-based strand whereby A is prevented from denying the truth of a representation made as to a matter of fact, or mixed fact and law, where B has acted on the basis of the truth of that representation.

[13] *Walton v Walton* CA, 14 April 1994.

IV. JUSTICE, FORMAL LAW AND LEGAL FORMALITIES

The lively judicial debate in *Guest v Guest* – whether proprietary estoppel remedies are expectation- or reliance-based – is of considerable importance. But in this chapter I will concentrate on the more abstract question of the tension between the goals of providing legal certainty through strict formalities and achieving justice, and the way that concepts such as detrimental reliance can be relevant to arriving at some accommodation between the two. With that in mind, I will first consider the role that formalities play in the law. The great virtue of formalities is that they reduce the scope for legal dispute by providing a degree of certainty lacking from purely informal arrangements.

This is particularly apt in the context of land, of course, where Parliament has long held that most transactions must be executed in a formal, predictable and certain way.[14] There are very good reasons for this. Proprietary rights are capable of affecting land through generations and the state and members of society generally must have certainty as to their existence and effect. This includes the people who live and work on the land. People should have a high degree of notice so that they know when they are conveying land or creating property interests in relation to it. The formalities associated with land transactions provide certainty as to what the relevant property rights are after the event of a transaction. Moreover, they enable lawyers confidently to advise clients as to their rights, on the basis of which people can plan their affairs.

Although not generally required to be in writing, similar concerns for legal certainty lie behind the strict common law requirements for contract formation. Contract has over the last two centuries become the central legal category for reciprocal promise-based relationships between private individuals. Contracts are now so commonplace in our lives that we can overlook that entering into a contract entails a significant commitment which can have sizeable financial repercussions. The expectation-based approach to contractual damages, for example, means that a party can be liable for non-performance even where the other party has suffered no loss. Potentially severe repercussions such as these make it important that the rules of contract formation are sufficiently precise such that individuals can reasonably know when they have entered into a contract and what they are required to do to abide by it.

On the whole, therefore, strict formalities promote justice for society as a whole, and at a general level, by promoting legal certainty and reducing the scope for costly disputes. They provide people with workable frameworks through which to manage their affairs, with the knowledge that – provided they have done what is required of them – the law will provide protection to them. In an important sense, therefore, formalities rules are facilitative tools which promote individual freedom and autonomy. If I comply with the rules I will

[14] Now, for contracts to convey land see the Law of Property (Miscellaneous Provisions) Act 1989, s 2.

produce particular intended effects; I can do so with assurance that the law will give effect to my intentions; and if I do not use the tools, then I will keep my property and not be affected by obligations which I did not intend to assume.

Life is not always so simple, however. To state the obvious, people are usually not lawyers and their ideas of what is just are not based, or at any rate not closely based, on whether legal criteria are complied with. The strictness of legal rules comes under strain where they meet real life situations in which their application conflicts with common understandings of justice. It might be difficult to explain to many, for example, why the law will uphold an agreement supported by even the tiniest amount of consideration but will provide no recourse for gratuitous promises no matter how ardently expressed.

One response to this is simply to say that such instances are the unfortunate yet necessary byproduct of the imperative of legal certainty. Yet law cannot be wholly divorced from common conceptions of what is just, for if it is it will lose its legitimacy. Certainly the approach of equity is that common conceptions of what is just and in accordance with 'conscience' should feed into the law, rather than be sacrificed always at the altar of maintaining the purity of the rule-based regime. It is a fact of life that people form reciprocal relationships which they understand to carry mutual obligations outside of the confines of contract and outwith the prescribed formalities for land transactions. For the law to wash its hands where the breakdown of those relationships and application of the strict legal rules would produce results offensive to widespread conceptions of what is right would be an abdication of the court's ultimate responsibility to achieve justice. Law (by which I mean equity here) has to meet real life half-way, by trying to find a just path which accommodates a basic social conception of justice as appropriate in the individual case with the more formal legal conception of justice, which is rule-based and directed to providing guidance across the full range of cases which might arise in future.

I suggest that equity's contemporary role remains to provide an essential channel by which broad social understanding of justice, as applicable to the individual historic case, can affect the application of laws directed to the general set of future cases. This is equity's historic and established role. It grew from the fourteenth century because of the reification and rigidity of the common law, which had split apart from social understandings of justice and acceptable conduct. The common law tended to favour strict, bright-line rules of property and obligation, whereas equity in its early period afforded the Lord Chancellors considerable freedom to do as they thought right. But it should be emphasised that their freedom was constrained, in the deeply Christian social context of that period, by quite a high degree of customary specificity about what might be required by 'conscience'. Although one can say that equity has tightened up its approach since the nineteenth century, eroding reliance on vague standards combined with a socially constrained idea of 'conscience' and moving towards an increased reliance on rules or discretions framed by rules, it retains its function to keep the underlying values and rationales of law in line with the actual application of the law, by providing relief against opportunistic misuse of the strict rules of the common law.[15]

Equity therefore overlays the common law, mitigating the harshness that would ensue were strict legal rules to be applied without any exception. It operates to bridge the tension between the bright-line rules favoured by the common law and a need for a sense of moral legitimacy in the application of the law.[16]

An analogy can be drawn with aspects of the law of tort, which can fulfil a similar function. For example, in identifying an exception to the rule against recovery for pure economic loss in *Hedley Byrne v Heller*,[17] Lord Devlin observed that a duty of care would arise in

> relationships which … are 'equivalent to contract', that is, where there is an assumption of responsibility in circumstances in which, but for the absence of consideration, there would be a contract.[18]

Although through the machinery of tort rather than equity, one can perceive the House of Lords straining to find a way around the unforgiving requirements of contract in order to do what it perceived as justice. Certain types of contract terms implied at law in a way similar to that by which a duty of care is identified fulfil an equivalent role. For example, in an employment relationship, the implied duty to maintain trust and confidence[19] operates as a local form of equity, preventing an employer from operating the express terms of the contract in an opportunistic and unfair way.

In this regard, the law of unjust enrichment provides another important analogy with proprietary estoppel. Both assumed increased prominence over a similar period and can be equally analysed as forms of equity or 'epieikeia' to ameliorate the potential harshness of the strict rules of property law or contract. Those rules mean, for example, that in most cases the making of a mistake by a party to a property transaction will not prevent the transfer of a right even where the other party is aware of the mistake. Unjust enrichment cannot undo the transaction, as this would undermine legal certainty in circumstances where the property may have been passed on to third parties. But it can offer a means of redress which can mitigate the harshness of that conclusion by providing a mechanism to meet the justice of the case between the immediate parties, adjusting the remedy to reflect the extent to which the enrichment was unjust.

There are a good many other examples of equity acting in such a way. The law of constructive trusts is a large topic which lies outside the scope of this chapter. But it can be argued that they can be understood as having a similar function

[15] See Sales (n 2) 53; I Samet, *Equity: Conscience Goes to Market* (Oxford, Oxford University Press, 2018) ch 2.

[16] See also P Sales, 'The Interface between Contract and Equity'(Lehane Memorial Lecture, Sydney, 28 August 2019) www.supremecourt.uk/docs/speech-190828.pdf (accessed 6 December 2022).

[17] *Hedley Byrne v Heller* [1964] AC 465.

[18] ibid 529.

[19] *BCCI v Malik* [1998] AC 20.

to soften and adjust the rigours of a strict application of bright-line formalities and common law rules. On one view of the case, the doctrine in *Rochefoucauld v Boustead*,[20] for example, holds that a constructive trust will arise to enforce an informal agreement in relation to a trust of land despite the absence of compliance with statutory formality requirements. Where B informally agrees to hold land on trust for A, and A transfers or allows their land to be transferred to B in reliance on B's promise, it has been argued that *Rochefoucauld* holds that a constructive trust arises to ensure that B takes only a qualified interest once they acquire A's land. On this view, therefore, as with proprietary estoppel, equity steps in to avoid an unconscionable outcome arising from a strict application of formality rules. As with proprietary estoppel, the doctrine has promises and reliance at its heart.[21]

The interactions of equity and equity-substitutes with the common law are therefore multifarious. In certain areas, the common law has incorporated an equity-type approach into itself. In others, equity overlays the common law to provide relief in circumstances where the application of strict formality rules would produce unconscionable results. Predictability and stability in the law is achieved by application of the common law's bright-line rules in the vast majority of cases. Nonetheless, when faced with the exceptional case where the application of a bright-line rule produces a result antithetical to justice, there is the possibility of avoiding this.

I think there is also much to be said for Irit Samet's argument in her book, *Equity: Conscience Goes to Market*,[22] that equity as a distinct body of doctrine laid over the common law serves to narrow the gap between law and morality and thus to legitimise the law and secure loyalty to it. On this reading, equitable doctrines such as proprietary estoppel do not undermine formality rules, but actually serve to legitimise them and their application in the ordinary run of cases. As described by Henry Smith, equity has the ability to offer a limited 'safety valve' that, by preventing opportunistic uses of strict formality rules, can in fact strengthen the force of those formal rules by softening their harshness in marginal cases, thus rendering them more palatable as the governing framework in ordinary circumstances.[23] Equity takes the pressure off the courts to try to modify or bend the underlying strict rules in an effort to do justice in the individual case.[24]

[20] *Rochefoucauld v Boustead* [1897] 1 Ch 196.

[21] See YK Liew, *Rationalising Constructive Trusts* (Oxford, Hart Publishing, 2017) ch 4. For a contrasting view, interpreting the case as being an example of an express trust, see W Swadling, 'The Nature of the Trust in *Rochefoucauld v Boustead*' in C Mitchell (ed), *Constructive and Resulting Trusts* (Oxford, Hart Publishing, 2010) ch 3.

[22] Samet (n 15).

[23] See H Smith, 'Property, Equity, and the Rule of Law' in L Austin and D Klimchuk (eds), *Private Law and the Rule of Law* (Oxford, Oxford University Press, 2014). For an extended treatment of this subject, see H Smith, 'Equity as Meta-Law' (2021) 130 *Yale Law Journal* 1050.

[24] *Cf* KLlewellyn, *The Theory of Rules: edited with an introduction by Frederick Schauer* (Chicago, University of Chicago Press, 2011) Introduction, 23–27, where Schauer observes that scepticism about rules is a strong theme in US legal thought, where a focus on purposive interpretation tends to redefine the real rule to be applied as a combination of the text and background principles

There is no avoiding, however, that any qualification to the requirement for formal rules also creates challenges for the law. The interaction of the formal *rules* and the justice *standard* has to be managed effectively so that the predictability associated with legal rules is not compromised too readily, thereby undermining the facilitation of individuals' autonomy which they tend to promote. Legal rules which can be circumvented too easily are hardly rules at all, and as I have stressed there are good reasons why the strict rules should be difficult to displace. The challenge for the law, therefore, is to give definition to the circumstances in which it is permissible to depart from the bright-line rules in order to achieve interpersonal justice, but to limit those circumstances sufficiently so as still to give primacy to the bright-line rules and their guidance function for wider society. Flexibility is undoubtedly one of equity's great virtues, enabling the law to reflect broad standards of fairness in very different factual scenarios. Nonetheless, to ward off the old charge that equity is measured by the length of the Chancellor's foot,[25] it is also critical for the law to define sufficiently the circumstances in which equity will intervene to qualify formality rules.

V. RULE OF LAW VALUES AND PROPRIETARY ESTOPPEL

This task of sufficiency of definition of the circumstances in which equity will intervene to give relief is particularly necessary in the context of proprietary estoppel, where the stakes can be very high for those involved. Although the law has since progressed, this extrajudicial observation of Lord Walker in 2008 remains relevant:

> in order to be compatible with the rule of law, the court's discretion must have an aim fixed by law; it must be necessary; and it must be susceptible to audit. There is still a lot of ground to be covered in fully achieving these objectives in connection with proprietary estoppel. But recognising that there are important questions of principle to be answered is a step towards establishing that the estoppel is indeed a principled doctrine, and not a matter of palm-tree justice, or the judge's intuition as to which side ought to win.[26]

It is fortunate that Lord Walker had the opportunity to contribute to this effort by way of his judgment in *Thorner v Major* just one year later. With this judgment a principled basis for the intervention of equity began to be delineated in

which taken together generate a just result: 'a long tradition, with Llewellyn as one of the pioneers, seeks to redefine prescriptive rules so that they incorporate what are in reality anti-rule perspectives'.

[25] On this tension, see Sherwin (n 10), especially chs 3 and 4.

[26] Lord Walker, 'Which side 'ought to win'? Discretion and certainty in property law'(Speech at Chancery Bar Association Conference, 2008). Lord Walker made a similar point in *Cobbe v Yeoman's Row Management Ltd* [2008] 1 WLR 1752, [46]: '[proprietary estoppel] is not a sort of joker or wild card to be used whenever the court disapproves of the conduct of a litigant who seems to have the law on his side. Flexible though it is, the doctrine must be formulated and applied in a disciplined and principled way. Certainty is important in property transactions.' See also S Gardner, 'The Remedial Discretion in Proprietary Estoppel – Again' (2006) 122 *LQR* 492.

a more concrete way, although the doctrine still retains its critics on grounds of unpredictability.[27]

As Lord Walker made clear, at the heart of the proprietary estoppel doctrine, and a crucial basis for the intervention of equity, is detrimental reliance. That is, the detriment that would arise from B's reasonable reliance on A's promise were A able to renege on that promise. What has led the law to identify this as the principled basis on which equity can intervene, such that the formalities relating to contracts and land transactions can be qualified?

The presence of detrimental reliance in a given situation will not necessarily result in the court giving relief which has the effect that the claimant's expectations arising from a promise made to them are realised. Once a claimant has demonstrated the requirements of promise, reliance and detriment, then, as it was put by Scarman LJ in *Crabb v Arun District Council*,[28] the court's task becomes to identify 'the minimum equity to do justice' and give relief accordingly. Where awarding a remedy which meets the claimant's expectation would be disproportionate – perhaps because the degree of detriment suffered by the claimant was, in the event, fairly low – then it is open to the court to fashion a different remedy. In *Ottey v Grundy*,[29] for example, the extent of the detriment was limited because the period in which the claimant had acted in reliance on the promise made was limited and had not led to the giving up of any alternative opportunities. As a result, the court awarded the claimant significantly less than what had been promised to him. However, it does not necessarily follow that the relief granted should always be limited only to the amount of detrimental reliance which has been suffered. Whether that should be so is a matter for exploration as the case-law stemming from *Thorner v Major* develops. *Guest v Guest* is a major step in that journey. The majority judgment of Lord Briggs takes as its foundation the historical development of the doctrine and cognate doctrines in equity, leading to the conclusion that a claimant's expectation interest will often be the interest which is protected. On this view, in the interaction between decided cases and legal theory, the decided cases have been taken to give an important steer. Lord Briggs' judgment contains an extended review of the cases in the nineteenth and twentieth centuries.

VI. PRECURSORS TO THORNER v MAJOR IN EQUITABLE DOCTRINE AND COMMON LAW ANALOGIES

The notion of detrimental reliance as a basis for recovery has a long history and is woven into many aspects of the law of private obligations. Perhaps the clearest

[27] See, eg, J Mee, 'Proprietary Estoppel and Inheritance: Enough is Enough?' [2013] *Conv* 280 and M Dixon, 'Painting Proprietary Estoppel: Howard Hodgkin, Titian or Jackson Pollock?' [2022] *Conv* 30.

[28] *Crabb v Arun District Council* [1976] Ch 179.

[29] *Ottey v Grundy* [2003] EWCA Civ 1176.

precursor to modern proprietary estoppel was the equitable doctrine of 'making representations good', which had detrimental reliance at its heart. As set out by the House of Lords in *Hammersley v De Biel* in 1845, the doctrine permitted the court to intervene where a representation is made by one party 'for the purpose of influencing the conduct of another and acted upon by him'.[30]

An example of the application of the doctrine which seems very close to the field now occupied by proprietary estoppel is the 1862 case of *Loffus v Maw*.[31] A young widower went to look after her unwell uncle. She found the work for her uncle grueling. After she threatened to leave, her uncle promised that he would provide to her for life the rents and profits of two houses owned by him in Hull. Upon his death, however, the niece discovered that her uncle had produced a new will in which the uncle had left the promised rents and profits to his son rather than to her. By a codicil to his will executed just 16 days before his death, the uncle made void all gifts contained in his will in favour of his niece and directed that his will should be read as if her name were expunged. In finding for the niece to enforce the promise made to her, the Vice-Chancellor stated:

> … the present plaintiff is entitled not to have relief out of the general assets, but out of that specific property which the testator represented to her that she was to enjoy after his death, she having acted upon the faith of that representation and performed those services which he, by the representation, induced her to render.[32]

Although 'making representations good' did not have exactly the same backwards-looking character possessed by modern proprietary estoppel, the essential normative principle that it is unconscionable to allow someone to suffer a detriment as a result of their reliance upon a promise which is reneged upon sits at the centre of both doctrines. One can only assess the existence and extent of detriment arising from reliance on a promise by looking back from the point when the promisor reneges on that promise.

Another forerunner of proprietary estoppel in which detrimental reliance features is the limited equitable jurisdiction to perfect a failed gift, discussed in *Dillwyn v Llewelyn*.[33] The relevant estoppel, sometimes known as estoppel by encouragement,[34] affects the donor of property who makes an imperfect gift – ie without compliance with proper formalities – and then induces the donee to act on the assumption that the gift is effective or will be perfected.

A further equitable doctrine which merits close attention as a precursor of proprietary estoppel is the doctrine of part performance as the basis for an

[30] *Hammersley v De Biel* (1845) 8 ER 1312, 1320.

[31] *Loffus v Maw* (1862) 66 ER 544.

[32] ibid 549.

[33] *Dillwyn v Llewelyn* (1862) 4 De G, F & J 517. This has been described as 'one of the leading cases on proprietary estoppel'; G Owen and M Parker Jones, '*Dillwyn v Llewelyn* – a Fresh Perspective on a Misconceived Approach' [2022] *Conv* 1.

[34] J Heydon, M Leeming and P Turner, *Meagher, Gummow & Lehane's Equity: Doctrines and Remedies*, 5th edn (Chatswood, Aus, Butterworths, 2015) 519.

award of specific performance of a contract (typically for the sale of land) where relevant formalities were not complied with.[35] This doctrine was abolished for England in 1989,[36] but this does not mean we should ignore lessons which can be drawn from it. The basis for the doctrine was that acts of detrimental reliance in performance of the contract could provide a basis for equitable relief, if the other party relies upon lack of formality to deny the contract. The leading case was *Maddison v Alderson* in 1889.[37] It fits the classic fact pattern in the modern proprietary estoppel cases. The defendant was induced to work for years as housekeeper to Alderson on the promise he would leave her a life estate in certain land. This agreement was void for want of writing. Alderson died without having made an effective will to leave the life estate, and his heir sued to recover the title deeds held by the housekeeper. Her defence was the agreement she had made and performed, which she sought to enforce in equity. Lord Selborne said,

> In a suit founded on such performance, the defendant is really 'charged' upon the equities resulting from the acts in execution of the contract, and not ... upon the contract itself. If such equities were excluded, injustice of a kind which the statute cannot be thought to have had in contemplation would follow.[38]

One does not need to look too far below the surface to see notions of detrimental reliance in other precursors to the modern law of obligations. Among the family of the so-called assumpsit causes of action, for example, was the action for misperformance of an undertaking. In seminal cases such as *Coggs v Barnard*,[39] the courts found that a defendant could be liable where a claimant had relied upon a gratuitous undertaking to carry goods which the defendant had subsequently misperformed. Notwithstanding the absence of any consideration, the claimant could recover on the basis that they had relied on the undertaking to their detriment.

VII. THE CHANGING PREOCCUPATIONS OF LEGAL DOCTRINE

These old forms of action infused by ideas of detrimental reliance fell into abeyance as the law became increasingly systematised around the law of contract and tort as the nineteenth century went on. In particular, the rise of Will Theory led the law of obligations to coalesce around a doctrine of contract based on the parties' expectations, with liability for breach of contract fixed irrespective

[35] See *Maddison v Alderson* [1883) 8 App Cas 467; *Steadman v Steadman* [1976] AC 536; and discussion in Heydon, Leeming and Turner (n 34) 678–687.

[36] The Law of Property (Miscellaneous Provisions) Act 1989, s 2(8); see Heydon, Leeming and Turner (n 34) 678 and references.

[37] *Maddison v Alderson* (1883) 8 App Cas 467.

[38] ibid 475.

[39] *Coggs v Barnard* (1703) 92 ER 999.

of whether there had been any detrimental reliance.[40] Moreover, in light of the prestige of the natural sciences and Benthamite philosophy, the law increasingly became seen as a science, with an emphasis on it consisting of definite formulae with intellectual coherence a priority. No longer could an appeal to the old forms of action be regarded as a satisfactory way of ordering the law. They left too many questions unanswered and applied in what had come to seem a fairly random way. More intellectual coherence was required to provide predictability. So the common law increasingly focused on bright-line rules, epitomised by its strict requirements in relation to the formation of contracts.

But as I have sought to show, the interaction of these bright-line rules with the unpredictability of real life inevitably created tensions. Crudely put, mid-twentieth century judges began to look for ways to ameliorate the harshness that ensued from people largely having to fit their disputes within the tightly defined doctrines of contract and tort. In doing so they drew creatively on case law preceding the arrival of Will Theory and the scientific understanding of law to fashion doctrines able to meet the tensions they perceived. This provides the context for the emergence of promissory estoppel, the constructive trust, unjust enrichment and the *Hedley Byrne* run of cases to name just a few.

Although often awkwardly categorised as an unjust enrichment case, *Brewer Street Investments v Barclays Woollen*[41] is another case in which detrimental reliance was central. It can be seen as a case which revives an older view of the equities rising where services are provided without a contract being in place, but where it is expected one will be entered into thereafter. The ruling that the services were provided on a conditional basis, that they would not be paid for separately if the contract was entered into (because the contract price would cover the cost), so that a quantum meruit was payable when that condition failed, seems to hark back to the approach in the old case of *Planché v Colburn*.[42] In that case the parties had agreed a price to be paid on the completion of a book. The plaintiff duly performed a large amount of work in writing the book, only for the defendant to cancel the contract before completion. The Court of King's Bench held that the defendant could not withhold payment on a quantum meruit basis: 'the plaintiff ought not to lose the fruit of his labour'.[43] The relief in both cases responded to the fact of detrimental reliance upon an assurance given, albeit the remedy was not limited to the

[40] See D Ibbotson, *A Historical Introduction to the Law of Obligations* (Oxford, Oxford University Press, 1999) ch 12.

[41] *Brewer Street Investments Ltd v Barclays Woollen Co Ltd* [1954] 1 QB 428.

[42] *Planché v Colburn* (1831) 8 Bing. 14; 131 ER 305.

[43] ibid 306 (Tindal CJ). see C Mitchell and P Mitchell, 'Planché v Colburn'in C Mitchell and P Mitchell, *Landmark Cases in the Law of Restitution* (London, Bloomsbury 3PL, 2006). The authors consider that the case was determined on a restitutionary basis; they argue, however, that the case is awkwardly categorised as such because the defendant received no discernible benefit. This aligns with the view that the case is better analysed in terms of detrimental reliance: See McFarlane and Sales (n 12) 627.

detriment as such, but was fashioned by reference to the reasonable market price of the services provided.

The reassertion of ideas of detrimental reliance in modern proprietary estoppel – and indeed in the *Hedley Byrne* cases concerning assumption of responsibility – falls squarely within this story. Re-emerging first in proprietary estoppel's acquiescence and representation-based strands,[44] the force of detrimental reliance when coupled with a promise has since evolved to become a powerful cause of action capable of allowing for the enforcement of agreements notwithstanding the absence of formalities.

But why should detrimental reliance be so important in this particular context? After all, the law could adopt any number of alternative bases for when it will recognise rights and obligations despite the absence of formalities. Lord Denning MR in *Greasley v Cooke*,[45] for example, suggested that mere reliance on a promise could be sufficient to 'activate the equity' without any detriment. Or it might be argued that proprietary estoppel should be confined to being a species of constructive trust or alternatively a remedy for unjust enrichment without detrimental reliance being necessary.

Much of this disquiet arises from a concern that detrimental reliance is somehow poised to displace consideration and by doing so undermine the law of contract. This concern is misplaced, as it overlooks critical differences between the promise-detriment strand of proprietary estoppel and contract law. Most obviously, the promise-detriment remedy is backward-looking in nature and does not impose obligations at the time of the relevant promise, whereas contract looks forward by imposing obligations as soon as the bargain is struck.

VIII. EXPECTATION, RELIANCE AND RESTITUTION INTERESTS

Concepts such as 'detrimental reliance' and 'unjust enrichment' are really proxies which we use for an underlying moral question. That is, they are used in an attempt to delineate the threshold at which the law can justifiably intervene in private – typically reciprocal – relationships, to enforce them or to give relief arising out of them. Naturally, this is a question which is not limited to the proprietary estoppel context. It sits at the heart of the entire law of obligations. As put by Fuller and Perdue in their famous 1936 article 'The Reliance Interest in Contract Damages', concepts like detrimental reliance are ultimately the basis

[44] See, eg, the first judicial use of the term in *E R Ives Investment v High* [1967] 2 QB 379, 405 (Winn LJ): 'where estoppel applies, the person entitled to wield it as a shield has, ex hypothesi, suffered a past detriment or other change of position; he is not asserting any positive right but is invoking law or equity to afford him procedural protection to avert injustice'.

[45] *Greasley v Cooke* [1980] 1 WLR 1306, 1311.

for moral claims about when it is appropriate 'to unlock the impulse to compel men to make good their promises'.[46]

Fuller and Perdue were grappling with this question in the context of damages for breach of contract, but it has wider application. Put simply, what circumstances are sufficiently unpalatable to legitimise the law in intervening in private reciprocal arrangements so as to compel one party to pay money or convey property to another? Fuller and Perdue's tripartite analysis of the expectation, reliance and restitution interests has proved to be remarkably influential. It offers a useful schema for considering why detrimental reliance is a relevant factor in the doctrine of proprietary estoppel.

As Fuller and Perdue point out, the classic model for contract remedies is based on expectation, with the object being to put the innocent party in as good a position as they would have been in had the defendant performed their promise. This remedy flows from the moral basis that it is unjust for a party not to receive what they had been promised. There are good reasons why this should not be taken to provide the basis for proprietary estoppel. To make available a claim in proprietary estoppel for frustrated expectations would seriously undermine the operation of contract law and the strict requirements which have been developed to police the formation of contractual bonds which have such far-reaching legal effects regarding the enforcement of promises. There are good reasons to restrict contractual rights on the expectation-basis to the cases where contractual formalities have been complied with, and this regime would be undermined if proprietary estoppel led simply to the enforcement of gratuitous promises.

Fuller and Perdue's version of the restitution interest is based on a different moral premise, ie of preventing unfair gain by a defaulting promisor at the expense of a promisee. There are proprietary estoppel cases which adopt an approach approximating to this. In *Jennings v Rice*,[47] for example, the Court of Appeal simply calculated the market cost of the labour received by the promisor as a result of the promisee's reliance without considering any distinct question of detriment.

The problem with a restitutionary approach for proprietary estoppel, however, is that it does not seem accurately to capture the unconscionability inherent in proprietary estoppel cases. The benefit received by a promisor may be disproportionate to the extent of the detriment suffered by the promisee. Consider the situation in *Crabb v Arun DC*.[48] There the promise related to a grant of a right of access on which Mr Crabb relied by selling the land on which his only other access point was located. The defendant council did not benefit in any obvious way from Mr Crabb's reliance on the assurance it gave. The restitutionary approach therefore fails to reflect what made the council's conduct

[46] L Fuller and W Perdue, 'The Reliance Interest in Contract Damages: I' (1936–37) 46 *Yale Law Journal* 52, 69.
[47] *Jennings v Rice* [2002] EWCA 159.
[48] *Crabb v Arun DC* [1976] Ch 179.

unconscionable, which was the combination of the breaking of a promise or assurance with the detriment which ensued for Mr Crabb as a result of this. Again, however, it is worth pointing out that it is not obvious that there was an exact correspondence between the relief given (the grant of the right of access) and the extent or value of the detriment suffered by him.

Therefore, from Fuller and Perdue's tripartite analysis, we are left with the reliance interest. That corresponds with the unconscionability of permitting someone to suffer a detriment by virtue of their reliance on a promise if that promise is reneged upon. This is a claim with a strong moral basis. Indeed, it may be argued that it is stronger than either the expectation interest or even the restitution interest (at least where the enrichment of the defendant is greater than the extent of the claimant's detrimental reliance). As Fuller and Perdue observe:

> the promisee who has actually relied on the promise, even though he may not thereby have enriched the promisor, certainly presents a more pressing case for relief than the promisee who merely demands satisfaction for his disappointment in not getting what was promised him.[49]

Patrick Atiyah made a similar point in his *Essays on Contract:*

> Consider next the possibility of detrimental reliance by the promisee. Is it not manifest that a person who has actually worsened his position by reliance on a promise has a more powerful case for redress than one who has not acted in reliance on the promise at all? A person who has not relied on a promise (nor paid for it) may suffer a disappointment of his expectations, but he does not actually suffer a pecuniary loss … no definitional jugglery can actually equate the position of the party who suffers a diminution of his assets in reliance on a promise, and a person who suffers no such diminution.[50]

It is this heightened claim on conscience which detrimental reliance carries which makes it the appropriate starting point for an analysis of the basis for application of the doctrine of proprietary estoppel. It is only where unconscionability is made out to this high standard that there is sufficient justification to allow qualification of strict adherence to the formalities associated with property and contract rights. Through detrimental reliance the law is able to provide redress for the most pressing instances of unconscionability, while leaving intact the primacy of the ordinary formality rules.

Where third parties receive property which may be affected by equitable claims based on proprietary estoppel, their interests will be protected by the usual rules governing when equities bind them. In particular, the bona fide purchaser of a legal interest for value and without notice – equity's darling – will be fully protected. In this way, equity protects against the limited disruption of the apparent property rights of the claimant and the defendant in a proprietary

[49] Fuller and Perdue (n 46) 56.
[50] PS Atiyah, *Essays on Contract* (Oxford, Oxford University Press, 1986) 20.

estoppel case, which is appropriate between the two of them, rippling out and creating an undue impact on the rights of third parties.

However, there is an additional element that informs the unconscionability analysis in many of the proprietary estoppel cases beyond simple detrimental reliance. The moral claim for adjustment of the strict legal rules may be all the stronger where the detrimental reliance occurs in the context of reciprocal relationships based on trust and what the parties objectively appear to regard as an acceptance of mutual obligations. Fuller and Perdue's tripartite schema does not adjust for this significant feature, which is present in some but not all cases of detrimental reliance.

Detrimental reliance can of course occur in circumstances where there is no reciprocity between the parties. A person may simply rely to their detriment on a promise without having given any undertaking to provide anything in return for that promise: see *Hedley Byrne*.[51] What is materially different about most of the proprietary estoppel cases, however, is that, despite not meeting the requirements for having a binding contract, they involve reciprocal relationships where the parties exchange promises and perform what they take to be obligations to one another.[52] For example, in *Gillet v Holt*, Robert Walker LJ recorded that the promisee and his wife had

> devoted the best years of their lives to working for Mr Holt and his company, showing loyalty and devotion to his business interests, his social life and his personal wishes, on the strength of clear and repeated assurances of testamentary benefits.[53]

It is not clear that the account of unconscionability here is limited to the feature of detrimental reliance. Should the reciprocity of the relationship, as understood by both parties, be factored in as well? Certainly it seems that the moral argument in favour of qualification of any right to rely on the absence of the usual formalities is all the stronger in a case of detrimental reliance in the context of the working out of a reciprocal relationship. The existence of a reciprocal arrangement between individuals is important in other contexts where equity intervenes to impose a constructive trust to give effect to the arrangement despite non-compliance with formalities: such as in *Rochefoucauld v Boustead*,[54] the *Pallant v Morgan* trust[55] and the doctrine of mutual wills,[56] for example. So there may be an argument for confining proprietary estoppel to these sort of cases. But would it be right to take the imperfect gift cases outside the scope of the doctrine?

[51] *Hedley Byrne* (n 17).

[52] This was also, of course, a feature of *Maddison* (n 35): one might say that the modern doctrine of proprietary estoppel has developed and expanded to take over the work once done, in part, by the doctrine of part performance.

[53] *Gillet v Holt* [2001] Ch 210, 235.

[54] (n 20). At least, on one interpretation of the case.

[55] *Pallant v Morgan* [1953] Ch 43. See Liew (n 21) ch 6.

[56] Liew (n 21) ch 12.

Related to this point is the question of whether the addition of this reciprocity element should affect the remedy to be granted. Should the relief be confined purely to making good any element of detrimental reliance, perhaps including adjustment to require the defendant to pay the market rate for any services rendered, as in *Brewer Street*?[57] Or should there be scope for enforcement of the promise in some cases, where, looking back in the way proposed by Hoffmann LJ in *Walton v Walton*, it can be seen that the promisor has in fact got the substance of what they took themselves to be seeking in the reciprocal relationship in which they made the promise? This might be a basis on which one could seek to explain the cases in which the promise has been enforced on the hybrid model which Professor McFarlane and I proposed in 2015.[58] Going down this route might also allow one to recognise the imperfect gift type of cases as falling within the doctrine, while at the same time acknowledging that it might be appropriate to limit the relief to be granted in such a non-reciprocal context to a remedy which purely reflects the extent of the detrimental reliance alone. According to the majority judgment of Lord Briggs in *Guest v Guest*, the emphasis to be given to satisfaction of the expectation interest may be greater still.[59]

IX. CONCLUSION

I make these points to draw out two aspects of the law in this area. First, the modern law of proprietary estoppel needs to stand on its own feet as a distinct basis for the creation of obligations affecting property rights. To call it an estoppel, which suggests that a party is estopped from refusing to fulfil their promise, conceals a good deal more than it reveals about the basis of this species of obligation. I would suggest that academia and the courts need to examine with great care the factors which do, and conversely those which do not, provide a justification for departure from the usual rules of formalities and contract formation. There are potentially important distinctions to be drawn between different cases, depending on precisely which factors may be present.

Detrimental reliance in the context of the working out of a reciprocal arrangement seems to provide the strongest justification for equity's intervention to qualify formality rules in the proprietary estoppel cases. The case for intervention becomes weaker when one moves away from that model. The law of proprietary estoppel is attempting to do two things. First, the case law is developing in an effort to ensure that the principles by which the ordinary formalities regarding property and contract-formation are departed from are given reasonably determinate form, in the interest of promoting consistency and fairness.

[57] *Brewer Street* (n 41).
[58] McFarlane and Sales (n 12).
[59] *Guest* (n 1).

The law here cannot be a terrain of palm-tree justice with no principles, as laid down authoritatively by the superior courts, to guide judicial discretion. Second, the law is attempting to strike a balance between addressing the unconscionability caused by opportunistic reliance on strict formality rules while at the same time specifying a sufficiently high threshold for equity's intervention so as not to undermine those rules fatally. It is this need for a high bar that has pushed the law towards a focus on detrimental reliance.

The second point is that we need to think more carefully about the relationship between the justification for equity's intervention under the doctrine of proprietary estoppel and the relief which is granted when such an estoppel is found to exist. The law should marry the relief granted with the grounds for applying the doctrine in the first place. The judgments in *Guest v Guest* are an important contribution to this task, whose implications will need to be considered carefully and digested. This is another important way in which the law and its rationale can be kept in line with each other, in true Aristotelian fashion, while also striving for a reasonable degree of certainty and predictability.

11

The Essential Similarity of Express Trusts in England, Japan and Quebec

JOYMAN LEE

THE TRUST IS historically viewed as an institution unique to common law, notwithstanding the long pedigree enjoyed by the Roman institution of the *fiducia* and the German *Treuhand*.[1] In the civil law context, it is often in legal systems shaped by a dual legal heritage in both common law and civil law where the trust has had the greatest impact.[2] Whereas in continental European countries such as France, the trust usually takes a contractual form – in other words, a contract inspired by the *fiducia* is often envisioned as a strengthened form of agency arrangements such as the mandate[3] – it is in jurisdictions which do not confine the trust within contract where local trusts with genealogical roots in the English trust are given full expression against the backdrop of civil law property systems. As a result of the choice to emphasise the

[1] C Witz, 'La fiducie en Europe: France, Suisse, Luxembourg, Allemagne, Liechtenstein: analyse des lois existantes et des projets en cours' in J Herbots and D Philippe (eds), *Le trust et la fiducie: implications pratiques* (Brussels, Bruylant, 1998); H Kötz, *Trust und Treuhand: Eine rechtsvergleichende Darstellung des anglo-amerikanischen trust und funktionsverwandter Institute des deutschen Rechts* (Gottingen, Vandenhoeck & Ruprecht, 1963).

[2] As Madeleine Cantin Cumyn observes, trusts in 'mixed' legal systems including Scotland, Quebec and South Africa had taken shape by the nineteenth century, reflecting an earlier and deeper historical interaction with the English trust focusing on family and succession contexts. In doing so, they demonstrate greater conceptual coherence than continental European trusts used primarily in the commercial context. MC Cumyn, 'Reflections Regarding the Diversity of Ways in which the Trust has been Received or Adapted in Civil Law Countries' in L Smith (ed), *Re-imagining the Trust* (Cambridge, CUP, 2012) 27. While Japan does not fall tidily into this group, its trust law is rooted in common law and the country is exposed to American legal and economic hegemony in the Western Pacific.

[3] C Witz, 'Les caractères distinctifs de la fiducie' in STEP France (ed), *Trusts & fiducie: concurrents ou compléments? Actes du colloque tenu à Paris les 13 et 14 juin 2007* (Geneva, Academy & Finance, 2008) 67, 71. The new Italian proposal for a domestic trust to replace the *trust interno* is also strongly influenced by the mandate. I Caggiano, 'A Trust Law for Italy? From the Chimera to the Phoenix' (February 2022) Global Seminar in Private Law Theory.

'absoluteness' of the concept of ownership,[4] it is often difficult to accommodate the trust in civil law countries. What is striking about legal systems with a long historical exposure to the English trust, therefore, are the stronger mechanisms which exist for controlling the trustee. The availability of such mechanisms is vital for express trusts to perform effectively their role as agreement-based institutions designed to deliver flexibility to property owners.[5]

In emphasising the commonalities between trusts which transcend contract, this chapter does not suggest that there is a doctrinal unity to institutions which, after all, differ significantly in institutional design. To take the question of ownership: whereas ownership falls to the trustee in many trusts including in England and Japan, in the South African *bewind* the beneficiary is the legal owner of property.[6] In Quebec, the legislator has gone even further in declaring that there is no legal 'owner' of the trust fund, by depriving any party of a property right.[7] Yet, from a socio-legal standpoint, what these systems share is a historical exposure to English law, which has been a significant source of influence at the level of procedure as well as the style of legal thinking.[8] Even if these structural features may not be a conscious factor in everyday legal practice, the specific pathways underpinning the development of these legal systems explain the key role of legal history in shaping institutions such as the trust.[9]

My chapter suggests that the English express trust and trusts as found in Japan and Quebec are functionally similar.[10] It aims to highlight that express trusts work as a system of rules, where robust mechanisms to subject trustees to effective control form a core feature.[11] In understanding this system, I focus on a number of specific doctrinal features highlighted by Jessica Hudson and Charles Mitchell as central to the English express trust. These include: first, the trustee's holding of legal title to property; second, the restriction of the trustee's

[4] See, eg, C civ (French *Code civil*), Art 544, Art 206 of the Japanese Civil Code and c 947 of the Civil Code of Quebec.

[5] H Dagan and I Samet, 'Express Trust as the Missing Piece in the Liberal Property Regime Jigsaw' (22 December 2020) in S Degeling, J Hudson and I Samet, *Philosophical Foundations of the Law of Trusts* (Oxford, OUP, forthcoming in 2023).

[6] T Honoré, 'Trust' in R Zimmermann and D Visser (eds), *Southern Cross: Civil Law and Common Law in South Africa* (Oxford, Clarendon Press, 1996) 865.

[7] Civil Code of Quebec (CCQ), CQLR c CCQ-1991, c 1261.

[8] A Popovici, 'Le droit civil, avant tout un style?' in N Kaisrer (ed), *Le droit civil, avant tout un style?* (Montréal, Éditions Themis, 2003) 214–218. In Japan, the direct influence of common law is more limited, and is confined to the greater discretion which courts enjoy relative to other civil law countries, and the role of scholars in moulding these judgements into doctrine (*hanrei kenkyū*).

[9] See, eg, S Normand, *Introduction au droit des biens*, 3rd edn (Montréal, Wilson & Lafleur, 2020) 423–425.

[10] I embrace the modern version of functionalism which pays close attention to social and cultural factors, at the same time as seeking to evaluate the selected legal systems in terms of their effectiveness in achieving a stated goal. See R Michaels, 'The Functional Method of Comparative Law' in M Reimann and R Zimmermann (eds), *The Oxford Handbook of Comparative Law*, 2nd edn (Oxford, OUP, 2019) 357–360, 379–382.

[11] By control, I mean that a trustee, unlike other titleholders of property, is not permitted to exercise their powers and discretion in any way they wish, and an effective system of trust law must provide enforceable rules that circumscribe their authority to do so.

authority in dealing with the property; and third, that the availability of the express trust always produces an impact on the property law of the host legal system.[12] The last point holds true whether property is defined pragmatically and relationally, in the case of English law, or against a firmer taxonomical and intellectual commitment in the cases of Japan and Quebec. While not all these features perform control functions independently, they nonetheless operate as a system, where the interactions between components contribute to the goal of maximising the trustee's powers and discretion at the same time as restricting their authority. Significantly, this restriction is only possible where the trust's relationship with underlying property laws is put on a sound conceptual basis that is recognised beyond the confines of trust law.

At this point, I would like to briefly explain my choice of jurisdictions. First, the selection of the English trust is straight forward. The large number of users means that the English trust retains a central role in the global development of trust law, even if a variety of other trajectories also exist. Second, while Japan might not have experienced the kind of formal influences from England comparable to Quebec, especially at the level of procedural law,[13] Japan has nonetheless been subjected to a greater degree of common law (specifically American) influences than jurisdictions in continental Europe. In addition to US-led constitutional and commercial law reforms after the Second World War, the country's location in the Western Pacific leads to greater exposure to American rather than European commercial practices, and the US remains the jurisdiction of choice for Japanese attorneys' overseas study.[14] Third, the intensity of doctrinal debates in Quebec is striking, as a result of Quebec jurists' allergic reaction to the trust's transplant in the province's predominantly civil law system. This historical context explains the radical choices made by the Quebec legislator in the Civil Code of 1994 in declaring the trust 'ownerless'.[15]

This chapter is divided into four sections. In the first section, I explore the structure of the English express trust and introduce to the reader the basic features of the trust in Japan and Quebec. I go on in the second and third sections to highlight two definitional components of express trusts, namely rules which allow the trustee as titleholder to enjoy full control over property and those which constrain her authority. The fourth section goes on to show that the ability to accommodate a modification of core property rules, whether defined relationally or according to strict taxonomical criteria, is crucial to the smooth functioning of the express trust.

[12] J Hudson and C Mitchell, 'Justificanda' (June 2021) Property Law Connections.

[13] For the contributions of civil procedure to mixity in Quebec, see J Plamondon, 'La procédure civile québécoise: à la recherche de la sérénité' (2020) 61 *Les Cahiers de droit* 1017.

[14] See, eg, Hatena Blog, 'Kigyō hōmu bengoshi no ryūgaku jijō ('Concerning overseas study of corporate attorneys')' (1 July 2021) law-trivia.hateblo.jp/entry/2021/07/01/225928 (accessed 2 March 2022).

[15] Civil Code (n 7) cc 2, 1261.

I. THE STRUCTURE OF THE EXPRESS TRUST

The first section of my chapter provides an overview of the structure of the express trust in the three jurisdictions. As suggested above, express trusts are the most effective where doctrinal rules give beneficiaries and other parties effective mechanisms to enforce their interests. While there is no reason why such trusts cannot be created by contract, legal systems must ensure that, once a trust is constituted, the effects of trust rules stem not from contract law but from trust law. This point is important because trust law differs from contract law in important areas such as the standing of beneficiaries and remedies, and in Japanese law – the closest to contract among the three trusts – there are also important differences with respect to the rules on trusts' constitutions.[16]

A. England

There is no consensus on the nature of the English express trust, which is a complicated question as the trust contains both personal and proprietary characteristics, and cuts across many different areas of law.[17] In recent years, the orthodox understanding of the beneficiary's interest as one stemming from split legal and equitable titles to property has largely fallen out of favour. As William Swadling points out, part of the problem of such a view is that the beneficiary's interest is simply not the equitable counterpart of the trustee's legal title: it contains a different kind of right, including the right to the due administration of the trust.[18] From a comparative standpoint, such a view is also unattractive because the reliance on equity's status as a source of law in justifying the trust strikes one as being excessively formalistic, and creates an unnecessary obstacle to the reception of the express trust outside common law systems.[19]

In England, with the exception of self-declared trusts, the creation of an inter vivos express trust involves the transfer of property from the settlor to the trustee, with the stipulation that the property is to be held in trust.[20] While the

[16] J Lee, 'Settlor's Retention of Powers in Civil Law Trusts' (2021) 35 *Trust Law International* 90, 99–100.

[17] Adam Hofri-Winogradow describes the trust as 'a particularly complex and conflicted legal site … [found] at a crossroads of family law, the law of succession and the law of commerce'. A Hofri-Winogradow, 'Zionist Settlers and the English Private Trust in Mandate Palestine' in L Smith (ed), *The Worlds of the Trust* (Cambridge, CUP, 2013) 253–4.

[18] W Swadling, 'Trusts and Ownership: A Common Law Perspective' (2016) 24 *European Review of Private Law* 951, 963–965; C Mitchell, '*Commissioner of Stamp Duties (Queensland) v Livingston* (1964): Rights of Estate Beneficiaries and Trust Beneficiaries Compared' in B Sloan (ed), *Landmark Cases in Succession Law* (Oxford, Hart Publishing, 2019) 274–276.

[19] B McFarlane and R Stevens, 'The Nature of Equitable Property' (2010) 4 *Journal of Equity* 1, 2, 28.

[20] *Milroy v Lord* [1862] 4 De GF&J 264 (Turner LJ). For self-declared trusts, see *Paul v Constance* [1977] 1 WLR 527; S Agnew and S Douglas, 'Self-Declarations of Trust' (2019) 135 *Law Quarterly Review* 67.

trustee's power to deal with property is prima facie coextensive with their powers as titleholder to property, they are disabled from dealing with property in any way they wish. This is because they are restrained by wide-ranging duties which courts are willing to enforce, including the duties to comply with the terms of the trust, to act honestly and in good faith, to account for their stewardship of trust property, and the beneficiary's entitlement to the due administration of the trust. Remedies for a breach of these duties also go beyond contract law, and include a wide range of equitable remedies such as injunctions, tracing, and claims in dishonest assistance and knowing receipt. Traditionally the trustee's duties are sourced from the settlor's intention to create a trust,[21] although the trustee and the beneficiary's consent also plays a role in creating the trust.[22] The fact that many trusts especially in the commercial context are created by contract has led John Langbein to argue that common law trusts are in fact contractual in nature.[23] This view, however, is difficult to apply to English trusts given its difficulty in explaining the beneficiary's *Saunders v Vautier* rights.[24]

While the English trust had always been a changing entity,[25] recent developments have changed the way English express trusts operate in significant ways. These changes are important because they show that the trust continues to function as a system in spite of the changing nature of trusts' use and juridical understanding of the institution. First, Langbein's theory of the trust highlights the important socio-legal reality that most express trusts are now found in the commercial context, where the trust's operation usually reflects an understanding based on parties' agreement rather than the donative intent of the settlor. Second, the proliferation of purpose trusts in offshore jurisdictions has increased both their profile and respectability, with significant implications for doctrinal developments in onshore jurisdictions.[26] Third, recent English cases such as *Akers v Samba Financial Group*[27] have clarified the nature of the trust by demonstrating English courts' recognition of the bifurcated nature of the beneficiary's interests. As Mitchell has pointed out, in a discretionary trust the beneficiary cannot be said to enjoy any economic interest, let alone property

[21] Agnew and Douglas (n 20) 87.

[22] YK Liew and C Mitchell, 'The Creation of Express Trusts' (2017) 11 *Journal of Equity* 133.

[23] J Langbein, 'The Contractarian Basis of the Law of Trusts' (1995) 105 *Yale Law Journal* 625.

[24] J Langbein, 'Why the Rule in *Saunders v Vautier* Is Wrong' in PG Turner (ed), *Equity and Administration* (Cambridge, CUP, 2016); P Matthews, 'The Comparative Importance of the Rule in *Saunders v Vautier*' (2006) 122 *Law Quarterly Review* 266.

[25] David Foster observes that the trust in the sixteenth and seventeenth centuries was highly personal, and it was only in the nineteenth century when it came to acquire proprietary characteristics. D Foster, 'Historical Conceptions of the Express Trust, c. 1600–1900', in Degeling et al (n 5).

[26] Examples include the abandonment of perpetuity rules in some North American jurisdictions or the weakening of the beneficiary principle in Australia. L Smith, 'Give the People What They Want? The Onshoring of the Offshore' (2018) 103 *Iowa Law Review* 2155, 2166; J Hudson, 'Mere and Other Discretionary Objects in Australia' in YK Liew and M Harding (eds), *Asia-Pacific Trusts Law: Theory and Practice in Context* (Oxford, Hart Publishing, 2021) vol 1.

[27] *Akers v Samba Financial Group* [2017] AC 424, [83] (Lord Sumption).

rights in the trust.[28] It follows that the beneficiary's right to the due administration of the trust is the more important of their two sets of rights.[29]

As a result of these changes, it is important to update our view of the express trust as an institution which operates primarily outside the donative context. Such a shift in emphasis highlights the trust's obligational characteristics,[30] which brings it closer to the characterisation of trusts outside common law. Yet, at the functional level this change does not necessarily alter the beneficiary's level of economic interest in the trust. Rather, a pragmatic and relational view of property means that trust interests understood as personal rights continue to affect rules which stand at highly 'interconnected' points within a legal system;[31] in other words, express trusts have de facto even if not de jure property effects. Conversely, a trust which does not affect interconnected points within a legal system, or pragmatically-defined 'property' rights, does not in fact perform the functions associated with the English express trust.

B. Japan

Unlike a number of European trusts, the Japanese trust has a clear English origin in the form of Indian and Californian trust statutes.[32] The Japanese trust was initially introduced to manage the proliferation of informal banking services in the first decades of the twentieth century.[33] As Japan emerged as a major world economy in the 1970s, the use of the trust increased greatly, especially in commercial settings including securitisation,[34] which mirrored trusts practice in the US and other parts of the world.[35]

In Japan trusts are usually created using contract, as permitted under Article 3(1) of the Trust Act 2006.[36] However, Article 3(2) and (3) also allow the creation of a trust by will or in the form of a self-declared trust.[37] Although the

[28] Mitchell (n 18) 274–276.

[29] *Akers* (n 27) [83]; ibid.

[30] D Hayton, 'Developing the Obligation Characteristic of the Trust' (2001) 117 *Law Quarterly Review* 96.

[31] H Smith, 'The Persistence of System in Property Law' (2015) 163 University of Pennsylvania Law Review 2055, 2067–2074; Yun-chien Chang, *Property Law: Comparative, Empirical, And Economics Analyses* (Cambridge, CUP) (forthcoming).

[32] S Tofaris, 'Trust Law Goes East: The Transplantation of Trust Law in India and Beyond' (2015) 36 *Journal of Legal History* 299, 323–326.

[33] A Yamada, *Shintaku rippō katei no kenkyū* ('A study on the legislative history of the trust') (Tokyo, Keisō shobō, 1981).

[34] H Dōgauchi, 'Atarashii shintakuhō riron no tenbō to kadai' ('The prospect of and topics in new trust law theory') (2007) 1261 *Kin'yū – shōji hanrei* 6, 7.

[35] L Ho and R Lee (eds), *Trust Law in Asian Civil Law Jurisdictions* (Cambridge, CUP, 2013); N Malumián, *Trusts in Latin America* (Oxford, OUP, 2009).

[36] Act No 108 of Heisei 18 (2006).

[37] Although the self-declared trust is now available under certain conditions, practitioners view its availability to be premature. Lee (n 15) 99–100; K Kimura, 'Shin shintakuhō no kadai' ('The Subject

latter forms of trust creation are less common than contract, the overall effect is that it would be inappropriate to understand Japanese trusts as contract. Where a trust is created by contract, it takes effect upon the conclusion of the trust contract, which must have as one of its terms the transfer of property or the grant of another property right, such as a security interest, to the trustee.[38] The Trust Act does not confer specific powers on the trustee, but rather grants trustees the general power to perform tasks necessary for fulfilling the purposes of the trust.[39]

In contrast to trustee powers, provisions on trustee duties are much more extensive. As I have discussed elsewhere, these include the duties of loyalty, care, to follow the terms of the trust, to inform beneficiaries of their beneficial interest and to keep accounts and provide information.[40] Trustees acting in breach of trust come under the liability to compensate the beneficiary or to restore the trust property.[41]

C. Quebec

In Quebec, the Quebec Act 1774 guaranteed the freedom of testation at the same time as preserving the province's civil law system in private law in the aftermath of British conquest. The trust first arrived in the province as a result of testamentary practices by English settlers. The Quebec trust was later codified and, sensing staunch opposition from French-speaking legal scholars, courts did much to restrict the institution to family and succession contexts.[42] From an English perspective, this would have been an unusual situation, given that the demand from users and legal practitioners for the trust form was robust. In 1994, after decades of debate led by the Office de révision du Code civil, the Quebec legislator put forward the radical model of an 'ownerless' trust. The trust was both unusual in its highly academic nature as an implementation of Pierre Lepaulle's heterodox theory,[43] while at the same time reflected important continuities with the old Quebec trust.[44]

of The New Trust Act') in M Arai (ed), *Shin shintakuhō no kiso to un'yō* ('The Foundations and Use Of The New Trust Act') (Tokyo, Nihon hyōronsha, 2007) 359–361.

[38] Trust Act (n 36) Arts 3(1), 4(1).

[39] ibid Art 26.

[40] ibid Arts 29–39; J Lee, 'The Irreducible Core of Trustee Duties in East Asian Trusts' (2021) 27 *Trusts and Trustees* 302, 304–308.

[41] Trust Act (n 36) Art 40.

[42] For example, the unit trust for investment purposes was rejected in *Crown Trust v Higher* [1977] 1 SCR 418, [425]–[426] (De Grandpré J).

[43] P Lepaulle, *Traité théorique et pratique des trusts en droit interne, en droit fiscal et en droit international* (Rousseau, 1932).

[44] P Charbonneau, 'Les Patrimoines d'affectation: vers un nouveau paradigme en droit québécois du patrimoine' (1983) 85 *La Revue du notariat* 491, 527–528.

Whereas the pre-1994 trust was held to be a case of a sui generis property right where formal ownership rights reposed with the trustee,[45] Quebec's new 'ownerless' patrimony is not built upon personal rights between parties, but is rather a mode of detaining property.[46] As no party has a property right,[47] a crucial element of the new Quebec trust is the trustee's role as the donee of a power.[48] Powers in the Franco-Quebec tradition of civil law are inherently fiduciary in nature,[49] and it is the notion of power which prevents the trustee from dealing with property in their own interest.[50] This move is important because, as explained further below, it is not possible for the holder of a right in Quebec law to be prevented from exercising the right in their own interest.[51]

Patrimony is a key idea underpinning the Quebec trust.[52] At the most basic level, patrimony refers to the totality of a person's assets and liabilities.[53] The Quebec and Scots trusts share the idea that the beneficiary's right is a personal right in a judicially-protected patrimony, which explains the insolvency protection offered by the trusts.[54] However, unlike in Scotland, the Quebec trust is rooted in the idea that the holder of a right cannot be prevented from exercising it in their self-interest, and hence protection can only be effectively rendered by declaring the patrimony 'ownerless'. As explained above, an 'ownerless' patrimony relies entirely on the exercise of fiduciary powers for its functioning. While the idea of 'ownerless' property as permitted by Article 2 of the Civil Code has not been further developed in practice, the Quebec trust's 'postmodern' character destabilises the very notion of ownership.[55] For the purpose of my argument,

[45] *Curran v Davis* [1933] SCR 283.

[46] A Popovici, 'Trust in Quebec and Czech Law: Autonomous Patrimonies?' (2016) 6 *European Review of Private Law* 929, 931.

[47] Civil Code (n 7) c 1261.

[48] M Cantin Cumyn and M Cumyn, *L'administration du bien d'autrui*, 2nd edn (Montreal, Editions Yvon Blais, 2014) 1; *Yared v Karam* (2019) SCC 62, [129] (Rowe J).

[49] E Gaillard, *Le pouvoir en droit privé* (Paris, Economica, 1985). As Alexandra Popovici notes, the fact that power in Quebec law exists only in a doctrinal rather than a codified form limits its force. A Popovici, *Êtres et avoirs: les droits sans sujet en droit privé actuel* (Montreal, Yvon Blais, 2019) 82.

[50] Civil Code (n 7) c 1283.

[51] The holder of a right can only be attacked via the restrictive doctrine of the *abus de droit*. Cantin Cumyn and Cumyn (n 48) 76.

[52] Notably, a slightly different version of the idea underlies the trust in Scotland. G Gretton, 'Trusts Without Equity' (2000) 49 *International and Comparative Law Quarterly* 599; K Reid, 'Patrimony Not Equity: The Trust in Scotland' (2000) 8 *European Review of Private Law* 427.

[53] The idea has its roots in the Roman idea of *universitas*, which had a similar meaning to the one given above. By the eighteenth century, patrimony came to be associated in French law with the idea of a person's assets and liabilities which were accessible to creditors. F Zenati and T Revet, *Les biens*, 3rd edn (Paris, Presses Universitaires de France, 2008) 23–26.

[54] J Brierley, 'Regards sur le droit des biens dans le nouveau Code civil du Québec' (1995) 1 *Revue internationale de droit comparé* 33, 48, 82; G Gretton, 'Constructive Trusts' (1997) 1 *Edinburgh Law Review* 281, 287.

[55] In particular, it attacks the idea of the *sujet de droit*, which is central to the organisation of private law in civil law countries. Popovici (n 49) 148–149; G Samuel, ''Le droit subjectif' and English law' (1987) 46 *Cambridge Law Journal* 264.

the Quebec trustee's control (*maîtrise*) of property is functionally equivalent to legal title to property in the English sense.[56]

II. POWERS OF THE TRUSTEE

As Frederic Maitland famously remarked, 'equity without common law would have been a castle in the air and an impossibility',[57] the English express trust cannot exist without the underlying rules of property found in common law. Legally, the trustee is the owner of property,[58] and in this capacity, they can exclude others from the property.[59] From the bundle of rights perspective popular in the US, the trustee enjoys a large number of rights associated with ownership.[60] For James Penner, the presence of a trust does not significantly affect the explanations offered by property theory because the trustee enjoys all the outward manifestations of an owner.[61] Even though 'ownership' is not always clearly defined in English law, in part because the 'owner' does not have special rights such as a monopoly of the ability to create subordinate property rights,[62] the trustee nonetheless holds all the legal rights associated with the interest held under trust. In particular, only the trustee is able to sue on behalf of 'the trust',[63] and trustee actions out of their authority are valid in law.[64]

It is perhaps for this reason that the French property jurist Frédéric Zenati-Castaing finds the removal of the 'owner' in the Quebec trust to be particularly unnecessary.[65] For Zenati-Castaing, without being vested in the law of ownership, which connects the right in a thing with its holder, the Quebec idea of patrimony exists in an uncertain and destabilised state. While there is no intrinsic need for a thing to be owned, modern civil law has evolved in such a way where 'ownership' is defined in relation to the capacity of its owner, rather than the physical attributes of the object.[66] Thus, the Quebec legislator's radical

[56] Civil Code (n 7) c 1278.

[57] FW Maitland, *Equity: A Course of Lectures*, rev edn (Cambridge, 1936) 19.

[58] For example, Trusts of Land and Appointment of Trustees Act (TOLATA) 1996, s 6(1) defines the trustee as the owner of property.

[59] Richard Nolan extends this idea to beneficiaries, arguing that the core function of equitable property is to exclude non-beneficiaries from trust assets. R Nolan, 'Equitable Property' (2006) 122 *Law Quarterly Review* 232, 264.

[60] T Honoré, 'Ownership' in AG Guest (ed), *Oxford Essays in Jurisprudence* (Oxford, OUP, 1961) identifies eleven incidents of ownership.

[61] J Penner, 'Purposes and Rights in the Common Law of Trusts' (2014) 48 *Revue juridique Thémis de l'Université de Montréal* 579, 583–584.

[62] SE Bartels and JM Milo, 'Contents of Real Rights: Personal or Proprietary. A Principled History' in Bartels and Milo (eds), *Contents of Real Rights* (Nymegen, Wolf Legal Publishers, 2004) 19–20.

[63] *Vandepitte v Preferred Accident Insurance Corporation of New York* [1933] AC 70, 79.

[64] *Rolled Steel Products (Holdings) Ltd v British Steel Corp* [1986] Ch 246, 303; *Akers v Samba Financial Group* [2017] AC 424, [51].

[65] F Zenati-Castaing, 'L'affectation québécoise, un malentendu porteur d'avenir. Réflexions de synthèse' (2014) 48 *Revue juridique Thémis de l'Université de Montréal* 623.

[66] Zenati and Revet (n 53) 26.

move is problematic because Quebec rules on patrimony are now potentially disassociated from the rules of ownership regulating the powers of the owner developed over the course of centuries.

In the absence of equity as a separate source of law, it is important for non-common law systems to ensure that the trustee is able to function as the legal owner of property, or at least as the party with the greatest custodial power over the property. This is not inherently difficult to achieve, although it may require the conferral of specific powers to trustees.[67] In the Roman *fiducia* it was the complex formalities associated with the transfer of ownership, rather than the notion that the transferee was the owner of property, which led to its replacement by more specialised methods.[68] Similarly, in medieval England, there was also no difficulty associated with the trustee's status as the owner of property at common law; rather, equity's role was to ensure that the trustee's obligations to the beneficiary were respected.

In Japan, the trustee is the outright legal owner of property, and their obligations to the beneficiaries or the settlor are personal in nature. In Quebec, as explained above, the absence of property rights does not preclude the trustee's control of property. In making the trustee the legal titleholder of property or its functional equivalent, two rules are particularly important. The first rule requires the transfer of property to the trustee. The second is the idea that a curtailment of the settlor's powers is necessary in order to defeat the normative intuition in civil law systems that, as the provider of property, the settlor ought to enjoy direct and continuing control over the trust.[69] I also discuss the question of powers held by the trustee.

A. Transfer of Property to the Trustee

At one level, the importance of requiring the settlor to transfer property to the trustee should be self-evident, and this rule is generally respected by different trust laws. While Article 4 of the Japanese Trust Act specifies that a trust is constituted when a trust contract comes into effect, jurists take the view that insolvency protection does not take effect until the trust property is transferred.[70] In Quebec, Article 1265 specifies that the trustee's acceptance divests the settlor of property.[71]

[67] For example, Trusts (Scotland) Act 1921, ss 3–5. Alternatively, these powers can also be conferred through the trust instrument.

[68] Witz (n 1) 52.

[69] A Hofri, 'Shapeless Trusts and Settlor Title Retention: An Asian Morality Play' (2013) 136 *Loyola Law Review* 135.

[70] M Arai, *Shintakuhō* ('Trust Law') 4th edn (Tokyo, Yūhikaku, 2014) 124–125.

[71] Civil Code (n 7); *Bank of Nova Scotia v Thibault* [2004] 1 SCR 758, 773.

B. Settlor's Retention of Control

The settlor's retention of control is rarely raised as an issue in England, in part because taxation considerations incentivise settlors to relinquish both the substance and appearance of continuing control. Where the issue appears, for example, in the Privy Council appeal of *Webb v Webb* from the Cook Islands,[72] it is often in the context of the sham trust doctrine, which requires collaboration between the settlor and trustee in creating a device which is not intended to be a trust in a meaningful sense.[73] The settlor's retention of control through appointing a protector or non-binding letters of wishes is not usually viewed as problematic, as it does not diminish the scope of the trustee's powers.

Outside common law systems, the question is more significant as the relative unfamiliarity with the institution raises the question of whether the trustee is really in control. In Japan, tax structures are not usually sensitive to the specificities of a trust structure, but rather the trust beneficiary is liable for paying tax on trust property, even in the case of a discretionary trust where trust property is not yet appointed to beneficiaries.[74] The lack of tax advantages means that there is no a priori incentive for settlors to relinquish control over trust assets. In the commercial context, there may also be a practical benefit relating to the settlor's reservation of an active role, for example by serving as a residuary beneficiary to absorb any shortfalls in trust income.[75]

Thus, in Japan, it was at the level of practical problems in securitisation which led the legislator to make changes to reduce the settlor's powers. In particular, it was the question of 'true sale', more specifically the ability of the trustee in bankruptcy to deny a trust arrangement in the event of insolvency, which gave the issue much of its urgency.[76] In the new Trust Act, the residual powers of the settlor now fall into the categories of a monitoring role over trustees, a power of veto over fundamental changes to the trust, and the settlor's residual interest.[77] These reductions are significant, given that it is difficult to justify the insolvency protection available in a trust where the trustee's exercise of their powers does not amount to overall control. Where the settlor is prepared to name themselves a direct beneficiary, or to reserve to themselves a power which is non-fiduciary in nature, there is enough clarity to suggest that the settlor is deriving benefit from their status as a beneficiary rather than as a settlor.

[72] *Webb v Webb* [2020] 8 WLUK 8.

[73] M Congalen, 'Sham Trusts' (2008) 67 *Cambridge Law Journal* 176; S Douglas and B McFarlane, 'Sham Trusts' in H Conway and R Hickey (eds), *Modern Studies in Property Law*, Vol 9 (Oxford, Hart Publishing, 2017).

[74] H Satō, *Shintaku to sozei* ('Trust and taxation') (Tokyo, Kōbundō, 2000).

[75] The Japanese practice is adopted from the American one described in S Schwarcz, 'Commercial Trusts as Business Organizations' (2003) 58 *Business Law* 559, 563.

[76] M Hamada, *Shōkenka no shinten ni tomonau shomondai: tōsan kakuri no meikakuka nado* ('Various problems related to the progress of securitisation: the clarification of bankruptcy remoteness, etc') (Tokyo, Nihon shōken keizai kenkyūjo, 2004).

[77] Lee (n 16) 94.

In Quebec too courts have been sensitive to the settlor's retention of powers, although the issues raised are largely the same as those covered under the sham trust doctrine. *In Bank of Nova Scotia v Thibault*, the Supreme Court of Canada held that the settlor's retention of full powers amounted to the 'reverse' of a trust.[78] In Quebec, the fiduciary nature of the concept of power means that the settlor cannot reduce the trustee's powers by subjecting them to mandatory directions, given that a trustee who exercises a power in ways other than in the best interests of the trust's purpose would be acting out of the scope of the power. In *Yared v Karem*, it was held that Article 1283's nature as a rule of public order meant that it was impossible for the settlor to make himself a beneficiary through a power of appointment.[79]

C. Trustee Powers

Unlike in Scotland, in Japan the Trust Act does not confer specific powers on trustees, but rather confers a general power to achieve trust purposes.[80] This is itself a departure from the old Trust Act, where the concept of power was thought to be unnecessary in view of the trustee's full ownership of property.[81] Beneficiaries are entitled to rescind the trustee's actions in excess of their powers.[82] In Quebec, the Civil Code grants trustees control and exclusive administration of the trust property,[83] presumes that trustees hold the power of appointment,[84] requires them to make the property productive and allows them to alienate it,[85] and contains a set of criteria concerning sound investment.[86] The trustee's powers come with the obligation to conform to the object of the powers.[87]

III. RESTRICTION OF AUTHORITY: TRUSTEE DUTIES

In all the jurisdictions studied, trust law's substantive intervention in the trustee's 'ownership' of property takes place at the level of constraining their authority

[78] See (n 71) 773–774 (Deschamps J).
[79] *Yared v Karem* (2019) SCC 62, [121] (Rowe J).
[80] Trust Act (n 36) Art 26.
[81] H Watanabe, 'Jutakusha no gimu/sekinin (2)' ('Trustee duty/liability') (2019) 280 *Shintaku* 35, 35–36.
[82] Trust Act (n 36) Art 27. One of the following requirements must be satisfied: the counterparty is aware that the property in question is trust property or the property is registered, or the trustee is acting in excess of their powers or grossly negligent.
[83] Civil Code (n 7) c 1278.
[84] ibid cc 1282, 1283.
[85] ibid cc 1306, 1307.
[86] ibid cc 1339–1344; John Claxton, *Studies on the Quebec Law of Trust* (Toronto, Thomson Carswell, 2004) ch 22.
[87] Cantin Cumyn and Cumyn (n 48) 283.

to deal freely with property. Trustee duties play a central role in this, both by defining how the trust is supposed to function and by guiding the trustee in their exercise of powers. While most duties are designated in the trust instrument, thus reflecting the intention of the settlor, there are also default duties which are imposed by general law. These rules, which apply unless parties opt out expressly, perform a gap filling function, and support the operation of the trust by pre-empting situations which parties might not have foreseen.[88] In aggregate terms, they add to the effectiveness and attractiveness of the express trust as an institution, by allowing users to benefit from a highly developed set of rules which are constantly adapted to changing circumstances and which benefit from significant network effects.

Although there is no agreement on their precise content, there is general agreement that duties including good faith and the duty to provide information stand at the 'core' of the trustee's duties.[89] Where these duties do not exist, for example where the powers granted to the trustee are 'limited to the point that they become something else entirely',[90] the existence of a trust can be called into question. The reason for this is that it suggests that the parties in question might not have intended to create a trust after all. However, as Hudson and Mitchell have observed, there is no suggestion by proponents of the idea of the irreducible core that core trustee duties are coterminous with 'the trust'.[91] From a comparative standpoint, the full set of features associated with trustee duties in English law is not required for the successful restriction of trustee authority.[92] Ying-chieh Wu, for example, has observed that the remedies associated with the constructive trust in common law are dispersed in civil law systems, which in his view present an 'epistemological gap'.[93]

Consequently, in this section I focus on the core set of trustee duties in the Japanese and Quebec trusts and the beneficiaries' ability to enforce these duties, rather than the features of the English trust which go beyond a narrow definition of the express trust.

[88] Robert Sitkoff describes these as rules which a well-informed party is unlikely to bargain away. R Sitkoff, 'An Economic Theory of Fiduciary Law' in A Gold and P Miller (eds), *Philosophical Foundations of Fiduciary Law* (Oxford, OUP, 2014) 205.

[89] C Mitchell, 'Good Faith, Self-Denial and Mandatory Trustee Duties' (2018) 32 *Trust Law International* 92; D Hayton, 'The Irreducible Core Content of Trusteeship' in AJ Oakley (ed), *Trends in Contemporary Trust Law* (Oxford, OUP, 1996); Lee (n 40); A Hofri, 'The Irreducible Cores of Trustee Obligations' *Law Quarterly Review* (forthcoming); New Zealand Trust Act 2019, ss 22–27.

[90] *Thibault* (n 71) 773 (Deschamps J).

[91] Hudson and Mitchell (n 12).

[92] By this I refer to areas such as tracing, dishonest assistance and knowing receipt, which are not usually available as a part of the express trust in civil law countries. In Japan, while Trust Act (n 35) Art 27(1) allows beneficiaries to rescind trustee actions in the case of bad faith or gross negligence, there is little discussion on counterparties' liability. For an overview of real subrogation as a concept similar to tracing in Quebec, see L Smith 'Unauthorized Dispositions of Trust Property: Tracing in Quebec Law' (2013) 58 *McGill Law Journal* 795.

[93] Ying-chieh Wu, 'Constructive Trusts in the Civil Law Tradition' (2018) 12 *Journal of Equity* 319.

A. Japan

In Japan a core set of trustee duties resembling the core duties in common law trusts exist. In spite of the reduction of core trustee duties under the 2006 Act, the fact that regulatory law applies to many trusts means that the level of duties has in fact not been lowered.[94] As explained above, these duties include the duties of loyalty and care not exceeding good faith, to register property where it is registerable and to keep it identifiable, and to provide information subject to restrictions.[95] While there is little explicit discussion on the prophylactic dimensions of fiduciary duties in Japan, the duty of loyalty captures some of the ideas inherent in the English concept.[96] Although there are concerns that such duties may not be enforced by courts in practice,[97] it has been argued elsewhere that good faith should be used to deny trustees' allegations that beneficiaries have in fact consented to a breach.[98]

As trustee duties are broadly similar to English trusts, another important point is that in Japan beneficiaries are able to enforce their interests. This stems from the muscular remedies which accompany the beneficiary's interest. Under the Trust Act, Article 2(6) and (7) defines the beneficiary as the party with the power to require the trustee to transfer property to them, in addition to other rights such as standing to petition the court, to oppose compulsory execution against the trust fund and to access information relating to the trust.[99] A clear set of rules on the beneficiary's rights signals both to courts and users that beneficiaries have a strong interest in property, which helps to justify beneficiaries' ability to hold trustees to account at the normative level.

B. Quebec

In Quebec, default trustee duties are imposed by the chapter on administrators of the property of another (*administrateur du bien d'autrui*), which is rooted in the law of mandate but similar in content to English trustee duties.[100] According to Article 1278, the trustee's control of trust property is explicitly subjected to the duties set out in the chapter.[101] These include the duties of prudence and

[94] Lee (n 40) 304.

[95] ibid 304–308.

[96] See, eg, Hiroto Dōgauchi, *Shintakuhō* ('Trust Law') (Tokyo, Yūhikaku, 2017) 203–221.

[97] Lee (n 40) 305–306; Osaka High Court, Heisei 22-5-14, Kinho 1935–59 (2010).

[98] J Lee, 'Structure and Rulemaking in English, Japanese and Quebec Trusts' (PhD thesis, UCL 2022) ch 8.

[99] J Lee, 'The Nature of the Beneficiary's Interest in English, Japanese and Quebec Trusts' (2021) 27 *European Review of Private Law* 611, 617–618.

[100] While there had been disagreements concerning the extent to which common law fiduciary duties should apply in Quebec, in *Provigo Distribution Inc v Supermarché ARG Inc* [1998] RJQ 47 the Court of Appeal rejected the application of common law fiduciary duties under that name.

[101] Civil Code (n 7) cc 1299–1370 (Title VII); Cantin Cumyn and Cumyn (n 48).

diligence, to not enter into a situation of conflict, and not to use powers for the trustee's own benefit.[102] Whereas under the old Quebec trust, the characterisation of the trustee as the 'owner' of property meant that beneficiaries were unable to hold trustees to their duties,[103] under the new trust, the trustee's possession not of legal rights but of fiduciary powers means that the trustee's actions in breach of trust would be ultra vires and void. As Alexandra Popovici has observed, however, the granting to the settlor, the beneficiary and 'any other interested' party of the right of enforcement does not by itself achieve the goal of constraining the trustee's authority, given that 'any other interested party' is not defined in the Civil Code.[104] Furthermore, in *Khouzam (succession de)* the Superior Court continued to require gross negligence, bad faith, malice or chagrin for imposing liability on trustees,[105] which demonstrated the limits of doctrinal reform as a way of controlling the trustee.

C. Conclusion on Trustee Duties

The similarities in the content of trustee duties between express trusts in England, Japan and Quebec are an important reason behind the institution's effectiveness. The imposition of a consistent set of trustee duties achieves the effect of restraining the trustee's authority to freely dispose of property. Without a coherent and relatively comprehensive set of duties, trust law would not be effective in transforming a claimed trust relationship from one of outright trustee ownership.

IV. MODIFICATION OF PROPERTY RULES

A. Effects of the English Trust on Property

The express trust is an institution designed to facilitate property owners' intentions with respect to property. Even if many of the features of the trust pertain to personal rights,[106] it is a requirement that the subject matter of trusts takes the form of property rights, or property-like rights such as a chose in action over money.[107] Furthermore, the trust has important third party effects which lie beyond purely personal rights, such as the ability to exclude non-beneficiaries

[102] ibid cc 1309, 1310, 1283.
[103] Cantin Cumyn and Cumyn (n 48) 122.
[104] Civil Code (n 7) c 1290; Popovici (n 49) 161.
[105] BE 2004Be-864 (CS).
[106] W Swadling, 'Property: General Principles' in A Burrows (ed), *English Private Law*, 3rd edn (Oxford, OUP, 2013) 4.140.
[107] ibid (fn 216) notes, many trusts textbooks do not notice that very often trust property consists of personal rights.

from enjoyment,[108] and the remedies associated with overreaching.[109] While trust rules have their origins in the law of obligations,[110] these rules came to acquire proprietary characteristics over the course of the seventeenth and eighteenth centuries. This historical process was expressed through the propertisation of rules on privity, which came to be strongly associated with the estate and allowed to bind the trustee's successors in title.[111] The association of the trust with the doctrine of estates was matched by the hardening of conscience into a body of technical rules which controlled norms of conveyancing. This not only gave conscience a different character as it came to be used to resolve priority conflicts,[112] but the Chancery's modelling of equitable ownership upon the common law also led to the development of a parallel system of equitable interests in land which rested upon the doctrine of purchaser for value without notice.[113]

What, then, are the effects of the English trust on today's property law? This question is important because it demonstrates both the implications of the successful restriction of the trustee's authority, and the requirement for trusts to destabilise underlying property rules in order to be effective. The Chancery's involvement in property disputes as a result of its recognition of the trust was in many ways responsible for the fundamental architecture of English land law as collections of legal and equitable interests, even though many of these interests have little to do with the express trust.[114] The codification of English land law in 1925 has not eliminated the role of the trust, which continues to govern areas such as co-ownership, albeit in a heavily modified form. Although this was in many ways a separate story, statutory regulation also curtailed the application of equitable doctrines to real property, such as notice which now exists only in an 'attenuated' form.[115] In 1996, the English legislator codified the trustee's duties in relation to land based on the rules of the trust for sale.[116] While the statutory trust in relation to land may differ from the traditional

[108] Nolan (n 59).

[109] D Fox, 'Overreaching' in P Birks and A Pretto (eds), *Breach of Trust* (Oxford, Hart Publishing, 2002).

[110] Lionel Smith, for example, has argued that the trust is best understood as a massive extension of rules against third party interference in the trustee's performance of *in persona* duties. L Smith, 'Transfers' in Birks and Pretto (n 109) 134–35, 138.

[111] Foster (n 25); D Fox, 'Purchase for Value Without Notice' in P Davies, S Douglas and J Goudkamp (eds), *Defences in Equity* (Oxford, Hart Publishing 2018) 56–57; Maitland (n 57) Lectures IX.

[112] Fox (n 109) 69.

[113] AWB Simpson, *A History of the Land Law*, 2nd edn (Oxford, OUP, 1986) 206–207. Note in this subsection 'common law' is used in its narrow sense in opposition to equity, whereas in the rest of the chapter the term usually refers to legal systems with roots in English law.

[114] In English land law the trust has historically played a key role in regulating successive and concurrent interests, specifically through strict settlements and trusts for sale before 1926. S Bridge, E Cooke and M Dixon, *Megarry & Wade: The Law of Real Property*, 9th edn (London, Sweet & Maxwell, 2019) ch 9.

[115] Fox (n 109) 74.

[116] Bridge, Cooke and Dixon (n 114) 11-002.

trust, by giving land trustees the rights of an 'absolute owner',[117] and restricting the trustee's authority by subjecting them to the duty to 'give effect to the wishes of … beneficiaries',[118] the legislator's choices support the view of the express trust adopted in this chapter.

Although many of equity's influences in English property law lie outside the realm of the express trust,[119] courts' willingness to recognise and enforce a wide range of trustee duties took place at a deep level in English property law.[120] When English land law was put on a statutory basis in 1925, the statute controlled trusts only to the extent of providing a rule of evidence which allowed trusts to be proved solely through signed writing, which meant that the presence of a trust allowed the de facto circumvention of the burdensome formality requirements needed to evidence ownership of a legal estate.[121] In some cases, even if the writing requirement were not met, a constructive trust might arise on the basis of the trustee's breach of trust.[122] Similarly, the impact of equity on personal property is deep rooted and allows the circumvention of the principle that ownership cannot be divided.[123] While the impact of equity on these areas can be characterised as a legal technique needed to achieve outcomes which are generally necessary in a modern legal system, rather than having an organic relationship with the trust, one cannot completely dissociate the modern shape of English property law from the Chancery's intervention in property law, which the proprietarisation of the trust necessitated.

It is important to emphasise that the above observations do not imply a commitment to the view that the English express trust as it currently operates affects ongoing changes in English property law; certainly, many of these influences are historical in nature. What they do highlight, however, is the inutility in English law of the taxonomical categories which preoccupy civil lawyers in understanding concepts such as property.[124] In the absence of an 'absolute' owner, 'ownership' in England is defined by the relativity of title, which leads some scholars to view equitable interests both within and beyond the trust as

[117] TOLATA (n 58) s 6.

[118] ibid s 11.

[119] Examples include equitable rules which deal with defects in formalities or the doctrine of conversion. M Dixon, 'Confining and Defining Proprietary Estoppel: The Role of Unconscionability' (2010) 30 *Legal Studies* 408. *Fletcher v Ashburner* (1779) 1 Bro CC 497. Significantly, conversion was abolished in TOLATA (n 58) s 3.

[120] While the use as a historical antecedent of the trust was the dominant form of landholding prior to its abolition in the Statute of Uses 1536, the precise reasons for the Chancery's willingness to enforce trusts in the subsequent periods remain unclear. In its new form, trusts became a common feature in conveyancing by the end of the seventeenth century. Simpson (n 111) 200.

[121] Law of Property Act 1925, s 53(1)(b).

[122] B McFarlane, 'Constructive Trusts on a Receipt of Property Sub Conditione' (2004) 120 *Law Quarterly Review* 667; S Gardner, 'Reliance-Based Constructive Trusts' in C Mitchell (ed), *Constructive and Resulting Trusts* (Oxford, Hart Publishing, 2010).

[123] M Bridge, *Personal Property Law*, 4th edn (Oxford, OUP, 2015) 48–49.

[124] Foster (n 25) has argued that taxonomical classifications from Roman law ought not be applied to a 'quintessentially common law concept as the English trust'.

'a proprietary interest ranking at the bottom of a hierarchy of proprietary interests'.[125] Furthermore, unlike in civil law, English property law had not experienced a redefinition of 'ownership' from the perspective of a natural or legal person's capacity, but rather rights continue to be defined in relation to a thing.[126] Thus, the express trust's ability to achieve significant effects deep inside the structure of property is seldom posed as a problem because the idea of an absolute property right upon which the trust encroaches does not itself exist. That said, from a civil law or functional perspective, property structures are clearly modified in the very manner in which equity interacts with common law.

B. Patrimony and Property in Japan and Quebec

In contrast, in many non-common law systems, property law has a unitary structure. Although historically property law in Europe was highly varied, the strong reaction to 'feudal' and invisible forms of landholding led to the dominance of a singular and unitary vision of property law in the form of the French *Code civil* 1804.[127] At the same time, the restriction of property rights to a circumscribed list in the form of the *numerus clausus* principle has fundamental implications for legal systems' ability to accommodate the trust. In this context, it is simply not possible to have a right which circumvents ownership: lesser property rights such as usufruits or servitudes may bind third parties, but they are granted by and are subordinate to the rights of the owner. The 'absolutist' view of property rights can also be detected in the approach taken by civil law towards agency-type arrangements. In the law of mandate, for example, the mandator's ability to revoke a mandate is central to the institution.[128] Where property is transferred permanently out of the settlor's control, this is equally problematic because the civil law jurist simply sees the new titleholder as the owner.

i. Japan

In Japan the proprietary effects of the trust are found in rules preserving the integrity and content of the trust fund. In the old Trust Act 1922, Article 31 provided the powerful remedy of rescission, which for the leading Japanese

[125] M Neave and M Weinberg, 'The Nature and Function of Equities' (1978–80) 1 *University of Tasmania Law Review* 6, 24, 38.

[126] Zenati and Revet (n 53) 26.

[127] See, eg, Anne-Marie Patault, *Introduction historique au droit des biens* (Paris, Presses Universitaires de France, 1989).

[128] For example, C civ, Art 2004 (France).

trusts jurist Kazuo Shinomiya could not be explained as a personal right.[129] Unlike English law, Japanese law does not provide extensive proprietary remedies against third parties such as tracing and claiming. As Shinomiya highlights, the proprietary effects of the Japanese trust are largely internal to the trust, and have relatively limited impact on the trust's relationship with third parties.[130] Furthermore, the beneficiary's right is explicitly defined as a personal right in the new Trust Act.[131]

Like other trusts which rely on the patrimony theory, Japanese law sees segregation as the core feature of trusts.[132] While patrimony is arguably a part of the law of persons,[133] the definition is semantic as the concept pertains to the way in which property is held, and can be classified either way. Particularly important is the idea of Hiroto Dōgauchi, who has argued based on the English trust concept that trust remedies should be extended to similar arrangements in civil law, such as the mandate, so long as the arrangement meets the requirement of segregation.[134] Dōgauchi's argument focuses on the idea that segregation should lead to a right in a protected fund. Thus, whether or not a right is defined as personal or proprietary, patrimony indicates a willingness to accept the express trust's intervention into legal relations at a structural and interconnected level, which subverts the static view embraced under the early nineteenth-century model of ownership in the *Code civil*.

ii. Quebec

Developments in Quebec reveal a fundamental willingness on the part of the Quebec legislator to adopt radical notions of property, building upon a historically open approach to property rights (*numerus apertus*).[135] In spite of a shared intellectual heritage in private law, Quebec property law is far from identical to French law. In Quebec, 'patrimony' has become the mainstream view of ownership rights in Quebec law, in the sense that property rights are now synonymous

[129] The right of rescission posed significant problems for many authors writing on the East Asian trust, for example Ying-chieh Wu, who suggested that the rule was hard to justify. Wu, 'Trusts Reimagined: The Transplantation and Evolution of Trust Law in Northeast Asia' (2020) 20 *American Journal of Comparative Law* 1, 20–21. The rule is not fundamentally different from *Actio Pauliana* available under many civil codes, which allows creditors to void prejudicial acts where the debtor knew that her act would be detrimental to the creditor or was outrightly fraudulent. Under Trust Act (n 36) Art 27, the right has been restricted by requiring the third party to know that the trustee was dealing with trust property or that they were either acting in excess of their powers or grossly negligent.

[130] Lee (n 99) 622.

[131] Trust Act (n 36) Art 2(7).

[132] For Scotland, see Reid (n 52) 431.

[133] Gretton (n 52) 614.

[134] H Dōgauchi, *Shintaku hōri to shihō taikei* ('The principles of trusts law and the structure of private law') (Tokyo, Yuhikaku, 1996).

[135] One example is the possibility to create an innominate real right (*droit réel innommé*) beyond the list of property rights in the Civil Code. Normand (n 9) 348.

with patrimonial rights.[136] In any event, while it is possible to criticise Lepaulle's view of the English trust as a fundamental misunderstanding, it is difficult to dispute that the emphasis on *flexibility* as the trust's key attribute was his creative contribution to the trust discussion.[137]

Even if the practical effects of the new Quebec concept of the 'ownerless' patrimony are unclear, the departure from the alignment of ownership with personal status is an important change, which reflects an indirect English influence in the form of the widespread use of the express trust. While the Quebec trust is not truly 'ownerless' as the underlying personal rights constituting the patrimony must still be held by a natural or legal person,[138] the idea that purposes may replace legal subjects as 'owners' of property is taxonomically radical. While a full discussion of its practical implications lies beyond the scope of the chapter, the idea that property can be owned by purposes rather than living beings may help us discover new solutions to contemporary problems, such as the use of Quebec's version of the charitable trust (*fiducie d'utilité sociale*) to protect the environment or to provide social housing.[139]

The classification of the Quebec 'ownerless' patrimony as property, rather than a part of the law of persons, supports the idea that an effective express trust *always* modifies property law. Whereas the weaker pre-1994 express trust had fewer effects on property, the modern Quebec trust has taken a largely contrary position. While it may be the case that such discussions are of limited interest to English trusts lawyers interested in *how* the trust operates, from a comparative perspective the Quebec approach reveals powerfully the potential which the trust – rooted in the English express trust in its spirit of user-driven flexibility rather than in a specific set of codifiable rules – has in transforming private law.

V. CONCLUSION

In this chapter, I have attempted to show that the effects of the English express trust are reproduced in Japan and Quebec through a restriction of the trustee's authority and a modification of civil law notions of property. While the Quebec trustee does not hold de jure title to property, in functional terms one can identify clearly that the trustee's legal title to property, burdened by similar sets of trustee duties, provides the clearest explanation of the operation of the express trust in all three jurisdictions. Similarly, an effective express trust affects property relations deeply, in other words at a level where the trust interferes with interconnected parts of the system. For English law, the pragmatic

[136] Popovici (n 49) 166 (fn 649).
[137] ibid 45–46.
[138] A Popovici, 'Le patrimoine d'affectation: nature, culture, rupture' (LLM thesis, Université Laval 2012) 93.
[139] On the wider application of '*affectation*' in Quebec property law, see S Normand, 'Affectation et biens communs urbains' (February 2022) Les communs urbains saisis par le droit.

definition of the very notion of property means that a strict distinction between property and personal rights is not necessary for appreciating the effects of the trust within property law. For Japanese and Quebec law, the absolutist view of 'ownership', a feature shared by most civil law property systems, presents a prima facie insurmountable obstacle to the development of the trust, as was clearly the case in Quebec before 1994. It is interesting in this regard that the theory of patrimony, whether characterised as a property or personal right, can be used to better rationalise the trust's intervention into property law. In doing so, the express trust both in Japan and Quebec has a significant impact on the ways in which property is held in the two jurisdictions, given that patrimony as a protected fund is inherently amenable to classification as property.

12

Elucidating Equity in Pallant v Morgan

JOSHUA TENG*

I. INTRODUCTION

A CURIOUS FEATURE of English law, the *Pallant v Morgan*[1] equity is said to arise where two parties interested in the acquisition of an interest in land, namely A, the acquiring party, and B, the non-acquiring party, agree in the context of a joint venture or other arrangement that A is to acquire the land on the understanding that upon the aforementioned acquisition, A is to grant a portion of the interest in land to B. However, the joint venture or arrangement fails to materialise into or constitute a legally enforceable contract. Subsequent to A's successful acquisition of the property, A refuses to dispose any part of the interest in the land to B.

This chapter seeks to examine the alternative bases for the *Pallant v Morgan* equity, namely under the explanations for the equity founded on the common intention constructive trust and under the law of agency. In this chapter it will be argued that the approach taken by the Court of Appeal in *Banner Homes Group plc v Luff Developments Ltd*[2] as understood by the majority in *Crossco No 4 Unlimited v Jolan Ltd*[3] in formulating the *Pallant v Morgan* equity as a species of common intention constructive trust is inapt and undesirable in the circumstances in which the *Pallant v Morgan* equity may typically arise. Thereafter, this chapter will consider if the equity arises on the basis of agency. While there may be some explanatory force to analysing the *Pallant v Morgan* equity as purely arising as a result of an agency relationship, it is suggested that even at its highest, the agency analysis is unlikely to fully be able to account for the varied circumstances in which the *Pallant v Morgan* equity may be thought to justifiably arise.

* I am grateful to William Swadling, Brian Sloan, Andreas Televantos, the participants of the Modern Studies in Property Law Conference 2022, and the anonymous reviewer for their comments on an earlier draft of this chapter. All errors and omissions remain my own.

[1] *Pallant v Morgan* [1953] Ch 43.

[2] *Banner Homes Group plc v Luff Developments Ltd* [2000] Ch 372.

[3] *Crossco No 4 Unlimited v Jolan Ltd* [2012] 2 All ER 754.

Finally, this chapter seeks to propose a basis for the *Pallant v Morgan* equity, in particular one founded upon the breach of fiduciary duty owed by the party acquiring the property to the other party to whom a promise of an interest in the property, whether enforceable under contract or otherwise, was made by the former. In doing so it is suggested that the basis for the unidirectional or mutual fiduciary duties owed by one party to the other, or between the parties, may be derived from the incomplete or 'failed' joint venture or arrangement and whose existence, scope, and consequences of breach are to be assessed on a case-by-case basis on the criteria applicable for the imposition of fiduciary duties in commercial joint ventures on a similar basis to those imposed on particular joint ventures akin to that in *Ross River Ltd v Waveley Commercial Ltd*.[4]

II. THE *PALLANT v MORGAN* EQUITY

The salient facts of *Pallant v Morgan* merit a mention in setting out the basis for the discussion which will follow. The acquisition of the property in question took place at an auction which was attended by the agents of the plaintiff and defendant. The plaintiff, Pallant, was the non-acquiring party, B, whereas the defendant, Morgan, was the acquiring party, A. The property in question was known as Lot 16. There were discussions between A and B prior to the day of the auction on how they were to approach bidding for Lot 16, but these discussions failed to materialise in a formal agreement.

The auction was attended by A's agent and B's agent. In this case, A's agent was authorised (by A) to bid up to £3,000 for Lot 16 whereas B's agent was authorised (by B) to bid up to £2,000. In the discussions prior to the day of the auction, it had been understood by A and B that 'if they bid one against the other no one would profit except the owner, and that it was preferable if possible that they should agree before the sale not to compete'.[5]

Although no agreement was reached before then, this sentiment had carried through to A and B's agents respectively such that A and B's agents had agreed in the auction room that should A be successful in acquiring Lot 15 and Lot 16, A would sell part of Lot 16 to B. On the assurance by A's agent, B's agent refrained from bidding in the auction for Lot 16 and A acquired the same for under £2,000. A had also successfully acquired Lot 15.

When it came time to divide the property, however, A and B had failed to agree on a division of the land, and as such A kept the property to himself without regard to B's interest in the property. The High Court found that the agreement reached between A's agent and B's agent was incomplete and too uncertain to be specifically enforceable and thus declined to grant the primary

[4] *Ross River Ltd v Waveley Commercial Ltd* [2014] 1 BCLC 545.
[5] *Pallant* (n 1) [45].

remedy of specific performance sought by B in the proceedings.[6] However, the High Court held that 'the proper inference from the facts is that [B]'s agent, when he bid for lot 16, was bidding for both parties on an agreement that there should be an arrangement between the parties on the division of the lot if he were successful'.[7] As the parties had failed to agree on a division, the Court could not compel them to agree but was able to decree that the property was held by A jointly for A and B, and if an agreement could not be reached on the division even then, the property must be resold.[8]

The primary principle underlying the *Pallant v Morgan* equity was pithily formulated by Megarry J in *Holiday Inns Inc v Broadhead*[9] as follows:

> It seems to me that if A and B agree that A will acquire some specific property for the joint benefit of A and B on terms yet to be agreed, and B, in reliance on A's agreement, is thereby induced to refrain from attempting to acquire the property, equity ought not to permit A, when he acquires the property to insist on retaining the whole benefit for himself to the exclusion of B. If on the facts it would be inequitable for the quantum of B's interest to be a moiety, I do not doubt that equity could determine what justice required the quantum to be; but where the facts suggest no other basis, then there should be equality.

The Court of Appeal had the opportunity to consider the basis of the *Pallant v Morgan* equity in *Banner Homes Group plc v Luff Developments Ltd.*[10] In the leading judgment of the Court of Appeal, Chadwick LJ enumerated a number of key propositions on the scope and application of the *Pallant v Morgan* equity which are as follows:[11]

> (i) The Pallant v Morgan equity arises from an arrangement or understanding which precedes the acquisition of the relevant property by one party to the arrangement. The pre-acquisition arrangement has the effect of colouring the subsequent acquisition by the acquiring party (by treating him as trustee) if he seeks to act inconsistently with the arrangement.
> (ii) The arrangement or understanding need not be contractually enforceable, and it is no bar if the arrangement is too uncertain to be enforced as a contract or is plainly not intended to have contractual effect.
> (iii) It is necessary that the pre-acquisition arrangement or understanding should contemplate that one party (the acquiring party) will take steps to acquire the relevant property; and that, if he does so, the other party (the non-acquiring party) will obtain some interest in that property. Any desire by one of the parties (in particular the acquiring party) to resile from the arrangement must be informed to the other before it is too late for the parties to be restored.

[6] ibid [48].
[7] ibid [50].
[8] ibid.
[9] *Holiday Inns Inc v Broadhead* (Ch, 19 December 1969), as approved by Chadwick LJ in *Banner Homes Group* (n 2). See also (1974) 232 EG 951.
[10] *Banner Homes Group* (n 2).
[11] ibid 397–9.

(iv) It is necessary that, in reliance on the arrangement or understanding, the non-acquiring party should do or refrain from doing something which confers an advantage to the acquiring party in relation to the acquisition of the property, or is detrimental to its ability to acquire the property on equal terms. A concurrent advantage to one party and a detriment to the other is not a necessary component.

(v) The essential element is 'that the circumstances make it inequitable for the acquiring party to retain the property for himself in a manner inconsistent with the arrangement or understanding on which the non-acquiring party has acted'. It is not strictly necessary for the non-acquiring party to keep out of the market, nor is the existence of both advantage and detriment as either one would suffice.

The *Pallant v Morgan* equity also came to be considered before the Court of Appeal in *Crossco No 4 Unlimited v Jolan Ltd*.[12] As observed below, the majority of the Court of Appeal took the view that the *Pallant v Morgan* constructive trust was an extension to the common intention constructive trust as a result of Chadwick LJ's analysis in *Banner Homes Group*.

In opposition to that position, however, Etherton LJ (as His Lordship then was) formulated the *Pallant v Morgan* equity as arising out of the existence and breach of fiduciary duty.[13] Examples of the existence and breach of fiduciary duty could be found in the agency relationship as well as in 'joint venture cases in which it is to be inferred that the particular nature of the relationship between joint venturers was such as to give rise to fiduciary duties'.[14] In effect, it would have the effect of fitting the category within the broader, and more conventional, application of cases of breach of fiduciary duty.

While what precisely constituted breach was not clearly defined by Etherton LJ in *Crossco*, it is suggested that the reference to the case of *Paragon Finance plc v Thakerar & Co* suggests that the event of breach turns upon the subsequent appropriation of property to the defendant's (ie acquiring party's) own use.[15] It was also suggested that the '*Pallant v Morgan* equity … can be seen as cases in which the court is, pursuant to the constructive trust, depriving the defendant of the advantage obtained in breach of trust'.[16] In that vein, the lack of complete agreement is an irrelevant factor and, additionally, the court has a broad latitude in devising the best way to deprive the acquiring party of an unconscionable advantage. These were said to be consistent with the breach of fiduciary duty analysis espoused by Etherton LJ.[17]

[12] *Crossco* (n 3).
[13] ibid [88].
[14] ibid.
[15] ibid [93] citing the judgment of Millett LJ (as His Lordship then was) in *Paragon Finance plc v Thakerar & Co* [1999] 1 All ER 400: 'His possession of the property is coloured from the first by the trust and confidence by means of which he obtained it, and his subsequent appropriation of the property to his own use is a breach of that trust.'
[16] ibid [95].
[17] ibid.

III. ALTERNATIVE CONCEPTIONS OF THE *PALLANT v MORGAN* EQUITY

It has been suggested that the *Pallant v Morgan* equity has its basis in the common intention constructive trust. Indeed, this was the position maintained by the majority of the Court of Appeal in *Crossco No 4 Unlimited v Jolan Ltd.*[18] The common intention constructive trust spoken of in this context is the one recognised in the line of cases beginning with *Gissing v Gissing.*[19]

Etherton LJ, in the minority in *Crossco* on this point, disagreed with the formulation of the *Pallant v Morgan* equity as a species of the common intention constructive trust and preferred the justification of the *Pallant v Morgan* equity on the basis of a breach of fiduciary duty owed by the acquiring party to the non-acquiring party. This proposition advanced by Etherton LJ has been referenced in section II above and will be discussed further in section V below.

At this juncture, it should be noted that Etherton LJ in *Crossco*[20] opined that the common intention constructive trust is a 'distinctive area … driven by policy considerations and special facts that normally apply in the dealings between those living in an intimate relationship'.[21] The policy rationale and underpinnings of the common intention constructive trust, being in the purely domestic context, are at their very highest inapposite to the context of commercial dealings, regardless of the level of formality in which these commercial dealings are undertaken. As aptly noted, commercial parties 'do not expect the court to determine their respective property rights and interests by the imputation of intentions which they did not have but which the court considers they would have had if they had acted justly and reasonably and thought about the point'.[22]

It is suggested here that the criticism of the suggestion that the *Pallant v Morgan* equity has as its basis the common intention constructive trust is justifiable. In the first instance, the majority in *Stack v Dowden* recognises that the domestic context within which the common intention constructive trust operates is a very different one from the commercial world. A panoply of varied factors, both in existence at the time of the agreement or understanding to acquire the property as well as those relating to conduct after the relevant property had been acquired up until the time the constructive trust is sought to be enforced, are considered relevant in determining the intention of the parties in relation to the apportionment of beneficial ownership to the property.[23] The breadth of these

[18] See the judgments of Arden LJ and McFarlane LJ in *Crossco* (n 3) which suggest that the ratio of the decision in *Banner Homes Group* (n 2) is best understood as being founded upon the common intention constructive trust.

[19] *Gissing v Gissing* [1971] AC 886.

[20] *Crossco* (n 3) [85]–[87]; in particular the references to the common intention constructive trust as 'ambulatory'.

[21] ibid [85].

[22] ibid [87].

[23] *Stack v Dowden* [2007] 2 AC 432 [69] (Lady Hale).

factors in determining whether there had been an original intention to hold the property on different proportions at the time the property was transferred, and their effect on varying the share of ownership was subject to some doubt and criticism by Lord Neuberger in *Stack v Dowden*.[24]

That the domestic context which forms the backdrop of the common intention constructive trust is starkly different from those of commercial dealings, however informal or incipient, is made clear by the acknowledgement by Lady Hale in *Stack v Dowden* that:

> There may also be reason to conclude that, whatever the parties' intentions at the outset [of the acquisition of the property in question], these have now changed. An example might be where one party has financed (or constructed himself) an extension or substantial improvement to the property, so that what they have now is significantly different from what they had then.[25]

By contrast, commercial dealings, however informal, are scarcely meant to be ambulatory to the extent recognised in *Stack v Dowden*. Furthermore, it would be antithetical to the certainty required in commercial dealings for factors taking place after the relevant period of acquisition to inform the bargain struck or agreement reached prior to the acquisition of a plot of land and a fortiori to alter that pre-existing bargain on the basis of an imputed understanding from conduct.

It may be contended that, in more recent times, common intention constructive trusts have also been invoked in increasingly commercial contexts, for instance in the Privy Council's decision in *Marr v Collie*[26] and before the Court of Appeal in *Kahrmann v Harrison Morgan*.[27] There was arguably, however, a domestic element in both cases, and the context was thus not purely commercial. In *Marr* the parties were in a personal relationship with each other, albeit the properties concerned were better characterised as investment properties.[28] *Kahrmann* was described by the Court of Appeal as an 'intermediate' case where the parties were personally known to each other as well as involved in a business relationship.[29] However, it should be noted that the decision in *Marr* has been subject to significant criticism for, among others, its expansion of the common

[24] *Stack* (n 23) [140]–[144] (Lord Neuberger).

[25] *Stack* (n 23) [70] (Lady Hale). That said, substantial improvements to the property which raise the value of the property could legitimately be a basis for proprietary estoppel in an appropriate case where a sufficiently clear and unequivocal promise to confer property is made accompanied by detrimental reliance upon such an unequivocal representation; alternatively under the law of unjust enrichment, albeit without a sufficient proprietary base or connection the remedy ought to be personal and may be more similar to a case of *negotiorum gestio*.

[26] *Marr v Collie* [2018] AC 631, in particular [39], [40], and [49] where *Stack* (n 23) is said to not be 'confined exclusively to the domestic setting'.

[27] *Kahrmann v Harrison Morgan* [2019] EWCA Civ 2094, in particular [98]–[101]. It is noteworthy that the claim based on *Pallant v Morgan* was abandoned in the first instance proceedings in *Kahrmann* and was therefore not considered on appeal, see [127].

[28] *Marr* (n 26) [1], [49], [58]–[61].

[29] *Kahrmann* (n 27) [100].

intention constructive trust to cases beyond the acquisition of the property for a 'domestic purpose'.[30] Separately, the fact that the Court of Appeal in *Kahrmann* found that there were enforceable agreements, the meaning of which was determined and construed, may shed some light on why the *Stack* analysis was not applied in disposing the appeal.[31] As such, both these cases ought not to be understood as altering the legal landscape applicable to the typical *Pallant v Morgan* facts.[32]

With particular reference to common intention constructive trusts arising in the commercial context, however, the evidential inquiry instead appears to centre around whether the parties considered themselves legally bound by what had been agreed, in spite of the lack of formalities. In *Kahrmann* the Court of Appeal found that despite the fact that 'the parties may well have envisaged that their agreement should be notarised … [the evidence did not negate] any intention to enter into legal relations until that formality was complied with',[33] whereas in *Cobbe v Yeoman's Row Management Ltd*, the specific finding of the House of Lords was that Mr Cobbe 'never expected to acquire an interest in property otherwise than under a legally enforceable contract'.[34]

Further, substantial differences may be seen between the *Pallant v Morgan* equity and the typical common intention constructive trust. First, the common intention constructive trust has detrimental reliance by the plaintiff (claiming the common intention constructive trust) as an essential component.[35] On the

[30] See, for instance, AYS Georgiou, '*Marr v Collie*: The Ballooning of the Common Intention Constructive Trust' (2019) 82 *MLR* 145.

[31] As observed, in respect of the *Kahrmann* (n 27) decision, in B Sloan, 'Informal Trusts of Land: W(h)ither different approaches for domestic and commercial contexts?' (Faculty of Law Blogs, University of Oxford, 17 December 2019) www.law.ox.ac.uk/research-and-subject-groups/property-law/blog/2019/12/informal-trusts-land-whither-different (accessed 15 May 2022).

[32] Although they arguably represent a broad expansion within the field of common intention constructive trusts, see also Georgiou (n 30) above.

[33] *Kahrmann* (n 27) [104].

[34] *Cobbe v Yeoman's Row Management Ltd* [2008] 1 WLR 1752 [37]; see also [87] where Mr Cobbe was said to be 'expecting a contract'. See also: *Thorner v Major* [2009] 1 WLR 776 [93]. A similar position is taken in *Dowding v Matchmove Ltd* [2017] 1 WLR 749 [32] and [38] and *Herbert v Doyle* [2010] EWCA Civ 1095 [57]–[58] and [79] where the claimants in those cases are said to have intended the agreements entered into to be legally binding notwithstanding that the formalities, including those under s 2(1) of the Law of Property (Miscellaneous Provisions) Act 1989, were not complied with.

[35] Note that in *Hudson v Hathway* [2022] EWHC 631 (QB), the High Court decided that detrimental reliance by the claimant was not a necessary element in a claim for a common intention constructive trust, see in particular [58]–[81]. This decision is surprising given that in the absence of any detriment suffered by the claimant in reliance upon the common intention, it is difficult to see how the conditions for the trust would be satisfied and that it was not a mere gratuitous promise. While unconscionability is referred to by the High Court in [73], it is difficult to see how *sans* the requisite detriment suffered by the claimant in reliance upon the common intention, it would be unconscionable to deny an interest in the common intention constructive trust. *Cf Kahrmann* (n 27) [89], [97]–[99] where the Court of Appeal in a 'commercial' or 'intermediate' case (ie, between the purely commercial and domestic contexts) nevertheless required a finding of detriment to give rise to the common intention constructive trust. I am indebted to Brian Sloan for bringing the *Hudson* decision to my attention.

other hand, the facts of *Pallant* are inconsistent with a requirement of detrimental reliance on the part of the non-acquiring party seeking the constructive trust.[36] This was so because it could not be said that the non-acquiring party had suffered a detriment as a result since, by the scope and limits of authority given to the non-acquiring party's agent, the non-acquiring party would have nevertheless failed to successfully acquire that property.[37] This is further buttressed by the majority judgment of Chadwick LJ in *Banner Homes Group*, namely that detrimental reliance is not an essential element of the *Pallant v Morgan* equity provided that an advantage was conferred on the acquiring party, A. Second, the evidential thresholds for demonstrating (detrimental) reliance[38] is markedly different in both the common intention constructive trust, especially those not involving a 'commercial context', and the *Pallant v Morgan* equity.[39] As elaborated above, the common intention constructive trust assessment takes into account evidence both of matters directly relevant to the acquisition of the property as well as background factors in the management of the financial affairs of the parties.[40]

Alternatively, it has also been suggested that the *Pallant v Morgan* equity is best formulated and understood as a species of agency whereby the agency relationship in question is one in which the acquiring party is said to be the agent of the non-acquiring party in the acquisition of the property.[41] It has been said that the particular agency is not one of a 'contracting agent' but is instead a 'property acquiring agent'.[42] It was also noted by the Court of Appeal in *Crossco* that there may be an agency relationship between the acquiring party and the non-acquiring party, where the acquiring party (or its agent) acts as the agent for the non-acquiring party in the acquisition of the relevant property.[43]

[36] *Pallant* (n 1) [46]–[47] (Harman J); See also J Grower, 'Explaining the *Pallant v Morgan* equity' [2016] *Conv* 434; YK Liew, 'Making Sense of Agreement-Based Constructive Trusts in the Commercial Context', [2022] *JBL* 330, 351–352. Detrimental reliance is a relevant factor in *Pallant v Morgan* but not a necessary one, unlike for the common intention constructive trust.

[37] *Pallant* (n 1). The non-acquiring party's agent had been given a limit of authority to bid up to £2,000 whereas the acquiring party's agent had been given a limit of authority to place a bid on the relevant property for up to £3,000, meaning that the resultant position in either case would have left the non-acquiring party in want of the property.

[38] For reasons set out at n 35 above, the *Hudson* (n 35) decision is anomalous in its dispensation of the requirement for the claimant to suffer a detriment in reliance upon the common intention.

[39] Grower (n 36).

[40] Although in *Kahrmann* (n 27) [89], the instances of detrimental reliance found to have been established in the case were more closely related to the acquisition of the desired interest in the property and not in the management of the financial affairs of the parties prior to the acquisition.

[41] *Pallant* (n 1) [50] (Harman J): 'In my judgment, the proper inference from the facts is that the defendant's agent, when he bid for lot 16, was bidding for both parties on an agreement that there should be an arrangement between the parties on the division of the lot if he were successful.' Arguably the formulation of the proper inference by Harman J could be said to be a form of an agency relationship.

[42] Grower (n 36).

[43] *Crossco* (n 3) [88] (Etherton LJ) and [128] (Arden LJ), where the defendant's agent [in *Pallant v Morgan*] was said to act for both the plaintiff and defendant at the auction in acquiring the relevant Lot 16.

The argument from agency requires that there be a form of undertaking or scope of authority on the part of the acquiring party, A, to act for the non-acquiring party, B. This undertaking or scope of authority must necessarily be for the acquisition of the property in question by A for the benefit of B (or A and B jointly), otherwise it would be difficult to ascertain how and why the agency relationship exists in the first place, and what the scope of agency would be such that it would permit or cause the 'acquiring party-agent', A, to acquire on behalf of B (whether singularly or jointly) in the first place. The other thing to note is that this conception is necessarily unidirectional in the owing of duties from A to B and would not result in the case of mutual duties being owed by A to B and vice versa.

There are two main points in response to the agency conception as described immediately above. Chiefly, an agency relationship may not be able to account for all the circumstances in which the *Pallant v Morgan* equity arises. This is notwithstanding that an agency relationship may well able to account for the factual matrix in existence in *Pallant* given that was arguably a clear sense in which the acquiring party's agent in *Pallant* could be said to be acquiring the property, Lot 16, for both the plaintiff and defendant since the content of their agreement was found to be that the non-acquiring party's agent 'had agreed not to bid on the faith of an assurance from [the acquiring party's agent] that, if he refrained, the [acquiring party] would convey over the portions "C" and "A" to the [non-acquiring party] at a price to be settled in accordance with the formula arrived at …'.[44]

On the other hand, the agency relationship would likely be inapt to account for the factual matrix in *Holiday Inns Inc v Broadhead* where the non-acquiring party's expectation in the joint venture with the acquiring party was to receive a lease from the acquiring party to operate a hotel on the property.[45] In that scenario, there could not be any meaningful way of describing the acquiring party's position as one of an agent with the scope of authority to acquire the property on behalf of or for the benefit of the non-acquiring party, since the interest actually acquired from the vendor of the property by the acquiring party, A, was different from the interest that was agreed to be granted by A to the non-acquiring party, B. In that sense, it would be artificial to speak of A as B's agent for the purpose of acquisition of the property, since there was no agreement to acquire the beneficial interest in the property for their mutual benefit in the first place.

[44] *Pallant* (n 1) [46]. At [48], Harman J observed: '[The non-acquiring party, B's, agent's] conversation with [the acquiring party, A's, agent] was, as I find, to the following effect. [A's agent] observed that if agreement was to be reached [B] would have to give way, not only on Ordnance No. 107, but on "B", and [B's agent], having express authority to that effect, agreed to do so. [A's agent] then said that [A] would not be willing to sell any part of "A" which affected certain water rights by which he set store, and [B's agent] agreed that, in so far as the boundaries of "A" as drawn did affect them, [B] would give way here also. [A's agent] thereupon intimated that in that case everything would be all right, and thereupon [B's agent] said he would not bid and did not do so.'

[45] *Holiday Inns Inc* (n 9) as, inter alia, observed by Etherton LJ in *Crossco* (n 3) [95].

In fact, the High Court in *Holiday Inns Inc* granted B a beneficial interest, and not a lease (which was B's original expectation under the agreement).[46]

The agency conception described above is thus difficult to reconcile with both what was agreed by the parties that would be done (and the non-acquiring party's expectations thereunder) as well as the remedies eventually awarded by the court.

Further, the agency analysis would not survive a situation where there was an express intention that A was not B's agent, or if on the facts of *Pallant* the agent did not have authority to delegate its authority (ie, authorise another to act as agent on behalf of their principal), notwithstanding that on normative terms, the *Pallant v Morgan* equity might be thought to be justified.

In that same vein, the second point in response is that the insufficiency of the agency conception above is that the scope of the 'agent's' authority or mandate of the 'agent', ie the acquiring party, A, are such that a reciprocal duty may never arise between A and the non-acquiring party, B.

This point is elaborated further in section V below. For the moment it will have to suffice to say that it would be artificial to delineate between a scenario where A undertakes to acquire property for the benefit of A and B, but goes on to do so only for itself and not for B (Scenario 1) and the scenario where A undertakes to acquire property for the benefit of A and B, and where B agrees to refrain from bidding on or acquiring that property for the purpose of that agreement, but nevertheless B goes on to acquire the property and refuses to make an appropriate disposition to A (Scenario 2).

In both Scenario 1 and Scenario 2, the undertakings of A and B are in respect of the same property, and further in the *acquisition* of the same property from a third party for their mutual benefit. It is only the exact specifics of the breach which are different: for A, it is in the acquisition of the property without accounting for or providing for the interests of B (arguably coupled with a failure to make a further transfer to rectify the same); for B, it is in the act of stepping into the fray where it had previously agreed to refrain, which enabled its acquisition of the property in question (and additionally the misuse or taking advantage of information obtained through the 'joint venture' with A[47] for its own benefit). The content of both these undertakings are in respect of the same property and, further, are in respect of the effort to acquire the same property.

On the agency analysis as referred to above, however, it would not be possible to accommodate Scenario 2 within the *Pallant v Morgan* equity as B's agreement to refrain from bidding on or acquiring the property could not be properly described as a form of 'agency' undertaking.

Accordingly, it is suggested that there is no good justification for the contrasting outcomes in Scenario 1 and Scenario 2. However, such a divergent outcome

[46] ibid.

[47] For instance, information about A's bidding strategy and limits of authority of A's agent in the acquisition.

would arise from the conception of the *Pallant v Morgan* equity as arising out of an agency relationship as described above.

IV. FIDUCIARY OBLIGATIONS IN COMMERCIAL JOINT VENTURES

The invocation of a 'joint venture' and its concomitant factual matrices often lie at the heart of a claim for a *Pallant v Morgan* equity. As such, it is apposite at this juncture to consider the circumstances in which joint ventures may give rise to fiduciary obligations owing from one party to the other (or mutually by both parties), and how these fiduciary obligations may interact with a *Pallant v Morgan* equity.

The definition of a fiduciary has commonly come to be understood as:

> … simply, someone who undertakes to act for or on behalf of another in some particular matter or matters. That undertaking may be of a general character. It may be specific and limited. It is immaterial whether the undertaking is or is not in the form of a contract. It is immaterial that the undertaking is gratuitous. And the undertaking may be officiously assumed without request.[48]

A number of broad propositions may be derived from the cases on commercial joint ventures and their corresponding fiduciary duties, if any. First, it is worth bearing in mind that the 'phrase "joint venture" is not a term of art either in a business or in a legal context, and each relationship which is described as a joint venture has to be examined on its own facts and terms to see whether it does carry any obligations of a fiduciary nature'.[49] The rights and duties between parties are to be determined 'by reference to their agreement or relationship rather than by reference to some abstract classification such as "partnership" or "joint venture"'.[50]

A similar point is made in *Ross River Ltd v Cambridge City Football Club Ltd*[51] where Briggs J (as His Lordship then was) observed that:

> in relationships falling short of partnership, but having in them elements of joint enterprise or joint venture, there is no hard and fast rule as to the existence or otherwise either of a duty of good faith, a fiduciary duty or a duty of disclosure. Each case will turn on its own facts, but if the relationship is regulated by a contract, then the terms of that contract will be of primary importance, and wider duties will not be lightly implied ….[52]

[48] PD Finn, *Fiduciary Obligations* (Pyrmont, The Law Book Company, 1977) 201.

[49] *Ross River Ltd* (n 4) [35] (Lloyd LJ).

[50] BH McPherson, 'Joint Ventures' in PD Finn (eds), *Equity and Commercial Relationships* (Pyrmont, The Law Book Company, 1987) 26 referring to *Walker v Hirsch* [1884] 27 Ch D 460 [468]–[470].

[51] *Ross River Ltd v Cambridge City Football Club Ltd* [2007] EWHC 2115 (Ch), [2008] 1 All ER 1004.

[52] This proposition is also supported by *Hospital Products Ltd v United States Surgical Corporation* (1984) 156 CLR 41 [97] (Mason J): 'That contractual and fiduciary relationships may co-exist

Second, it may be said that a fiduciary duty on the part of a commercial joint venturer arises where the parties had been associated on the basis of 'the mutual trust and confidence of each partner in the skill, knowledge and integrity of every other party',[53] at least to the extent that it affects the particular subject of the joint venture or undertaking. In *Murad v Al Saraj*, the fiduciary duties were held to arise because the parties were in the position of joint venturers, the relationship between the parties was one of trust and confidence, the defendant [acquiring party] had taken on responsibilities in connection with the joint venture, and that the claimants had no relevant experience and knowledge of the arrangements made by the defendant with third parties, entrusting them with discretion to act.[54]

It was on that similar basis, it appears, that *United Dominions Corp. Ltd v Brian Pty Ltd*[55] was decided. United Dominions Corp sought to retain profits under collateralisation clauses in a mortgage agreement that it had entered into with one of the other joint venturers, SPL, over the land which was the subject of the joint venture. The third joint venturer, Brian, asserted that the mortgages were taken in breach of a fiduciary duty owed by each of them to him. The High Court of Australia agreed with this analysis, finding that the relationship between the joint venturers was 'one between persons who, intending to become partners, had already embarked on the partnership venture of which the execution of the mortgage was an incident'.[56]

The case of *United Dominions Corp* further supports the proposition that the matter which is complained of as a 'breach of fiduciary duty' must fall within the scope of that joint venture relationship of trust and confidence, thus explicating the particular finding that the execution of the mortgage was an incident of the partnership venture in question.[57]

Some authors have suggested that fiduciary obligations are imposed in circumstances where a person 'acquires control over a part … of another person's autonomy.'[58] The possession of legal power or holding of the legal controls for (but not merely over) the second person by the first person justifies the imposition of a requirement of loyalty on the part of the first person to the

between the same parties has never been doubted. Indeed, the existence of a basic contractual relationship has in many situations provided a foundation for the erection of a fiduciary relationship. In these situations it is the contractual foundation which is all important because it is the contract that regulates the basic rights and liabilities of the parties.'

[53] *Baird's Case* [1870] LR 5 CH App 725 [732]–[733].

[54] *Murad v Al Saraj* [2004] EWHC 1235 (Ch) [247].

[55] *United Dominions Corp. Ltd v Brian Pty Ltd* (1985) 157 CLR 1, as noted in McPherson (n 50) 33–4.

[56] ibid 744.

[57] ibid.

[58] L Smith, 'Fiduciary relationships: Ensuring the Loyal Exercise of Judgement on Behalf of Another' (2014) 130 *LQR* 608, 614.

second, such that the levers of power are exercised by the first in the second's best interest.[59]

This conception may, at best, only partially explain the landscape of fiduciary obligations in commercial joint ventures. First, it may be peculiar to think of one party to a commercial joint venture as acquiring control over a part of its counterparty's autonomy, particularly where the joint venture obliges the second person *to do something or not to do something*. It is not simply the case that something is done *for* the second party, with the second party being an idle bystander in its own affairs. Second, in a *Pallant v Morgan* type case, where the main object of the venture is to ostensibly acquire property not presently belonging to either party involved in the venture, it may be difficult to think of the acquiring party, A, as having any legal power over the non-acquiring party, B, or its affairs.[60]

On another conception of fiduciary duties, it is suggested that the imposition of fiduciary duties responds to a need to 'remove or neutralise incentives that might tempt or otherwise motivate a fiduciary not to perform properly his non-fiduciary duties'[61] and is 'concerned to reduce the likelihood of a fiduciary acting in breach of [a] non-fiduciary duty'.[62] This conception, however, may be inapt to capture and explain those instances of a fiduciary duty where there is no enforceable non-fiduciary duty owed by the person sought to be classified as the fiduciary, as may be the case in the *Pallant v Morgan* equity.[63] If the view espoused above were correct, we would expect that A's failure to make any acquisition of the property would also be actionable by B in the same way that A's acquisition of the property solely for its own benefit (and to the exclusion of B) would be actionable. However, this is unlikely to be the case.

Returning to the question of trust and confidence on the part of co-joint venturers. It is suggested that this relationship of trust and confidence forms the basis for the recognition of fiduciary obligations between the co-joint venturers. Where the relationship of trust and confidence could be said to permeate and

[59] ibid 614–16. See, in particular, at 616: 'the fundamental question is whether a person holds powers in the role or capacity of a manager or administrator, rather than as a form of personal wealth'.

[60] Admittedly, where the venture involves the surrender or disposition of an interest from X to Y to achieve a further, joint purpose, it may be more readily said that Y now holds a power over the interest that X previously had, or that Y now holds a power that X previously had.

[61] M Conaglen, 'The Nature and Function of Fiduciary Loyalty' (2005) 121 *LQR* 452, 469.

[62] ibid 475.

[63] For instance, Chadwick LJ in *Banner Homes Group* (n 2) [400E] states: 'the Pallant v Morgan equity does not seek to give effect to the parties' bargain, still less to make for them some bargain which they have not themselves made', thus suggesting that absent the *Pallant v Morgan* equity, there is no otherwise-enforceable (non-fiduciary) duty the breach of which requires prevention. Similarly, a trustee of a bare trust without any power to invest or disburse may have no non-fiduciary duty (see J Edelman, 'The Importance of the Fiduciary Undertaking' (presented at the conference on fiduciary law, University of New South Wales, 22 March 2013)).

inform the mutual undertakings[64] between the parties, this would colour them with the hue of fiduciary obligations from the onset of the relationship. Within the content of the undertaking may be found the need for the suborning of one's interest to that of the other and the mutual reliance on each other insofar as they relate to the subject matter of the venture.

V. JURIDICAL BASIS AND FUTURE DEVELOPMENTS

As stated above, this chapter seeks to advance the proposition that the basis for the *Pallant v Morgan* equity may be found in the pre-existing fiduciary obligations owed by one party to the other, or between the parties, and the breach of these fiduciary obligations. This proposition finds some support in the observations of Etherton LJ in *Crossco v Jolan* that the decisions in *Holiday Inns Inc v Broadhead*,[65] *Time Products Ltd v Combined English Stores Group Ltd*,[66] and *Island Holdings Ltd v Birchington Engineering Ltd*[67] were 'joint venture cases, in which it is to be inferred that the particular nature of the relationship between the joint venturers was such as to give rise to fiduciary duties'.[68]

It may be argued that a commercial joint venture may involve a relationship of trust and confidence in the dealings between the parties, or dealings with third parties which affect the rights and obligations of the parties. Based on the foregoing analysis in section IV above, it is possible to argue that those cases in which the *Pallant v Morgan* equity is thought to apply may be as a result of a finding that fiduciary obligations were owed by one party to the other, or between both parties. These may result from undertakings made or given against the factual backdrop of a relationship of trust and confidence established or subsisting between the parties.

In the quintessential form of the *Pallant v Morgan* fact scenario, the parties are said to have reached some form of agreement, albeit invariably it will be an informal or incomplete one.[69] The terms of the agreement involve the undertaking by the acquiring party, A, to seek to acquire the property for the benefit of A and B (broadly speaking) and for the non-acquiring party, B, to refrain from entering the fray with regards to the acquisition.[70] Otherwise, there is usually an advantage conferred by the arrangement or relationship in respect of the

[64] On the importance of undertakings to the fiduciary obligation see, inter alia, J Edelman, 'The Role of Status in the Law of Obligations: Common Callings, Implied Terms and Lessons for Fiduciary Duties' (presented at the University of Alberta, 18 July 2013 and DePaul University conference, Chicago, 19–20 July 2013).

[65] *Holiday Inns Inc* (n 9).

[66] *Time Products Ltd v Combined English Stores Group Ltd* (unreported, 2 December 1974).

[67] *Island Holdings Ltd v Birchington Engineering Ltd* (unreported, 7 July 1981).

[68] *Crossco* (n 3) [88] (Etherton LJ).

[69] Eg, such as in *Pallant* (n 1) where the agreement reached was too incomplete and left too much undetermined for there to be specific performance.

[70] Albeit note that in *Banner Homes Group* (n 2) [399], it is not a necessary feature for the non-acquiring party to keep out of the market.

acquisition of the property. There may also be the sharing of information between the parties relating to the acquisition.

While trust and confidence reposed is necessarily a factual question, it stands to reason that both A and B may be said in some way to rely upon the other and to repose a degree of trust and confidence in the other. This is manifestly arguable from the default position that A and B may be competitive rivals to the other, as was the case in *Pallant v Morgan*.[71] They are competitive rivals in that the default position was that each of the parties had sought to acquire the property themselves, and only sought to set aside the competitive rivalry (for the particular property sought to be acquired) to serve their joint mutual benefit. In other words, they each had an individual interest in acquiring the property individually which they set aside in favour of acquiring it together.

Thus, the agreement between the parties, albeit informal and incomplete, constitutes a mutual reliance upon the other to do or not to do what was promised in respect of the acquisition. One part of the reliance is the 'delegation' by B to A of the task of acquiring the property from the vendor; the other part of the reliance is the 'trust' by A to B to refrain from acting in its own interests and to pursue the common interest by refraining from the acquisition. Unsurprisingly the cases in which a fiduciary duty may be thought to arise would be found where either what is undertaken to be done is something which: (i) both parties seek to achieve together, but would be more advantageous to be done alone (eg, bidding on a plot of land at an auction);[72] or (ii) one party is unable to do alone and requires the assistance of the other party as a partner (eg, obtaining planning permission to operate a hotel).[73]

To add to this, both facets of this mutual reliance are not untethered but are expressly on the particular subject of the acquisition of a specific piece of land or property. That further defines the scope of the fiduciary duties, the reliance placed upon the other, and the relevant breaches of fiduciary duty that may be actionable.

As seen earlier, there is a level of judicial recognition or consideration of the 'terms' of the informal or incomplete agreement in determining the scope of relief to be granted in the case where the *Pallant v Morgan* constructive trust has been recognised.[74] This position was similarly taken by Etherton LJ in *Crossco*:

> If the cases in which the Pallant v Morgan equity has been applied are interpreted as I suggest, then they can be seen as cases in which the court is, pursuant to the

[71] *Pallant* (n 1).

[72] ibid.

[73] *Holiday Inns Inc* (n 9).

[74] *Banner Homes Group* (n 2) (Chadwick LJ) approving of Megarry J in *Holiday Inns Inc* (n 9): 'If on the facts it would be inequitable for the quantum of B's interest to be a moiety, I do not doubt that equity could determine what justice required the quantum to be; but where the facts suggest no other basis, then there should be equality.' Reference to the 'facts' giving rise to the inequity or otherwise of the quantum of B's interest must necessarily include reference to the 'terms' of the incomplete or failed agreement between A and B.

> constructive trust, depriving the defendant of the advantage obtained in breach of trust. The irrelevance or lack of complete agreement, whether documented or not, is then easily explained as is the latitude with which the court devises the best way to deprive the defendant of the unconscionable advantage: compare the *Holiday Inns* case … (where the plaintiff's expectation was to receive a lease, but it was granted a beneficial interest) and *Yaxley v Gotts*… (in which the plaintiff was granted a 99-year lease rent free).[75]

What these cases suggest is that while the *Pallant v Morgan* equity does by no means seek to give effect to the parties' bargain or to make a bargain for the parties,[76] that does not consign the substance of what was agreed, albeit not enforceable as a contract, to irrelevance. In *Pallant v Morgan*, the contract was found to be too incomplete in substantial part to avail the plaintiff of the remedy of specific performance,[77] yet the agreement that the acquiring party would convey to the non-acquiring party some portion of the property[78] at a price to be agreed was relevant to the finding of the equity in favour of the non-acquiring party. If the 'terms' of the informal or incomplete agreement are an important factor for deciding on the grant of relief, it ought to follow that these terms are also relevant in any consideration on the existence of liability on the part of the acquiring party to the non-acquiring party. While this does not necessarily mean that those 'terms' are conclusive or determinative, it would be artificial to suggest that their relevance is confined only to the question of relief but not liability.

In that event, it is suggested here that those 'terms' of the informal or incomplete contract – but which, notwithstanding the incipient state of the contract, can be said with a measure of certainty to have existed – ought rightly to form the basis of any determination on the existence and scope, if any, of the fiduciary duties owed by the acquiring party, A, to the non-acquiring party, B, or mutually between A and B.

Without seeking to detract from the position set out above, it must nevertheless be borne in mind that the propositions here are subject to the bright line set out in *Generator Developments Ltd v Lidl UK GmbH* governing 'subject to contract' joint ventures. Where an informal or incipient agreement has been expressed to be 'subject to contract', this would mean that both 'neither party intends to be bound either in law or in equity unless and until a formal contract is made and that each party reserves the right to withdraw until such time as a binding contract is made'.[79] In such a case, both parties would have been taking a commercial risk that its counterparty would back out from the contract.[80]

[75] *Crossco* (n 3) [95] (Etherton LJ).
[76] *Banner Homes Group* (n 2) [400E] (Chadwick LJ).
[77] *Pallant* (n 1) [48].
[78] Marked 'C' and 'A' on the Ordnance plan used by the parties' respective agents when engaged in the discussions leading to the agreement which formed the basis of the plaintiff's claim.
[79] *Generator Developments Ltd v Lidl UK GmbH* [2018] EWCA Civ 396 [79].
[80] ibid.

The requirement of a positive intention to not be bound appears to be important, if not necessary, in defeating the existence of an agreement which formed the basis for the *Pallant v Morgan* equity.[81] It is suggested here that this applies where the only inference to be drawn from the use of the 'subject to contract' formula is that the express or implied intention of the parties, in the totality of the circumstances, is that they would not be bound by any bargain sought to be struck or any agreement, informal or incipient, that had been entered. To put it differently, the first element of the *Pallant v Morgan* equity itself, namely the requisite arrangement or agreement, would not have been satisfied.

It has been suggested, contrary to the conception of the *Pallant v Morgan* equity being founded upon a breach of fiduciary duty as espoused by Etherton LJ in *Crossco*, that the justification premised upon a breach of promise is not a prerequisite; otherwise, the constructive trust could not arise immediately upon the acquisition of the relevant property by the acquiring party, A.[82] In effect, in this instance the primary characterisation of the breach which causes the *Pallant v Morgan* equity to arise or, in other words, be actionable is the failure to make the transfer of the property or the interest in that property to the non-acquiring party, B following a demand by A or, alternatively, in accordance with the terms of the agreement reached between B and A.

This characterisation of the breach of fiduciary duty as the suggested triggering event may not be the appropriate one. The event of breach is better understood as the act or fact of acquisition of the property in a manner that does not account or provide for the interest of the non-acquiring party (or the lack of an intention to do so on the part of the acquiring party at the time of acquisition) or if the act or fact of acquisition of the property represents an acquisition of the interest absolutely for the benefit of the acquiring party only. This would be the case even if this fact is not known to the non-acquiring party at the time that the acquisition is made by the acquiring party, or until a demand for a transfer of the interest in property is made by the non-acquiring party against the acquiring party.

This would be consistent with the principles enumerated by Chadwick LJ in the *Banner Homes Group* case which is premised on the idea that 'the *Pallant v Morgan* equity does not seek to give effect to the parties' bargain, still less to make for them some bargain which they have not themselves made'.[83] The bargain in the case of the incomplete or imprecise agreement in the *Pallant v Morgan* equity would typically require a further disposition of an interest in the property by the acquiring party to the non-acquiring party: in *Pallant v Morgan* this was the disposition of parts of the lots acquired by the acquiring party, A, to

[81] *London & Regional Investments Ltd v TBI plc* [2002] EWCA Civ 355 [47]–[50] (Mummery LJ).

[82] Liew (n 36) 353–54. It is understood that the 'breach of promise' referred to in the main text could refer to a variety of situations including that of a 'breach of fiduciary duty'.

[83] *Banner Homes Group* (n 2) [400E].

the non-acquiring party, B;[84] in *Holiday Inns Inc v Broadhead* this was the grant of a lease over the land by the acquiring party, A, to the non-acquiring party, B.

Since, however, the *Pallant v Morgan* equity does not seek to give effect to the parties' bargains, the necessity to conceive of the breach of fiduciary duty in terms of the failure to adhere to the specific terms of the incomplete or failed agreement would, at its highest, be inapposite. Accordingly, there would be no compelling reason to either define or confine the breach of fiduciary duty by reference to the 'breaches' of the terms of the agreement. Instead, it is suggested here that it is the act of acquisition without accounting for or providing for the interest of the non-acquiring party or an acquisition of the property solely and absolutely for the benefit of the acquiring party itself that would constitute the sufficient breach of fiduciary duty to give rise to the *Pallant v Morgan* equity.

A further argument in support of the proposition that the *Pallant v Morgan* equity may be best justified as being premised upon the breach of fiduciary duty owed by the defendant to the plaintiff lies in the fact that such a conceptualisation of the *Pallant v Morgan* equity is better placed to capture all possible factual permutations of the *Pallant v Morgan* equity.

To illustrate this point, it may be worth considering the converse scenario: as before, A promises B that A will seek to acquire land for the benefit of A and B; in return, B promises A that B will not seek to acquire that land independently of or to the exclusion of A. No formal agreement is concluded, albeit the value of the offer to be made by A is discussed or even, some may say, 'agreed'. Suppose that the sale of the property takes place by way of a sealed-bid auction. As in the *Pallant v Morgan* scenario, A makes an offer to acquire that land, ostensibly independently or for its own benefit only – for the reasons which follow this is broadly immaterial; however, unlike *Pallant v Morgan*, B, armed with this knowledge of A's offer or at the very least a fairly reliable approximation of A's offer, makes a rival offer in excess of A's offer. Unsurprisingly, A's offer is rejected; B successfully acquires the land and seeks to retain the beneficial interest over the whole of it.

Should a constructive trust over the land in A's favour (or more accurately, A and B jointly depending on the terms of the 'agreement') arise in the circumstances above? The answer to this question is likely to be in the affirmative. After all, the facts establishing the informal agreement and their concomitant duties are the same as those in the *Pallant v Morgan* scenario; the only material differences are the specifics of the breach (albeit, it is argued below, not the true content of the undertaking) and the party said to be committing the breach of duty. In this alternative scenario, the actionable breach of fiduciary duty giving rise to the *Pallant v Morgan* constructive trust may be said to arise out of two factors taken in combination: first, in the breach of the agreement by B, the 'non-acquiring party' (or more specifically the party who undertook

[84] *Pallant* (n 1).

to refrain from acquiring the party for its own benefit but who nevertheless goes on to acquire the property); and second, in the use of knowledge or information obtained in confidence and subject to a fiduciary duty, viz. the sum that A was intending to bid in, for example, a sealed auction or the bidding strategy agreed between A and B. This would also be of some importance in protecting A in a scenario where A's particular knowledge, effort, or confidential information was the basis of the joint venture or endeavour between the parties and utilised by B to make the acquisition. As such, any attempt to distinguish between the two scenarios would potentially be artificial in nature.

Nevertheless, it may be contended that the precise content of the undertaking by B does not avail A of the constructive trust remedy in relation to the specific property in question. This could be due to the fact that there was no specific undertaking that B was to undertake the task of acquiring the property for the benefit of A and B jointly or on terms as agreed. The undertaking was one made by A and not B. The specificity of the content of the promise could be said to be a determining factor.[85]

As against this objection, it is pointed out that even if the mutual undertakings of the parties do not include one for B, as the non-acquiring party, to acquire the property in question for the benefit of A and B jointly (or on some other terms), this ought not to militate against the justification for the *Pallant v Morgan* equity.[86] The fact remains that even in such a case, the content of the undertaking by B is plainly still to do with the specific property relevant to the *Pallant v Morgan* equity and additionally to the specific effort or initiative to *acquire* that specific property. This is explicable when the undertaking by B is properly analysed as having a content of an 'assurance to refrain' which is directly tied to the acquisition of the property in question, and would thus be capable of attracting a duty in relation to the acquisition of the property. Further, as pointed out above in section III, the same cannot be said for an 'acquiring' agency, even a voluntary one. Whereas in the breach of fiduciary duty analysis, it may be said that B's actions are a breach of a fiduciary duty owed to A; under the agency analysis, B, having never agreed or been appointed by A to acquire the property on behalf of A and B could not be said to have been an agent with authority.

In the light of the foregoing, it would stand to reason that the breach of fiduciary duty analysis better accommodates the broader range of circumstances in

[85] Liew (n 36) 346: 'This background fact leading up to [the acquiring party's] acquisition of the property indicates the autonomy-related logic behind the law's ordinary hesitancy to deprive owners of their property does not apply here. The reason for this is that, through the parties' agreement, [the acquiring party] does not make an ordinary promise but a specific one, exhibiting two crucial features .... Secondly, the content of [the acquiring party's] promise is specific: [the acquiring party] promises to qualify her interest in the property acquired as a result of [the non-acquiring party's] advantage-conferring reliance.'

[86] *Cf* Liew (n 36) 353.

which the finding of a *Pallant v Morgan* constructive trust would be justified. Rather than the fiduciary duties owing under the *Pallant v Morgan* equity be purely unidirectional in their nature, namely owing from A (ie the 'nominated acquirer') to B, it is argued that the justification proposed herein recognises that the duties can be reciprocal and bidirectional in nature in the appropriate cases. In doing so, it is suggested that this strengthens the basis the *Pallant v Morgan* equity and the consistency of its application to substantially similar-fact situations.

VI. CONCLUSION

It has been argued that the *Pallant v Morgan* equity has the pre-existing fiduciary obligations owed by one party to the other, or by both parties to each other, as its basis. It is suggested that these duties arise out of an understanding or agreement, to use the term loosely, giving rise to a nascent or incipient joint venture notwithstanding that this fails to materialise in a formal contract. It is suggested that the nature of the *Pallant v Morgan* equity and its corresponding remedies and reliefs in the known instances where the equity has been recognised is consistent with the approach taken to identifying and remedying a breach of pre-existing fiduciary duties.

Naturally, as has been suggested above, the terms of what has been 'agreed' will depend on the assessment of the facts of the case, subject to the established bright line[87] that where the agreement or understanding is expressly said to be 'subject to contract', that the proper finding to be reached in such a circumstance would be the necessary underlying agreement or understanding which could form the basis of the pre-existing fiduciary obligation would not in the first place exist.

It is suggested here that the *Pallant v Morgan* equity could potentially be engaged upon the breach by B, the 'non-acquiring party', who goes on to make a successful acquisition of the property in question in breach of the understanding that A would be the party who makes the acquisition for the benefit of A and B (jointly, as the case may be). It remains to be seen whether this reciprocal version of the *Pallant v Morgan* equity will be recognised by the courts in future equivalent cases.

[87] *Generator Developments Ltd* (n 79).

13

Subrogation, Marshalling, and Property

RORY GREGSON*

I. INTRODUCTION

SUBROGATION AND MARSHALLING are two controversial sources of property rights. They are both said to allow one party to stand into another's place and exercise the latter's property rights.[1] This is strange. Why should the law allow one person to take the benefit of another's property rights? Are there any good reasons for subrogation and marshalling, or should they be abolished?

Furthermore, subrogation and marshalling have a controversial relationship with each other. Sometimes, marshalling is treated as an example of subrogation[2] or 'akin to subrogation'.[3] At other times, marshalling and subrogation are distinguished and analysed separately.[4] So what is the relationship between subrogation and marshalling; is marshalling an example of subrogation or not?

To answer these questions, this chapter considers subrogation and marshalling separately, before considering their relationship. The central argument is that subrogation describes a particular form of rights, of which marshalling is

* I thank Lorren Eldridge, Clara Hurley, Nick McBride, Ben McFarlane, Lionel Smith, Robert Stevens, and Alexander Waghorn for their comments. The usual disclaimers apply.

[1] Subrogation: eg, *Drew v Lockett* (1863) 32 Beav 499, 503–04; 55 ER 196, 197–98 (Sir John Romilly MR); *Patten v Bond* (1889) 60 LT 583 (Ch) 585–86 (Kay J). Marshalling: eg, *Aldrich v Cooper* (1803) 8 Ves Jun 382, 497; 32 ER 402, 408 (Lord Eldon LC).

[2] Eg, *Chase Corporation (Australia) Pty Ltd v North Sydney Brick and Tile Co Ltd* (1994) 35 NSWLR 1 (NSWSC) 25B–C (Cohen J); C Mitchell, *The Law of Subrogation* (Oxford, Clarendon Press, 1994) 143; C Mitchell, 'Book Review' [2000] *Lloyd's Maritime and Commercial Law Quarterly* 589, 590; JD Heydon, MJ Leeming and PG Turner, *Meagher, Gummow and Lehane's Equity: Doctrines and Remedies*, 5th edn (Chatswood NSW, Butterworths, 2015) para 11-20.

[3] *Highbury Pension Fund Management Co v Zirfin Investments Ltd* [2013] EWHC 238 (Ch), [2014] Ch 359 [15] (Norris J).

[4] Eg, *Re Dent Co* [2016] EWHC 2650 (Ch), [2017] Ch 422 26, [29]–[30] (Norris J); PAU Ali, *Marshalling of Securities* (Oxford, Oxford University Press, 1999) ch 4; C Hare, 'Marshalling Marshalling' in PS Davies, S Douglas and J Goudkamp (eds), *Defences in Equity* (Oxford, Hart Publishing, 2018) 242.

an example. However, marshalling has a different justification to other instances of subrogation. Marshalling is justified by preventing a private party determining the distribution of assets on insolvency. By contrast, other instances of subrogation are justified by properly distributing the burden of a debt.

II. SUBROGATION

A. What is Subrogation?

There are two forms of subrogation: subrogation to subsisting rights and subrogation to extinguished rights.[5] This chapter is only concerned with the latter, which it calls 'subrogation' for short, as it is this form of subrogation which is said to have a relationship with marshalling.[6]

Subrogation describes a particular form of rights: C's new rights against D have the same content as X's extinguished rights against D.[7] So if X's rights against D were secured, then so too are C's new rights against D.[8] Similarly, if X's rights had priority in the event of D's insolvency, then C's new rights have the same preferential status.[9] Again, D's new debt to C incurs interest at the same rate as D's extinguished debt to X.[10] However, where C voluntarily[11] becomes D's creditor, subrogation will not give C more than it bargained for.[12] Thus, if C agreed to make an unsecured loan to D, then subrogation will not give C security.

The classic example of subrogation is *Butler v Rice*.[13] Mrs Rice owned a house subject to a bank's charge. Acting behind his wife's back, Mr Rice asked

[5] C Mitchell and S Watterson, *Subrogation: Law and Practice*, rev edn (Oxford, OUP, 2007) paras 1.04–1.10; C Mitchell, P Mitchell and S Watterson, *Goff and Jones: The Law of Unjust Enrichment*, 10th edn (London, Sweet & Maxwell, 2022) para 19-45. See also *Ibrahim v Barclays Bank Plc* [2011] EWHC 1897 (Ch), [2011] 2 CLC 589 [7] (Vos J); *Alliance Bank JSC v Aquanta Corp* [2011] EWHC 3281 (Comm), [2012] 1 Lloyd's Rep 181 [21] (Burton J).

[6] Mitchell (n 2) 590.

[7] Mitchell and Watterson (n 5) para 1.05.

[8] Eg, *Butler v Rice* [1910] 2 Ch 277 (Ch); *Boscawen v Bajwa* [1996] 1 WLR 328 (CA).

[9] *Hodgson v Shaw* (1834) 3 My & K 183, 40 ER 70; *Re M'Myn* (1886) 33 ChD 575 (Ch) 578 (Chitty J); *Re Lord Churchill* (1888) 39 ChD 174 (Ch); *Re Lamplugh Iron Ore Co Ltd* [1927] 1 Ch 308 (Ch). *Cf Copis v Middleton* (1823) Turn & R 224, 37 ER 1083.

[10] *Western Trust & Savings Ltd v Rock* (CA, 26 February 1993); *Castle Phillips Finance v Piddington* (1995) 70 P & CR 592 (CA) 602 (Peter Gibson LJ); *Filby v Mortgage Express (No 2) Ltd* [2004] EWCA Civ 759 [63]–[67] (May LJ); *Cheltenham & Gloucester Plc v Appleyard* [2004] EWCA Civ 291 [76]–[77] (Lord Neuberger MR).

[11] *Cf, Mayhew v Crickett* (1818) 2 Swans 185, 191; 36 ER 585, 587 (Lord Eldon LC); *Duncan Fox & Co v North & South Wales Bank* (1880) 6 App Cas 1 (HL); *Boscawen* (n 8) 338B–340A (Millett LJ); *Insol Funding Co Ltd v Cowlam* [2017] EWHC 1822 (Ch) [120] (Master Bowles).

[12] Eg, *Re Wrexham Mold & Connah's Quay Railway Co* [1899] 1 Ch 440 (CA); *Paul v Speirway* [1976] Ch 220 (Ch) 233B (Oliver J); *Banque Financière de la Cité SA v Parc (Battersea) Ltd* [1999] 1 AC 221 (HL) ('*BFC*') 235D (Lord Hoffmann), 237H (Lord Clyde), 242F–G (Lord Hutton); *Appleyard* (n 10) [38], [41] (Neuberger LJ); *Swynson Ltd v Lowick Rose LLP* [2017] UKSC 32, [2018] AC 313 [31]–[34] (Lord Sumption), [86] (Lord Mance).

[13] *Butler* (n 8).

Butler for a loan to pay off the bank's charge. Butler thought that Mr Rice owned the house, so agreed to the loan in exchange for a mortgage over the house. Butler therefore paid the loan monies to Mr Rice, who paid the bank, discharging the bank's charge. When Mrs Rice discovered the arrangement, she refused to execute a mortgage in favour of Butler. On the face of it, then, Butler was unsecured.

However, the court held that because Butler's loan had been used to pay off the bank's charge, Butler was subrogated to the bank's extinguished charge. In other words, Butler acquired a new charge with the same content as the charge that the bank used to have. Subrogation meant that Butler was secured after all.

B. What Justifies Subrogation?

Butler illustrates that the form of rights created by subrogation are difficult to justify in two ways. First, subrogation did not just give Butler personal rights; it gave him a charge. What justified giving Butler this powerful equitable proprietary right? Second, even if Butler deserved a charge, why should it have the same content as the charge that the bank used to have?[14] A justification for subrogation must explain both of these aspects of its form.[15]

In *Butler*, the court justified subrogation on the basis that Butler intended to keep the bank's charge alive for his own benefit.[16] Today, this reasoning is recognised as unpersuasive. Butler's intention was to acquire a new legal mortgage. It was a fiction to say that Butler intended to keep alive the bank's equitable charge.[17]

Indeed, Mitchell and Watterson explain that if the parties want C to acquire X's rights then they can choose to transfer X's rights by assignment; in practice parties never intend subrogation.[18] Consequently, it seems that subrogation cannot be justified by the parties' intention or agreement.

Instead, the dominant view is that subrogation is a remedy for D's unjust enrichment at C's expense.[19] On this view, the form of rights created by

[14] *Menelaou v Bank of Cyprus UK Ltd* [2015] UKSC 66, [2016] AC 176 [109] (Lord Carnwath); P Jaffey, *The Nature and Scope of Restitution* (Oxford, Hart Publishing, 2000) 270; C Rotherham, *Proprietary Remedies in Context* (Oxford, Hart Publishing, 2002) 245, 248.

[15] B McFarlane, 'Form and Substance in Equity' in A Robertson and J Goudkamp (eds), *Form and Substance in the Law of Obligations* (Oxford, Hart Publishing, 2019) 198; B McFarlane, 'Equity and the Justification of Private Rights' in S Degeling, M Crawford and N Tiverios (eds), *Justifying Private Rights* (Oxford, Hart Publishing, 2020) 222–23.

[16] *Butler* (n 8) 282.

[17] *Halifax Mortgage Services Ltd v Muirhead* (1998) 76 P&CR 418 (CA) 425 (Evans LJ); Mitchell, Mitchell, and Watterson (n 5) para 39-07.

[18] Mitchell and Watterson (n 5) para 3.01.

[19] *BFC* (n 12) 228C-F (Lord Steyn), 231H (Lord Hoffmann), 238H (Lord Clyde); *Menelaou* (n 14) [37], [49]–[50] (Lord Clarke), [78]–[99] (Lord Neuberger); *Swynson* (n 12) [19], [22], [30] (Lord Sumption), [55]–[90] (Lord Mance); P Birks, *An Introduction to the Law of Restitution*, rev edn (Oxford, Clarendon Press, 1989) 93–97, 191–92; Mitchell and Watterson (n 5) para 3.02; A Burrows,

subrogation – giving C rights with the same content as X's extinguished rights – carries little if any significance. Indeed, Birks wrote that 'within the law of restitution [subrogation] really adds nothing' and 'is in the nature of a metaphor which can be done without'.[20]

Thus, courts should approach claims for subrogation like any other claim for a remedy for unjust enrichment and ask the four unjust enrichment questions (is D enriched? At C's expense? Is D's enrichment unjust? Are there any defences?).[21] Subrogation is said to be triggered by the same unjust factors,[22] and subject to the same defences,[23] as other remedies for unjust enrichment.[24] In fact, Burrows begins his chapter on subrogation by suggesting that the chapter should not exist:

> [S]ubrogation … is triggered by a range of unjust factors. In principle, therefore, it ought to be dispersed throughout this book into the chapters on those unjust factors. However at the present time, when subrogation has only recently begun to be properly understood, it is too hard, as a matter of exposition, to go straight to that advanced position.[25]

Overall, then, subrogation is treated as one of many remedies for unjust enrichment, downplaying the particular form of the rights created by subrogation.

This chapter takes a different approach. It argues that subrogation's distinctive form reflects a distinctive justification. Subrogation is justified by ensuring that the burden of debts are distributed as they should be. If C bears the burden of D's debt to X and this burden should have been borne by D, then the burden needs to be lifted from C and reinstated upon D. Subrogation achieves this by reinstating the debt and having D now owe the debt to C. Thus, the particular form of rights created by subrogation reflects subrogation's particular role in ensuring interpersonal justice. Subrogation gives C new rights against D with the same content as X's extinguished rights against D because this ensures that the burden of D's extinguished debt to X is distributed as it should be.

For example, in *Forbes v Jackson*, a debtor borrowed £200 from a creditor, secured by a mortgage over the debtor's property.[26] A surety guaranteed the debt. The debtor defaulted so the surety paid £200 to the creditor, discharging

The Law of Restitution, 3rd edn (Oxford, OUP, 2011) 144; A Burrows, *A Restatement of the English Law of Unjust Enrichment* (Oxford, OUP, 2012) 173; Mitchell, Mitchell, and Watterson (n 5) para 39-01.

[20] Birks (n 19) 93.

[21] Eg, *BFC* (n 12) 234B–G (Lord Hoffmann); *Menelaou* (n 14) [18] (Lord Clarke); *Swynson* (n 12) [56] (Lord Mance), [110] (Lord Neuberger); Mitchell and Watterson (n 5) paras 3.02–3.03; Burrows, *The Law of Restitution* (n 19) 145; Mitchell, Mitchell, and Watterson (n 5) para 39-25.

[22] Mitchell and Watterson (n 5) para 6.02; Burrows, *The Law of Restitution* (n 19) 147, 148, 167; Burrows, *A Restatement of the English Law of Unjust Enrichment* (n 19) 173. *cf* Mitchell, Mitchell, and Watterson (n 5) para 39-29.

[23] Mitchell and Watterson (n 5) paras 7.01, 7.68, 8.07; Mitchell, Mitchell, and Watterson (n 5) para 39-38.

[24] See also Mitchell, Mitchell, and Watterson (n 5) para 37-57.

[25] Burrows, *The Law of Restitution* (n 19) 147.

[26] *Forbes v Jackson* (1882) 19 ChD 615 (Ch).

the debtor's debt and the mortgage. Hall VC held that the debtor owed £200 to the surety and that the surety was 'entitled to have all [X's] securities preserved for him, including the mortgage'.[27] In other words, the surety was subrogated to X's mortgage.

This can be justified as an instance of subrogation properly distributing the burden of a debt. The debtor agreed to mortgage his property as security for the creditor's loan. Consequently, the debtor agreed that his title to the property would be encumbered until the loan was repaid. A surety agrees to pay only if the principal debtor cannot do so; as between the debtor and the surety, the debtor agreed to bear the burden of repaying the loan and releasing the mortgage. Meanwhile, the debtor's other voluntary creditors did not bargain for security over the property. They therefore agreed not to have recourse to the property until the debtor had borne the burden of the debts secured over the property.[28]

The surety then paid the creditor, discharging the debt and the mortgage. The surety therefore bore the burden of discharging the debt and the mortgage, whereas this burden should have been borne by the debtor. The other creditors now had recourse to the property, whereas they should not have done so before the debtor had borne the burden of the debt which had been secured over the property.

To put all this right, the surety was subrogated to the creditor's extinguished mortgage. This lifted the burden of discharging the debt and the mortgage from the surety and reinstated it upon the debtor. It denied the other creditors recourse to the property, until the debtor had borne the burden of the debt which had been secured over the property. Thus, subrogation was justified by properly distributing the burden of a debt. As Smith puts it:

> The surety has guaranteed the risk of non-payment by the debtor to the creditor. He has not guaranteed any larger risk. If the creditor has real security for the debt, then the creditor's risk is reduced; so then should be the surety's. The only way to ensure that the surety's risk is no greater than the risk taken by the creditor is to provide that the surety shall have the benefit of any security, once he has paid the creditor.[29]

This justification is also reflected in the reasoning of many cases.[30] For example, in *Duncan Fox & Co v North & South Wales Bank*, Lord Selborne LC said that subrogation is justified when

> there is a primary and a secondary liability of two persons for one and the same debt, the debt being, as between the two, that of one of those persons only, and not equally

[27] *Forbes* (n 26) 621.

[28] *Cf*, *Drew v Lockett* (1863) 32 Beav 499, 505; 55 ER 196, 198 (Sir John Romilly MR); C Rotherham, 'Subrogation' in S Hedley and M Halliwell (eds), *The Law of Restitution* (London, Butterworths, 2002) para 8.14.

[29] L Smith, 'Book Review' (1995) 9 *TLI* 133, 134. See also L Smith, 'Security' in A Burrows (ed), *English Private Law*, 3rd edn (Oxford, OUP, 2013) para 5.178.

[30] Eg, *Yonge v Reynell* (1852) 9 Hare 809, 818–19; 68 ER 744, 748–49 (Sir GJ Turner VC); *Re Downer Enterprises* [1974] 1 WLR 1460 (Ch) 1468C–69A (Pennycuick VC); *Bofinger v Kingsway*

> of both, so that the other, if he should be compelled to pay it, would be entitled to reimbursement from the person by whom (as between the two) it ought to have been paid.[31]

C. Why should D Bear the Burden?

The reason why, and extent to which, D ought to bear the burden of a debt varies from case to case.[32] In some cases, there is an agreement about where the burden should fall. In *Forbes*, for example, the parties agreed who was the guarantor and who was the principal debtor, making it clear that the burden of the debt should fall on the principal debtor.[33]

In other cases, a debt is assumed involuntarily and so there is no agreement about where its burden should fall.[34] In *Niru Battery Manufacturing Co v Milestone Trading Ltd (No 2)*, X was a victim of a fraud which occurred because of C's negligence, and which left D unjustly enriched at X's expense.[35] X obtained judgment against C and D. C owed X a duty to compensate X for the losses caused by its negligence, while D owed X a duty to make restitution of its unjust enrichment at X's expense. C and D were therefore jointly and severally indebted to X under a court judgment. C paid the whole of the judgment, discharging both parties' debt to X. C then sought to be subrogated to X's extinguished rights against D.

Here, no agreement decided who should bear the burden of the debt. Instead, the Court of Appeal explained that if C bore the burden of the debt to X, then X's losses would be compensated but D would remain unjustly enriched. By contrast, if D bore the burden of the debt to X, then D would no longer be unjustly enriched and X's losses would be compensated. The Court therefore held that D ought to bear the burden of the debt as this remedied both injustices: D's unjust enrichment and the losses caused by C's negligence. C was therefore subrogated to X's extinguished rights against D.

Group Ltd [2009] HCA 44, (2009) 239 CLR 269 [7]–[8] (Gummow, Hayne, Heydon, Kiefel, and Bell JJ). See also C Mitchell, *The Law of Contribution and Reimbursement* (Oxford, OUP, 2003) paras 1.01, 1.09, 1.11, 3.28–3.29; R Stevens, 'The Unjust Enrichment Disaster' (2018) 134 *LQR* 574, 588; L Smith, 'Restitution: A New Start?' in P Devonshire and R Havelock (eds), *The Impact of Equity and Restitution in Commerce* (Oxford, Hart Publishing, 2019) 106–08.

[31] *Duncan Fox* (n 11) 11.

[32] Mitchell (n 30) ch 10; Mitchell, Mitchell, and Watterson (n 5) paras 20-82–20-104; Smith, 'Restitution' (n 30) 107; C Mitchell, 'Other Reasons for Restitution' in E Bant, K Barker, and S Degeling (eds), *Research Handbook on Unjust Enrichment and Restitution* (Cheltenham, Edward Elgar Publishing, 2020) 391.

[33] *Forbes* (n 26) 621 (Hall VC).

[34] See also *Brook's Wharf & Bull Wharf Ltd v Goodman Bros* [1937] 1 KB 534 (CA).

[35] *Niru Battery Manufacturing Co v Milestone Trading Ltd (No 2)* [2004] EWCA Civ 487, [2004] 1 CLC 882.

To sum up, subrogation is justified where C bears the burden of a debt which ought to have been borne by D. The reason why D ought to bear the burden of the debt varies from case to case. The remainder of this section makes three controversial claims about this justification for subrogation.

D. Terminology

To start, unjust enrichment theorists often label this justification 'legal compulsion' or 'secondary liability'. This chapter's first controversial claim is that these labels are distracting and unnecessary.

i. Legal Compulsion

Birks argued that, where C pays C and D's common debt to X, subrogation was justified to reverse D's unjust enrichment. D was enriched at C's expense because C paid X, discharging D's debt to X. D's enrichment was rendered unjust by the unjust factor of 'legal compulsion': C was under a duty to pay X so the legal system compelled C to pay X, vitiating C's intention to enrich D.[36]

However, legal compulsion is not unjust. As Hilliard explained, a 'threat to have recourse to legal process is not objectionable, quite the reverse in fact'.[37] Mitchell gives a telling example:

> People routinely bind themselves by contract to perform obligations, and no question arises of their recovering the value of their performance via an action in unjust enrichment on the ground that their performance was compelled by the law of contract.[38]

As a result, Burrows writes that 'legal compulsion is better viewed as a policy-motivated unjust factor designed to ensure that liability is ultimately borne by the appropriate party in the appropriate amount'.[39] Burrows therefore endorses the idea that subrogation can be justified by C bearing the burden of a debt which ought to have been borne by D.[40] However, labelling this idea 'legal compulsion' is misleading given that this compulsion is not unjust and it plays no role in justifying subrogation.

36 Birks (n 19) 185–93. See also *Samsoondar v Capital Insurance Company Ltd* [2020] UKPC 33, [2021] 2 All ER 1105 [21] (Lord Burrows); G Virgo, *The Principles of the Law of Restitution*, 3rd edn (Oxford, OUP, 2016) 233–53.

37 J Hilliard, 'A Case for the Abolition of Legal Compulsion as a Ground of Restitution' (2002) 61 *CLJ* 551, 553. See also JA Dieckmann, 'The Province of Subrogation Determined: Some Corrections – A Functional Analysis of the Guarantor's Right to Derivative Recourse, Comprising a Critique of the Restitutionary Thesis' (2012) 20 *European Review of Private Law* 989, 1031–33.

38 Mitchell (n 30) para 3.27.

39 Burrows, *The Law of Restitution* (n 19) 437. See also Burrows, *A Restatement of the English Law of Unjust Enrichment* (n 19) 99.

40 Burrows, *The Law of Restitution* (n 19) 148; Burrows, *A Restatement of the English Law of Unjust Enrichment* (n 19) 173.

ii. Secondary Liability

Mitchell, Mitchell, and Watterson label the same idea 'secondary liability':

> [D] is the person who should ultimately bear some or all of the burden of paying [X]: in the language of the cases, because [D] is 'primarily' and [C] only 'secondarily' liable for [D]'s share of their common obligation.[41] Mitchell, Mitchell, and Watterson therefore also endorse the idea that subrogation can be justified by C bearing the burden of a debt which ought to have been borne by D.[42]

Calling this idea 'secondary liability' works well in cases like *Forbes* where C and D shared a common debt which arose under an agreement.[43] D agreed to take primary responsibility for paying X and C agreed to take secondary responsibility by agreeing to pay X if D failed to do so. The reason for subrogation was enforcing this agreement about who had 'primary' and 'secondary liability' for the burden of a common debt.

However, the language of 'secondary liability' is less apt in cases like *Niru Battery* where no agreement decided who had 'primary' and 'secondary liability' for the debt.[44] Instead, the reason that D ought to bear the burden of the debt to X, and thus the reason for subrogation, was to ensure that both injustices (D's unjust enrichment at X's expense, and X's loss caused by C's negligence) were remedied. This led the Court to describe D as primarily and C as secondarily liable for the debt. But this was merely a conclusory label which did no justificatory work.[45]

In sum, this chapter agrees with the substance of Burrows' and Mitchell, Mitchell, and Watterson's position: subrogation can be justified by ensuring that the burden of debts are distributed as they should be. However, labelling this justification 'legal compulsion' or 'secondary liability' is inaccurate and unnecessary.

E. Did C Bear the Burden of D's Debt?

It is often thought that properly distributing the burden of a debt can only justify subrogation where C was obliged to pay D's debt,[46] such as the guarantor case of *Forbes*.[47] This chapter's second controversial claim challenges that

[41] Mitchell, Mitchell, and Watterson (n 5) para 19-01. See also *Niru Battery Manufacturing Co v Milestone Trading Ltd (No 2)* [2003] EWHC 1032 (Comm), [2003] 2 All ER (Comm) 365 [31] (Moore-Bick J).

[42] Mitchell and Watterson (n 5) para 6.04; Mitchell, Mitchell, and Watterson (n 5) para 39-30.

[43] *Duncan Fox* (n 11); *Forbes* (n 26).

[44] *Niru* (n 35). See also Burrows, *A Restatement of the English Law of Unjust Enrichment* (n 19) 99.

[45] *Niru* (n 35) [69] (Clarke LJ), [85] (Sedley LJ).

[46] Mitchell and Watterson (n 5) para 6.07; Burrows, *The Law of Restitution* (n 19) ch 17; Burrows, *A Restatement of the English Law of Unjust Enrichment* (n 19) 98–99; Mitchell, Mitchell, and Watterson (n 5) paras 20-01–20-02.

[47] *Forbes* (n 26).

assumption: almost all cases of subrogation are justified by properly distributing the burden of a debt.

To substantiate this claim, this subsection proceeds in three steps. First, it controversially argues that the justification extends to cases where C pays D's debt, even though C was not obliged to do so. Second and more controversially still, it argues that this justification also operates where C does not pay D's debt but C can trace into the payment used to discharge of D's debt. Third, it argues that subrogation's availability may then be cut back by countervailing considerations.

i. C Pays D's Debt, even though C was not Obliged to do so

Turning first to cases where C pays D's debt, even though C was not obliged to do so, two questions must be distinguished:

(1) Can C's payment to X discharge D's debt, even if C was not obliged to pay the debt or authorised by D to do so?
(2) If so, is C subrogated to X's extinguished rights against D?

The answer to the first of these questions is controversial.[48] A legal system may reasonably choose one of a range of options on the matter[49] and so this chapter does not take a position on the first question. Instead, it argues that the answer to the second question is 'yes': subrogation can be justified whenever C bore the burden of a debt which ought to have been borne by D, even if the debt was D's alone and C was not obliged to pay it.

This is illustrated by *Cunliffe Brooks & Co v Blackburn and District Benefit Building Society*.[50] There, the Blackburn Building Society had an overdrawn account at its bank. The Society instructed the bank to pay the Society's creditors and the bank did so, making the Society's account further overdrawn. It then transpired that the Society had acted ultra vires in borrowing from the bank, and so was not contractually obliged to repay the bank. Nevertheless, the House of Lords held that the Society was obliged to repay the bank 'as far as it

[48] *Cf*, eg, *Butler* (n 8) 282 (Warrington J); *B Liggett (Liverpool) Ltd v Barclays Bank Ltd* [1928] 1 KB 48 (KB); *Barclays Bank Ltd v WJ Simms Son & Cooke (Southern) Ltd* [1980] QB 677 (QB); *Crantrave Ltd v Lloyds Bank Plc* [2000] QB 917 (CA) 923G–H (Pill LJ); P Birks and J Beatson, 'Unrequested Payment of Another's Debt' (1976) 92 *LQR* 188, 188–202; D Friedmann, 'Payment of Another's Debt' (1983) 99 *LQR* 534; Birks (n 19) 189–191; J Beatson, *The Use and Abuse of Unjust Enrichment: Essays on the Law of Restitution* (Oxford, Clarendon Press, 1991) 200–05; Mitchell and Watterson (n 5) para 2.05; Burrows, *The Law of Restitution* (n 19) 460–68; Burrows, *A Restatement of the English Law of Unjust Enrichment* (n 19) 100; Mitchell, Mitchell, and Watterson (n 5) para 5-62.

[49] S Hedley, *Restitution: Its Division and Ordering* (London, Sweet & Maxwell, 2001) 140–44.

[50] *Cunliffe Brooks & Co v Blackburn and District Benefit Building Society* [1884] 9 App Cas 857 (HL) ('*Blackburn* (HL)'). See also *Re Wrexham* (n 12); *Brocklesby v Temperance Permanent Building Society* [1895] AC 173 (HL).

can be made out that the moneys which were advanced by the bankers simply went to pay the legitimate debts and liabilities of the society'.[51]

Importantly, the bank was not indebted to the Society's creditors. The Society and the bank did not share a common debt to the creditors. Nevertheless, the House assumed without discussion that the bank's payments had extinguished the Society's debts, and held that the Society was obliged to repay the bank. Lord Blackburn said that 'Any person, whether the bankers or anyone else, might pay off the creditors and stand in the shoes of the creditor who is paid off.'[52]

Similarly, in the Court of Appeal Lord Selborne LC said that:

> [T]hose who pay legitimate demands which they are bound in some way or other to meet, and have had the benefit of other people's money advanced to them for that purpose, shall not retain that benefit so as, in substance, to make those other people pay their debts.[53]

Lord Selborne LC's reasoning echoes his judgment two years earlier in *Duncan Fox*. In *Duncan Fox*, C paid C and D's common debt to X. Lord Selborne LC justified subrogation on the basis that C was 'entitled to reimbursement from the person by whom … [the debt] ought to have been paid'.[54] In *Blackburn*, the bank paid the Society's debts, even though the bank was not indebted to the creditors. Lord Selborne LC justified subrogation on much the same basis: the Society 'shall not … make those other people pay their debts'.[55] Thus, Lord Blackburn and Lord Selborne LC recognised that subrogation is justified whenever C pays a debt which D ought to bear the burden of, and that this justification is not limited to cases where the debt is C and D's common debt.

Again, the reason why D ought to bear the burden of the debt is the same reason why D was originally indebted to X. In *Blackburn*, the Society's debts paid by the bank included 'the payment of members who had given notice of withdrawal, and the balance in payment of salaries of officers or legal expenses'.[56] The Society's debts to its members and staff had been assumed voluntarily, so the Society had consented to bearing the burden of these debts. The same might be true of the 'legal expenses' if they were debts to the Society's lawyers. Alternatively, the 'legal expenses' may have arisen under a court order to pay costs, in which case the court order would be the reason why D ought to bear the burden of this debt.

Blackburn provides further evidence against using the labels 'legal compulsion' or 'secondary liability' to describe the idea that C bore the burden of a debt which ought to be borne by D. The bank had no duty or liability to pay the

[51] *Blackburn Building Society v Cunliffe Brooks & Co* (1882) 22 ChD 61 (CA) ('*Blackburn* (CA)') 71 (Lord Selborne LC) affd *Blackburn* (HL) (n 51).

[52] *Blackburn* (HL) (n 51) 866.

[53] *Blackburn* (CA) (n 51) 71 (Lord Selborne LC).

[54] *Duncan Fox* (n 11) 11.

[55] *Blackburn* (CA) (n 51) 71.

[56] ibid 64.

Society's creditors; it is inaccurate to say that the bank was 'legally compelled' or had 'secondary liability' to pay. Nevertheless, subrogation was justified because the bank bore the burden of debts which ought to have been borne by the Society. The labels 'legal compulsion' and 'secondary liability' are therefore under-inclusive: they do not capture all the cases in which subrogation is justified because C bore the burden of a debt which ought to have been borne by D.

In sum, there is good reason for subrogation whenever C pays D's debt, even if the debt was not C and D's common debt.

ii. C can Trace into the Payment Used to Discharge D's Debt

In fact, this justification may be pushed even further, beyond cases where C pays X, and to cases where C can trace into the payment used to discharge D's debt.

For example, in *Boscawen v Bajwa*, Bajwa owned a house subject to the Halifax's charge.[57] Bajwa agreed to sell the property to purchasers. The Abbey National agreed to loan the purchasers funds for the purchase, in exchange for a charge over the property. The Abbey National paid the loan to the purchasers' solicitors, who paid it to Bajwa's solicitors. Bajwa's solicitors were authorised to pay the monies to the Halifax on completion of the sale of the property. However, Bajwa's solicitors acted too soon and paid the monies to the Halifax before completion, partially discharging the Halifax's charge.

The sale then fell through and completion never took place. This left Bajwa with unencumbered title to the house. Meanwhile, the Abbey National had paid out the loan monies but had not received any security. To remedy this, Millett LJ held that the Abbey National was subrogated to the Halifax's extinguished charge.

Unlike the bank in *Blackburn*, the Abbey National had not itself paid the defendant's debt. Instead, it was Bajwa's solicitors who had paid Bajwa's debt to the Halifax. Nevertheless, the Abbey National still bore the burden of Bajwa's debt, and so subrogation was still justified, because the Abbey National could trace into the payment used to discharge the debt. Millett LJ explained that when the Abbey National paid the loan monies to the purchasers' solicitors, the solicitors held the monies on trust for the Abbey National.[58] The Abbey National could then trace the monies from the purchasers' solicitors, through Bajwa's solicitors, and into the payment to the Halifax which discharged the charge.[59] This enabled the Abbey National to show that it had borne the burden of Bajwa's debt. As a result, the Abbey National was subrogated to the Halifax's extinguished charge.[60]

[57] *Boscawen* (n 8).
[58] ibid 332F.
[59] ibid 335F–338A.
[60] ibid 334B–35F.

Boscawen is an example of a case where the court explicitly showed that C was entitled to subrogation because it could trace into the payment used to discharge of D's debt. However, in many cases, subrogation was awarded even though C did not pay D's debt and the court did not investigate whether C could trace into the payment used to discharge D's debt.[61] Nevertheless, the results of some of these cases are defensible because, if the court were to conduct this investigation, C would indeed be able to trace into the payment used to discharge D's debt.

Butler v Rice illustrates this.[62] Butler paid the loan monies to Mr Rice, who paid the bank, extinguishing the bank's charge. Unlike *Blackburn*, then, Butler did not himself pay the debt. Unlike *Boscawen*, the court did not investigate whether Butler could trace into the discharge of the debt. What would have happened had the court conducted this investigation?

Birks argued that 'Mr Rice had misrepresented the facts. The contract with him was therefore voidable.'[63] Butler therefore had a mere equity to rescind the contract with Mr Rice, allowing Butler to trace any monies paid under the contract.[64] Butler could therefore trace through Mr Rice's payment to the bank, and into the payment that discharged the bank's charge. This showed that Butler bore the burden of Mrs Rice's debt to the bank, entitling Butler to subrogation. *Butler* was therefore correctly decided, albeit incorrectly reasoned.

iii. Countervailing Considerations

So far, it has been argued that properly distributing the burden of a debt provides a reason for subrogation whenever C can trace into the discharge of D's debt to X. Nevertheless, this does not necessarily mean that subrogation will be awarded. The availability of subrogation may be cut back by countervailing considerations. Two examples illustrate this.

First, a legal system may want a rule against malicious intervenors. The classic example is *Norton v Haggett*.[65] Norton and Haggett had two arguments and Norton was 'desirous of harming' Haggett. Norton paid off a bank's mortgage over Haggett's home, then sought to be subrogated to the bank's mortgage. The

[61] Eg, *Baroness Wenlock v River Dee Co (No 2)* (1887) 19 QBD 155 (CA); *Chetwynd v Allen* [1899] 1 Ch 353 (Ch); *Butler* (n 8); *Menelaou* (n 14) [50], [53] (Lord Clarke), [85], [92], [96]–[98] (Lord Neuberger); S Watterson, '"Direct Transfers" in the Law of Unjust Enrichment' (2011) 64 *Current Legal Problems* 435, 464; S Watterson, 'Subrogation' in G Virgo and S Worthington (eds), *Commercial Remedies: Resolving Controversies* (Cambridge, CUP, 2017) 459–61.

[62] *Butler* (n 8). For the facts see section II.A. See also *Chetwynd* (n 61).

[63] P Birks, *Unjust Enrichment*, 2nd edn (Oxford, OUP, 2005) 97. See also Birks (n 19) 392–93; *cf* B McFarlane, 'Unjust Enrichment, Property Rights and Indirect Recipients' [2009] *Restitution Law Review* 37, 49.

[64] *Banque Belge Pour L'Etranger v Hambrouck* [1921] 1 KB 321 (CA); *El Ajou v Dollar Land Holdings Plc (No 1)* [1993] 3 All ER 717 (Ch) 734C–E (Millett J); Birks (n 19) 392–93; Birks, *Unjust Enrichment* (n 63) 97.

[65] *Norton v Haggett* 85 A 2d 571 (Vermont SC 1952).

Supreme Court of Vermont held that the bank's mortgage was extinguished but denied Norton's claim to be subrogated to it. The Court explained that Norton 'was an intermeddler, and officiousness is not to be encouraged' and that Norton's 'good faith was apparently questionable'.[66]

Second, insofar as C consented to bearing the burden of D's debt, C cannot complain about this and so subrogation will not come to C's aid. If C agreed to make an unsecured loan to D to pay off D's debt to X, then C consented to bear the burden of D's debt to X in exchange for purely personal rights, and so subrogation will not give C security.[67] Hence the rule that subrogation will not give C more than it bargained for.

iv. Summary

Subrogation is prima facie justified whenever C bears the burden of a debt which ought to have been borne by D. It is uncontroversial that this justifies subrogation where C pays X, discharging C and D's common debt to X.

This section pushed that justification further, arguing that it can also justify subrogation in two further scenarios. First, the justification applies where C pays D's debt to X, even though C was not obliged to do so. Second, the justification applies even where C did not pay X, so long as C can trace into the payment used to discharge D's debt to X. However, the availability of subrogation may then be cut back by countervailing considerations, such as a rule against malicious intervenors.

F. Is Subrogation a Remedy for Unjust Enrichment?

This chapter's third and final controversial claim about subrogation is that subrogation is not a remedy for unjust enrichment. Subrogation describes a particular form of rights: C's new rights against D have the same content as X's extinguished rights against D. This distinctive form reflects a distinctive justification. Where C bore the burden of a debt which should have been borne by D, that burden needs to be lifted from C and reinstated upon D. Subrogation achieves this by reinstating D's debt, and having D now owe that debt to C. Subrogation's form and its justification are therefore tied together. Subrogation gives C new rights against D with the same content as X's extinguished rights against D because this puts the burden of D's extinguished debt to X where it ought to be.

Other rights take a different form because they have a different justification. For example, take Birks' 'core case' of unjust enrichment: the right to restitution

[66] *Norton* (n 65) 547 (Blackmer J). See also *Exall v Partridge* (1799) 8 TR 308, 310; 101 ER 1405, 1406 (Lord Kenyon CJ); *Owen v Tate* [1976] 1 QB 402 (CA).

[67] See n 12 above.

of a mistaken payment.[68] This takes the form of a right against the payee to recover the mistaken payment.[69] Unlike subrogation, it does not take the form of a right with the same content as someone else's extinguished right. The justification for the right to restitution of a mistaken payment is controversial.[70] The leading theories say that it is justified by the payor's vitiated intention[71] or the absence of basis for the payment.[72] On either view, the form of the right and its justification are again tied together. The right takes the form of reversing the payor's payment because the payment was an imperfect expression of the payor's autonomy[73] or because there is no reason for a legal system to uphold the payment.[74] Thus, subrogation and the right to restitution of a mistaken payment take different forms because they have different justifications. Furthermore, because they have different justifications, they are governed by different rules.[75]

It is therefore dangerous to treat subrogation as a remedy for unjust enrichment. Subrogation creates rights of a distinctive form because it has a distinctive justification. Grouping subrogation with rights which take a different form obscures the important relationship between the form of rights and their justification.[76] Furthermore, it obscures the distinctiveness of each form of rights and the distinctiveness of each justification. This creates a mirage of similarities which do not exist. It becomes easy to slip into the error of thinking that subrogation cases are governed by the same rules as other unjust enrichment cases.[77]

In short, subrogation has a different form, justification, and rules to other remedies for unjust enrichment. Nevertheless, one might think that unjust enrichment still has a role to play as a 'high level normative principle'[78] or 'organising concept'.[79] However, so far as subrogation is concerned, this principle or concept is redundant since unjust enrichment is neither sufficient nor necessary for subrogation to occur.

[68] Birks, *Unjust Enrichment* (n 63) ch 1 'A Core Case'.

[69] *Prudential Assurance Co Ltd v Revenue and Customs Commissioners* [2018] UKSC 39, [2018] 3 WLR 652.

[70] F Wilmot-Smith, 'Should the Payee Pay?' (2017) 37 *OJLS* 844.

[71] Birks (n 19) 100–01; Burrows, *The Law of Restitution* (n 19) 86; Burrows, *A Restatement of the English Law of Unjust Enrichment* (n 19) 5, 30; Mitchell, Mitchell, and Watterson (n 5) para 1-29.

[72] Birks, *Unjust Enrichment* (n 63) chs 5–6; Stevens (n 30) 581.

[73] Birks (n 19) 100–01, 140; H Scott, *Unjust Enrichment in South African Law: Rethinking Enrichment by Transfer* (Oxford, Hart Publishing, 2013) 210.

[74] Birks, *Unjust Enrichment* (n 63) chs 5–6; Stevens (n 30) 581.

[75] R Gregson, 'Is Subrogation a Remedy for Unjust Enrichment?' (2020) 136 *LQR* 481.

[76] McFarlane, 'Form and Substance in Equity' (n 15) 198; McFarlane, 'Equity and the Justification of Private Rights' (n 15) 222–23.

[77] Gregson (n 75).

[78] A Burrows, 'In Defence of Unjust Enrichment' (2019) 78 *CLJ* 521, 529.

[79] Mitchell, Mitchell, and Watterson (n 5) para 1-08. See also *Mann v Paterson Constructions Pty Ltd* [2019] HCA 32, (2019) 267 CLR 560 [199] (Nettle, Gordon, and Edelman JJ); Birks (n 19) 19–20; H Scott, 'Change and Continuity in the Law of Unjust Enrichment' [2019] *Acta Juridica* 469, 488–89; Mitchell, 'Other Reasons for Restitution' (n 32) 380–84.

Unjust enrichment is not sufficient because even those who support the idea that subrogation is a remedy for unjust enrichment concede that it is an incomplete justification for subrogation's creation of property rights. For instance, Mitchell and Watterson's leading text on subrogation says that 'further inquiry is required before the law affords [subrogation to proprietary rights]. It is not sufficient to conclude that [D] has been unjustly enriched at the expense of [C].'[80] In light of this, the authors suggest that the 'authorities reveal a surprising readiness to award proprietary subrogation'.[81] Similarly, Burrows writes that:

> Although subrogation to proprietary rights ... is commonplace, this is generally difficult to justify because [C] has taken the risk of [D]'s (or X's) insolvency and therefore does not appear to merit priority over unsecured creditors.[82]

Thus, even those who argue that subrogation is a remedy for unjust enrichment concede that this is insufficient to explain why subrogation creates property rights. Subrogation's creation of property rights can only be explained by recognising that its role is to properly distribute the burden of a debt.

Furthermore, once this role is understood, any reference to unjust enrichment is unnecessary. As Hilliard explains:

> [T]he burden of payment has fallen unfairly .... This rationale is sufficient in itself both to determine the measure of relief and explain why such relief should be granted. It is unnecessary to go on to enquire as to the extent of [D]'s gain, whether such gain was at [C]'s expense and whether any defences are available: the rationale above takes care of everything. ... Unjust enrichment adds needless complexity, replacing a one stage process (Is the distribution of liability equitable?) with a four-stage version (Is [D] enriched? Is this at [C]'s expense? etc).[83]

In short, subrogation has a different form, justification, and rules to remedies for unjust enrichment. Unjust enrichment is neither necessary nor sufficient for subrogation to occur. Subrogation is not a remedy for unjust enrichment.

G. Summary

Subrogation describes rights of a particular form: C's new rights against D have the same content as X's extinguished rights against D. This particular form

80 Mitchell and Watterson (n 5) para 8.39. See also Mitchell, Mitchell, and Watterson (n 5) para 39-41.

81 Mitchell and Watterson (n 5) para 8.46.

82 Burrows, *The Law of Restitution* (n 19) 167. See also 149–50.

83 Hilliard (n 37) 554 (footnote omitted). See also, eg, *Trades House of Glasgow v Ferguson* 1979 SLT 187 (IH) 192 (Lord Justice-Clerk Wheatley); S Meier, 'No Basis: A Comparative View' in A Burrows and Lord Rodger of Earlsferry (eds), *Mapping the Law: Essays in Memory of Peter Birks* (Oxford, OUP, 2006) 359–61; NJ McBride, *The Humanity of Private Law: Part I: Explanation* (Oxford, Hart Publishing, 2019) 213; S Meier, 'Enrichment "At the Expense of Another" and Incidental Benefits in German Law' [2019] *Acta Juridica* 453, 460–61.

reflects a particular justification: properly distributing the burden of D's extinguished debt to X.

Recognising this as the justification for subrogation has three important implications. First, labelling this justification 'legal compulsion' or 'secondary liability' is misleading and unnecessary. Second, this justification is not limited to cases where C pays C and D's common debt. C bears the burden of D's debt, and so subrogation is prima facie justified, whenever C can trace into the discharge of D's debt. Finally, subrogation is not a remedy for unjust enrichment.

III. MARSHALLING

A. What is Marshalling?

Marshalling is best explained by way of example. Say D owes £1 million to X, secured over two properties, Whiteacre and Blackacre, which are each worth £1 million. D also owes £1 million to C who has security over Whiteacre, ranking behind X's security. However, C does not have security over Blackacre. This is illustrated by the following diagram.

WHITEACRE	BLACKACRE
Value £1m	Value £1m
X's first charge for £1m	X's first charge for £1m
C's second charge for £1m	

If D is solvent, then both creditors can be paid. The problem arises if D is insolvent.[84] If X chooses to realise its security over Blackacre, then C can realise its security over Whiteacre and so both creditors will be paid. However, if X chooses to realise its security over Whiteacre, then X's right to £1 million will exhaust Whiteacre (which is only worth £1 million), leaving C unsecured. C would then compete with D's unsecured creditors and so may not be paid in full. As such, X's choice of which security to realise can affect whether or not C will be paid.

Marshalling prevents X's choice prejudicing C. If X chooses to realise its security over Whiteacre, then C 'can look to the other property to satisfy the debt owed to him'.[85] In other words, C acquires security over Blackacre with

[84] *National Crime Agency v Szepietowski* [2013] UKSC 65, [2014] AC 338 [32] (Lord Neuberger).

[85] ibid [31] (Lord Neuberger). See also *Aldrich* (n 1); *Ex p Kendall* (1811) 17 Ves Jun 514, 520; 34 ER 199, 201 (Lord Eldon LC); *Webb v Smith* (1885) 30 ChD 192 (CA) 200 (Cotton LJ); *Re Bank*

the same characteristics as X's extinguished security.[86] Marshalling therefore fits the definition of subrogation: it gives C new rights with the same content as X's extinguished rights. Marshalling is indeed an example of subrogation.

B. What Justifies Marshalling?

Marshalling is difficult to justify. C did not bargain for security over Blackacre, so why should marshalling give C more than it bargained for?[87] Why should marshalling favour C over the unsecured creditors?[88]

Unlike other cases of subrogation, marshalling cannot be justified because C bore the burden of a debt which should have been borne by D. In marshalling cases, D pays its debt to X; the burden of this debt is already properly distributed before marshalling.

Consequently, if marshalling is to be justified, one must look beyond the justification for other cases of subrogation. In the leading Supreme Court decision of *National Crime Authority v Szepietowski*, Lord Neuberger suggested that:

> [T]he right to marshal is an incident of the second mortgage when it is granted …. It is normally easy to imply a common intention on the part of the parties to the second mortgage (the mortgagor and the second mortgagee) that there should be a right to marshal where the second mortgage secures a debt due from the mortgagor, because such a right is to the manifest advantage of the second mortgagee and of no significance either way to the mortgagor.[89]

However, marshalling is an arcane doctrine and most parties are unlikely to be aware of it. If the contract is silent about marshalling, it seems fictitious to interpret this silence as agreement to marshalling.[90]

In his monograph on marshalling, Ali argues that:

> In the absence of such a device as security, which gives secured creditors preferential rights of recourse to the assets of a debtor, many debtors would be either unable to obtain credit on an unsecured basis or would only be able to do so at relatively high rates of interest, because of the risk of loss to the creditor. … Security reduces the risk of loss to creditors and, as a consequence, they are willing to lend funds at lower

of Credit and Commerce International SA (No 8) [1996] Ch 245 (CA) 271F–H (Rose LJ); *Re Bank of Credit and Commerce International SA (No 8)* [1998] AC 214 (HL) 230H–31B (Lord Hoffmann); *Szepietowski* (n 84) [1]–[2], [31]–[32] (Lord Neuberger).

[86] In Australia, C only acquires this security once there is a court order giving effect to marshalling: *Commonwealth Trading Bank v Colonial Mutual Life Assurance Society Ltd* (1970) 26 FLR 338 (Tas SC); *Chase* (n 2) 18G–21B (Cohen J); *Sarge Pty Ltd v Cazihaven Homes Pty Ltd* (1994) 34 NSWLR 658 (NSWSC) 664D–65G (Young J).

[87] Mitchell (n 2) 591.

[88] Rotherham (n 28) para 8.72.

[89] *Szepietowski* (n 84) [54] (citation omitted).

[90] See also Hare (n 4) 244–46.

> rates of interest. Under the conventional theory, the law accords secured creditors priority over unsecured creditors because it recognises that security allows debtors access to credit which might not otherwise have been available. … As a corollary …, the law will do all it can to protect security and preserve the preferential status of secured claims, for by so doing it protects the supply of credit to debtors. It is this policy imperative which underpins the doctrine of marshalling of securities.[91]

However, this is not a justification for marshalling specifically; it is a general argument for giving advantages of any form to secured creditors in order to incentivise lending. The 'policy imperative' of allowing 'debtors access to credit' could equally justify giving C a floating charge over all of D's rights, or a state compensation scheme for creditors in C's position. Thus, Ali's argument fails to justify the particular form of the rights created by marshalling: giving C security over Blackacre with the same characteristics as X's extinguished security over Blackacre.

Neyers argues that marshalling is one manifestation of a prohibition on abuse of rights. He explains:

> the only point of [X] insisting on realising its security [over Whiteacre] can be to harm [C] without any gain for itself. [X] is not allowed to do this when its obligations can be met perfectly through the realisation of another security [over Blackacre].[92]

The problem with this argument is that it cuts both ways. One could deploy exactly the same argument for the opposite result:

> the only point of [X] insisting on realising its security [over Blackacre] can be to harm [the unsecured creditors] without any gain for itself. [X] is not allowed to do this when its obligations can be met perfectly through the realisation of another security [over Whiteacre].

Neyers' argument is therefore ambiguous about whether C should have priority over the unsecured creditors to the proceeds of Blackacre, or whether the proceeds should be distributed between C and the unsecured creditors. It is therefore ambiguous as to whether marshalling should occur.

A better argument for marshalling focuses on the fact that, were it not for marshalling, X would have the ability to determine the distribution of the insolvent debtor's assets. On the one hand, if X chooses to realise its security over Blackacre, then C's security over Whiteacre allows it to be paid before D's unsecured creditors. On the other hand, if X chooses to realise its security over Whiteacre, then C loses its security and competes with the unsecured creditors for the proceeds of Blackacre. In effect, then, X's choice determines how the insolvent debtor's assets are distributed between C and unsecured creditors.

[91] Ali (n 4) paras 6.35–6.37.

[92] JW Neyers, 'Explaining the Inexplicable? Four Manifestations of Abuse of Rights in English Law' in D Nolan and A Robertson (eds), *Rights and Private Law* (Oxford, Hart Publishing, 2012) 316.

However, it is the role of the state to determine how an insolvent debtor's assets are distributed. Allowing a private party to determine this would undermine the insolvency regime.

Furthermore, a private party could abuse their power. As Lord Neuberger explained:

> [T]here are also good practical reasons for equity adopting the doctrine, namely the unattractive and adventitious benefit which would otherwise be accorded to [X]. If marshalling was not available to [C], [X]'s free right to choose the property against which he enforced could have substantial value. In effect, he could auction that right as between [C] (who would be prepared to pay him to enforce against [Blackacre]) and the unsecured creditors of the mortgagor (who, especially where the mortgagor was actually or potentially insolvent, would be prepared to pay him to enforce against [Whiteacre]).[93]

Consequently, the law should step in and determine how the insolvent debtor's assets are distributed between C and unsecured creditors, rather than leaving it to X's whim.

Marshalling achieves this. If X chooses to realise its security over Blackacre, then C's security over Whiteacre allows it to be paid before the unsecured creditors. To take the power out of X's hands, the law must ensure the same result if X makes a different decision. Thus, if X chooses to realise its security over Whiteacre, marshalling gives C security over Blackacre with the same characteristics as X's extinguished security. This ensures that C and unsecured creditors end up in the same position, regardless of the decision X makes.

IV. CONCLUSION

Having analysed subrogation and marshalling separately, it is now possible to understand the relationship between the two. The key is that subrogation describes a distinctive form of rights: C's new rights against D have the same content as X's extinguished rights against D. Most instances of subrogation are justified by properly distributing the burden of a debt. If C bears the burden of a debt which ought to be borne by D, then that burden needs to be lifted from C and reinstated on D. Subrogation achieves this by reinstating D's debt and having D now owe that debt to C.

Meanwhile, marshalling gives C security with the same characteristics as X's extinguished security. It therefore creates rights which fit the definition of subrogation; marshalling is an example of subrogation. However, marshalling has a different justification to other instances of subrogation. Marshalling is justified by preventing a private party, X, determining the distribution of an insolvent debtor's assets. To take the distribution out of X's hands, the law must ensure

[93] *Szepietowski* (n 84) [36]. See also Heydon, Leeming, and Turner (n 2) para 11-180.

the same result whatever choice X makes. This justifies giving C property rights with the same content as X's extinguished property rights.

There is certainly a familial resemblance between these justifications: both are concerned with preventing private parties changing how the benefit and burden of debts are distributed.[94] Ultimately, however, they are distinct. The justification for marshalling is premised on X having a choice and an ability to decide the distribution of the debtor's assets. By contrast, subrogation can be justified to properly distribute the burden of a debt, even if C was not obliged to pay D's debt.[95] In these cases, X had no right against C; X had no choice to make and no ability to decide the distribution of assets.

Consequently, there is some truth in both views about the relationship between subrogation and marshalling. On the one hand, subrogation describes a particular form of rights, of which marshalling is an example. On the other hand, marshalling has a different justification compared to other instances of subrogation. This justification operates in different circumstances, so marshalling is available in different circumstances compared to other instances of subrogation. As such, it is correct to analyse the availability of marshalling and other instances of subrogation separately.

[94] Smith, 'Book Review' (n 29) 134, fn 4.
[95] See section II.E.

Index

www.ingramcontent.com/pod-product-compliance
Ingram Content Group UK Ltd.
Pitfield, Milton Keynes, MK11 3LW, UK
UKHW020240290926
15470UKWH00002B/648

9 781509 963669